NATURE IN FRAGMENTS

AMERICAN MUSEUM OF NATURAL HISTORY
CENTER FOR BIODIVERSITY AND CONSERVATION
NEW DIRECTIONS IN BIODIVERSITY CONSERVATION

AMERICAN MUSEUM ᴼꜰ NATURAL HISTORY

Center for Biodiversity and Conservation
New Directions in Biodiversity Conservation
■ ■

ELEANOR J. STERLING, SERIES EDITOR

The books in this series are based on annual symposia presented by the American
Museum of Natural History's Center for Biodiversity and Conservation and partners.
Each symposium reviews a topic critical to biodiversity and conservation, and provides
diverse perspectives by scientists, resource managers, policymakers, and others.

EDITED BY
Elizabeth A. Johnson
& Michael W. Klemens

NATURE IN
FRAGMENTS

THE LEGACY OF SPRAWL

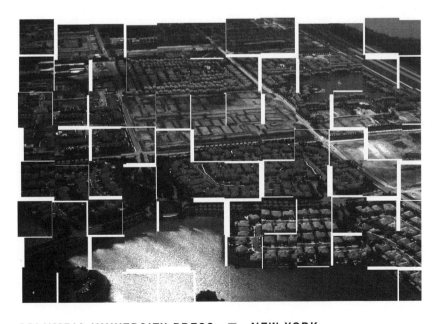

COLUMBIA UNIVERSITY PRESS ■ NEW YORK

COLUMBIA UNIVERSITY PRESS
Publishers Since 1893
New York Chichester, West Sussex

Library of Congress Cataloging-in-Publication Data
Nature in fragments : the legacy of sprawl / edited by Elizabeth A. Johnson and Michael W.
  Klemens.
      p. cm. — (New directions in biodiversity conservation)
  Includes bibliographical references (p.).
  ISBN 0-231-12778-2 (cloth : alk. paper)
  ISBN 0-231-12779-0 (pbk. : alk. paper)
    1. Cities and towns—Growth—Environmental aspects—Congresses. 2. Fragmented
  landscapes—Congresses. 3. Biological diversity conservation—Congresses. I. Johnson,
  Elizabeth A. (Elizabeth Ann), 1954 Aug. 29– II. Klemens, Michael W. III. Series.
QH545.C545N38 2005
577.27—dc22   2005041415

Printed in the United States of America
c 10 9 8 7 6 5 4 3 2 1
p 10 9 8 7 6 5 4 3 2 1
Designed by Lisa Hamm

■ ■

To our children Karla, Daniel, and Robert, with whom we share our joy of nature and our hopes for a more sustainable world.

CONTENTS

■ ■

PREFACE

T his book is based in part on the symposium "Nature in Fragments: The Legacy of Urban Sprawl," held in April 2000 at the American Museum of Natural History and co-sponsored by the museum's Center for Biodiversity and Conservation and the Wildlife Conservation Society's Metropolitan Conservation Alliance. The impetus behind the conference—and this book— was to create a platform from which to integrate biodiversity issues, concerns, and needs into the growing number of antisprawl initiatives, including the "smart-growth" and "new urbanist" movements. Our goal is to add biodiversity to the agenda of all who are creating more sustainable human environments, but who may not be fully considering ecological issues and opportunities associated with more informed development. A second, related goal is to deepen and broaden the discussion about sprawl's impacts on biodiversity and to include looking at ways in which sprawl affects species and alters or modifies natural communities, ecosystems, and processes.

There is widespread acknowledgment that biodiversity on Earth is imperiled and that we are in the midst of an extinction spasm of unprecedented proportions, caused primarily by human activities (Wilcove et al. 1998). Overpopulation and overconsumption, the roots of this crisis, are generally discussed in terms of the following threats: habitat loss, fragmentation, and degradation; invasive species; pollution; overexploitation of biological resources; and global climate change. Sprawl creates and contributes significantly to these threats, thus both directly and indirectly causing the decline of biodiversity.

For the purposes of this book, we define sprawl as poorly planned, land-consumptive development, regardless of where it is located. It occurs at the edges of cities or in rural fringes within commuting distance of metropolitan centers. But sprawl also can be found in more remote areas. Second-home development and recreational sprawl can be found in backcountry areas with significant natural features and wildlife. Sprawl also includes single-family homes and tract developments, megahouses found in upscale communities throughout the United States, as well as commercial and industrial development. The unifying features of these developments are that they all are placed haphazardly and wastefully on the greater landscape.

Although this book presents examples primarily from the United States, the link between sprawl, energy and resource consumption, and increasing affluence and population growth is a worldwide phenomenon. As global citizens, we need to act decisively to develop more sustainable ways to live within the dwindling resources of our planet. The Western nations, especially the United States, have the additional responsibility to lead by example because we are exporting (intentionally or not) this sprawl-dependent lifestyle throughout the world.

Citizens, politicians, and municipalities are increasingly interested in addressing sprawl, and myriad individuals and organizations are working to find solutions to the social and economic challenges presented by a decentralized, sprawl-created environment. Interest groups are trying to rechannel development into more productive avenues, to enhance quality of life and community cohesion, to reinvest in established urban centers, and to discourage wasteful patterns of development and land use.

Discussions about the biological effects of sprawl have centered on its impact on pollution, on both air quality and water quality, and on the protection of open space. Open space is an umbrella term that typically includes undeveloped land we consider "valuable," such as farmland, scenic vistas, recreational parks and corridors, and natural areas, as well as ecologically constrained land such as steep slopes and wetlands. Each of these open-space components has its constituencies, most of which are focused on meeting human wants and needs, including farmland and watershed protection, scenic vista protection, and recreational interest. Some efforts have been focused on the protection of threatened and endangered species, but in general there is little advocacy for biodiversity: for the protection of ecosystem processes on the landscape and for the protection of the community of common and uncommon plants, animals, fungi, and microbes living among us in the landscape. Yet biodiversity—nature—is vital to our survival.

This book contains four parts. Part I provides the introduction to the topic. In chapter 1, Barbara L. Lawrence presents an overview of sprawl and how we got where we are today. In chapter 2, the volume editors provide an introduction to biodiversity and discuss the ways in which sprawl threatens the planet's biological foundation.

Parts II and III of the book explore in more detail some of the impacts of sprawl on biodiversity at different organizational levels, with part II looking at sprawl's effects on ecosystems and ecosystem processes, and part III examining sprawl's impacts at the species level. In chapter 3, Nicholas A. Miller and Michael W. Klemens discuss the impacts of sprawl on wetland ecosystems. Although focusing on wetlands, the conclusions they draw can be applied to terrestrial systems. In chapter 4, Seth R. Reice explains sprawl's effects on the processes of ecosystem disturbance. In chapter 5, James H. Cane presents an introduction to the process of pollination with an in-depth discussion of sprawl's effects on our most important pollinators, the bees. Chapter 6, by Margaret M. Carreiro, illustrates the way in which sprawl alters forest decomposer communities and soil processes. In chapter 7, Fred W. Koontz and Peter Daszak broaden the discussion of processes to emphasize sprawl's impacts on disease and disease transmission. Opening part III, Diane L. Byers and Joseph C. Mitchell begin the discussion of sprawl's impact on species by focusing in chapter 8 on plants and animals with limited dispersal capability. Justina C. Ray follows in chapter 9 with an introduction to wide-ranging and area-sensitive species. Stephen DeStefano and Elizabeth A. Johnson remind readers in chapter 10 that some species tolerate and even benefit from the changes that sprawling development brings to the landscape.

Part IV presents the challenges we face in our efforts to conserve biodiversity by addressing the causes and effects of sprawl and by offering some examples of what is successfully being undertaken and where we can go further in our efforts. In chapter 11, M.A. Sanjayan and Kevin R. Crooks clarify the importance of landscape connectivity. Stephen Farber discusses in chapter 12 the role of economics in developing more effective land-use plans for biodiversity. Jessica Wilkinson, Sara Vickerman, and Jeff Lerner look at the role of planning and conservation at the state and national level in chapter 13, and in chapter 14 Jayne Daly and Michael W. Klemens focus on the complementary value of local planning efforts for biodiversity conservation. Effective communication is a key to addressing sprawl; Cynthia Coffin and Jane Elder discuss this topic in chapter 15. Last, in chapter 16, the volume editors offer some additional recommendations to incorporate biodiversity concepts more effectively into land-use planning in the future.

In an editorial in the journal *Conservation Biology*, John Marzluff wrote that we need to "develop an understanding of how settlement affects the richness and relative abundance of species, what motivates people to develop and settle land the way we do, how land use policy is crafted, implemented, and informed by economic and ecological reality and how planners, managers, developers and architects respond to human desire and policy to create settlements" (2002:1176). This volume should be an important step in attaining that understanding.

REFERENCES

Marzluff, J. M. 2002. Fringe conservation: A call to action. *Conservation Biology* 16:1175–1176.

Wilcove, D.S., D. Rothstein, J. Dubow, and E. Losos. 1998. Quantifying threats to imperiled species in the United States. *BioScience* 48:607–615.

■ ■

ACKNOWLEDGMENTS

W e thank the American Museum of Natural History's Center for Biodiversity and Conservation (CBC) and the Wildlife Conservation Society's Metropolitan Conservation Alliance (MCA) for convening the symposium "Nature in Fragments: The Legacy of Urban Sprawl," on which this book is based. We also acknowledge the contributions of the symposium presenters, who laid the groundwork for this volume. Although not all of them are represented in this volume, all contributed significantly to the evolution and synthesis of our position on this topic.

To our contributing authors we owe a special debt for generously sharing their scholarly work and for their patience during the revision and editorial process. Their contributions have added depth to the understanding of biodiversity, the challenges of sprawl, and the ways we can make a meaningful contribution to reversing the frightening trajectory of ecological waste that characterized the closing decades of the twentieth century. We are indebted to all those individuals and organizations working toward solutions to the sprawl crisis—they have established a solid platform on which to build a new land-use paradigm.

We also appreciate the efforts of our many chapter reviewers, who gave their time and expertise to ensure the accuracy and clarity of each chapter and provided thoughtful feedback. Many thanks to Dana Beach, Diane Byers, Donald Chen, Ray Curran, Eric Davidson, Richard DeGraaf, Amanda Dey, Joan Ehrenfeld, Paul Epstein, Peggy Fiedler, James Gibbs, Frank Golet, John Gowdy, Jodi Hilty, Roland Kays, William Kemp, Linda Kervin, Claire Kremen, Gretchen LeBuhn, Jay Malcolm, R. William Mannan, Carl McDaniel, Nick Miller, Martha Monroe, Gerry Moore, Marya Morris, Reed Noss, T'ai Roulston, Eric Sanderson, Elizabeth Schilling, Sacha Spector, Gary Tabor, Vince Tepedino, Adrian Treves, Thomas Wright, Jianguo Wu, and Wayne Zipperer.

We value your help in creating a better book that is not only well grounded in science, but more closely linked to the planning and public-policy processes.

Special thanks to CBC and MCA staff and volunteers who assisted us in various ways throughout the writing and editing process. In particular, we thank Josh Berman, Fiona Brady, Elizabeth Cornell, Melina Laverty, Marc LeCard, Jim McDougal, Timon McPhearson, Ho-Ling Poon, Kevin Ryan, Jennifer Schmitz, and Jennifer Stenzel. We also appreciate the in-depth contribution of CBC director and series editor, Eleanor Sterling.

The MCA acknowledges financial support provided by the Doris Duke Charitable Trust, the Surdna Foundation, the Westchester Community Foundation, and Vivian and Strachen Donnelly. The CBC acknowledges financial support provided by the Sarah K. de Coizart Article TENTH Perpetual Charitable Trust.

Thanks to all the individuals and organizations that contributed their photographic work to this volume: Diane L. Byers, Stephen DeStefano, James Glinski, Keith Hackbarth, Fred W. Koontz, Gene Magee, Nicholas A. Miller, Joseph C. Mitchell, Michael B. Morrissey, Michael Reuter, Biodiversity Project and Green Team Advertising, Defenders of Wildlife, Florida Greenways Commission, Leyland Alliance LLC, Regional Plan Association, Rhode Island Geographical Information System and MIT, and Wildlife Conservation Society/Metropolitan Conservation Alliance. Special thanks to James Lui for his original cover design and to Patricia Wynne for her fine artwork.

Many thanks also to Robin Smith, Irene Pavitt, and Lisa Hamm at Columbia University Press and to Annie Barva for patiently guiding us through the book-writing, -editing, and -design process.

Finally, we are also indebted to our friends and families, for their patience and understanding as we worked on this book. Elizabeth Johnson would especially like to thank her husband, Dave, for his love and support and for the many insightful discussions they shared about conserving the natural world that so enriches their lives.

CONTRIBUTORS

Diane L. Byers
Associate Professor in Evolutionary Biology
Behavior, Ecology, Evolution, and Systematics Section
Department of Biological Sciences
Campus Box 4120
Illinois State University
Normal, Illinois 61790

James H. Cane
Research Entomologist
USDA-ARS Bee Biology and Systematics Lab
Utah State University
Logan, Utah 84322–5310

Margaret M. Carreiro
Associate Professor of Biology
Department of Biology
139 Life Sciences Building
University of Louisville
Louisville, Kentucky 40292

Cynthia Coffin
Partner
About Place Consulting
225 Merry Street
Madison, Wisconsin 53704

Kevin R. Crooks
Assistant Professor
Department of Fishery and Wildlife Biology
Colorado State University
115 Wagar
Fort Collins, Colorado 80523

Jayne Daly
Attorney
Jacobowitz and Gubits, LLP
158 Orange Avenue
Walden, New York 12586

Peter Daszak
Executive Director
Consortium for Conservation Medicine
460 West Thirty-fourth Street
New York, New York 10001

Stephen DeStefano
Leader, Adjunct Professor
U.S. Geological Survey
Massachusetts Cooperative Fish and Wildlife Research Unit
Holdsworth Natural Resources Center
University of Massachusetts
Amherst, Massachusetts 01003

Jane Elder
Executive Director
Biodiversity Project
214 North Henry Street, Suite 201
Madison, Wisconsin 53703

Stephen Farber
Professor
Graduate School of Public and International Affairs
University of Pittsburgh
Pittsburgh, Pennsylvania 15260

Elizabeth A. Johnson
Manager, Metropolitan Biodiversity Program
Center for Biodiversity and Conservation
American Museum of Natural History
Central Park West at 79th Street
New York, New York 10024

Michael W. Klemens
Senior Conservationist, Director
Wildlife Conservation Society
Metropolitan Conservation Alliance
2300 Southern Boulevard
Bronx, New York 10460

Fred W. Koontz
Executive Director
Teatown Lake Reservation
1600 Spring Valley Road
Ossining, New York 10562

Barbara L. Lawrence
Executive Director
Henry and Marilyn Taub Foundation
300 Frank W. Burr Boulevard
Teaneck, New Jersey 07666

Jeff Lerner
Director, Conservation Planning
Defenders of Wildlife
National Headquarters
1130 Seventeenth Street, NW
Washington, D.C. 20036

Nicholas A. Miller
Program Manager
Wildlife Conservation Society
Metropolitan Conservation Alliance
2300 Southern Boulevard
Bronx, New York 10460

Joseph C. Mitchell
Research Biologist
Department of Biology
University of Richmond
Richmond, Virginia 23173

Justina C. Ray
Associate Conservation Zoologist,
  Director
Wildlife Conservation Society Canada
720 Spadina Avenue, Suite 600
Toronto, Ontario M5S 2T9
Canada

Seth R. Reice
Associate Professor
Department of Biology
Campus Box 3280, Coker Hall
University of North Carolina
Chapel Hill, North Carolina 27599–3280

M. A. Sanjayan
Lead Scientist
The Nature Conservancy
4245 North Fairfax Drive, Suite 100
Arlington, Virginia 22203–1606

Sara Vickerman
Director, West Coast Office
Defenders of Wildlife
1880 Willamette Falls Drive, Suite 200
West Linn, Oregon 97068

Jessica Wilkinson
Director, State Biodiversity Program
Environmental Law Institute
2000 L Street NW, Suite 620
Washington, D.C. 20036

PART I

BIODIVERSITY AND THE GENESIS OF SPRAWL

1

THE CONTEXT AND CAUSES OF SPRAWL

Barbara L. Lawrence

Americans living in the sprawling twenty-first century face a Three Bears' dilemma, but with fewer choices: the places where we live, work, and play are too far apart to offer the option of walking from one activity to another, but too close together to move about without regular traffic snarls. Our housing is too expensive for many to own, but too poorly built to survive the turn of the next century. Our open space is too fragmented for wildlife habitat and efficient farming, but abundant enough to attract even more sprawling development.

Viewed from the air, the curves of cul-de-sacs and intricate patterns of the highway interchanges that open new land to development are too clearly planned to have been accidental. Planners and government officials have helped pave the way for development with deliberate decisions that have resulted in the rapid, unsustainable consumption of green fields and forests and the abandonment of older communities. This is not a natural occurrence, nor is it inevitable, as some would argue.

Rather, sprawl is driven by a set of public policies at the national, state, and local levels. Many growth policies, but not all, were developed on sound logic that fit the economic needs of the previous century. Today, such policies not only are obsolete, but have a profound and adverse affect on both the long-term health of our environment and the daily quality of life for millions of Americans.

These policies—which govern housing, transportation, taxation, public investment, and even neighborhood zoning—make discarding existing homes and communities for new ones seem the natural choice. It is not. The sprawling land-use pattern we developed in the twentieth century has no single cause and no single cure, which makes tackling the causes of sprawl complicated and difficult, but not impossible.

FIGURE 1.1. Sprawling development around Miami, Florida. (Photo by Elizabeth A. Johnson)

SPRAWL: THE MYTHS ABOUT CAUSE

Sprawl is a dispersed pattern of single-use, low-density land uses, most evident as developments of large-lot, single-family homes, office campuses, and strip malls (figure 1.1). It frequently leapfrogs, jumping beyond established settlements onto farm- or forestland. Roads and highways play an important role as incubators of retail strip development, much of which is indistinguishable from one place to another. Roads are also precursors and companions to sprawl because sprawl favors the automobile over all other travel options. Sprawl not only stakes its claim to open lands, but also is clearly linked to urban and suburban decline, as economic investment moves from older cities and suburbs to newer green-field development sites. These sites frequently offer lower construction costs and some form of lower taxation, at least in the initial stages of development.

This movement to new locations is unassociated with overall regional population growth, contrary to the popular myth that sprawl is a natural result of population growth. A look at any number of sprawling metropolitan regions in the country shows that urban population declines frequently cancel out the suburban increases. Overall, between 1982 and 1997, land in the United States was developed at approximately 1.8 times the rate of population growth. However, this national figure greatly underestimates the impact of sprawl in particular states and regions. In Wyoming between 1982 and 1997, the state *lost* 5.2 percent of its population but *increased* developed acres by 17.1 percent. In the same time period, New York State saw 3.2 percent population growth and 0.8 percent increase in developed acres (Department of Agriculture 1992; Bureau of the Census 2000). Nor is there truth in the myth that sprawl is solely an artifact of the market or of affluence, a consequence of decisions made by millions of Americans to maximize their well-being by choosing a place to live or work that best suits their taste. This explanation ignores the omnipresent government policies and regulations—at the federal, state, and local levels—that largely prescribe what choices are available.

THE POLICIES THAT CAUSE SPRAWL

Sprawling, low-density expansion is a relatively new state of affairs whose pattern derives from advances in transportation technology. The history of civilization is one of compact, walkable communities surrounded by open lands. For most of human history, travel was by foot or animal. Both required relatively compact communities settled at relatively high densities. Animals brought the added requirement of preserving nearby open land for the provision of fodder and waste disposal. Even the addition of water and rail transport did not dramatically alter this pattern because after passengers departed a train or boat, they again faced foot or animal travel to reach their destinations.

Indeed, compact, walkable communities prevailed in the United States until the early years of the twentieth century, when technological innovations and a series of public-policy decisions created both opportunities and incentives for development to spread out from central cities. The rise of the automobile, the almost magical invention of a "one-seat" all-weather ride from one's home to a location of choice at any time of the night or day, was destined to have a major impact on American life. However, the revolution it brought in social form was largely unpredicted and unseen until a plethora of public policies fully embraced the technology. As the century progressed, planning and other policies overwhelmingly favored an automobile-centric highway paradigm to the utter exclusion of traditional patterns of urban development, in which walking and transit had played the key roles.

At the same time that these new opportunities for development were being created along highways instead of sidewalks, disincentives were put into place that discouraged—and in some cases prohibited—more compact urban development. Changes in the policies governing housing, infrastructure (transportation, water, and sewers), and taxation were the primary drivers. On the local level, zoning was invented to protect private-property owners from the impact of nearby factories and other noisy, unsafe, and noxious facilities. However, the unintended consequences of single-use zones provided a means of closely regulating undeveloped land, locking in a segregation of land uses and locking out the flexibility of the marketplace.

The public-policy influences on the use of land are manifold. Each level of government has contributed some incentives and some restrictions. In sum total, federal, state, and local government policies for much of the twentieth century have produced sprawl for the most part as a largely unintended consequence.

FEDERAL POLICIES

The federal government is the level of government farthest away from the decisions made in town halls about the exact shape and location of the next development. Yet federal policy decisions, many made years earlier, serve as the catalyst for the land-use proposals facing local decision makers. A multitude of federal programs have the potential to influence land-use patterns. Two of the most critical are housing and transportation.

HOUSING POLICY Beginning in the early 1930s, new federal housing policies evolved that effectively discouraged urban investment and spurred suburban home ownership. These policies, established 70 years ago and amplified by the GI Bill in 1944, lured middle-class families out of older urban places by making new suburban home ownership the most inexpensive living option for this group of Americans.

Among the first in this series of policy decisions was the creation of the Homeowners Loan Corporation in 1933. Its laudable goal was to protect homeownership by stemming the tide of foreclosures resulting from the Great Depression. It did so by refinancing mortgages with lower interest rates and longer terms—the very system we use today. In addition to improving the mortgage as an instrument for financing housing, the Homeowners Loan Corporation created the first standardized national system for appraising real estate. Unfortunately, this system was based on ideas about what constituted a "good" neighborhood. The appraisals devalued much of what we know as urban life—areas with older housing stock and mixed uses, including retail and office uses, and areas with dense populations and nonwhite residents. These areas were considered high risk for mortgages. The maps resulting from this classification system were used not only by the federal government, but also by private bankers, ensuring that the potential for urban decline was fulfilled.

A year after the Homeowners Loan Corporation enabled longer mortgage terms, the National Housing Act of 1934 was signed into law, creating the Federal Housing Administration (FHA). The act's immediate goal was to increase employment in the building trades without direct government expenditures. However, its long-lasting impacts went far beyond unemployment relief. Among the key features of the FHA were federal insurance for homes that met certain building and location standards, a longer payback period for mortgages, and a substantially lower down-payment requirement. As a result of these public-policy changes, the costs of homeownership dropped dramatically, enlarging the number of American families seeking and able to buy a house. According to Kenneth T. Jackson in his classic work *Crabgrass Frontier*, "it often became cheaper to buy than to rent" (1985:205).

Built into this new system of insuring mortgages were blatant antiurban and antiblack provisions that made cookie-cutter, whites-only suburban subdivisions the norm. The FHA, in an effort to ensure that the mortgages it backed were for a "quality" product, established minimum requirements for "lot size, setback from the street, separation from adjacent structures, [and] even for the width of the house itself" (Jackson 1985:208). These standards discouraged the purchase of traditional urban homes. The FHA also established standards for the property, the neighborhood, and the mortgage holder. The exclusion of blacks from its insured homes was based on the notion that homes would lose value in an integrated neighborhood.

This codification of antiurban bias pulled resources from cities, leaving behind the people for whom choice was most limited, because of either race or financial status. It made building a new house on a cornfield or in a forest easier and more affordable than finding the funds to renovate an existing structure. As the middle class moved itself to the suburbs because of these incentives, impoverished families were moved into public housing clustered in already poor neighborhoods. Federal housing policy allowed municipalities to choose if they wanted to build public housing. Given this choice, newer suburbs declined to house the poor. These policies persisted into the late 1960s. By then, the desirability of many cities as places to live was substantially reduced, continuing the downward urban spiral that fueled further sprawl.

Amplifying these midcentury housing policies were two tax policies that continue to reduce the cost of home ownership: the mortgage interest deduction and the tax treatment of capital gains from sale of a residence. Homeownership was and is seen generally as a net benefit to society. It was thought that where people own their homes, they will have a stronger stake in the community. Although this conclusion may be debatable, home ownership has clearly been an effective form of wealth creation—the most substantial savings that middle-class families have after several decades of living, working, and raising a family are often the appreciated values of their homes.

This benefit was relatively modest when it was first introduced, but over time marginal tax rates substantially rose on upper-income families, increasing the financial benefits of home ownership. In 1955, the highest marginal federal tax rate was 22 percent. By 1981, before Ronald Reagan pushed through a tax cut, it had risen to 40 percent. The higher the tax rate, the greater the incentive for upper-income Americans to go for the tax deduction by buying a large house and taking out a large mortgage. (And looking ahead, as the alternative minimum tax becomes the critical determinant for an increasing number of Americans, once again the attractiveness of the interest deduction will be even greater.)

Although no specific provision in the tax code prohibits the application of these benefits to urban residents, in practice most new housing is being built in sprawling suburbs, according to a Brookings Institution study of housing built between 1986 and 1998: "In each of the years studied, more than 80 per cent of the new housing took place in the suburbs" (Von Hoffman 1999:1).

TRANSPORTATION POLICY The road to sprawl was paved when trolley tracks were torn up and concrete was poured for one of the largest public-works projects in world history—the interstate highway system. Policymakers in Washington began talking about creating transcontinental highways beginning in the 1930s, when state governments were already building a few grade-separated highways with limited access points (Weingroff 1996). But World War II and then the Korean War curtailed any serious attempt at creating an interstate system.

When Dwight D. Eisenhower became president, he took up the cause of building a vast interstate highway network. He saw such construction not only as an economic development tool, but as a necessity for moving people and weapons in a time of great nuclear threat. In 1956, the Interstate Highway Act was signed. It called for the construction of 41,000 miles (66,129 kilometers) of roads (this number was later expanded), built to standards that would ensure seamless transitions from highway to highway. Limited access meant that speeds could be much higher, which thus extended the distance that could be traveled in a given time period. Debate around creating this highway network centered only on how to finance the system, not on its potential impact on cities or on alternative means of transport.

The means chosen to finance the system was an increase in the federal gas tax and the dedication of those funds to highway construction. Federal funds would cover 90 percent of construction costs. At the same time, a conscious decision was made to disinvest in existing public-transit infrastructure in favor of new roads. Trolleys, streetcars, and commuter rail lines had provided the backbone of the transportation infrastructure through World War II. Little investment was made in these systems during the war; they were beginning to deteriorate at the very time that massive federal investments were being made in new roads. As a result, across the country in the 1950s and into the 1960s, trolleys and many trains made their last runs.

The new highways changed the nature of accessibility. Until that point, accessibility meant proximity, and it gave urban areas a major advantage both for housing and for businesses. That advantage literally hit the road with the extension of highways through buildable open lands. The long-term commitment that U.S. government leaders have shown for low energy prices—gas prices in Europe are consistently two and one-half to three times higher than they are in the United States (Energy Information Administration 2004)—has amplified the highways' impact. Although some will argue whether highways and cheap gas are a cause or a consequence of sprawl, there is no doubt about the inextricable nature of the connection.

The American legacy delivered by decades of highway building is a country with the highest dependence on auto use in the world. Some change has finally come with recognition of the economic dependence this distinction brings and of the adverse impact highway building has had on the American landscape. The passage of the Intermodal Surface Transportation Efficiency Act (ISTEA) of 1991 marked the first time a federal transportation bill did not use the word *highway* in its title. This act explicitly recognized the link between land use and transportation and provided a mechanism for public participation in preparing comprehensive transportation plans. It also offered states considerably more flexibility in spending to meet particular needs, including for transit improvements left out of previous federal legislation. ISTEA's successor, the Transportation Equity Act for the 21st Century (TEA-21), is built on this shifted paradigm (Surface Transportation Policy Project 1996).

STATE POLICIES

Despite these powerful federal policy directions, the most profound powers to spur or control sprawl are the state governments. Under our federal Constitution, powers not assigned to the federal government rest with the states; this is the case with land use. State policies fall into three categories: *taxation*, specifically how local governments are financed; *spending*, especially how transportation and other infrastructure financing decisions are made; and *regulation*, including the extent to which state governments set controls on local land-use decision making.

TAXATION Local governments are essentially self-financed, independent entities competing with one another for sources of revenue. Depending on the state, this revenue may be received from property tax, sales tax, income tax, or user fees. This system has promoted an unending chase, without regard to the source, for ratables (taxable properties) of some sort. High-income residents, shopping malls, and office and industrial complexes bring some form of revenue to the municipality. Over time, local governments have made determinations about what type of development is a "cost center" and what type is a "profit center." To the extent politically feasible, planning and zoning have been adjusted to achieve a more fiscally desirable outcome. Where permitted, annexation of surrounding suburbs by central cities has been another way to incorporate the revenue from new development.

This focus on financial benefits of certain types of development has also insidiously promoted single-use projects. By viewing land use solely through the fiscal lens, leaving social and environmental considerations out of the mix, states have failed to promote diverse land-use types and mixed-use communities. The single-use nature of most new development has further exacerbated sprawl.

In a few places, most notably the Minneapolis–St. Paul metropolitan area, tax sharing has been introduced to reduce local competitive instincts and to redress the inequity between the growing suburbs and the older places left behind (Orfield 1992). In states such as New Jersey, where there is great reliance on the property tax to fund both local government and schools, the perfect ratable is an office campus or a mall, preferably located at the edge of the municipality, which generates no school children and for which traffic can be routed through an adjoining municipality. Second best is perhaps age-restricted housing for affluent seniors, where it is hoped the demand for municipal services will be low, the taxes high, and any traffic generated will be at off-peak hours.

To the extent that local political leaders are judged by their ability to keep taxes from rising in their terms of office, and given that it is easier and less expensive to build on green fields and in forests than it is to redevelop, the tax inducements toward sprawl continue to be strong. It is almost impossible for older suburbs and central cities to win under such a system.

SPENDING ON INFRASTRUCTURE For the most part, state government spending on infrastructure—especially sewer, water, and transportation—has followed the federal lead. For decades, it was less expensive to build a new sewer with state and federal funding than it was to repair the old systems. Transportation funding also mirrored the federal pattern, with the state money making up the small difference between the cost of a new road and the federal contribution.

Many state departments of transportation have maintained a strict policy of asserting that they are not in the land-use business. This hands-off approach has undermined many efforts to reduce roadway delays and to increase transit services. By continuing to expand roads to serve sprawl, transportation officials have perpetuated the notion that it is possible to build our way out of congestion. But because these roadway expansions are not tied to appropriate land uses, they will ultimately fail to alleviate congestion. Anthony Downs (1992) of the Brookings Institute often cites the "triple convergence" of people shifting their trips to the new facility from (1) other routes, (2) other times of day, and (3) other modes of transportation.

In the 1990s, some states began to move toward more coordination between infrastructure provision and land use. Maryland was the acknowledged leader in tying state spending for infrastructure, including schools, to a determination about where development is appropriate and where it is not. This approach is in marked contrast to the bureaucratic isolation that characterizes most state governments. Each state agency—environmental protection, public health, education, housing, economic development, and transportation—is allowed to focus on its own actions largely without regard for the consequences to any other agency's mission. It is not uncommon for transportation policies to undermine environmental protection and public-health goals, which would call for more compact walkable communities, because transportation spending is focused on highway widening.

REGULATIONS AND CONTROLS ON LOCAL DECISION MAKING State governments have made a significant difference on their own in promoting sprawl through their regulatory programs. In some cases, regulations have proactively promoted sprawl, as in a state's inability or unwillingness to deny permits for new water and sewer infrastructure. For at least 25 years, environmentalists have argued that irreversible damage to aquifers and aquifer recharge areas is being caused by inappropriately sited development made possible by the construction of new water and sewer infrastructure. Yet state governments across the country have continued to permit these projects and, indeed, sometimes subsidize them through their economic development arm.

Closely linked to these spending and regulating decisions are the parameters that state governments set on local land-use decision making and on the level of local government empowered to make decisions. One of the prime accelerators of sprawl is the fragmentation of local government and state government's unwillingness to create mechanisms to ensure that land-use decisions are made at an appropriate level. In most states today, there continues to be a mismatch between the effects of a decision and the power of the body making the decision. A notable exception is Oregon, where local governments must plan and zone in accordance with overall state goals. Such a system requires local governments to make decisions in a larger context, making it possible to plan land uses on a level that protects regional resources and stimulates regional economies. In the New Jersey Pinelands, which accounts for 22 percent of New Jersey's land area, a very effective regional planning system is in place that requires local plans to conform to a regional plan. Other states have taken steps in this direction, but none has progressed as far in its development.

LOCAL POLICIES

Local land-use decision making is at the forefront in creating and controlling sprawl. Each night across the United States, tens of thousands of local officials make the decisions on where and how development will happen. Many of these decision makers have little or no formal training in planning, architecture, public policy, ecology, or engineering. Most of them are well-intentioned volunteers giving their time to make their piece of the country a better place.

The purview of each of these local bodies—known as planning commissions, planning boards, community boards—is by definition local. In few places do they have the legal power to look beyond their community to the region. In practice, night after night, they are looking at site plans, not at community or regional plans. These decision makers respond to the proposals that developers set before them. The developers, in turn, are responding to zoning.

Zoning is the skeleton on which sprawl is hung. The power to zone rests on government's responsibility to protect the health, welfare, and safety of its citizens. Begun in the late nineteenth century and gaining great momentum in the early twentieth century, zoning locked in values and ideas from the industrial era through a philosophy that favors separation of uses.

Zoning was first used in the United States in San Francisco in the late nineteenth century to separate noxious industries seen as a health hazard to nearby residents and to protect residents' property values. In 1916, New York City became the first fully zoned municipality. The New York City approach created a pyramid of zones, with the residential zone at the top. In this top zone, only residential uses were permitted. In the next lower zone, commercial and residential uses were permitted. At the base of the pyramid were residential, commercial, and industrial zones. The New York City approach was interesting in that within all but the top zone, uses were mixed.

On the West Coast, Los Angeles was also an early zoning pioneer. Its contribution was twofold. Unlike New York City, Los Angeles zoned large areas of undeveloped land. In these areas, the city government created a multitude of new types of zones, including zones for single-family housing only. As these concepts spread to other areas, initial zones were relatively small and tightly defined. But as automobile ownership increased, it allowed single-use zones to get larger so that vast sections of undeveloped land were reserved for a single use (Gerckens 1994).

Zoning began to be used throughout much of the country in the 1920s. When the town of Euclid, Ohio, passed a zoning ordinance that resulted in the devaluation of 68 acres (28 hectares) of land owned by the Ambler Realty Company, Ambler Realty sued the town, claiming that the zoning ordinance violated the Fifth Amendment of the Constitution, which reads "nor shall private property be taken for public use, without just compensation." The case went all the way to the Supreme Court, which ruled in the landmark case *Village of Euclid, Ohio v. Ambler Realty Company* (1926) that zoning is constitutional provided that it is designed to protect the public health, welfare, and safety—recognizing a city's right to place restrictions on the use of private land in order to deal with the complications of urban living. For the most part, states adopted legislation promoted by the U.S. Department of Commerce model-planning and zoning-enabling acts. The impact of zoning has been debated since its inception. Does it protect the general welfare or the neighbors' property values? One fact seems clear: local zoning tends to "result in lower overall urban densities and [to] encourage urban sprawl" (Knaap et al. 2001:8).

IS SPRAWL INEVITABLE IN THE TWENTY-FIRST CENTURY?

Much of what we see around us is the legacy of nearly a century spent charting a policy course that made sprawl and urban decline the inevitable outcome. However, toward the end of the twentieth century, a consensus started to build for the notion that we must seek another, more economically efficient, socially sound, and environmentally sustainable outcome before it is too late. The movement toward smart growth is not guaranteed, and it will not occur without many setbacks and detractors.

According to Don Chen, executive director of Smart Growth America, "Smart growth is development that protects farmland and open space, revitalizes neighborhoods, keeps housing affordable and provides people with more transportation choices" (personal communication, April 2002). It is something of a back-to-the-future vision, with several key differences from the past. Smart growth does envision communities where there are "all kinds of diversity, intricately mingled in mutual support" (Jacobs 1961:241). But it also recognizes where we are today. The smart-growth movement comes at a time when a great deal of sprawling development has taken place. It does not envision a future where all people live in cities. Rather, it works to make in-fill and redevelopment easier than building on farmland and forests. It works to see that new development, regardless of where it takes place, is designed to advance the values of environmental conservation, strong healthy communities of all types, more convenient access, and lower costs.

It is important to recognize that as we enter the twenty-first century, the problems of sprawl are not as bad as they might have been had we not already achieved some success through earlier movements—in particular, the civil rights, the environmental, and the growth-management movements. The evils of redlining and the most blatant policies that discouraged or prevented urban revitalization were reversed through the work of thousands of activists in the 1960s and 1970s. The first Earth Day in 1970 brought another group of innovators to what would become the fight against sprawl. Most of these early environmentalists did not regard sprawl as the major environmental problem that we see today. One exception was Ian McHarg, author of the landmark book *Design with Nature* (1969). McHarg, a landscape architect by training, was an early advocate for a more holistic way of thinking about the environment and about the importance of land use as a determinant of environmental quality.

Also gaining currency in the 1970s was the concept of growth management. Although initially thought of as describing the "no growth" or "slow growth" techniques, the term *growth management* gained support in the 1980s as describing the way to make infrastructure and development fit responsibly together. In the 1970s, seven states adopted or extended some form of statewide or regional growth management (DeGrove and Miness 1992). It is on this basis that the current more comprehensive smart-growth movement has been built.

Several other hopeful signs indicate that the tide is turning against sprawling land use. This turn begins with the accumulation and spread of new scientific knowledge. The extension of geographic information systems to state and local governments and to nonprofit organizations has a democratizing and empowering affect on land-use planning, the impacts of which we cannot yet completely see.

As shown by the shift in federal transportation policies, we are also seeing the early benefits of renewed investment in rail. Communities from California to Atlanta are taking tentative steps toward relieving the traffic congestion brought by sprawling development with investment in public transit. With such investment come new interest in redeveloping the older communities served by rail and rises in property values. Research done by the Washington Metro system shows that "local jurisdictions prosper from new taxes (currently more than $20 million per annum) which help them to recapture some of their investment in the Metro system" (Washington Metropolitan Area Transit Authority n.d.)

Antisprawl advocates often claim that how we grow is as important as "where." The drive for a "new urbanism" is led by architects and planners who want to reform all aspects of real-estate development. This idea was codified into the charter of "new urbanism": "We stand for the restoration of existing urban centers and towns within coherent metropolitan regions, the reconfiguration of sprawling suburbs into communities of real neighborhoods and diverse districts, the conservation of natural environments, and the preservation of our built legacy" (Congress for the New Urbanism 1996). This movement is being aided by changes in the market: "Nontraditional households—including baby boomer empty nesters, divorcees, singles, and unmarried and/or childless couples—want to live in the city, closer to work and without cars. Since such households will represent the majority over the next two decades as the population grows by more than 60 million, well organized, high-density projects are needed" (Dymi 2002:22).

New urbanism is one aspect of what is perhaps the most interesting and powerful change in the antisprawl drive: the creation and spread of the smart-growth movement. For the first time, the United States has a national movement that encompasses environmentalists, supporters of affordable housing and transit, elements of the building and farming industries, equity advocates, architects and planners, public-health proponents, and many others. It has an umbrella group, Smart Growth America, in Washington, D.C., pushing the research agenda and communicating with Congress, federal agencies, and the press. It has a national coalition of state and regional advocates for smart growth, the Growth Management Leadership Alliance. The movement has ignited a lively academic debate, a sure sign of legitimacy.

The smart-growth movement also has begun to send roots into the political establishment of both major political parties. Beginning in the latter half of the 1990s, Republican and Democratic governors began to embrace the smart-growth label and its ideas. The trend began on the East Coast, with the governors of New Jersey and Maryland, and has been picked up by other governors, using their state of the state and inaugural speeches to stake their claims as sprawl fighters. Fighting sprawl is also bipartisan at the local level. Many mayors and mayoral candidates, especially on the suburban fringe, have determined that opposing sprawl is good politics.

CONCLUSION

A mix of federal, state, and local land-use, tax, and spending laws and regulations has resulted in a land-use system that makes it easier and more profitable to create new automobile-dependent, single-use, low-density locales rather than to rebuild existing communities within cities. As a result, for the majority of us in the United States today, sprawling newer suburbs and declining cities and older suburbs mark a pattern to which we are accustomed. The school bus is the way to get to school, the regional mall is the place to shop, the strip-mall convenience store is the place to drive to where we can buy a quart of milk, the office park is the place to work, and the single-family house with attached garage and backyard is the place to live. For most middle-class Americans, the "choice" has become which look-alike suburb to live in, not whether to live in a city or ride transit or walk to work. Although for some people this suburban lifestyle may be attractive, for many it is not a matter of choice, but rather a matter of what is available.

The status quo is a powerful force. And today's status quo perpetuates a self-reinforcing pattern of new office campuses, which draw new suburban housing, which draw new highway-based retail stores. At this point, it is not clear which wave came first or which is coming next. It is not likely, however, that we will see again the convergence of factors that pushed sprawling growth in the mid-twentieth century: the policy framework from the New Deal; the postwar baby boom and pent-up demand for housing; the clean new ribbons of concrete that allowed workers to travel quickly from job to home.

New forces are now at work. In 1950, 90.1 percent of all households were "family households." By 2000, that percentage had dropped to 68.8 percent. In these same 50 years, the average number of persons in a household dropped from 3.37 to 2.62. The percentage of women in the workforce nearly doubled from 1950 to 1990 (Bureau of the Census 2000). These changes have profound impacts on the type of housing and transportation we require. The nature of the land-use system is such that we have locked in policies and regulations that were meant for another age. Unless we change those policies, our environment, economy, and society will suffer.

CONSERVATION RECOMMENDATIONS

The question that conservationists must grapple with is: If not "here," then "where"? It is neither sufficient nor responsible to oppose sprawl without supporting an alternative. Development can bring important benefits when done with a healthy regard for environmental resources, economic impact, and social consequences. The U.S. population is expected to grow by another 100 million people before the middle of the twenty-first century. How and where are these people to be accommodated?

Conservationists must recognize the necessity of taking equally aggressive steps to make development happen in the right places as they do to stop development in the wrong places. This means lending environmental support to the growth of transit and to the funding that goes with that growth. It also means supporting development built in accordance with smart-growth principals—higher-density, mixed-use development, where people have choices to walk or bike, where environmental damage is minimized.

Support is needed for scientific research and for new policy and regulatory tools for applying that research. We know much more now about the impact of development than we did 50 years ago, when the first sprawling suburbs were bursting on the landscape. The importance of protecting whole systems—watersheds, ecosystems, landscapes, farmland "critical mass" regions—is gaining adherents in both the political and the scientific arenas.

Achieving these kinds of landscape protections will take money and regulatory systems. Neither alone will be enough. Traditional conservation tools such as purchasing land outright and acquiring development rights are fine, but changes in the policy and regulatory framework at the federal, state, and local levels of government are essential for success. There is not enough money to buy all the land that needs protecting for our own well-being and for that of generations that follow us.

REFERENCES

Bureau of the Census. 2000. Census 2000. Washington, D.C.: Bureau of the Census.

Congress for the New Urbanism. 1996. Charter of the new urbanism. Available at: www.cnu.org.

DeGrove, J. M., and D. A. Miness. 1992. Planning and Growth Management in the States. Cambridge, Mass.: Lincoln Institute of Land Policy.

Department of Agriculture, Natural Resources Conservation Service. 1992. National Resource Inventory. Washington, D.C.: Department of Agriculture.

Downs, A. 1992. Stuck in Traffic. Washington, D.C., and Cambridge, Mass.: Brookings Institution and Lincoln Institute of Land Policy.

Dymi, A. 2002. Demand grows for high-density housing. National Mortgage News, March 18, 22.

Energy Information Administration. 2004. Weekly premium gasoline prices. Available at: www.eia.doe.gov/emeu/international/gas1.html (accessed May 19, 2004).

Gerckens, L. C. 1994. American zoning and the physical isolation of uses. Planning Commissioners Journal 15:10.

Jackson, K. T. 1985. Crabgrass Frontier. New York: Oxford University Press.

Jacobs, J. 1961. The Death and Life of Great American Cities. New York: Random House.

Knaap, G., E. Talen, R. Olshansky, and C. Forrest. 2001. Government Policy and Urban Sprawl. Urbana: Department of Urban and Regional Planning, University of Illinois.

McHarg, Ian. 1969. Design with Nature. Garden City, N.Y.: Natural History Press.

Orfield, M. 1992. Metropolitics. Washington, D.C., and Cambridge, Mass.: Brookings Institution and Lincoln Institute of Land Policy.

Surface Transportation Policy Project. 1996. TEA-21 user's guide. Available at: www.stpp.org.

Von Hoffman, A. 1999. Housing Heats Up: Home Building Patterns in Metropolitan Areas. Center on Urban and Metropolitan Policy Survey Series. Washington, D.C.: Brookings Institution.

Washington Metropolitan Area Transit Authority. n.d. Metro means smart development. Available at: www.wmata.com.

Weingroff, R. F. 1996. Federal-Aid Highway Act of 1956: Creating the interstate system. Public Roads 60:10–17, 45–51.

THE IMPACTS OF SPRAWL ON BIODIVERSITY

Elizabeth A. Johnson and Michael W. Klemens

BIODIVERSITY

Biological diversity (or *biodiversity*, for short) is the variety of life on Earth and the interactions, cycles, and processes of nature that link it all together. In its broadest definition, biodiversity includes individual species, the genetic diversity within species, the natural communities in which these species interact, and the ecosystems and landscapes in which species evolve and coexist (Noss and Cooperrider 1994). Although conservation efforts to protect biodiversity tend to focus on unique plants or rare animals, biodiversity actually encompasses all nature, including both common and rare components and even more obscure organisms such as fungi and microbes.

Humans depend on biodiversity in myriad ways. Our food, fuel, shelter, clothing, and medicine rely on diverse natural resources. Indeed, more than 57 percent of the 150 most commonly used drugs in the United States originate from living organisms (Grifo et al. 1997). We make new discoveries every day about ways in which biodiversity benefits humans. For example, scientists recently discovered that the saliva of the Gila monster (*Heloderma suspectum*) contains a compound that may serve as a model drug to counteract the debilitating effect of diabetes (Nielson, Young, and Parkes 2003).

Biodiversity provides invaluable ecosystem services, or the ecological processes that sustain life on Earth, including decomposition, nutrient cycling and soil formation, pollination, filtration of pollutants from water, regulation of global temperature and precipitation, and flood and erosion control. At the genetic level, biodiversity allows species to adapt to changing environmental conditions. It also provides a genetic "library," a source of information to create better agricultural crops or livestock, which is, in essence, insurance for human food production. Biodiversity also teaches us how to solve problems. *Biomimicry* is the study of how humans solve problems in medicine, agriculture, manufacturing, and commerce using models from the natural world, such as the invention of Velcro, modeled on the seed-spreading strategies of cockleburs (*Xanthium* spp.), a common plant.

People look to the natural world as a source of beauty, inspiration, and renewal; it also serves as an outdoor laboratory that educates us about life processes. However, apart from the tangible (and often monetarily valuable) benefits that biodiversity provides for humans and other life-forms (Farber, chapter 12, this volume), biodiversity is also intrinsically valuable. Recent work by the Biodiversity Project (2001, 2002) has demonstrated the strong ethical and faith-based relationship that many people and cultures have with the natural world. Faith-based affirmations of stewardship, rooted in the need to respect processes and life-forms that transcend the human experience, are at the heart of many people's belief systems. Whether respect for "God's creation" or respect for all life because of its intrinsic worth as espoused by secular ethicists (e.g., humanists), such belief systems are often more powerful in moving people to action than scientific reasoning alone.

The diversity of life on Earth is severely threatened, however, despite widespread recognition of its critical importance. One-third of all plant and animal species in the United States is at risk of extinction (Stein, Kutner, and Adams 2000). Entire groups of organisms (e.g., primates, turtles, orchids) are under threat worldwide (IUCN 1989, 1996; Oates 1996). In fact, scientists predict that 30 percent of species globally may become extinct by 2050 (Novacek and Cleland 2001). Earth's biomes are under threat as well. For example, in the United States almost 97 percent of the tallgrass prairie has been destroyed by human activity, mainly for agricultural purposes, as well as more than half of the nation's wetlands (Stein, Kutner, and Adams 2000). Similar losses are occurring worldwide. The five major threats to biodiversity are (1) habitat loss, fragmentation, and degradation (including disruption of ecological processes); (2) invasive species; (3) pollution; (4) overexploitation; and (5) global climate change (Wilcove et al. 1998).

SPRAWL

Patterns of development associated with sprawl lead directly to habitat loss and fragmentation, with a concomitant reduction in biodiversity. In addition, sprawl plays a significant role in amplifying other threats to biodiversity. Humans alter the Earth's natural landscape in three main ways: through agriculture, natural-resource extraction, and urban and rural settlement (Vitousek et al. 1997; Marzluff and Hamel 2001). In many areas in the United States, settlement is replacing agriculture and resource extraction as the major land use (Heinz Center 2002). Sprawl and urbanization endanger more species than any other human activity in the United States and are more geographically widespread than all activities except for agriculture (Czech, Krausman, and Devers 2000). According to Meyer and Turner (1992), human dwellings and infrastructure now occupy 2.5 to 6 percent of the Earth, and approximately 10 percent of this area is covered with impervious surfaces.

Sprawl typically occurs in ever-widening bands surrounding large urban centers. Disconnected developments and single-family homes are established outside urban areas, well beyond city limits, but usually within commuting distances. In many areas of the United States, commutes of several hours have become the norm. Over time, the areas between the urban core and isolated satellite developments begin to fill in with buildings, parking lots, and manicured lawns, creating a dense suburb (Daniels 1999). These newly developed areas have also been called "peri-urban areas" (Imhoff 2000) and the "intermetropolitan periphery" (Berry 1990). The "exurban areas" beyond the suburbs are sometimes called "fringe" developments (Daniels 1999) and "extended places" (Bureau of the Census 2000). For the purposes of this chapter, we refer to all of it as *sprawl*.

Surprisingly, sprawl is also found in remote wilderness settings, around national parks, and near other scenic and recreational areas. According to Hart (1998), before World War II the countryside "belonged" primarily to the rich and famous. Today, postwar affluence and the creation of the Eisenhower Interstate Highway System have made the countryside available to a much wider segment of the population. Second homes abound in once undeveloped areas that are now accessible by car. In sum, sprawl has many forms, from a 1-acre (0.4 hectare) lot housing development to a strip mall to single-family vacation homes on isolated hilltops or on 40-acre (16-hectare) "ranchettes."

Much of what we know and hypothesize about the impacts of sprawling development on biodiversity comes from studies on the effects of urbanization on species and ecosystems. We know that biodiversity within cities differs significantly from that found in more rural, natural areas. Although there are exceptions related to both individual taxa and biomes, most studies looking at these differences have shown that urban environments tend to be species and ecosystem poor, supporting on average less than half the diversity found in natural habitats. Weedy plants and adaptable animal species tolerant of pollution and other environmental stresses characterize urban areas, whereas undeveloped lands in more rural areas support a suite of natural communities and a larger array of plants and animals, many of which have more specialized life history requirements (biological needs for food, shelter, reproduction, etc.) (McKinney 2002). There are some notable exceptions to this generalization. For example, in Tucson, Arizona, certain specialized bee species persist in urban areas because of increased nesting opportunities (Cane, chapter 5, this volume).

The physical environments in developed and undeveloped land often differ dramatically, and the biodiversity found in each place reflects these differences. Urban environments typically have more polluted water and air, compacted soils that impede root growth, increased artificial lighting, and increased disturbance by humans and their vehicles (Adams 1994). Cities are dominated by permanent structures, such as buildings and impervious pavement. These hardened surfaces alter the movement of water through the city, increasing runoff and channelizing stream flows (L'vovich and White 1990; Adams 1994). They also affect the city's climate. Most buildings and pavement absorb more of the sun's heat during the day than nonurban, vegetated land, making cities on average warmer than surrounding areas (Landsberg 1956; Berry 1990). Termed the *heat island effect*, this increase in temperature is also characteristic of suburban habitats, though to a lesser degree (Stone and Rodgers 2001). Sprawl-dominated environments fall somewhere along the gradient from wild to urban in terms of environmental characteristics.

Until the Industrial Revolution, cities were compact, with well-defined urban centers surrounded by rural agriculture and wild land. Even during much of the postindustrial era, cities remained relatively compact, constrained by transportation and the lack of a central authority directing growth and development of transportation infrastructure (Mumford 1956). Today, transportation and communication limitations no longer constrain us, and agricultural production has become globalized and divorced from local economies. This shift away from dependence on local agriculture has allowed people to move beyond city centers and to build homes on former agricultural lands. In addition, by fostering development in a sprawling fashion, we also alter more and more of the surrounding natural communities. These sprawling suburban environments ultimately have a greater impact on biodiversity than the once compact city because they affect a significantly larger area in a more dispersed fashion.

To many people, suburban environments may offer the best of both worlds — the amenities of an urban area in a more natural setting. These newly developed areas may also appear to benefit biodiversity because they often support elevated levels of species diversity, having both "sensitive" species that still survive in remnant natural habitats and generalist species characteristic of developed areas. However, as more and more of the remaining natural lands are developed, the end result is an increasingly simplified environment, no longer able to support sensitive species and overall having a severely diminished suite of species. In addition, as Marzluff and Hamel (2001) explain, although increases in generalist taxa may increase species biodiversity at the local level, we are losing species at a global level as more sensitive species are extirpated.

The remainder of this chapter examines some of sprawl's ecological impacts in relation to the five key threats to biodiversity:

- Habitat loss, fragmentation, and degradation
- Invasive species
- Pollution
- Overexploitation
- Global climate change

Although these overall threats are universal, certain effects may be site specific, reflecting the varied ecological systems and biomes where sprawl occurs.

HABITAT LOSS, FRAGMENTATION, AND DEGRADATION

Sprawl causes direct habitat loss as well as habitat fragmentation and degradation, affecting all levels of biodiversity, from species to ecosystems.

HABITAT LOSS

A *habitat* is the physical and biological environment used by an individual or a population of a species (Hall, Krasuman, and Morrison 1997). As defined by biologists, *habitat loss* is the conversion of one habitat type to another such that the new type no longer supports a given species. Development drastically and often permanently alters natural communities and ecosystems outright as wetlands are drained or filled and forests and farmlands are cleared for construction.

HABITAT FRAGMENTATION

Habitat fragmentation occurs when natural or human processes break large, contiguous areas into smaller, isolated patches. Although fragmentation is often associated with humans, it is also a natural process. Landscapes are fragmented over time by geologic forces, such as erosion and glaciation, and also by the workings of natural features such as rivers and mountains. Natural patchiness creates heterogeneous landscapes that support complex biological systems. However, fragmentation by human activities, a key characteristic of sprawling development, usually creates more simplified landscapes that interfere with ecosystems processes, disrupt species movement, and remove critical habitats.

Road construction is often the first stage of the human-caused fragmentation process. According to Forman and colleagues, "The road system ties the land

EFFECTS OF ROADS AND POWER LINES

Vehicles kill an estimated 1 million vertebrates per day in the United States (Forman and Alexander 1998). Similar impacts have been observed in the United Kingdom, where millions of birds and 20 to 40 percent of the amphibian breeding population are reported to die each year on roads (Juniper 2002). Impacts on invertebrates are less well known, although road traffic has been shown to lead to substantial mortality in butterflies (Samways 1994; McKenna, McKenna, and Malcolm 2001). Species mortality depends on traffic speed and volume and on species behavior and ecology. For example, mortality will be greater for individuals of species that have an intrinsically greater likelihood of crossing roads (e.g., greater for leopard frogs [*Rana pipiens*], which move about on land, than for green frogs [*Rana clamitans*], which remain in ponds) (Carr and Fahrig 2001). Species that move from a central breeding or hibernation place each year are particularly susceptible (e.g., timber rattlesnake [*Crotalus horridus*]). Also, species that are attracted to roads for basking, such as snakes and some insects, or for feeding, such as birds of prey, will also be subject to greater mortality. Such road mortality may actually jeopardize population persistence of species groups such as turtles (Gibbs and Shriver 2002).

Roads also alter or prevent species movement. On some highways, traffic is separated by "New Jersey" barriers—3-foot concrete lane dividers that few animals are able to cross. Some sections of highway, particularly in suburban areas, also have noise barriers that completely block roadsides for considerable distances. But even a level, seemingly narrow two-lane road without dividers restricts animal movement. Small road clearances less than 9 feet (3 meters) wide act as barriers to prairie voles (*Microtus ochrogaster*) (Swinhart and Slade 1984) and land snails (*Arianta arbustorum*) (Baur and Baur 1990). The presence of roads affects even larger, more mobile mammals (Ray, chapter 9, this volume). In contrast, carabid beetles and lycosid spiders move along roads rather than crossing them, illustrating another way in which roads change movement patterns (Mader, Schell, and Kornacker 1990). Preventing or altering these patterns means keeping these animals from carrying out their daily activities—finding food and shelter, encountering mates for reproduction, and dispersing and colonizing new habitats.

Roads, power lines, and other development-related infrastructure can also facilitate dispersal, but often with unintended effects on species and individuals. Predators such as crows and related birds (Corvidae) and mesocarnivores (smaller predators, such as foxes and raccoons) use power line rights-of-way to penetrate deeply into undisturbed habitats. Ravens (*Corvus corax*) prey on young desert tortoises (*Gopherus agassizii*) in the Mojave Desert from perches provided by power line poles. This novel habitat allows ravens to extend their foraging areas into previously inaccessible portions of the desert (Boarman 1997). Similarly, Boarman reported that two other desert tortoise predators, coyotes (*Canis latrans*) and kit foxes (*Vulpes macrotis*), were increasing their range into desert tortoise habitat by way of bridges and other artificial structures associated with development.

Roads also alter the quality of the surrounding environment by increasing pollution and noise and by increasing disturbance. This affected area is known as the *road-effect zone*. Forman and Deblinger (2000) found that the road-effect zone for a suburban highway in Massachusetts averaged 1,968 feet (600 meters) in width and varied in shape, depending on natural landscape features. Because of these secondary effects, living near roadways can be stressful to many organisms. For example, levels of stress-induced hormones were higher in northern spotted owls (*Strix occidentalis caurina*) living adjacent to highways than in populations living farther away (Wasser et al. 1997).

together for us, yet slices nature into pieces" (2003:xiii). Roads divide natural landscapes, increase access, and open the way for further development. Today it is estimated that roads ecologically affect 15 to 20 percent of the land area in the United States (Forman and Deblinger 2000) by associated pollution, noise, and other disturbances (for a detailed discussion, see the box "Effects of Roads and Power Lines"). Although the rate of increase in road density has slowed overall in this country, the road network in suburban areas is still rapidly expanding. People are driving more, and the total miles traveled per year are increasing, mostly as a result of increased commuting in sprawled development. As driving miles increase, road construction and improvements lead to changed traffic patterns and new bypasses. The new roads being built in sprawled areas are wider, of greater density, and better connected to larger highways, resulting in even greater traffic volume (Forman et al. 2003).

Once roads are established, habitat fragmentation accelerates with land clearing for agriculture or the construction of isolated vacation homes or large-lot subdivisions scattered here and there in otherwise undeveloped wild lands. This "early-stage" fragmentation, where a number of small developed areas are set within a larger natural ecosystem, is called a *perforated landscape* (Forman 1995). As development proceeds and intensifies over time, these remaining natural-habitat patches are built on, broken up, and divided even further. Ultimately, fragmentation irreversibly changes the larger landscape into a human-dominated matrix of impervious pavement, strip malls, and housing developments with only scattered patches of natural vegetation (figure 2.1).

HABITAT DEGRADATION

Sprawl also causes habitat degradation. *Habitat degradation* is the alteration of a species's habitat such that it reduces the habitat's ability to meet that species's needs. A degraded environment, although harmful to many species, may benefit others that are more tolerant (DeStefano and Johnson, chapter 10, this volume). Pollution and the introduction of invasive species to a landscape, two threats that also degrade habitats, are addressed later in this chapter.

HABITAT LOSS, FRAGMENTATION, AND DEGRADATION: EFFECTS ON SPECIES

Each species—whether plant, animal, fungi, or microbe—is adapted to a particular quantity and quality of environments. Each individual's survival depends on various environmental factors, including food quality and abundance; soil quality and availability of nutrients; light or shade; shelter; moisture or dryness; windiness or calmness; depth of leaf litter; presence and number of

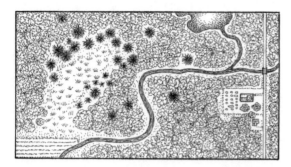

(a)

(b)

FIGURE 2.1. Roads lead to habitat conversion (*a*) initially with agriculture and isolated housing, (*b*) followed over time by more extensive development. (Artwork by Patricia Wynne)

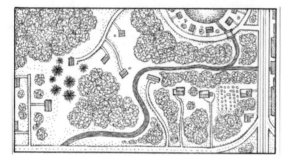

predators, parasites, and diseases; presence of mates; availability of seed dispersers (e.g., birds, ants); and quality of the surrounding landscape, including the connectivity between natural-habitat patches.

Habitat loss, fragmentation, and degradation affect these factors in three main ways: by reducing the size or amount of habitat available for species, by altering and degrading the environmental conditions within those remaining habitat patches, and by altering individual movement patterns among patches.

As natural-habitat patches decrease in size and area because of sprawling development, they initially appear to support a greater number of species and individuals, all seeking refuge in the remaining undeveloped habitat patch (Collinge and Forman 1998). Over time, however, these smaller fragments support fewer and fewer species. Loss of species is nonrandom, with large predators that require extensive areas of habitat typically disappearing first from a landscape (Ray, chapter 9, this volume).

The quality of the environment in these isolated patches degrades, also affecting species numbers and the quality of the ecological processes within the patch. Smaller patches have a greater ratio of edge habitat to interior habitat. *Edge habitats* are found at the interface of two ecosystems or areas of land use. In natural communities, edges or transitions between habitats, such as between field and forest, are gradual, whereas in human-dominated landscapes the transition between field and housing development or tropical rainforest and grazing fields is abrupt. A more gradual transition between landscape types provides a buffer to the interior patch environment from external physical and biological impacts (Forman 1995).

This buffering is important because edges often have environmental characteristics that are different from those of either of the two ecosystems they separate, and these altered conditions may affect the interior habitat. For example, in the middle of a deciduous forest, the environment is shady and more humid, with little wind, and the organisms living there are adapted to these habitat qualities. However, forest edges are exposed to warmer, drier, brighter, and often windier conditions. These different environmental conditions influence the kinds of plants and animals that can live at the edge, often supporting more generalist predators and invasive plant species (Forman 1995). The altered microclimate, predation rates, plant and animal communities, and ecosystem processes at the edge have an effect on the interior habitat. For instance, the extension of drier soil conditions into the forest from the edge may prevent certain seeds from germinating or invertebrates from finding shelter. New predators frequenting the edge habitat may encroach deeper into the forest. These influences (called *edge effects*) often extend for some distance into the habitat patch, with smaller fragments often having greater relative penetration. In fact, a very small fragment can be composed entirely of edge environment. Sprawl and its associated habitat fragmentation create abrupt boundaries between patches that dramatically increase the proportion and extent of edge habitat, with negative consequences for many sensitive species that are not able to thrive under such conditions.

Species movement and dispersal are also altered as habitat patches become further fragmented by development. This increased fragmentation makes it difficult for individuals of a species to find food and mates. Because many plant seeds are dispersed by animals (fruits, sticky seeds), reduced animal mobility affects plant populations as well. Without connections to one another, populations of many plants and animals unable to disperse become susceptible to genetic inbreeding and possibly to local extinction. Some species spend their entire lives in a single habitat, such as orchids growing deep in a northern white cedar swamp or dung beetles living in an Amazonian forest (Klein 1989). The quality of that single habitat is a key to population persistence. Other species, including most amphibians and dragonflies, require multiple habitat types at various life stages. Dragonflies and damselflies have an aquatic larval stage and as adults forage on land and over water. Amphibians also have an aquatic larval stage complete with gills, but as adults, most species develop lungs and many move out onto land for the remainder of their lives, returning to water only to breed (figure 2.2). Migratory birds and large herbivores such as elk move between summer breeding and wintering territories. And some larger carnivores

FIGURE 2.2. Spotted salamanders (*Ambystoma maculatum*) use many habitats, moving between upland forests and vernal pools, where they breed each spring. (Photo by Joseph C. Mitchell)

range widely over the landscape, visiting many habitat patches in order to meet their daily food and shelter requirements. In these cases, several natural communities are necessary for the survival of individuals and populations.

If the single habitat required by those orchid and beetle species is divided into smaller pieces that become increasingly separated, or if the multiple habitats required, for example, by amphibians and elk are also spatially isolated within the larger landscape, the structure of the fragmented landscape must permit safe passage of individuals between habitat patches for these individuals and populations to survive (on connectivity, see Sanjayan and Crooks, chapter 11, this volume). Human-dominated habitat matrices are inhospitable to many native species (see the box "Human Activities and Novel Disturbances"). Therefore, these sprawl-generated patterns of habitat patches alter and prevent seed dispersal in plants as well as natal and daily or seasonal movements and migration by animals (Byers and Mitchell, chapter 8, and Ray, chapter 9, this volume).

HABITAT LOSS, FRAGMENTATION, AND DEGRADATION: EFFECTS ON ECOSYSTEMS AND PROCESSES

Important ecosystem functions include *biogeochemical cycles*, such as the water and carbon cycles; *life cycles*, including photosynthesis, soil formation, and decomposition; and processes critical to the persistence of life, such as

HUMAN ACTIVITIES AND NOVEL DISTURBANCES

Sprawl brings people closer to the natural world. Although this may be beneficial for humans, our everyday activities create novel disturbances and impacts to the landscape. Even seemingly small-scale or short-term recreational activities, such as walking through the woods, bicycling, and off-road vehicle riding, take their toll on plant and animal species, even when these activities are confined to designated trails. These activities occur with greater frequency in natural lands that are adjacent to development. Trails affect the distribution, abundance, and reproductive success of bird species (Miller, Knight, and Miller 1998). Soil trampling related to human use has been shown to affect invertebrate fauna adversely (Duffey 1975), potentially altering food webs, nutrient cycling, and other ecosystem functions. Garber and Burger (1995) found that opening a previously closed forest to human access for fishing and hunting led to the rapid decline and extinction of wood turtle (*Clemmys insculpta*) populations. In fact, Boyle and Samson (1985) found that nonconsumptive outdoor recreation had negative effects on wildlife in 81 percent of the studies reviewed. Impacts to wildlife from recreational activities include the intentional or unintentional harassment of wildlife, which changes their behavior, in turn altering predator–prey relationships or reproductive behavior (Knight and Cole 1995). Certain human activities have measurable stress impacts on wildlife. Snowmobiles cause physiological stress responses in elk and wolves, measurable by glucocorticoid levels in their feces, which can translate into reduced reproduction and fitness (Creel et al. 2002).

   Plant communities are also affected by public access into natural areas. Impacts include soil compaction, altered drainage patterns, soil erosion and associated loss of nutrients, and trampling, all of which increase plant mortality (Adkison and Jackson 1996; Bhuju and Ohsawa 1998). Studies have shown that human impacts to forest floor vegetation can extend up to 262 feet (80 meters) into suburban forests from areas of human use (Matlack 1993), whether that use is related to recreation (campsites, trees cut for firewood) or to proximity to homes (dumping of yard waste or other debris).

pollination. Ecosystems are said to have integrity when the full complement of species and processes are in place, functioning sustainably within a normal range of variation. Such healthy ecosystems are often more resilient, better able to maintain key processes over time in the face of natural ecological change (Naeem and Li 1997). For instance, Tilman and Downing (1994) found that grassland communities in the midwestern U.S. prairies that supported a greater suite of species were better able to withstand the effects of sustained drought.

   Habitat loss, fragmentation, and degradation owing to development may reduce integrity by altering ecosystems and their associated processes. The hydrologic cycle is highly altered in developed areas as a result of channelization and the impervious nature of streets, sidewalks, and packed turf (L'vovich and White 1990). Sprawl and urbanization have also been shown to affect annual photosynthetic activity, reducing annual productivity by the equivalent of as much as 20 days (Imhoff 2000). According to Imhoff, although urbanization can lengthen the growing season in part because of the warmer temperatures found in cities (i.e., the urban heat island effect), it still reduces overall productivity in a region by reducing the amount of land available for plants to grow and hence reducing photosynthetic activity.

Species have integral roles to play in each of Earth's ecological processes and functions—for example, as pollinators (Byers and Mitchell, chapter 8, and Cane, chapter 5, this volume), as nutrient cyclers and decomposers (Carreiro, chapter 6, this volume), as seed dispersers, and even as top consumers. In some ecosystems, certain species have dominant roles. *Keystone species* are those on which entire communities of plants and animals depend. Many vertebrate species, such as the eastern indigo snake (*Drymarchon corais couperi*), and more than 300 species of invertebrates are intimately associated with the burrows of the gopher tortoise (*Gopherus polyphemus*) (Diemer 1992). In fact, the survival of some of these invertebrates at a site is entirely dependent on the presence of these burrows. The presence or absence of important interactive species such as the gopher tortoise significantly affects ecosystem functioning. Their loss resulting from changes in habitat caused by sprawl means that they either are no longer present at all or are no longer found at sufficient densities to be ecologically effective in carrying out their roles in the larger ecological process. In another example, the decline and disappearance of top consumers such as wolves from many landscapes has resulted in greater abundances of large herbivores such as white-tailed deer (*Odocoileus virginianus*), moose (*Alces alces*), and elk (*Cervus canadensis*). In turn, increased grazing pressure by these herbivores is altering the forest environments in which each lives, with trickle-down impacts on other species that also depend on the forest habitat. Maintaining predator–prey interactions is a key to ecosystem health (Soulé et al. 2003). Fragmentation owing to sprawl also contributes to the loss of these top predators, with similar repercussions in many ecosystems.

An important characteristic of ecosystems and communities is that they are dynamic; they change over time. These changes can be driven by natural succession, such as the slow filling of wetlands with sediments and associated changes in plants, or by disruptions or disturbances such as tree falls, hurricanes, and fire. Disturbances that bring about ecosystem change contribute to biodiversity, benefiting (increasing) some components or harming (decreasing) others. Some natural communities depend on disturbance, and occasional, unpredictable events may be a key to long-term environmental health (Kendle and Forbes 1997). For instance, some species are adapted to only one specific stage of ecological transition (i.e., successional stage) in an ecosystem and depend on some level of disturbance or habitat modification to maintain a particular habitat on the landscape. The bog turtle (*Clemmys muhlenbergii*) requires wet meadows with an open canopy. It moves between opening and closing habitat patches within a dynamic wetland system (Klemens 1993; Fish and Wildlife Service 2001). Kirtland's warblers (*Dendroica kirtlandii*) are dependent on periodic fire to maintain the ideal-aged jack pine (*Pinus banksiana*) stands in which they breed. Piping plovers (*Charadrius melodius*) and other beach-nesting birds depend on coastal storms and dune blowouts to create unvegetated back-dune areas where they nest. Other species adapt over time to prevailing environmental conditions. Some coniferous trees in fire-prone environments have evolved cones that open to release seeds only after heated by fire. Many of these pine trees are also able to regenerate by sprouting from bark and shoots.

Because disturbances have such an important role in community and landscape formation, any change to a disturbance regime may have far-reaching repercussions throughout the entire system. Human activity has not only introduced new agents of change to the land in the form of agriculture, forestry, and other resource extraction and development, but also altered the rates of change to natural lands and affected natural disturbance processes. In particular, sprawl disrupts the frequencies of large-scale disturbances, such as fire and flooding, that are critical to the maintenance of certain ecosystems (Reice, chapter 4, this volume). In some cases, the proximity of development to natural lands increases the frequency of a disturbance—for example, fire frequency increased in the chaparral in California (Keeley, Fotheringham, and Morias 1999). In other cases, fires and floods are suppressed to protect human interests, with potentially harmful effects on the species that require these natural disturbances for survival.

In the past, the consequences of natural changes in ecosystems were mitigated somewhat by the presence of nearby unaltered lands that either provided refuge to species affected by the disturbance itself or served as sources of individuals for recolonization after the disturbance. However, as sprawl converts more land to development, there are few or no adjacent undeveloped lands to meet these needs. In addition, sprawl and many other human activities typically alter natural habitats on a much larger scale than most natural disturbance events and, in the case of development, result in changes to the land that are often more severe and permanent (Walker and Willig 1999).

HABITAT LOSS, FRAGMENTATION, AND DEGRADATION: CHALLENGES POSED TO PLANNERS AND SCIENTISTS

As discussed in this chapter (and in chapter 10), although some plant and animal species readily adapt and even flourish in fragmented, human-dominated landscapes, most plants and animals exhibit sensitivities to human-induced disturbances. These sensitivities are determined in part by species-specific life history characteristics, by the characteristics of the ecosystem in which the alteration occurs, as well as by the type and severity of the habitat modification. For this reason, it is sometimes difficult to predict the effect of a specific habitat alteration on a particular species or ecosystem at any point in place and time. However, the more-sensitive species tend to be animals that are highly mobile, including neotropical migratory birds, or those with large home range requirements, such as the black bear (*Ursus americanus*) and gray wolf (*Canis lupus*) (Ray, chapter 9, this volume). Animals that use a mosaic of wetland and upland habitats during their life cycle, such as the Blanding's turtle (*Emydoidea blandingii*) and red-spotted newt (*Notophthalmus viridescens*); plants with limited dispersal capability, such as orchids; or species with small home ranges, such as carabid beetles and small mammals such as voles, are also sensitive to changes brought about by development (Byers and Mitchell, chapter 8, this volume). Other species very sensitive to human-induced environmental change include those with specific habitat requirements, such as old-growth forests or wetlands, or those with high site fidelity for nesting or migration; those with life history characteristics such as long generation times or nonpersistent seed banks or ground nests; those that are the focus of more intense human interest, such as collectible species or species considered to be overabundant or injurious; and those that compete with humans for habitat (e.g., beach-nesting birds, such as the piping plover).

Another challenge to biologists and planners alike is that changes that may be imperceptible to us can drastically alter the habitat for some plants and animals. For example, in New England, sprawl in rural areas is degrading forest habitats without obviously altering forest cover or shrub vegetation, so impacts are not as noticeable. However, ground-nesting birds, such as the ovenbird (*Seiurus aurocapillus*), are in decline, with the likely culprit being increased predation by nest predators attracted to the edges created by construction of new homes (Kluza, Griffin, and DeGraaf 2000). A similar phenomenon has been observed in native small mammal populations in Colorado grasslands. In this case, the densities of native rodents were significantly lower in grasslands near suburban edges than in interior grasslands, even though the grasslands themselves did not differ in vegetation attributes. Again, although on the surface the habitat appeared quite suitable, predation by domestic and human-tolerant predators may have been a key factor in the decline (Bock et al. 2002). Even something as seemingly minor as a single-family home tucked into an otherwise intact natural ecosystem has been shown to have a zone of negative impact on some nearby native wildlife as a result of combinations of factors, such as the presence of pets, yard lights, and backyard bird feeders. Odell and Knight (2001) observed that a house-distance effect alters bird densities up to 590 feet

(180 meters) from homes in rural areas in Colorado, with increases in human-adapted species (e.g., American robin [*Turdus migratorius*] and black-billed magpie [*Pica pica*]) and declines in human-sensitive species (dusky flycatcher [*Empidonax oherholseri*] and blue-gray gnatcatcher [*Polioptila caerulea*]).

In sum, sprawl plays a primary role in habitat loss, fragmentation, and degradation. Some impacts to species and ecosystems are well defined, others are more subtle, and some impacts will not become evident until many years after development of a landscape has occurred.

INVASIVE SPECIES

Sprawl exacerbates the spread of invasive species and disease. *Invasive species* are defined as those species whose populations have expanded dramatically and are affecting native species and communities in significant ways. Conservation biologists have identified invasive species, in particular nonnative species (those not originally occurring at a locale) introduced into natural habitats, as the second major threat to biodiversity (Vitousek et al. 1996; Wilcove et al. 1998; Stein, Kutner, and Adams 2000). Invasive species impact natural ecosystems and biodiversity by reducing the number of native species through competition for resources, predation and grazing, hybridization, and the introduction of new parasites and diseases. Invasive species also alter the frequency of disturbances such as fire regimes (e.g., cheat grass [*Bromus tectorum*] in the western United States), change soil chemistry (e.g., Japanese barberry [*Berberis thunbergii*] and Japanese stilt grass [*Microstigeum vimineum*] in the eastern United States), and alter hydrology (e.g., Brazilian pepper [*Schinus terebinthifolius*] in the Florida Everglades and salt cedar [*Tamarix* spp.] in the southwestern United States and Australia). Over the long term, these disruptions will alter the Earth's biota, change the role of native species in communities, cause radical changes in abundance, disrupt evolutionary processes, and cause the extinction of some species (Mack et al. 2000). In fact, nonnative fishes have been implicated as a causal factor in 68 percent of North American fish extinctions over the past 100 years, during which we lost 27 species and 13 subspecies of fishes (Miller, Williams, and Williams 1989). According to Wilcove and colleagues (1998), nonnative invasive species are partially responsible for the endangerment of 49 percent of imperiled species in the United States.

Disturbance such as sprawl accelerates the spread of invasive species. According to the St. Louis Declaration on Invasive Plant Species, "People are major dispersers of plants" (Fay 2001:29), even unwittingly by what they plant in their own backyards. In fact, half the plants considered to be most invasive in North America were introduced intentionally for horticultural use (Marinelli 1996). Developers also tend to overuse a small suite of nonnative species (e.g., Bradford pear [*Pyrus calleryana* "Bradford"] lining the streets of East Coast developments). These suburban monocultures are vulnerable to disease, create uniform habitats suitable for few species, and sometimes invade natural areas.

Suburban homes adjacent to natural areas are perfect places for invasive species, such as Japanese barberry or purple loosestrife (*Lythrum salicaria*), to "escape" into the wild because sprawl-type development creates habitat "steppingstones" that allow these species to disperse into unaffected areas. This spread is exacerbated when people dump yard wastes, which often contain seeds and tubers, along forest or stream edges, thereby facilitating the spread of invasive plants. Scotch broom (*Cytisus scoparius*), now a major problem in California and the Pacific Northwest, invaded in many places from home gardens (Hoshovsky 1986). Another effect of invasive species introduction is that the presence of one invasive species often facilitates the invasion of another, leading to what Simberloff and Van Holle (1999) have called "invasional meltdown." Sprawl is likely to increase this effect because so many invasive species are often found in housing developments.

Roads also contribute to the spread of invasive species. In Australia, the nonnative cane toad (*Bufo marinus*) dispersed along roadways into new habitats (Seabrook and Dettmann 1996), with negative effects on native fauna. Vehicles transport plant seeds into uninfested areas (Gelbard and Belnap 2003), and the movement of wind-dispersed seeds is often enhanced along roads (Forman et al. 2003). In New York State, purple loosestrife has reportedly spread via roadside ditches and culverts (Wilcox 1989). Furthermore, roadsides are often dominated by weedy, nonnative plant species. Extensive road building and suburban development have been identified as two of the three main factors in the spread of the yellow star thistle (*Centaurea solstitialis*) (Gerlach, Dyer, and Rice 1998), a nonnative plant particularly troublesome to natural communities in the western United States.

Invasive species that have negative ecological effects have been dubbed *disruptive species*, formally defined as "those species that have negative effects on natural areas and native species or cause damage to people and property" (Heinz Center 2002:192). Most often, these taxa are introduced, nonnative species. But even native species can become disruptive. This is especially likely if their populations expand out of control in human-dominated landscapes. Mitchell and Klemens (2000) coined the term *subsidized species* to describe species that are overabundant because of human activities. Some of these species can become disruptive. White-tailed deer are one example. They adapt readily to human-dominated, sprawling areas, and when they overpopulate an area, the intense grazing pressure impacts ecosystem function and, in turn, other species (including humans). Yet the landscape they favor is one created and maintained in part by sprawl (Allan, Keesing, and Ostfeld 2003).

Other subsidized species include predators such as raccoon (*Procyon lotor*), skunk (*Mephitis mephitis*), crow (*Corvus brachyrhynchos*), and red fox (*Vulpes vulpes*). They readily exploit urban or suburban environments where there are abundant food and den sites (created by habitat alteration), concentrated garbage, and a lack of competition with species sensitive to humans (DeStefano and Johnson, chapter 10, this volume). House cats (*Felis catus*) allowed to roam outdoors are also included in this category. Feral and free-ranging domestic cats, well subsidized by humans, are a significant factor in the mortality of small mammals, birds, reptiles, amphibians, and invertebrates. Estimates indicate that hundreds of millions of birds are killed by domestic cats annually (Coleman, Temple, and Craven 1997).

For the purposes of this chapter, we also consider many emerging infectious diseases to be a specialized form of invasive species. The spread of some of these diseases has also been exacerbated by sprawl as developments bring us closer to the "wild," increasing disease transmission between wild animals, humans, and their pets and domestic livestock. The synergistic impacts of sprawl development and forest fragmentation in the northeastern United States have led to decreased mammalian diversity (predominantly a decrease in predators on or competitors with white-footed mice); thus elevated population densities of white-footed mice occur in small forest fragments, which is leading to increased human exposure to Lyme disease. Smaller habitat fragments lead to even greater Lyme disease transmission (Allan, Keesing, and Ostfeld 2003) because the density of nymphal blacklegged ticks (*Ixodes scapularis*) and prevalence of nymphal infection are correlated with habitat patch size. Allan, Keesing, and Osfeld recommend that fragmenting forests into patches smaller than 2.5 to 5 acres (1–2 hectares) should be avoided (Koontz and Daszak, chapter 7, this volume).

In addition, with increased sprawl and subsequent habitat loss, fragmentation, and degradation, animals become physically concentrated in smaller and smaller areas, thus increasing population densities. This crowding, coupled with additional stress from human disturbance, leads to increased susceptibility to infection (Flanagan 2000). For example, ducks and other waterfowl become concentrated into smaller ponds as their wetland habitats are destroyed. Crowding leads to increased incidences of botulism, cholera, and other diseases (Friend 1995).

Sprawl also increases the spread of some plant diseases, with implications for the horticulture and forest industry as well as for the integrity of our native forests. For example, the rapid spread of oak wilt disease and its pathogen (*Ceratocystis fagacearum*) into forests in the midwestern United States has been attributed to the increasing construction of homes in formerly undeveloped forested areas (Blair 2001). When trees are damaged during development or pruned inappropriately by homeowners, the disease invades. Each home site then subsequently serves as a site for dispersal into the surrounding forest. Port Orford cedar root disease and the pathogen that causes it, *Phytophthora lateralis*, spreads by movement of contaminated soil, facilitated by land clearing and construction (E. Hansen, personal communication, January 2004).

POLLUTION

Sprawl increases and broadly disperses pollution. *Pollution* is defined as the contamination of air, water, or soil with undesirable amounts of material or heat as a direct or indirect result of human activity (Nebel and Wright 1998). It often refers to the release of synthetic substances from industrial or transportation sources, substances that are toxic to living organisms or that modify their habitats in ways harmful to them. However, even natural, nontoxic substances, such as excessive sedimentation or increased nutrients, can be harmful to species and alter community composition and ecosystem function. In addition, many pollutants are widely dispersed and often persist in the environment. Pollution is probably one of the most visible and most researched threats to biodiversity, particularly as it relates to humans, whether in the form of air pollution, water pollution, or toxic waste.

Pollution affects biodiversity at all levels. It can be toxic to organisms at certain concentrations or life stages. For example, larval dragonflies may be more susceptible to water pollution than are adults (Corbett 1999). Certain pollutants bioaccumulate, meaning that more toxic concentrations build up in the tissues of animals higher up the food chain as predators eat prey. Such toxic buildups often interfere with life processes such as reproduction (e.g., effects of DDT on birds of prey). Pollution can even affect entire ecosystems (e.g., acid rain is detrimental to both aquatic and forest systems), alter major biogeochemical cycles such as the nitrogen cycle and sulfur cycles, and impair ecosystem processes such as water filtration.

In the past 30 years in the United States, we have made great strides in environmental cleanup and in creating legislation to this effect (e.g., the Clean Water Act, Clean Air Act, Environmental Cleanup Review Act). Other countries, particularly in Europe, have also developed strict environmental quality regulations that have led to substantial improvement in air and water quality. In Sweden, regulations have been successful in reducing pollution from industry, but there is still substantial pollution from excessive consumption and waste. As noted by the Swedish Institute, "Nowadays, it is the consumers who, like it or not, are responsible for the greatest harm being done to the environment" (1999:1).

WATER POLLUTION

Sprawling development patterns have clearly made the task of cleaning our environment more challenging, particularly in the case of water pollution. In the 1970s, water-pollution control in the United States focused on point-source pollution, or pollution with a single source, such as industrial pipes that discharged directly into rivers. Today the greatest threat to our water quality is from nonpoint sources (Environmental Protection Agency 1994), or pollution that comes from multiple locations such as lawns, roads, and agricultural fields rather than from a single discharge pipe. Nonpoint-source pollution occurs when contaminants such as fertilizers, pesticides, and pet waste from agriculture and lawns as well as gasoline, oil, dust, and heavy metals from roadways run off the land into adjacent waterways and ultimately end up in coastal waters, lakes, and underground aquifers.

Dispersed development increases the extent of nonpoint pollution. New construction in undeveloped areas facilitates the movement of pollutants into previously unpolluted waterways. Coupled with this development pattern is the style of development, in particular the creation of impervious surfaces by pavement and extensive turf. A 1-acre (0.4-hectare) parking lot produces 16 times more runoff than an undeveloped meadow (Schueler 1994), and roads account for 60 percent of total imperviousness in suburban areas. Surprisingly, lawns are almost as impervious to water infiltration as asphalt (Sauer 1997; Otto et al. 2002).

In addition, dispersed development often relies on septic systems rather than on sewer systems for waste disposal. Well-designed and -maintained septic systems do filter contaminants. However, poorly functioning septic systems discharge contaminants to the landscape in a more dispersed manner. Even sewer systems malfunction or overflow, particularly after heavy rains, releasing contaminants into the environment. In addition, neither septic nor municipal wastewater-treatment systems are designed for effective removal of the specialized organic compounds found in household pharmaceuticals and personal care products. These products, detergents, and lawn and garden pesticides pose a risk to human and environmental health. For example, those pesticides that are endocrine disrupters, or chemicals that mimic or inhibit the effects of hormones, have entered lakes, streams, and coastal areas in many parts of the United States. In Florida, they have been implicated in the feminization of male alligators (*Alligator mississippiensis*), which exhibit reduced male characteristics (Guillette et al. 2000). Household antibiotics and antimicrobial agents from wastewater have been shown to affect species richness of stream algae adversely, with negative effects to food web structure and to other stream-dependent species likely (Wilson et al. 2003).

Roads, parking lots, and the increased driving associated with sprawl also increase nonpoint pollution loads, in turn creating problems for natural systems. In a study of the road-effect zone along a Massachusetts highway, Forman and Deblinger (2000) estimated that the effects of road salt can extend anywhere from 656 feet up to 4,921 feet (200–1,500 meters) away from roads. Road salts alter soil structure and permeability and harm vegetation and wildlife (Environment Canada 2001). Oil, grease, and hydrocarbons emitted from cars and trucks and chemical pollutants emitted from paving material also contaminate soil and are toxic to plants and most aquatic life, even at low concentrations (Center for Watershed Protection 2001; Forman et al. 2003; for further discussion of pollution in wetlands, see also Miller and Klemens, chapter 3, this volume).

Pollution in contaminated runoff from dispersed home sites and roads also affects distant ecosystems. Land-based surface runoff contaminated with domestic cat feces has recently been implicated as the source of the parasitic *Toxoplasma gondii* infections found in coastal populations of the southern sea otter (Miller et al. 2002). According to Howarth (1981, as cited in Walker 1990), more than 90 percent of the oil input into marine environments comes from "mundane sources," including sewage effluent and stormwater runoff. A recent survey by the U.S. Geological Survey confirmed that caffeine was present in 70 percent of the waters tested across the United States (Kolpin et al. 2002). Studies also indicate that caffeine has been detected in surface waters worldwide (Habeck 2003). Although caffeine is not currently considered a pollutant, such a widespread occurrence is a further indication of the extent of our environmental reach into the natural world.

AIR POLLUTION

The effect of sprawl on air pollution has been well documented. Sprawl necessitates the use of automobiles. Car use doubled in the United States between 1970 and 1990 (EPA 1993a), and similar increases occurred in Canada over the same period. In developed areas in Europe, cars are replacing stationary sources (e.g., smoke stacks) as the main source of air pollution (UNEP 2000). The U.S. Environmental Protection Agency (EPA) has identified both the increased miles driven and longer commuting distance (with more solo commuting) as the primary and secondary reasons for the continued persistence of mobile source pollution (EPA 1993b). However, for short car trips, most emissions occur during vehicle start-up, which also makes low-mileage trips a problem (Department of Transportation 2002). Pollutants from car exhaust increase acid deposition, alter soil acidity, and change nutrient availability, leading to tree death. Such pollutants also affect human health. It is estimated that half of all human mortality caused by air pollution in Austria, France, and Switzerland is attributed to vehicle use (Kunzli et al. 2000). In sum, as Benfield, Raimi, and Chen (1999) state, the more we drive, the more fuel we use, and the more greenhouse gases and pollutants our vehicles emit.

In addition to increased pollutant loads from sprawl-related vehicle use, there is also the increased air pollution from the use of two-cycle, gasoline-powered engines associated with lawn care, such as mowers, leaf blowers, and chain saws. The EPA estimates that a gas-powered lawnmower generates 11 times the air pollution of a new car for each hour of operation (Northeast Illinois Planning Commission 1997), with significant negative effects on suburban air quality.

NOISE AND ARTIFICIAL-LIGHT POLLUTION

Transportation and industry are leading sources of noise pollution. Sprawl enhances the noise levels related to transportation owing to increased automobile use. It also facilitates the penetration of noise into previously unaffected areas. Two-cycle engines—used not only in lawn equipment, but also in recreational vehicles (jet skis, snowmobiles, and dirt bikes)—are another major source of noise in suburban and nearby natural areas. Most animals rely on hearing to communicate, avoid predators, and find food. Increased noise pollution may cause them to alter their behavior or to move to less-optimal habitat. Many breeding birds, such as the willow warbler (*Phylloscopus trochilus*), are negatively affected by traffic noise and exhibit reduced densities near highways (Reijnen and Foppen 1994). In some cases, excessive noise levels have even been shown to cause hearing loss. For example, the Colorado Desert fringe-toed lizard (*Uma notata*) and the endangered desert kangaroo rat (*Dipodomys desertii*) experienced hearing loss as a result of motorcycle noise (Bondello and Brattstrom 1979).

Artificial light is another consequence of sprawl and urbanization. Night lighting, such as around individual homes or in parking lots, fragments the darkness, resulting in changes to certain behaviors, which lead to reduced reproductive success; it also increases susceptibility to predation and mortality. The impacts stem not only from direct exposure to individual lights, but also from "sky glow," the overall brighter skies caused by the reflection of lights off clouds and buildings. Life on Earth has evolved over the millennia in response to predictable day–night cycles. The use of lights at night interferes with these adaptations.

In addition, artificial nocturnal lighting alters birds' migratory pathways, increases fishes' susceptibility to predation, alters aquatic invertebrates' feeding behavior, and prevents certain frog species from feeding (Longcore and Rich 2004). Artificial lighting from street lights and flood-lit sports facilities on Reunion Island in the Indian Ocean adversely affects fledglings of Barau's petrel (*Pterodroma baraui*), a small seabird. The number of lights has mushroomed with development on the island. The young birds are attracted to the lights during their first flights to the sea, apparently because they confuse the lights with bioluminescent squid (Le Corre et al. 2002). A similar phenomenon has been observed in hatchling loggerhead sea turtles (*Caretta caretta*). Rather than moving to the sea upon hatching, they instead move toward the light from nearby coastal developments. (Hatchling sea turtles typically use the moonlight reflected on the ocean to orient them to water.) The result of these altered movement patterns is death for the dispersing young (Peters and Verhoeven 1994).

Most people are aware that many insects are attracted to lights, but they may not be aware that these mass movements toward light might have profound impacts to individuals and populations. Some declines in moth populations may be linked to the effect of artificial lights on their reproduction because the energy they spend flying around lights may reduce their ability to find mates or good places to lay eggs. Moths are also more susceptible to predation when under streetlights (Frank 1988). Some species, in particular predators, may benefit from night lighting and actually take advantage of lit situations; for example, spiders build webs near street lights, certain bat species such as pipistrelles (*Pipistrellis pipistrellus*) catch moths around street lights, and many birds come in early morning to feed on resting moths at street lights (Outen 2003). Night lighting is more often a threat than a benefit, however.

Light cycles also affect plant growth, influencing seed germination, flower and fruit development, and leaf drop. Although laboratory studies have led to greater understanding of how photoreceptors work in plants, there has been little or no research on the impact of night lighting on plants in the wild (Briggs 2002). Anecdotal reports indicate that deciduous trees retain their leaves longer in the fall when growing under streetlights and that the presence of streetlights may reduce the productivity of certain crops. However, further research is needed to illuminate the full impact of artificial lights.

OVEREXPLOITATION

Sprawl facilitates overexploitation. Overexploitation of natural resources, such as overharvesting of fishes or overhunting of wildlife, is a major threat to biodiversity. In many places in the world, it is considered more of a threat to many species than invasive species or pollution. For instance, human use of turtles for food is the principal cause of turtle population declines and endangerment of South American river turtles (*Podocnemis* spp.), the Central American river turtle (*Dermatemys mawii*), the Madagascaran big-headed turtle (*Erymnochelys madagascariensis*), and many Southeast Asian species (Thorbjarnarson et al. 2000). At first glance, sprawl would not seem to have any effect on this particular threat to biodiversity, yet there are direct, though sometimes subtle ways in which sprawl exacerbates overuse of our natural resources.

By bringing the public closer to nature via scattered development, sprawl makes many species, in particular turtles and plants, more vulnerable to collection. This action might be the final straw that wipes out a local population already stressed by the proximity of development, fragmentation, and attendant pollution. In many parts of the developing world, the creation of roads and settlements in pristine areas, often associated with logging concessions and resource extraction, creates a huge increase in the exploitation of wildlife for the bushmeat trade by facilitating access (Robinson, Redford, and Bennett 1999). Whether in collecting by professional poachers or in "collecting" by children—for instance, when they bring box turtles (*Terrapene carolina*) home to live in their yards—the constant removal of individuals from a population over time, especially of slow-growing, long-lived species, can cause entire populations to become locally extinct (Byers and Mitchell, chapter 8, this volume).

Overconsumption, or consumerism, which Barrow describes as "the demand for material things which are not vital for adequate survival" (1999:664), is a major underlying factor leading to overexploitation and other environmental degradation. For instance, living in a more compact village or city setting has less impact on the environment than living in a sprawling housing development. According to Kolankiewicz and Beck (2001), the causes of sprawl are divided almost equally between population growth and our land-use and consumption choices. Liu and others (2003) report that the increase in household numbers worldwide and the resulting higher resource consumption per household are serious challenges for biodiversity conservation.

Driven not only by policy decisions that facilitate sprawl (Lawrence, chapter 1, this volume), the decision to live in a sprawled environment is based largely on personal and societal choices for a certain lifestyle. As Coffin and Elder explain in more detail in chapter 15 of this volume, this decision is often linked to a desire for greater mobility, improved schools, and the perception that the quality of life is better than in many urban areas. Ironically, although people care about and wish to live "close to nature," the sprawl they create ends up degrading the very nature and green space they crave.

Large single-family homes scattered over a landscape require more resource use and infrastructure support to maintain them. This not only affects the immediate environment but also has repercussions in faraway ecosystems. Deforestation rates increased dramatically during the twentieth century—in part for human settlement and agriculture, but also for extraction of forest products, including timber for large-home construction. A dispersed development pattern affects water resources and groundwater recharge, necessitating the use of individual wells and septic systems. In addition, the large properties typical of the suburbs consume almost 16 times more water than homes on smaller lots in urban settings (Otto et al. 2002). Consumptive use by humans takes water out of circulation in the hydrologic cycle more quickly than it can normally be returned to the atmosphere by evaporation. For example, lawn watering returns most water directly to the atmosphere through evaporation instead of allowing it to enter the ground to recharge aquifers. The lack of groundwater recharge is an especially pressing issue when development is sited in already arid regions (e.g., the southwestern United States, fynbos of South Africa).

Sprawl and suburban development also lead to increased energy use. According to Browning, Helou, and Larocque (1998), a household with the newest, most energy efficient design and appliances in a typical U.S. suburb consumes more energy than a traditionally older and smaller inner-city household because of the need for increased vehicle use in the suburbs. This sprawl-related vehicle use, along with other transportation, accounts for 70 percent of the total annual oil consumption in the United States (Department of Energy 2000). Once again, sprawl and its associated vehicle use lead directly to overconsumption of natural resources.

GLOBAL CLIMATE CHANGE

Sprawl contributes to and compromises species and ecosystem responses to global climate change. Scientists agree that the Earth's climate is indeed warming and that biodiversity will be affected worldwide (Malcolm and Pitelka 2000; IPCC 2001a, 2001b). Expected impacts include warming temperatures, rising sea level, changing rainfall patterns, declining water balances, and increased extreme climatic events. Scientists predict that human-induced climate change may become the greatest threat to biodiversity in some regions of the world and that 18 to 35 percent of species may face extinction in the future as a result of this anthropogenic warming of the Earth (Thomas et al. 2004). This overall change in climate has been attributed to a number of factors, the predominant one being the increase in carbon dioxide and other gases from the use of fossil fuels (IPCC 2001a, 2001b). Because a high dependence on automobile use is a major result of sprawl, sprawl is therefore an important factor in contributing to the conditions for climate change.

As the climate changes, species and subsequently ecosystems will respond. Some species and systems will adapt to the new conditions; others will migrate to areas with more favorable conditions; and still others will perish. Studies are already documenting changes in phenology (the seasonal timing of such events as flowering and germination), species ranges, and ecology. For example, reports indicate that amphibians are emerging from hibernation earlier in the spring (Beebee 1995; Gibbs and Breisch 2001), birds are breeding earlier (Crick et al. 1997), eastern European trees are blooming sooner, and some tropical birds and butterflies are shifting their ranges (Parmesan et al. 1999; Hughes 2000).

The extent of poorly planned development and its juxtaposition with natural habitat will determine, in part, the way in which climate change affects a landscape and the extent to which biodiversity is impacted by or can adapt to these changes. Ecosystem fragmentation and fragmenting agents such as roads, all a result of sprawl, will disrupt migratory pathways as species move in response to changing temperature and other climatic conditions. There will be particular challenges to species and habitats with restricted distribution, such as alpine areas that will become warmer and simply disappear. Coastal wetlands and estuaries and the species that depend on them will be particularly vulnerable to any rise in sea level. The intense development that exists along the coastal zone will create a barrier for the inland migration of tidal wetlands following a rise in sea level. There will also be challenges to species with limited dispersal capabilities. Migratory species, such as seabirds and shorebirds (e.g., red knot [*Calidris canutus*]), that depend on the availability of resources at specific times during the year may also have difficulties as the key resources they depend on en route may no longer be found or may not be present at the time needed (Myers and Lester 1992). This disconnect between the need for and the availability of such resources is in part owing to the fact that bird migration is triggered by changes in day length, whereas the hatching or spawning of many invertebrate prey species is cued by other factors, such as temperature.

One response to climate change may be adaptation to the new conditions, but this may be the only option for those species unable to migrate in response to the change. Whether adaptation is possible will depend in part on the speed of the environmental change and on the existence of suitable genetic variation in populations to enable adaptation. Sprawl and fragmentation will ultimately reduce genetic variability by increasing the likelihood of localized extinctions of small, now isolated populations and by diminishing the quality of the remaining habitat.

Another important factor to consider is that our existing system of parks and other protected areas may no longer serve to protect plants and animals whose ranges shift in response to climate change. As species move, their ranges will likely shift outside the boundaries of these protected areas into less hospitable, human-altered landscapes, ultimately leading to the demise of individuals and populations. For this reason, it is vital that our human-dominated environments remain as natural as possible.

CONCLUSION

In addition to sprawl's role as a leading cause of habitat loss and alteration and contributing substantially to the other threats to biodiversity, there is a synergy among all these threats and human actions related to sprawl.

Species or natural communities may persist and may tolerate the assault of one threat, but the additive or synergistic impacts of suburban sprawl and the resulting habitat fragmentation and degradation can completely decimate them. As Laurance and Cochrane (2001) explain, habitat fragmentation creates fragments more vulnerable to other stresses, whether those stresses are from air pollution, increased susceptibility to fire and storms, or invasion by nonnative species. Global warming has been cited as an example of an added stress with which many birds will have to cope in order to survive (Price and Glick 2002).

Indeed, it is usually not just one threat that causes a plant or an animal population to die out finally, but rather the cumulative effect of many stresses. In fact, a set of small changes may actually have a far greater effect on biodiversity than a single major change (Tilman and Lehman 2001). For example, the greatest threat to the world's swamp pink (*Helonias bullata*) populations is alteration of the natural hydrology of its stream and wetland habitats (figure 2.3). The proximity of housing and other development in adjacent upland habitats is a key factor in significantly altering water flow and groundwater levels. Such development also leads to increased spread of invasive nonnative plants into the wetlands, increased pollution of the stream and wetlands, outright destruction of the plants themselves from trampling and bank erosion, and increased browsing by deer that are thriving in sprawling developments (E. A. Johnson, personal observation; Fish and Wildlife Service 1991). Swamp pink populations may tolerate one or two of these threats and still remain stable, but the cumulative effects of so many stresses—competition for resources with exotic species, pollution that reduces habitat quality and thus leads to poor growth, altered hydrology and the grazing pressures from deer that prevent the plants from flowering and producing seeds—all take their toll. Ultimately, all the energy of individual plants is allocated to just surviving another day, another season, over time resulting in the loss of these populations.

All of Earth's ecosystems and associated species are linked by their processes, meaning that any change to one component will affect all interdependent systems, both proximal and distant. For example, any change to a headwater

FIGURE 2.3. Swamp pink (*Helonias bullata*) flowers in late April. Found in scattered populations from New Jersey south to North Carolina, swamp pink is threatened by altered hydrology and other impacts from adjacent development. (Photo by Elizabeth A. Johnson)

stream through water diversion or withdrawal or even excess sedimentation resulting from stormwater surges from adjacent developments will directly affect that individual stream section. In addition, these habitat alterations affect the downstream river ecosystems into which the stream feeds, the connected estuaries, and the coastal environments. In the same way, sprawl's impacts are also far-reaching. Not only is the upland environment where development occurs directly altered, but so are nearby wetlands (Miller and Klemens, chapter 3, this volume) and even coastal systems (Reice, chapter 4, this volume). According to Beach, "runaway land consumption, dysfunctional suburban development patterns, and exponential growth in automobile use are the real engines of pollution and habitat degradation on the coast" (2002:ii). Such degradation negatively affects estuarine habitat quality, in part by altering water temperatures and increasing pollutant loads, and is leading to severe and possibly irreversible declines in the health of many coastal ecosystems.

What does all this mean to us? Sprawl is leading to the loss of rare and common species and possible species extinctions. It is also leading directly to the loss of our natural environment, of ecosystem functioning, and of the quality of our lives. Urban and suburban biotic and cultural communities are also beginning to look the same everywhere, hosting not only similar species but the same chain stores and big-box retailers. According to Lockwood and McKinney, apart from the decline in biodiversity, "perhaps the most troubling aspect of biological homogenization is how it could degrade the human perception of 'nature.' . . . People begin to care less about the species they see, as more and more of the things they *do* see are as 'common as dirt.' . . . Biological homogenization creates more than an impaired global environment, it creates a biologically indifferent culture" (2001:viii). In addition, the loss of biodiversity from city and suburban landscapes reduces our children's ability to experience the fullness of nature and thereby to feel part of our natural world. Ultimately, this detachment from nature reduces the motivation to protect it.

In today's world, the move away from cities into single-family homes in a poorly planned fashion is coupled with increasing population growth and resource demand, making such a move unsustainable. Researchers from the Wildlife Conservation Society and Columbia University recently mapped the global "human footprint," the sum total of human population density, roads, human land use, and lights visible by satellite at night. The human footprint shows the patterns of sprawl on a global scale, but if we zoom in on specific areas, we can see few remaining wild areas, largely surrounded by rural lands, fragmented by road systems and human development, and punctuated by suburban and urban areas. This gradient reflects increases in human population density, road density, more intensive land use, and increased use of electrical lights, particularly in the developed world, including the United States, Europe, Australia, and Japan. At the high end, these factors are associated with sprawling development and, as time goes on, with a replacement of less-developed areas by more-developed ones: rural by exurban, exurban by suburban, suburban by urban. The global extent of the human footprint explains why sprawl is such a pervasive threat to biodiversity at both local and global scales (Sanderson et al. 2002).

This chapter provides an overview of some of the ways in which sprawl affects biodiversity. Although benefiting some species and creating novel habitats, sprawl and the lifestyles associated with it more often destroy, fragment, and degrade natural habitat; increase the spread of invasive species; lead to greater environmental pollution; add to overexploitation of our natural resources; and contribute greatly to global climate change. We are far from understanding the subtleties and synergies of the interactions between sprawl and other threats to biodiversity, but we cannot let that be an impediment to take action. As the creators and drivers of sprawl, we have the power to modify our practices and policies to live more sustainably. Our goal for cataloging these impacts is to create a foundation for meaningful change in our patterns of development and resource consumption that will help conserve the wealth and diversity of species and ecological processes on which all life, including our own, depends.

REFERENCES

Adams, L. W. 1994. *Urban Wildlife Habitats: A Landscape Perspective*. Minneapolis: University of Minnesota Press.

Adkison, G. P., and M. T. Jackson. 1996. Changes in ground-layer vegetation near trails in midwestern U.S. forests. *Natural Areas Journal* 16:14–23.

Allan, B. F., F. Keesing, and R. S. Ostfeld. 2003. Effect of forest fragmentation on Lyme disease risk. *Conservation Biology* 17:267–272.

Barrow, C. J. 1999. How humans respond to natural or anthropogenic disturbance. In L. R. Walker, ed., *Ecosystems of the World*. Vol. 16, *Ecosystems of Disturbed Ground*, 659–671. New York: Elsevier.

Baur, A., and B. Baur. 1990. Are roads barriers to dispersal in the land snail *Arianta arbustorum? Canadian Journal of Zoology* 68:613–617.

Beach, D. 2002. *Coastal Sprawl: The Effects of Urban Design on Aquatic Ecosystems in the United States*. Arlington, Va.: Pew Oceans Commission.

Beebee, T. J. C. 1995. Amphibian breeding and climate. *Nature* 374:219–220.

Benfield, F. K., M. D. Raimi, and D. D. T. Chen. 1999. *Once There Were Greenfields (How Urban Sprawl Is Undermining America's Environment, Economy, and Social Fabric)*. Washington, D.C.: Natural Resource Defense Council.

Berry, B. J. L. 1990. Urbanization. In B. L. Turner, W. C. Clark, R. W. Dates, J. F. Richards, J. T. Mathews, and W. B. Meyer, eds., *The Earth as Transformed by Human Action: Global and Regional Changes in the Biosphere over the Past 300 Years*, 103–119. Cambridge: Cambridge University Press.

Bhuju, D. R., and M. Ohsawa. 1998. Effects of nature trails on ground vegetation and understory colonization of a patchy remnant forest in an urban domain. *Biological Conservation* 85:123–135.

Biodiversity Project. 2001. *Building Partnerships with the Faith Community: A Resource Guide for Environmental Groups*. Madison, Wis.: Biodiversity Project.

———. 2002. *Ethics for a Small Planet: A Communications Handbook on the Ethical and Theological Reasons for Protecting Biodiversity*. Madison, Wis.: Biodiversity Project.

Blair, N. 2001. *The Surprising Connection Between New Housing and Oak Wilt*. St. Paul, Minn.: North Central Research Station and U.S. Forest Service. Also available at: www.ncrs.fs.fed.us/news/ncnewsarchives/2001JanFebMar.pdf.

Boarman, W. I. 1997. Predation on turtles and tortoises by a "subsidized predator." In *Proceedings: Conservation, Restoration, and Management of Tortoises and Turtles—An International Conference*, 103–4. New York: New York Turtle and Tortoise Society.

Bock, C. E., K. T. Vierling, S. I. Haire, J. D. Boone, and W. W. Merkle. 2002. Patterns of rodent abundance on open-space grasslands in relation to suburban edges. *Conservation Biology* 16:1653–1658.

Bondello, M. C., and B. H. Brattstrom. 1979. *The Experimental Effects of Off-road Vehicle Sounds on Three Species of Desert Vertebrates*. Washington, D.C.: Bureau of Land Management.

Boyle, S. A., and F. B. Samson. 1985. Effects of noncomsumptive recreation on wildlife: A review. *Wildlife Society Bulletin* 13:110–116.

Briggs, W. R. 2002. Plant photoreceptors: Proteins that perceive information vital for plant development from the light environment. Abstract presented at Ecological Consequences of Artificial Night Lighting Meeting, February 23–24, 2002, Los Angeles, Calif. Available at: www.urbanwildlands.org/conference.html.

Browning, R., M. Helou, and P. Larocque, 1998. Impacts of transportation on household energy consumption. *World Transport Policy and Practice* 4:36–39.

Bureau of the Census. U.S. Census Bureau definitions for urban and rural. Available at: www. census.gov/geo/www.tiger/glossary.html#urbanandrural.

Carr, L. W., and L. Fahrig. 2001. Impact of road traffic on two amphibian species of different vagility. *Conservation Biology* 15:1071–1078.

Center for Watershed Protection. 2001. Impacts of new development. In *New York State Stormwater Management Design Manual*, 2.1–2.15. Ellicott City, Md.: Center for Watershed Protection.

Coleman, J. S., S. A. Temple, and S. R. Craven. 1997. Cats and wildlife: A conservation dilemma. Available at: www.wisc.edu/extension/catfly3.htm.

Collinge, S. K., and R. T. T. Forman. 1998. A conceptual model of land conversion processes: Predictions and evidence from a field experiment with grassland insects. *Oikos* 82:66–84.

Corbett, P. S. 1999. *Dragonflies: Behavior and Ecology of Odonata*. Ithaca, N.Y.: Cornell University Press.

Creel, S., J. E. Fox, A. Hardy, J. Sands, B. Garrott, and R. O. Peterson. 2002. Snowmobile activity and glucocorticoid stress responses in wolves and elk. *Conservation Biology* 16:809–814.

Crick, H. Q. P., C. Dudley, D. E. Glue, and D. L. Thomas. 1997. UK birds are laying eggs earlier. *Nature* 388:526.

Czech, B., P. R. Krausman, and P. K. Devers. 2000. Economic associations among causes of species endangerment in the U.S. *BioScience* 50:593–601.

Daniels, T. 1999. *When City and Country Collide: Managing Growth in the Metropolitan Fringe*. Washington, D.C.: Island Press.

Department of Energy. Energy Information Administration. 2000. *Annual Energy Outlook 2001, with Projections to 2020*. DOE/EIA-0383(2001). Washington, D.C.: Department of Energy.

Diemer, J. E. 1992. Gopher tortoise. In P. E. Moler, ed., *Rare and Endangered Biota of Florida: Amphibians and Reptiles*, 123–127. Gainesville: University Press of Florida.

Duffey, E. 1975. The effects of human trampling on the fauna of grassland litter. *Biological Conservation* 7:255–274.

Environment Canada/Health Canada. 2001. *Canadian Environmental Protection Act, 1999 — Priority Substances List — Assessment Report — Road Salts*. Hull, Que.: Existing Substances Branch, Environment Canada.

Environmental Protection Agency (EPA). Office of Mobile Resources. 1993a. *Automobile and Ozone Factsheet*. EPA-400-F-92-006. Washington, D.C.: EPA.

———. Office of Air Quality Planning and Standards. 1993b. *The Plain English Guide to the Clean Air Act*. EPA-400-K-93-001. Washington, D.C.: EPA.

———. Office of Water. 1994. *The Quality of Our Nation's Water: 1992 United States*. EPA-841-S-94-002. Washington, D.C.: EPA.

Fay, K., ed. 2001. *Linking Ecology and Horticulture to Prevent Plant Invasions*. St. Louis: Missouri Botanical Garden.

Federal Highway Administration. 2002. *Transportation Air Quality: Selected Facts and Figures*. Washington, D.C.: Department of Transportation. Also available at: www. flhwa.dot.gov/environment/aqfactbk/facttoc.htm.

Fish and Wildlife Service. 1991. *Swamp Pink* (Helonias bullata) *Recovery Plan*. Washington, D.C.: Department of the Interior, Fish and Wildlife Service.

———. 2001. *Bog Turtle* (Clemmys muhlenbergii), *Northern Population, Recovery Plan*. Washington, D.C.: Department of the Interior, Fish and Wildlife Service.

Flanagan, J. 2000. Disease and health considerations. In M.W. Klemens, ed., *Turtle Conservation*, 85–95. Washington, D.C.: Smithsonian Institution Press.

Forman, R.T.T. 1995. *Land Mosaics: The Ecology of Landscapes and Regions*. Cambridge: Cambridge University Press.

Forman, R. T. T., and L. E. Alexander. 1998. Roads and their ecological effects. *Annual Review of Ecology and Systematics* 29:207–231.

Forman, R.T.T., and R.D. Deblinger. 2000. The ecological road-effect zone of a Massachusetts (U.S.A.) suburban highway. *Conservation Biology* 14:36–46.

Forman, R.T.T., D. Sperling, J.A. Bissonette, A.P. Clevenger, C.D. Cutshall, V.H. Dale, L. Fahrig, R. France, C.R. Goldman, K. Heanue, J.A. Jones, F.J. Swanson, T. Turrentine, and T.C. Winter. 2003. *Road Ecology: Science and Solution*. Washington, D.C.: Island Press.

Frank, K.D. 1988. The impact of lighting on moths: An assessment. *Journal of the Lepidopterists' Society* 42:63–93.

Friend, M. 1995. Increased avian diseases with avian change. In E.T. LaRoe, G.S. Farris, C. E. Puckett, P.D. Doran, and M.J. Mac, eds., *Our Living Resources: A Report to the Nation on the Distribution, Abundance, and Health of U.S. Plants, Animals, and Ecosystems*, 401–405. Washington, D.C.: Department of the Interior, National Biological Service.

Garber, S.D., and J. Burger. 1995. A 20-yr study documenting the relationship between turtle decline and human recreation. *Ecological Applications* 5:1151–1162.

Gelbard, J. L., and J. Belnap 2003. Roads as conduits for exotic plant invasions in a semiarid landscape. *Conservation Biology* 17:420–432.

Gerlach, J.D., A. Dyer, and K.J. Rice. 1998. Grassland and foothill woodland ecosystems of the Central Valley. *Fremontia* 26:39–43.

Gibbs, J.P., and A.R. Breisch. 2001. Climate warming and calling phenology of frogs near Ithaca, New York, 1900–1999. *Conservation Biology* 15:1175–1178.

Gibbs, J.P., and W.G. Shriver. 2002. Estimating the effects of road mortality on turtle populations. *Conservation Biology* 16:1647–1652.

Grifo, F., D. Newman, A.S. Fairfield, B. Bhattacharya, and J.T. Brupenhoff. 1997. The origins of prescription drugs. In F. Grifo and J. Rosenthal, eds., *Biodiversity and Human Health*, 131–163. Washington, D.C.: Island Press.

Guillette, L.J., D.A. Crain, M.P. Gunderson, S.A. Kools, M.R. Milnes, D.F. Orlando, A.A. Rooney, and A.R. Woodward. 2000. Alligators and endocrine disrupting contaminants: A current perspective. *American Zoologist* 40:438–452.

Habeck, M. 2003. Testing for caffeine reveals pollution. *Frontiers in Ecology and the Environment* 1:64.

Hall, L.S., P.R. Krasuman, and M.L. Morrison. 1997. The habitat concepts and a plea for standard terminology. *Wildlife Society Bulletin* 25:173–182.

Hart, J. F. 1998. *The Rural Landscape.* Baltimore: Johns Hopkins University Press.

Heinz Center. 2002. *The State of the Nation's Ecosystems: Measuring the Lands, Waters, and Living Resources of the United States.* Cambridge: Cambridge University Press.

Hoshovsky, M. 1986. *Element Stewardship Abstract for* Cytisus scoparius *and* Genista monspessulatus. Arlington, Va.: Nature Conservancy.

Howarth, R. W. 1981. Oil and fish: Can they coexist? In T. C. Jackson and D. Reische, eds., *Coast Alert,* 49–72. San Francisco: Friends of the Earth.

Hughes, L. 2000. Biological consequences of global warming: Is the signal already apparent? *Trends in Ecology and Evolution* 15:56–61.

Imhoff, M. L. 2000. The use of multisource satellite and geospatial data to study the effect of urbanization on primary productivity in the United States. *Transactions in Geoscience and Remote Sensing* 38:2549–2556.

Intergovernmental Panel on Climate Change (IPCC). 2001a. Climate change 2001: Impacts, adaptation, vulnerability. A report of Working Group II of the IPCC, approved at the Sixth Session of the IPCC, Geneva, Switzerland, February 13–16, 2001. Available at: www.ipcc.ch/pub/wg2SPMfinal.pdf.

——. 2001b. Climate change 2001: The scientific basis. Third assessment report of Working Group I of the IPCC, approved at the Eighth Session of the IPCC, Shanghai, China, January 17–20, 2001. Available at: www.ipcc.ch/pub/wg2SPMfinal.pdf.

International Union for Conservation of Nature and Natural Resources (IUCN). 1989. *Tortoises and Freshwater Turtles, an Action Plan for Their Conservation.* Gland, Switzerland: IUCN, Species Survival Commission, Tortoise and Freshwater Turtle Specialist Group.

——. Species Survival Commission. Orchid Specialist Group. 1996. *Orchids—Status Survey and Conservation Action Plan.* Gland, Switzerland: IUCN.

Juniper, T. 2002 . Public opinion, wildlife, and roads. In B. Sherwood, D. Cutler, and J. A. Burton, eds., *Wildlife and Roads: The Ecological Impact,* 101–111. London: Imperial College Press.

Keeley, J., C. J. Fotheringham, and M. Morias. 1999. Reexamining fire suppression impacts on brushland fire regimes. *Science* 284:1829–1932.

Kendle, T., and S. Forbes. 1997. *Urban Nature Conservation.* London: E & FN SPON.

Klein, B. C. 1989. Effects of forest fragmentation on dung and carrion beetle communities in central Amazonia. *Ecology* 70:1715–1725.

Klemens, M. W. 1993. *Amphibians and Reptiles of Connecticut and Adjacent Regions.* State Geological and Natural History Survey of Connecticut, bulletin no. 112. Hartford: Connecticut Department of Environmental Protection.

Kluza, D. A., C. R. Griffin, and R. M. DeGraaf. 2000. Housing developments in rural New England: Effects on forest birds. *Animal Conservation* 3:15–26.

Knight, R. L., and D. N. Cole. 1995. Wildlife responses to recreationists. In R. L. Knight and K. J. Gutzwiller, eds., *Wildlife and Recreationists: Coexistence Through Management and Research,* 51–69. Washington, D.C.: Island Press.

Kolankiewicz, L., and R. Beck. 2001. Weighing sprawl factors in large US cities. *Sprawl City.* Available at: www.sprawlcity.org/studyUSA/inex.html [Geo-2-222].

Kolpin, D. W., E. F. Furlong, M. T. Meyer, E. M. Thurman, S. D. Zaugg, L. B. Barber, and H. T. Buxton. 2002. Pharmaceuticals, hormones, and other organic wastewater contaminants in U.S. streams 1999–2000: A national reconnaissance. *Environmental Science and Technology* 36:1202–1211.

Kunzli, N., R. Kaiser, S. Medina, M. Studnicka, O. Chanel, P. Filliger, M. Herry, F. Horak Jr., V. Puybonnieux-Texier, P. Quenel, J. Schneider, R. Seethaler, J.-C. Vergnaud, and H. Sommer. 2000. Public-health impact of outdoor and traffic-related air pollution: A European assessment. *The Lancet* 356:795–801.

Landsberg, H. E. 1956. The climate of towns. In W. L. Thomas Jr., with C. O. Sauer, M. Bates, L. Mumford, eds., *Man's Role in Changing the Face of the Earth*, 584–606. Chicago: University of Chicago Press.

Laurance, W. F., and M. A. Cochrane. 2001. Introduction to the special section: Synergistic effects in fragmented landscapes. *Conservation Biology* 15:1488–1489.

Le Corre, M., A. Oliver, S. Ribes, and P. Jouventin. 2002. Light-induced mortality of petrels: A 4-year study from Reunion Island (Indian Ocean). *Biological Conservation* 105:93–102.

Liu, J. G., G. C. Daily, P. R. Ehrlich, and G. W. Luck. 2003. Effects of household dynamics on resource consumption and biodiversity. *Nature* 421:530–533.

Lockwood, J. L., and M. L. McKinney. 2001. Preface. In J. L. Lockwood and M. L. McKinney, eds., *Biotic Homogenization*, viii. New York: Kluwer Academy, Plenum.

Longcore, T., and C. Rich. 2004. Ecological light pollution. *Frontiers in Ecology and the Environment* 4:191–198.

L'vovich, M. I., and G. F. White. 1990. Use and transformation of terrestrial water systems. In B. L. Turner, W. C. Clark, R. W. Dates, J. F. Richards, J. T. Mathews, and W. B. Meyer, eds., *The Earth as Transformed by Human Action: Global and Regional Changes in the Biosphere over the Past 300 Years*, 235–252. Cambridge: Cambridge University Press.

Mack, R. N., D. Simberloff, W. M. Lonsdale, H. Evans, M. Clout, and F. Bazzaz. 2000. Biotic invasions: Causes, epidemiology, global consequences, and control. *Issues in Ecology* 5:1–20.

Mader, H. J., C. Schell, and P. Kornacker. 1990. Linear barriers to arthropod movements in the landscape. *Biological Conservation* 54:209–222.

Malcolm, J. R., and L. F. Pitelka. 2000. *Ecosystems and Climate Change: A Review of Potential Impacts on US Terrestrial Ecosystems and Biodiversity*. Arlington, Va.: Pew Center of Global Climate Change. Also available at: www.pewclimate.org/global-warming-in-depth/all_reports/ecosystems_and_climate_change/index.cfm.

Marinelli, J. 1996. Redefining the weed. In J. Marinelli and J. M. Randall, eds., *Invasive Plants: Weeds of the Global Garden*, 4–6. Brooklyn, N.Y.: Brooklyn Botanic Garden.

Marzluff, J. M., and N. Hamel. 2001. Land use issues. In S. A. Levin, ed., *Encyclopedia of Biodiversity*, 3: 659–673. San Diego: Academic Press.

Matlack, G. R. 1993. Environmental auditing—sociological edge effects: Spatial distribution of human impact in forest fragments. *Environmental Management* 17:829–835.

McKenna, D. D., K. M. McKenna, and S. B. Malcolm. 2001. Mortality of Lepidoptera along roadways in central Illinois. *Journal of the Lepidopterists' Society* 55:63–68.

McKinney, M. L. 2002. Urbanization, biodiversity, and conservation. *BioScience* 52:883–890.

Meyer, W. B., and B. L. Turner II. 1992. Human population growth and global landuse/cover change. *Annual Review of Ecology and Systematics* 23:39–61.

Miller, M. A., I. A. Gardner, C. Kreuder, D. M. Pardies, K. R. Worcester, D. A. Jessup, E. Dodd, M. D. Harris, J. A. Ames, A. E. Packham, and P. A. Conrad. 2002. Coastal freshwater runoff is a risk factor for *Toxoplasma gondii* infection of southern sea otters (*Enhydra lutris nereis*). *International Journal for Parasitology* 32:997–1006.

Miller, R. R., J. D. Williams, and J. E. Williams. 1989. Extinctions of North American fishes during the past century. *Fisheries* 14:22–38.

Miller, S. G., R. L. Knight, and C. K. Miller. 1998. Influence of recreational trails on breeding bird communities. *Ecological Applications* 8:162–169.

Mitchell, J. C., and M. W. Klemens. 2000. Primary and secondary effects of habitat alteration. In M. W. Klemens, ed., *Turtle Conservation*, 5–32. Washington, D.C.: Smithsonian Institution Press.

Mumford, L. 1956. The natural history of urbanization. In W. L. Thomas Jr., with C. O. Sauer, M. Bates, and L. Mumford, eds., *Man's Role in Changing the Face of the Earth*, 382–398. Chicago: University of Chicago Press.

Myers, J. P., and P. T. Lester. 1992. Double jeopardy for migrating animals. In R. Peters and T. Lovejoy, eds., *Global Warming and Biological Diversity*, 193–200. New Haven, Conn.: Yale University Press.

Naeem, S., and S. Li. 1997. Biodiversity enhances ecosystem reliability. *Nature* 390:507–509.

Nebel, B. J., and R. T. Wright. 1998. *Environmental Science: The Way the World Works*. 6th ed. Upper Saddle River, N.J.: Prentice Hall.

Nielson, L. L., A. A. Young, and D. G. Parkes. 2003. Pharmacology of exenatide (synthetic exendin-4): A potential therapeutic for improved glycemic control of type 2 diabetes. *Regulatory Peptides* 117:77–88.

Northeast Illinois Planning Commission. 1997. *A Source Book on Natural Landscaping for Public Officials*. Environmental Protection Agency (EPA) Region 5. Washington, D.C.: EPA. Also available at: www.epa.gov/glnpo/greenacres/toolkit/.

Noss, R. F., and A. Cooperrider. 1994. *Saving Nature's Legacy: Protecting and Restoring Biodiversity*. Washington, D.C.: Defenders of Wildlife and Island Press.

Novacek, M. J., and E. E. Cleland. 2001. The current biodiversity extinction event: Scenarios for mitigation and recovery. *Proceedings of the National Academy of Sciences* 98:5466–5470.

Oates, J. F. 1996. *African Primates: Status Survey and Conservation Action Plan*. Gland, Switzerland: International Union for Conservation of Nature and Natural Resources, Species Survival Commission, Primate Specialist Group.

Odell, E. A., and R. L. Knight. 2001. Songbird and medium-sized mammal communities associated with exurban development in Pitkin County, Colorado. *Conservation Biology* 14:1143–1150.

Otto, T., K. Ransel, J. Todd, D. Lovaas, H. Stutzman, and J. Bailey. 2002. *Paving Our Way to Water Shortages: How Sprawl Aggravates the Effects of Drought*. Washington, D.C.: American Rivers, National Resource Defense Council, and Smart Growth America.

Outen, A. R. 2003. The ecological effects of road lighting. In B. Sherwood, D. Cutler, and J. Burton, eds., *Wildlife and Roads: The Ecological Impact*, 133–155. London: Imperial College Press.

Parmesan, C., N. Ryrholm, C. Stefanescu, J. K. Hill, C. D. Thomas, H. Descimon, B. Huntley, L. Kaila, J. Kullberg, T. Tammaryu, W. J. Tennent, J. A. Thomas, and M. Warren. 1999. Poleward shifts in geographical ranges of butterfly species associated with regional warming. *Nature* 399:579–583.

Peters, A., and K. J. F. Verhoeven. 1994. Impact of artificial light on the seaward orientation of hatchling loggerhead turtles. *Journal of Herpetology* 28:112–114.

Price, J., and P. Glick. 2002. *The Birdwatcher's Guide to Global Warming*. Arlington, Va.: National Wildlife Federation and American Bird Conservancy.

Reijnen, R., and R. Foppen. 1994. The effects of car traffic on breeding bird populations in woodland. I. Evidence of reduced habitat quality for willow warblers (*Phylloscopus trochilus*) breeding close to a highway. *Journal of Applied Ecology* 31:85–94.

Robinson, J. G., K. H. Redford, and E. L. Bennett. 1999. Wildlife harvest in logged tropical forests. *Science* 284:595–596.

Samways, M. J. 1994. *Insect Conservation Biology*. London: Chapman and Hall.

Sanderson, E. W., M. Jaiteh, M. A. Levy, K. H. Redford, A. V. Wannebo, and G. Woolmer. 2002. The human footprint and the last of the wild. *BioScience* 52:891–904.

Sauer, L. 1997. *The Once and Future Forest*. Washington, D.C.: Island Press.

Schueler, T. 1994. The importance of imperviousness. *Watershed Protection Techniques* 1:100–111.

Seabrook, W. A., and E. B. Dettmann. 1996. Roads as activity corridors for cane toads in Australia. *Journal of Wildlife Management* 60:363–368.

Simberloff, D., and B. Von Holle. 1999. Positive interactions of non-indigenous species: Invasional meltdown? *Biological Invasions* 1:21–32.

Stone, B., Jr., and M. O. Rodgers. 2001. Urban form and thermal efficiency: How the design of cities influences the urban heat island effect. *American Planning Association* 67:186–198.

Soulé, M. E., J. A. Estes, J. Berger, and C. M. Del Rios. 2003. Ecological effectiveness: Conservation goals for interactive species. *Conservation Biology* 17:1238–1250.

Stein, B. A., L. S. Kutner, and J. S. Adams. 2000. *Precious Heritage*. New York: Oxford University Press.

Swedish Institute. 1999. *Fact Sheet on Sweden*. Report no. FS 58 sUh. Stockholm: Swedish Institute.

Swinhart, R. K., and N. A. Slade. 1984. Road crossing in *Sigmodon hispidus* and *Microtus ochrogaster*. *Journal of Mammalogy* 65:357–360.

Thomas, C. D., A. Cameron, R. E. Green, M. Bakkenes, L. J. Beaumont, Y. C. Clooingham, B. F. N. Erasmus, M. F. de Siqueira, A. Grainger, L. Hannah, L. Hughes, B. Huntley, A. S. van Jaarsveld, G. F. Midgley, L. Miles, M. A. Ortega-Huerta, A. Townsend Peterson, O. L. Phillips, and S. E. Williams. 2004. Extinction risk from climate change. *Nature* 427:145–148.

Thorbjarnarson, J., C. J. Lageux, D. Bolze, M. W. Klemens, and A. B. Meylan. 2000. Human use of turtles—A worldwide perspective. In M. W. Klemens, ed., *Turtle Conservation*, 33–84. Washington, D.C.: Smithsonian Institution Press.

Tilman, D., and J. A. Downing. 1994. Biodiversity and stability in grasslands. *Nature* 367:363–365.

Tilman, D., and C. Lehman. 2001. Human-caused environmental change: Impacts on plant diversity and evolution. *Proceedings of the National Academy of Sciences* 98:5433–5440.

United Nations Environmental Program (UNEP). 2000. *UNEP Global Environmental Outlook 2000*. Nairobi, Kenya: UNEP GEO Team.

Vitousek, P. M., C. M. D'Antonio, L. L. Loope, and R. Westbrooks. 1996. Biological invasions as global environmental change. *American Scientist* 84:468–478.

Vitousek, P. M ., H.A. Mooney, J. Lubchenco, and M. Melillo. 1997. Human domination of the earth's ecosystems. *Science* 277:494–499.

Walker, H.J. 1990. The coastal zone. In B. L. Turner, W. C. Clark, R.W. Dates, J.F. Richards, J.T. Mathews, and W.B. Meyer, eds., *The Earth as Transformed by Human Action: Global and Regional Changes in the Biosphere over the Past 300 Years*, 271–294. Cambridge: Cambridge University Press.

Walker, L.R., and M.R. Willig. 1999. An introduction to terrestrial disturbance. In L.R. Walker, ed., *Ecosystems of the World*. Vol. 16, *Ecosystems of Disturbed Ground*, 1–16. Amsterdam: Elsevier.

Wasser, S.K., K. Bevis, G. King, and E. Hanson. 1997. Noninvasive physiological measures of disturbance in the northern spotted owl. *Conservation Biology* 11:1019–1022.

Wilcove, D.S., D. Rothstein, J. Dubow, and E. Losos. 1998. Quantifying threats to imperiled species in the United States. *BioScience* 48:607–615.

Wilcox, D.A. 1989. Migration and control of purple loosestrife (*Lythrum salicaria* L.) along highway corridors. *Environmental Management* 13:365–370.

Wilson, B.A., V.H. Smith, F. Denoyelles Jr., and C.K. Larive. 2003. Effects of three pharmaceuticals and personal care products on natural freshwater algal assemblages. *Environmental Science and Technology* 37:1713–1719.

PART II

SPRAWL, ECOSYSTEMS, AND PROCESSES

3

FRESHWATER WETLAND BIODIVERSITY
IN AN URBANIZING WORLD

Nicholas A. Miller and Michael W. Klemens

Wetland habitats occupy between 4 and 6 percent of the world's land surface (Mitsch and Gosselink 2000). Despite such minimal coverage, these systems contain a disproportionate amount of the world's biodiversity and, in particular, the world's imperiled species. In the United States, wetlands account for only approximately 5.5 percent of all land area (Dahl 2000), but these habitats are required by 50 percent of animals and 28 percent of plants designated as federally endangered or threatened (Niering 1988). In addition to listed species, wetland diversity is supplemented by numerous hydrophytes (i.e., water-tolerant plants) and wildlife that specifically require wetland habitats throughout all or some of their life cycles. Because of the rich biological diversity that freshwater wetlands support, sprawl's impacts on these systems must be better understood. This is crucial to an overall understanding of conservation as it relates to land use.

This chapter explores the influences of sprawl on freshwater wetland habitats and processes. A portion of the chapter covers well-documented and more familiar impacts of sprawl on wetlands, such as wetland filling, but the primary focus is on the often unrecognized and poorly understood impacts that urbanization and insufficiently planned development have on wetlands. For example, sprawl severs vital ecological and functional links between wetlands and adjacent uplands. Regulatory frameworks and formulas (e.g., stormwater management, wetland mitigation)—intended to protect water quality and habitats—can negatively impact biodiversity.

In this chapter, we discuss the importance of freshwater wetlands, the mechanisms by which sprawl affects wetland systems, and the responses of wetland biodiversity to those impacts. Our intent is not simply to catalog human impacts on wetland biodiversity, but to lay a foundation for discussing options that can reduce and, in some instances, reverse sprawl-induced impacts. In that vein, the final section of this chapter examines steps already taken to maintain freshwater wetland biodiversity and provides additional recommendations.

The chapter provides a framework for the wetland conservation and planning efforts of local land-use decision makers, concerned citizens, and others. This framework is not intended to be comprehensive; instead, it highlights sprawl's impacts primarily on wetland fauna of the northeastern United States. However, most of the issues presented here can be extrapolated to other regions and other freshwater wetland habitats and species. Factors such as geologic setting and hydrology may vary, but many of the broad concepts presented here are relevant to developing areas throughout the United States and around the globe.

WETLAND DIVERSITY

The term *wetland* has been defined in a number of ways by scientists classifying and studying these ecosystems and by agencies responsible for regulation of activities within them. Most definitions stress that wetlands contain three basic elements: (1) wetland vegetation (hydrophytes), (2) wetland soil types (hydric soils), and (3) wetland hydrology (flooding or soil saturation). The U.S. Fish and Wildlife Service defines *wetlands* as "lands transitional between terrestrial and aquatic systems where the water table is usually at or near the surface or the land is covered by shallow water" (Cowardin et al. 1979:11), and it requires that a site exhibit one or more of the three elements listed here. Because different agencies responsible for managing and regulating wetlands have differing roles and agendas, their definitions of wetlands vary accordingly. Current issues, political agendas, agency missions, and scientific advances that increase our understanding of wetlands have shaped these definitions. Subtle differences in definitions are important because they can significantly influence the amount of land included in the jurisdictional extent of wetland regulations.

The National Research Council has developed a broad reference definition of wetlands, with the intent of including all the substantive issues required for regulatory and research purposes alike. This definition reflects an ecosystem approach, integrating physical, chemical, and biological aspects of wetland environments—all of which must be considered for effective identification, regulation, management, restoration, and protection of wetlands:

> A wetland is an ecosystem that depends on constant or recurrent, shallow inundation or saturation at or near the surface of the substrate. The minimum essential characteristics of a wetland are recurrent, sustained inundation at or near the surface and the presence of physical, chemical, and biological features reflective of

the recurrent, sustained inundation or saturation. Common diagnostic features of wetlands are hydric soils and hydrophytic vegetation. These features will be present except where specific physicochemical, biotic, or anthropogenic factors have removed them or prevented their development. (1995:59)

This chapter is concerned with habitats that meet this broad definition of wetlands. We focus on freshwater wetlands in particular, but address other habitats (e.g., coastal salt marshes and deepwater habitats), as appropriate. A remarkable array of habitat types is encompassed by this definition, and these habitats assume diverse forms and perform many important functions. Depending on the definition, wetland types range from streams and shallow ponds to densely vegetated forested swamps. Between these extremes are numerous other wetland types, including freshwater marshes, vernal pools, bogs, fens, wet meadows, and shrub swamps (Mitsch and Gosselink 2000). Many factors interact to produce this rich diversity of wetland types, including the frequency, duration, and extent of flooding or soil saturation; climate; geologic setting; soil chemistry; and the source of water (e.g., groundwater versus surface water). In turn, these numerous wetland types and variations in the key factors that produce them create profuse habitat niches that support an abundance of plant and animal life.

Wetlands occupy a position on the Earth's moisture continuum between dry land (upland ecosystems) and deepwater ecosystems. Although wetlands are considered ecosystems in their own right, their intermediate position on the moisture continuum confers properties similar to those of ecotones (i.e., habitats that constitute the boundary area and transition zone between core ecosystems). Because ecotones blend elements of multiple ecosystems, they tend to be characterized by high biodiversity (Holland and Risser 1991). The same principle holds true for wetlands. Neotropical migrant birds—most of which are considered upland species—tend to be more abundant where landscapes contain a greater proportion of wetland habitats (Flather and Sauer 1996). In the state of Washington, bird species richness (total number of species) in uplands was found to be lower than in wetlands, and wetlands contained a mixture of both upland- and wetland-dependent species (Richter and Azous 2001).

Wetlands protected for their biodiversity, in turn, can perform ecological functions—including many that directly benefit human communities (Smith et al. 1995; Mitsch and Gosselink 2000). For example, dense wetland vegetation slows floodwaters and serves as a coarse filter, removing sediments and pollutants, thus keeping waters clean. Mucky wetland soils remove hazardous nitrogen from groundwater, often at a much faster rate than upland soils remove it. Wetland plants purify water by uptaking pollutants, helping to maintain water quality in reservoirs and aquifers. The abundance of plants within wetlands serves as the foundation of a complex food web that radiates far beyond individual wetlands, bolstering wildlife and fish populations in adjacent upland and aquatic habitats. The horizontal and vertical structural complexity created by a diverse wetland flora also results in numerous wildlife niches, providing aesthetic benefits to people and numerous opportunities for both passive and active recreation, such as bird-watching and hunting.

In light of all these benefits—cleaner water, reduced flooding problems, diverse and healthy fish and wildlife populations, recreation opportunities—conservation of wetland resources should be a priority for a broad constituency. Not only conservationists but also community leaders, chambers of commerce, developers, and in fact all who desire to create a sustainable economic base for human communities should be concerned with these vital resources and champion wetland protection. But this is not the case, and wetlands continue to disappear at an alarming rate. By the 1970s, more than half of the wetlands in the conterminous United States had been destroyed by impacts such as filling and draining (Dahl 1990). Although the rate of wetland loss has slowed, almost 60,000 acres (24,291 hectares) of wetland continue to be lost each year in the United States (Dahl 2000). Agriculture was the primary cause of wetland loss until the 1980s; since then, wetland loss has been related primarily to urbanization and the patterns of sprawl that accompany consumptive land use.

HOW SPRAWL AFFECTS WETLANDS

The discussion in this section is divided into two broad categories: (1) impacts that occur directly within wetlands and (2) impacts that occur in or originate from the uplands surrounding wetlands. This distinction is made for two primary reasons. First, we tend to think of wetlands as discrete, functionally isolated ecosystems. Although it is true that wetlands support a unique assemblage of species and perform some functions not found in uplands, the biotic and abiotic interactions between wetlands and surrounding uplands are myriad. Second, the jurisdictional extent of most wetland regulations ends at or near the wetland boundary. Surrounding uplands are often completely unprotected or, at best, receive limited protection in the form of narrow "buffer" zones, or "setbacks," that typically extend 100 feet (30 meters) or less beyond wetland boundaries.

There is a need to think holistically, to recognize that most wetlands within a degraded upland context cannot function properly. Simultaneously, landscapes that have been stripped of their wetlands are ecologically bereft. The linkages between wetland and upland domains are vital; the fate of one rests on that of the other.

IMPACTS WITHIN WETLANDS

FILLING Filling raises the grade of a wetland to a point well above the seasonally high water table so that wetland hydrology, hydric soils, and hydrophytes may no longer be present. Fill materials may include construction and demolition debris, soil, sand, gravel, ash, trash, and other materials, including dredge spoil in coastal areas. Filled wetlands often function as upland habitat and can no longer provide ecological services associated with wetlands, such as water purification, to the same degree (Miller and Golet 2001). Plants and animals that require wetland habitats disappear from wetlands that have been converted to upland through filling. Invasive plant species often establish where wetlands have been disturbed (Mitsch and Gosselink 2000), including exposed substrates from filling activities; these invasives can persist as a significant component of the plant community for decades, compromising the site's ability to support diverse assemblages of native plant and animal populations. Sometimes wetlands are filled simply in an attempt to dispose of unwanted materials. However, wetlands are most often filled to increase the amount of buildable land. Impacts associated with development (i.e., structures and paved areas) are longer lasting than those associated with many other human land uses, such as agriculture and forestry (Heinz Center 2002). Therefore, wetlands that are filled and built on as a result of urbanization are unlikely to be capable of maintaining high levels of biodiversity now or in the future.

DRAINING Drainage—through ditching or other means—converts wetlands into uplands, or at least into drier wetland types. Plant and animal communities shift in response to these drier conditions, and many wetland-dependent species are excluded. Intentional drainage of wetlands is most commonly associated with agricultural land uses (Tiner 1984), but it also may occur as a result of urbanization, particularly in densely populated coastal regions (Mitsch and Gosselink 2000). Within the context of sprawl, wetlands may be drained as groundwater tables are lowered for construction of basements or to accommodate individual septic systems where municipal sewage lines are not available. In agricultural settings, it is often possible to restore drained wetlands by reintroducing the original water regime (Galatowitsch and van der Valk 1994); however, postagricultural lands are often prime sites for development. Like filled wetlands, drained wetlands that have been built on are unlikely to contribute significantly to the maintenance of biodiversity.

Wetlands are sometimes drained unintentionally by wells, especially larger municipal wells (Owen 1995). Such wells are often located in or near wetlands, and they can partially or fully drain wetlands by drawing down the local groundwater table. As rural areas are converted to higher-density residential land uses, water demands rise, leading to increased flow rates from existing wells, installation of new wells, and the potential for further wetland drainage. Gravel mines, which often accompany sprawl-associated road building, may also alter local groundwater hydrology. Where mines intersect the groundwater table, nearby wetlands may be deprived of groundwater inputs and dry up (M. W. Klemens, personal observation).

ALTERATION OF SURFACE HYDROLOGY When streams and rivers are dammed, wetlands associated with those watercourses may be lost in the process (Keddy 2000). Freshwater wetlands that have been flooded to depths greater than 3 to 4 feet (approximately 1 meter) generally cannot support emergent vegetation, shrubs, or trees. Flooding to more than 6 feet (2 meters) converts wetlands to deepwater habitats (Cowardin et al. 1979). Downstream of dams, the magnitude and frequency of flooding is reduced, causing shifts to drier wetland types and reductions in wetland extent (Keddy 2000). Damming accompanies urbanization for a number of reasons: to create drinking-water reservoirs, to increase recreational opportunities for growing communities, to prevent flooding, to generate electricity, or to change the aesthetics of an area. Damming can also occur inadvertently through blockage of culverts or lack of culverts, where roads intersect wetlands. Reservoirs are often created in response to increased water usage within urbanizing areas. The irony is that the wetlands lost to reservoirs might well have helped to purify water and made it more suitable for drinking.

Although deepwater habitat can support diverse aquatic biota—including ducks, fishes, and an array of invertebrates—the species composition of flooded sites changes, and overall site biodiversity may decline. For example, habitats that are flooded for longer durations tend to have lower plant species richness and abundance than habitats less frequently flooded (Keddy 2000). Klemens (1993) suggested that the decline of leopard frogs (*Rana pipiens*) in Connecticut is owing in part to permanent inundation of their floodplain habitats by damming. If deepwater habitats are lacking on a broad, landscape scale, shifts in species composition that accompany damming can result in increased biodiversity overall throughout the region. However, in recent decades, the acreage of open-water habitats has been increasing because—as a result of compensatory mitigation for permitted wetland alterations—open water bodies are restored and created disproportionately to the frequency in which they naturally occur (Kentula 1993). Therefore, reservoirs and other created water bodies are rarely in short supply. In addition, the ability of created habitats to support a diversity of plants and animals is, in general, less than that of their natural counterparts. For instance, Knutson and colleagues (1999) concluded that frogs and toads associated with permanent water bodies were much more likely to occur in natural lakes than in reservoirs.

FRAGMENTATION WITHIN WETLANDS Wetland fragmentation occurs as roads are built through wetlands. Fragmentation reduces overall biodiversity by dissecting habitats into units of insufficient size for area-sensitive species (Saunders, Hobbs, and Margules 1991). Fragmentation can also degrade remnant patches by increasing the amount of habitat "edge," thereby changing environmental characteristics such as light, wind, and moisture from levels occurring in habitat "cores." As with plants and animals of upland habitats, the dispersal of wetland organisms and seeds among remnant patches bolsters populations and maintains gene flow. As individual fragments become increasingly isolated as a result of continued fragmentation, dispersal of migrating animals and plant seeds among remnant patches becomes ever more difficult. For these reasons, wetland species may become extinct in small, isolated fragments.

For example, Canada warblers (*Wilsonia canadensis*) and northern water-thrushes (*Seiurus noveboracensis*), both neotropical migrant wood-warblers, are restricted to forested wetlands in the southeastern New England portion of their breeding ranges. Large forested swamps are more likely to contain these area-sensitive, forest-interior species than are smaller swamps (Miller 1999). Wetlands that have been dissected into small fragments by roads and other forms of development are unlikely to contain Canada warblers, which rarely occur within 325 feet (100 meters) of paved roads. Roads through wetlands can also cause direct mortality for many reptiles and amphibians that migrate seasonally in and among wetlands; animals crossing roads are often crushed by vehicles (Mitchell and Klemens 2000; Forman et al. 2003).

For further discussion of how fragmentation affects biodiversity, see chapter 2 in this volume. Details about the effects that roads and fragmentation in the *uplands* surrounding wetlands have on wetland biodiversity are provided later in this chapter.

CHANNELIZATION Channelization involves the widening, deepening, and straightening of streams or rivers (Brookes 1988). Channelized river bottoms and banks may be lined with concrete or riprap, or otherwise stabilized. Levees, or spoil banks, may also be created during the channelization process. The purpose of these modifications is to move water quickly out of an area to prevent floods during storm events. Once floodplains are developed for residential or commercial purposes, which is often the ultimate goal of channelization, restoration back to a natural river channel is highly unlikely. Channelization can be a very effective means to reduce flooding locally and to increase the amount of buildable land; however, the many environmental and economic costs that accompany channelization (Brookes 1988) offset localized benefits. In-stream and bankside habitats are destroyed during channel alteration. Lowered water tables and constructed levees, both associated with channelization, can dry or drain adjacent wetlands by reducing groundwater inputs and eliminating over-bank flow. In addition, channelization quickly moves floodwaters out of one area and into another, exacerbating flooding problems downstream. Numerous studies have demonstrated reduced biodiversity among riparian and wetland plants, mammals, birds, reptiles, and amphibians because of channelization (Brookes 1988).

REMOVAL OR ALTERATION OF WETLAND VEGETATION Where sprawl encroaches into wetland landscapes, landowners often attempt to "clean up" their wetlands by thinning dense vegetation and removing deadfall. Wetlands situated between houses and water bodies are often cleared to improve views. The thinning and clearing of wetland vegetation reduces structural complexity, which can in turn decrease biodiversity (Meffe and Caroll 1994). For example, trees that fall into ponds and streams provide important basking habitat for turtles (Klemens 1993), so removal of these snags negatively impacts turtle populations. Breeding bird communities are more diverse in structurally complex forested wetlands than in forested wetlands with sparser vegetation layers (Golet et al. 1993). Sustained clearing might theoretically create new niches for plants and animals that require early-successional, open habitats, but a number of factors interact to make this outcome unlikely:

1. "Cleanups" usually occur without regard to seasonality or to species' life history requirements and can lead to direct mortality or disruption of life cycles.
2. The context of wetlands "cleaned up" in this manner tends to be urban, so resulting habitats are fragmented and isolated.
3. The process of clearing vegetation disturbs wetlands, increasing the likeli-hood that invasive plants will become established.

INVASIVE PLANT SPECIES Many wetlands, in particular those in suburban and urban settings, have been invaded by exotic species or aggressively spreading native species. In the northeastern United States, two invasive plants that often dominate freshwater wetlands are the common reed (*Phragmites australis*) and purple loosestrife (*Lythrum salicaria*). Habitats disturbed by human activities tend to favor invasive species (Meffe and Carroll 1994; Mitsch and Gosselink 2000). Sprawl-related activities encourage the establishment and dominance of invasive plants by disturbing both wetlands and the uplands surrounding them; such disturbance factors include high nutrient loads, hydrologic altera-tions, vegetation removal, land clearing (Galatowitsch, Anderson, and Ascher 1999), and sedimentation (N. A. Miller, personal observation). These impacts are described elsewhere within this chapter. Where sprawl accelerates eutrophication, invasive species often colonize (Keddy 2000) and can form dense monocultures, which by definition have reduced plant biodiversity. Wetlands dominated by invasive plants also tend to have depauperate wildlife communities (Thompson, Stuckey, and Thompson 1987). A study in Connecticut's salt and brackish marshes found bird diversity to be lower in wetlands dominated by *Phragmites* compared with wetlands dominated by native vegetation (Benoit and Askins 1999).

However, these impacts do not justify the intensive removal and control methods that are often employed where these species have established a foothold (Hager and McCoy 1998; Kiviat 2001). Removal of the above-ground biomass of invasive plants can disturb and expose soils, creating ideal conditions for reinvasion by the same species; removal of roots and rhizomes requires excavation and a likely conversion of habitat type from vegetated wetlands to ponds; broadcast spraying of herbicides may degrade water quality and create a host of problems for native plants and wildlife; introduction of biological control agents can cause further environmental problems (e.g., nonnative insects introduced to control invasives might switch hosts and thus have an impact on native wetland vegetation). Because poor water quality can promote eutrophication, leading to the establishment of large, rhizomatous species such as *Phragmites australis* (Keddy 2000), attempts to restore a more diverse plant community in urban wetlands are likely to fail unless the quality of the water entering the wetland is first improved. Recent inquiries into invasive species management (Hager and McCoy 1998; Kiviat 2001) warn that the reported impacts of invasives on wetland biodiversity (e.g., Thompson, Stuckey, and Thompson 1987) may not be as severe as previously assumed. More research should be conducted to understand better the relationship between invasive species and overall biodiversity levels; this research can serve as a foundation for developing better-informed, less-destructive management alternatives tailored to individual site characteristics.

DISRUPTION OF THE FOOD CHAIN Sprawl can have an impact on wetlands in surprising ways. As residential neighborhoods expand into wetland landscapes, people interact more frequently with all aspects of wetlands, including those aspects that are often considered undesirable, such as mosquitoes. Although mosquitoes, which breed in wetlands, are considered pests to humans, they also play an important role in wetland ecosystems—they are an integral part of the wetland food web. In vernal pools, many amphibians depend on mosquito larvae as a food source; and bats consume adult mosquitoes.

Unfortunately, some mosquito species play another role—serving as vectors for diseases that affect humans, such as West Nile virus, malaria, and eastern equine encephalitis. Therefore, insecticides are widely used to eradicate mosquito populations. It has been suggested, however, that intensive application of insecticides may ultimately exacerbate mosquito-associated disease problems. For example, in the northeastern United States, vernal pools function as breeding habitat for both amphibians and mosquitoes. Eliminating mosquito larvae can remove critical food resources for larval salamanders and newts. Resulting crashes in amphibian populations may be followed by surges in mosquito populations. Whereas mosquitoes can rapidly reestablish breeding populations, amphibians cannot. For reliable, long-term control of mosquitoes, we must ensure that the habitats in which they breed are functional and can support their natural predators. More research is required to support this hypothesis, followed by innovative application of the research results to provide a scientific foundation for policy and management.

IMPACTS FROM OUTSIDE WETLANDS

LINKS BETWEEN WETLANDS AND UPLANDS Wetlands are the keystone of biodiversity in most landscapes, but it is vital to understand that wetlands do not occur in an ecological vacuum. Surface water flows from surrounding uplands into wetlands. Some wetlands recharge groundwater aquifers that underlie entire regions; other wetlands help to maintain water levels in nearby lakes and streams. Many wetland-dependent wildlife species use wetlands at certain times in their annual activity cycle; at other times of the year, they disperse far into the adjacent uplands (Semlitsch and Jensen 2001). These species, which span both land and water, often serve as the foundation of the food web within entire forested landscapes (Calhoun and Klemens 2002). For all these reasons, wetland ecosystems are inextricably linked to the upland matrices within which they occur, and the fate of any individual wetland depends on the condition of the upland habitat that surrounds it.

Local, state, and federal laws often regulate land uses in close proximity to wetlands, generally within 50 to 100 feet (15–30 meters) of a wetland edge. The intent of these regulations is to "buffer" the impacts of development on wetland functions and processes. But uplands often act as much more than just buffers or shields to protect wetland biodiversity from surrounding land-use changes. Wetland-dependent wildlife that alternate between wetlands and uplands throughout their life cycles require intact upland habitats adjacent to wetlands. For example, wood turtles (*Clemmys insculpta*) hibernate and mate in streams, but also spend a significant portion of each year foraging, basking, and nesting in adjacent uplands (Klemens 1993). Roads, fences, subdivisions, and other fragmenting elements can impede wood turtles as they move between wetland and upland habitats; these barriers can even exclude the turtles from habitats altogether, critically imperiling their populations.

The importance of healthy upland habitats surrounding wetlands is underscored by yet another example: vernal pool–breeding amphibians, as described in the box "The Upland–Wetland Continuum."

FRAGMENTATION OF UPLANDS SURROUNDING WETLANDS Fragmentation does not have to occur within wetlands to affect wetland biodiversity (figure 3.1). The basic building blocks of sprawl—houses, buildings, parking lots, roads, highways, and other infrastructure—dissect the uplands that surround wetlands into smaller fragments, which causes declines in species that require large tracts of relatively undeveloped land (Saunders, Hobbs, and Margules 1991). The fragmenting elements can also act as barriers to wildlife dispersal. Chapter 2 in this volume provides further details about the effects of fragmentation on biodiversity in general; this section illuminates the impacts of upland fragmentation specifically on wetland-associated species.

THE UPLAND–WETLAND CONTINUUM: VERNAL POOLS IN AN UPLAND FOREST MATRIX, NORTHEASTERN UNITED STATES

Vernal pools are seasonal or semipermanent bodies of water that usually attain maximum depths in spring and lack permanent surface-water connections with other wetlands or water bodies. Pools fill with snowmelt or runoff in the spring, although some may be fed primarily by groundwater sources. The duration of surface flooding, known as the *hydroperiod*, varies, depending on the pool and the year; vernal pool hydroperiods range along a continuum from less than 30 days to more than one year (Semlitsch 2000). Pools are generally less than 2 acres (0.81 hectare), but most are less than 0.5 acre (0.2 hectare), and the extent of vegetation varies widely. They lack fish populations, usually as a result of periodic drying, and support communities dominated by animals adapted to living in temporary, fishless pools. Vernal pools provide essential breeding habitat for a variety of wildlife species, including Ambystomatid salamanders (*Ambystoma* spp., called "mole salamanders" because they live in burrows), wood frogs (*Rana sylvatica*), and fairy shrimp (*Eubranchipus* spp.).

Spotted salamanders (*Ambystoma maculatum*) breed in vernal pools of North America and require intact forests in the surrounding uplands. In urbanizing areas, vernal pool–dependent species can be conserved only by combining wetland protection with careful land-use planning in adjacent uplands. (Copyright WCS/ Nicholas A. Miller)

Vernal pools are of great interest to ecologists because, despite their small size, they are characterized by high productivity and a unique assemblage of species adapted to breeding in seasonally flooded wetlands (Skelly, Werner, and Cortwright 1999; Semlitsch 2000). Within the past decade, interest in vernal pools has increased dramatically because of well-publicized

(continued)

declines of amphibians, many of which require vernal pools and other small wetlands (Pechmann et al. 1991; Lannoo 1998).

Conservation of pool-breeding amphibians requires that equal attention be
paid to the integrity of the upland landscape surrounding the vernal pools and to
the wetlands proper because these amphibians depend on both aquatic *and* terrestrial habitats for survival. Most adult vernal pool amphibians spend less than
a month in breeding pools; they spend the rest of their annual cycle in adjacent uplands and wetlands (Semlitsch 1981, 2000). The surrounding forest provides critical terrestrial habitat for adult amphibians and newly emerged juveniles throughout the year (Semlitsch 1998; Calhoun and Klemens 2002). In their
upland habitats, both young and adults need areas of loose, deep, organic litter;
coarse woody debris; and shade. These elements provide a suitable environment
for amphibians as they move through the forest, feed, and hibernate (deMaynadier and Hunter 1995; DiMauro 1998). This dependence on the surrounding
landscape for survival has prompted one researcher to refer to this critical terrestrial habitat around pools as a *life zone*, instead of a *buffer zone* (Semlitsch 1998).
Conservation strategies that focus on protecting only breeding pools and associated
wetlands will most likely fail to maintain healthy amphibian populations. Protection
of surrounding upland habitat must also be a priority (Marsh and Trenham 2001).

Amphibians, reptiles, and small mammals also need suitable upland habitat *connecting* wetlands. These animals live in small populations or small units that together
make a larger population (metapopulation). These small populations often intermix
through dispersal of juveniles. For example, small populations may replenish one
another with new breeding stock when natural catastrophes (e.g., drought or freez-
ing) eliminate breeding adults or cause larval failures in certain pools (Klemens
2000). The average distance that a spotted salamander moves from a pool into the
surrounding forest is nearly 400 feet (122 meters); Jefferson salamanders may travel
more than 450 feet (137 meters) (Windmiller 1996; Semlitsch 1998), with as much
as half the population in some instances traveling even greater distances. Wood frog
juveniles disperse on average approximately 1,550 feet (472 meters) from a breeding pool (Berven and Grudzien 1990). *Therefore, long-term persistence of vernal pool
amphibian populations depends on the availability of habitat that connects local populations and enables dispersal among them* (Semlitsch and Bodie 1998).

Many species depend on these small wetlands for numerous reasons. For example, beetles and water bugs that overwinter in permanent water migrate to vernal
pools to breed and feed during the spring and summer. Medium-size to large mammals—including raccoon, skunk, fox, deer, moose, and bear—visit pools to feed on
amphibian eggs and fresh green shoots emerging in spring or, later in the season, on
amphibians and insects. Therefore, the loss of individual vernal pools may weaken
the health of entire wildlife communities.

Source: Portions adapted from Calhoun and Klemens (2002).

Roads and highways—precursors and hallmarks of sprawl—can be particularly damaging to highly mobile or area-sensitive wetland species. Egan (2001)
reported significant decreases in spotted salamander egg masses where road
densities surrounding breeding pools exceeded only 39 feet (12 meters) per
hectare; the critical threshold for wood frogs was 62 feet (19 meters) of road per
hectare. Findlay and Houlahan (1997) found that species richness of plants,

FIGURE 3.1. Sprawling residential development severs wetland–wetland and upland–wetland connectivity, imperiling species that need to disperse among these habitats during various stages of their life cycles. In this image, upland habitats appear as light gray and wetlands appear as dark gray. (Image courtesy of Rhode Island Geographical Information System and MIT)

herpetofauna, and birds within wetlands of southeastern Ontario decreased with increasing density of paved roads in adjacent uplands; roads as far away as 1.24 miles (2 kilometers) appeared to influence wetland biodiversity. A Minnesota study reported lower amphibian species richness where road densities and urban land uses were greater surrounding wetlands (Lehtinen, Galatowitsch, and Tester 1999). Underpasses and overpasses have been installed on highways and roads to reduce wildlife mortality, but the effectiveness of such efforts varies widely among taxa, is in general uncertain, and requires further study (Forman et al. 2003). Because there is a time lag between the construction of a road and its impact on nearby wetland biodiversity (Findlay and Bourdage 2000), the impacts of rapid urbanization on wetland biodiversity may not be fully recognized for several decades.

Fragmentation of the uplands surrounding wetlands can have a deleterious effect on wetland species that do not even enter or use those upland habitats. For example, in a Rhode Island study, forested swamps surrounded by roads and residential subdivisions were much less likely to serve as breeding habitat for Canada warblers than swamps situated in extensively forested upland habitats with minimal development (Miller 1999). Although in Rhode Island Canada warblers do not use upland habitats during the breeding season, these uplands do shield the swamp-dwelling Canada warblers from the impacts of sprawl. Because development patterns within 1.24 miles (2 kilometers) of a swamp can negatively impact this species, regulatory "buffer" zones around wetlands are of insufficient size to ensure the continued viability of Canada warbler populations. Many researchers (e.g., Findlay and Houlahan 1997; Mitchell and Klemens 2000; Semlitsch and Jensen 2001) have expressed concern over the limitations of regulatory buffers and have stressed the need to protect larger swaths of habitat in order to maintain wetland biodiversity.

REMOVAL OR ALTERATION OF VEGETATION IN THE UPLANDS BORDERING A WETLAND Removal or alteration of upland vegetation along the wetland edge is often done to improve views or to increase the size of lawns in residential and commercial developments. This clearing can have negative impacts on wetland biodiversity. For example, trees or shrubs in the upland surrounding a marsh may provide nest sites (e.g., for wood ducks [Aix sponsa]) or roosting areas (e.g., for herons and osprey [Pandion haliaetus]). Such vegetation can also serve as a "screen" for wetland wildlife. This is particularly important for wildlife in urban wetlands, where, without a screen of trees or other dense vegetation, the species would be subject to traffic noise and frequent visual disturbance—factors that may eliminate these species from such sites. During storms, well-vegetated uplands surrounding wetlands also stabilize soils and filter runoff, removing sediments and pollutants before they can enter the wetland and degrade water quality (Lowrance 1998).

WATER QUALITY AND QUANTITY The quality and quantity of water can affect wetland biodiversity in many ways. This section does not attempt to cover exhaustively these topics. Instead, it provides a brief overview of the major issues and illustrates the effects of individual water-quality and -quantity impacts on wetland biodiversity.

Overview of Water-Quality Issues Wetlands may receive water inputs from a variety of sources, including precipitation, overbank flooding, overland flow (e.g., surface runoff), and groundwater (e.g., springs) (Mitsch and Gosselink 2000). Urbanization can affect these sources and degrade the quality of water entering wetland ecosystems, with repercussions for wetland-dependent biodiversity. In some instances, wetland water-quality degradation can be traced to a discrete source, such as a factory's effluent pipe or a municipal sewage pipe; this is termed *point-source pollution*. If the degradation emanates from diffuse sources, including fertilizer runoff from residential lawns and sedimentation from roads and construction sites, it is called *nonpoint-source pollution*.

Urbanized areas generate significantly more runoff than natural landscapes because of impervious surfaces, including paved roads, sidewalks, rooftops, and other surfaces that cannot absorb water (Schueler 1995). Most of this runoff is channeled into drains and sewer pipes that transport it directly to the nearest stream, lake, or wetland. In most urban areas, stormwater is viewed as a waste product, to be piped away from the developed area as quickly as possible, rather than as a vital part of the interdependent wetland–upland ecological continuum. Stormwater flowing off of the impervious urban landscape transports a variety of pollutants, including road salt and sand, pesticides, herbicides, lawn fertilizers, heavy metals, and other chemicals. The strategy of collecting stormwater into a system of curbs, catch basins, and pipes concentrates pollutants at the discharge point, often damaging wetlands and water bodies (Forman et al. 2003).

Sediment In northern climates, sedimentation often occurs where roads that intersect wetlands are sanded during snowy or icy conditions (Forman et al. 2003). As snow and ice melts, the sand runs off the roads and is deposited into adjacent wetlands. Unpaved roads also cause sedimentation problems if they are poorly designed, poorly maintained, or heavily traveled. Sediment traps are often installed beneath roadside drains to counteract this problem, but these traps may quickly fill up and are rarely maintained, often rendering them useless. Sedimentation also occurs from soil erosion as a result of improper soil-stabilization measures—or a complete absence of such measures—during land clearing and construction activities.

Sediments bury wetland soils and vegetation and may contain nutrients that accelerate the eutrophication process (Keddy 2000). In extreme situations, sediments may increase the elevation of the soil above the water table to a point where the site no longer functions as a wetland (i.e., the wetland has, in essence, been filled). Sedimentation also has direct impacts on biodiversity; for example, sediments smother fish and amphibian eggs and kill benthic (bottom-dwelling) aquatic invertebrates (Keddy 2000).

Nutrients Fertilizers—in the form of nitrogen, phosphorus, and other sources—are commonly applied to residential lawns and landscaped gardens, impacting water quality (Schueler 1995). These fertilizers promote lush plant growth, high yields, and aesthetically pleasing surroundings, but they are often applied in quantities that greatly exceed the uptake capacity of lawns and garden plants. This is particularly problematic in residential settings with extensive landscaping and expansive green lawns. When excess nutrients are washed away by rainwater, these nonpoint-source pollutants usually end up in wetlands and waterways. Accumulations of dog feces along suburban roads can also significantly degrade surface-water quality. In addition, roads—in particular major highways—can serve as a source of nitrogen. Car exhaust contains nitrogen oxides, which can increase nitrogen levels in habitats along highways and radically alter plant community composition (Angold 1997).

Another major source of nutrient pollution is effluent from septic systems—also referred to as individual sewage disposal systems (ISDSs)—especially where these units are poorly maintained and failing. The advance of development into unsewered areas has increased dependence on ISDSs. Although infill development within towns can make use of existing sewage systems, the decentralized pattern of human settlement caused by sprawl (i.e., spreading development thinly over greater land area) almost invariably increases reliance on ISDSs. Installation of these units is particularly problematic in areas where the ground-water table, bedrock, or dense till is located near the ground surface. In addition, highly permeable substrates such as gravelly soils enable rapid movement of nitrates away from ISDSs—potentially into wetlands or water bodies. Failing and improperly sited ISDSs pollute nearby wetlands and water bodies with nitrate and phosphorus, threatening both ecosystem health and human health, particularly where the systems are in close proximity to public drinking-water supplies. Many towns and states have established minimum setbacks for septic systems from wetlands and water bodies, ranging from 50 feet (15 meters) to more than 200 feet (62 meters); the effectiveness of these setbacks varies according to local geology, hydrology, and distance from wetlands.

The repercussions of increased nutrient inputs for wetland biodiversity can be dramatic. In a process known as *eutrophication*, nutrients in wetlands and open water bodies accelerate plant growth (Keddy 2000). This leads to the uncontrolled spread of plants such as algae and water milfoil (*Myriophyllum* spp.), which can choke waterways and exclude native species. In addition to shading out desirable plants and changing habitat composition and structure, the increased plant biomass—especially algae—consumes more oxygen in the water column. Reduced oxygen levels lead to die-offs in fish and other aquatic organisms, which, in turn, impact other organisms in the wetland food chain.

Other Chemical Pollutants In addition to sediment and nutrients, runoff may collect a variety of other chemicals and substances as it moves across impervious surfaces in urban areas (Horner et al. 1994). Roads and other impervious surfaces that are sanded for traction in winter are also usually salted to melt ice. Salt can severely damage roadside plant communities and can accumulate in high concentrations at the bottom of shallow roadside lakes, depriving the bottom layer of oxygen and excluding benthic organisms (Forman et al. 2003). However, spring snowmelt may sufficiently dilute and remove salts before the growing season for wetland plants. Impervious surfaces are the source of other pollutants, including heavy metals and chemical spills; although the ecological effects of many these substances are relatively unknown, some of them can impair reproductive capacity of wildlife, and others can cause direct mortality (Forman et al. 2003).

Pesticides are commonly applied on residential and commercial lawns and gardens to kill off undesirable pests. Herbicides may alter wetland vegetation composition and habitat structure; insecticides may kill animals or cause less direct impacts. For example, the insecticide DDT, formerly widely applied to control insect populations, biomagnified in the food chain (i.e., increased in concentration at each higher level in the food chain) and caused reproductive failure in top predators such as osprey (Andrle and Carroll 1988). The ecological effects of some of these chemicals are better understood than others, but in general they should be avoided or used conservatively to minimize potential and unforeseen impacts to nontarget plants and animals.

Thermal Alterations Pavement and other hard surfaces in urban areas absorb solar energy; therefore, water that runs off these surfaces tends to be warmer than more natural wetland water inputs (Schueler 1995). As sprawl spreads into and around wetlands, more and more of the wetlands' total water budgets are derived from temperature-raising impervious surface runoff. In addition, vegetation along the edges of streams, lakes, and wetlands—which helps to shade and cool the water—is often removed as lawns are established around new developments. For these reasons, the overall water temperature within urbanized wetlands rises.

Habitat composition and structure change in response to these thermal spikes; warmer waters exacerbate the eutrophication processes, leading to algal blooms and potentially the establishment of invasive plants such as *Phragmites australis* (Keddy 2000). Fish and wildlife populations are also affected. Trout and salmon require cool streams for breeding and tend to be replaced by largemouth bass and carp where waters are warmed. Spring salamanders (*Gyrinophilus porphyriticus*) are restricted to cool, oxygen-rich waters, which may account for their increasing rarity in the increasingly sprawl-dominated landscapes of southern New England (Klemens 1993).

Manipulation of Water Quantity Sprawling development brings with it enormous water demands and changes in local hydrology. These alterations to water quantity are caused by factors such as impervious surfaces, damming, inappropriate stormwater management techniques, loss of overall wetland acreage within a watershed, and pumping of water from wetlands and regional groundwater aquifers. Hydrologic impacts vary according to a number of factors, including site-specific land-use history, but urban wetlands tend overall to exhibit "flashy" characteristics (high-volume pulses of water and dramatic water-level fluctuations), and they tend to be drier (Ehrenfeld et al. 2003).

Impervious surfaces, combined with stormwater management techniques that aggregate and redirect floodwaters, can drastically alter the amount of water that reaches wetlands and water bodies (Horner et al. 1994). Precipitation falling on impervious surfaces does not slowly percolate through soils and reach wetlands in a steady, diffuse manner; instead, it is quickly transported to curbs and channeled via outfalls and storm sewer pipes, usually directly to wetlands and water bodies. Most wildlife species are not adapted to resulting "flashy" conditions. The precipitous decline of the dusky salamander (*Desmognathus fuscus*) in the suburban counties north of New York City has been correlated with increased flashiness and thermal spiking caused by runoff from impervious surfaces (Klemens 1993). Wetlands that receive influxes of stormwater are impaired in their ability to serve as appropriate breeding habitat for many invertebrates, fishes, and amphibians. Rapid fluctuations in water levels and water quality caused by concentrated stormwater runoff affect these species' sensitive egg and larval stages (Calhoun and Klemens 2002).

Flashy conditions can also cause scouring, which removes soil and vegetation, leading to erosion and sedimentation problems and denuded stream habitats (Brookes 1988). Increased erosion can deepen stream and river channels, resulting in lower water tables (Booth 1990), which also may reduce water inputs to adjacent wetlands. Filling of wetlands can increase flashiness downstream by reducing the overall floodwater storage capacity of wetlands within a watershed. Remaining wetlands are not equipped to offset the high volume of water that formerly would have been distributed over greater wetland acreage; they may be quickly inundated and overtaxed during storms. Floods made more severe through wetland loss, impervious surfaces, and hydrologic manipulations create hazards for downstream riparian biodiversity.

In many cases, precipitation falling on impervious surfaces is transported by storm drains *away* from wetlands, which eliminates or reduces overland flow entering wetlands and can also prevent or reduce groundwater recharge (Ferguson 1994). In addition, municipal wells, pumping stations, and an increase in the number of private wells can cause drawdowns in the local water table, reducing groundwater inputs to wetlands. These factors can alter the duration and depth of flooding or soil saturation in both wetlands that depend heavily on surface water inputs and those that receive most of their water from groundwater inflow. Stromberg, Tiller, and Richter (1996) found that the abundance of obligate wetland herbs in the southwestern United States decreases sharply as the depth to groundwater is increased. Groundwater depletion is particularly damaging to ephemeral and relatively drier wetlands, which can become too dry under such circumstances to support wetland-dependent plants and animals. Even small, subwatershed diversion caused by a housing subdivision can significantly impact vernal pools and small headwater wetlands. A reduction in groundwater inflow is especially critical to groundwater-fed habitats such as fens, on which a unique assemblage of species depend, including the imperiled bog turtle (*Clemmys muhlenbergii*) (Klemens 2001).

Stormwater Management Urbanized areas contain major economic investments, including buildings and related infrastructure. The presence of such structures can alter local hydrology and create flooding problems that, in turn, can threaten these investments. Where sprawl extends into and replaces wetland and floodplain habitats, downstream flooding problems are more severe (Smith et al. 1995). Flooding is exacerbated where impervious surfaces cover the uplands, compromising the substrates' ability to absorb stormwater and to slow overland flow (Schueler 1995). To address these issues, communities have established stormwater management systems that are designed to rapidly remove water from developed areas.

Runoff from roads and other impervious surfaces is often managed through systems of curbs, hydrodynamic separators, and catch basins (Forman et al. 2003). Vertical curbing—commonly used in subdivisions—efficiently channels stormwater but is an insurmountable barrier to small vertebrates and so traps turtles, frogs, salamanders, and small mammals in roadways. Animals not directly killed by traffic move along the curbing "wall" until they fall into a catch basin. Hydrodynamic separators, which remove particulate matter from stormwater with swirl chambers, are often installed in tandem with catch basins. These devices are particularly problematic because they cannot distinguish sediment from small vertebrates, potentially leading to thousands of amphibian deaths in a single unit (Calhoun and Klemens 2002). Because these small vertebrates serve as the basis of the food chain in wetland and forested ecosystems, population crashes resulting from conventional stormwater management practices can affect the entire local wildlife community. Roads that bisect wetlands or that are placed between the base of a forested slope and a wetland often cause unsustainable impacts to wetland-dependent wildlife (Mitchell and Klemens 2000). Low-impact stormwater management practices that take wildlife into account might mitigate some of these impacts (Calhoun and Klemens 2002).

Stormwater management regulations often require detention basins and biofiltration ponds in new construction, with the intent of removing pollutants before water flows off-site. In some instances, however, wetlands have inappropriately been used for detention and biofiltration (Keddy 2000). These practices create a degraded aquatic environment subject to sediment loading, pollutants, and rapid changes in water quantity and temperature. Construction of new wetlands for the sole purpose of treating stormwater would seem to be the logical solution to these problems. However, detention basins that have been excavated from upland habitat can also cause problems for wildlife of nearby small wetlands. These artificial wetlands can function as "decoy" wetlands, intercepting amphibians in search of breeding habitats (Calhoun and Klemens 2002). If amphibians deposit their eggs in these artificial wetlands, they rarely survive because of the habitat's degraded state. Creation of artificial wetlands also may alter local hydrology and dewater nearby natural small wetlands (Calhoun and Klemens 2002).

Stormwater regulations often also require the installation of silt fencing to control erosion on construction sites. Unfortunately, fencing is usually left in place long after construction is completed and substrates have stabilized, which creates barriers to the movement of amphibians and other small animals (Calhoun and Klemens 2002). This problem is easily fixed by removing silt fencing upon substrate stabilization. The duration for which silt fencing is needed can be minimized by reseeding the substrate immediately with the use of a coarse jute ground blanket. At sites where rapid stabilization is not possible, berms (low earthen mounds that act as barriers to stormwater) can be used instead of silt fencing to control erosion and runoff.

REDUCING THE IMPACTS OF SPRAWL ON WETLANDS

WETLAND REGULATIONS

Land-use activities within wetlands are often regulated. In the United States, wetland alterations are regulated at the federal level under Section 404 of the Clean Water Act. Many states have developed additional regulations for wetland resources that extend beyond federal limits. In the northeastern United States, where municipal governments have a high degree of self-determination, local ordinances may extend further protection to wetlands. The purpose of this section is not to describe this regulatory framework comprehensively, but to examine its effectiveness.

Without a doubt, wetlands have benefited greatly from local, state, and federal land-use laws and regulations. The rates of wetland destruction and degradation have slowed dramatically (Dahl 2000), beginning with the passage of wetland protection laws in the 1970s. Many of these laws were intended primarily to protect water quality, but they have also had a positive influence on wetland biodiversity.

Despite regulations, however, wetland loss and degradation—associated with cumulative permitted impacts, alteration or loss of unregulated (small and isolated) wetlands, and illegal alterations—continue to this day. It is important to remember that although these regulations are intended to protect certain wetland functions and values, they are not specifically designed to *preserve* wetland resources. Instead, they *permit* activities within wetlands; applications are made for permits to make alterations. Although the regulatory process often minimizes the impacts of individual development proposals, the cumulative number and acreage of wetlands that are legally altered through this process can be very large (Gosselink et al. 1990). In addition, regulations often have minimum size thresholds, leaving the smallest wetlands completely unprotected. For example, in the state of New York, wetlands must in general be at least 12.4 acres (5 hectares) to receive state regulatory protection. Small wetlands often perform unique functions (Gibbs 1993), however, and cumulatively can rival or surpass larger wetlands in functional capacity, but because of this regulatory deficiency they tend to rapidly disappear from our landscapes.

Most wetland regulatory programs require applicants to explore a sequence of alternatives—avoid, minimize, and compensate (National Research Council 2001). First, if at all possible, a wetland disturbance should be avoided completely. If the impact cannot be avoided, then it should be minimized to the extent practicable. Finally, unavoidable alterations often must be offset through one or more forms of "compensatory" mitigation, such as wetland creation or restoration. Although this sequence provides a logical solution to wetland impacts, the hierarchy of alternatives is not always observed; the potential for avoidance is sometimes not even considered before mitigation. For instance, federal guidance documents have relaxed the avoidance requirement for landowners with small properties and for sites deemed to be of low environmental value (National Research Council 2001). Another problem lies in the assumption that mitigation is always successful and can result in replacement of wetland functions lost to the permitted wetland alteration.

Mitigation is attractive in theory, but usually ineffective in practice. Literature reviews have demonstrated that although many mitigatory wetland restoration and creation activities have occurred, very little research has been done to measure their effectiveness; most of the limited research carried out so far suggests that mitigations are largely unsuccessful (Turner, Redmond, and Zedler 2001). A study of the success of wetland mitigation projects required by the Army Corps of Engineers in New England reported that of the 60 projects investigated, 67 percent met basic permit requirements; however, only 17 percent adequately replaced functions lost because of permitted impacts (Minkin and Ladd 2003). Mitigation rarely, if ever, results in the exact replication of habitat or other wetland functions; mitigation wetlands are often simplified versions of the wetlands they were designed to replace. Even mitigations that occur at a two-to-one or greater ratio (as is sometimes required) are often not adequate because functional capacity is based on more than just acreage. The many functions and ecosystem services performed by a shrub swamp or forested wetland are lost when the swamp is filled. Such complex, diverse habitats are often replaced with marshes or ponds, either intentionally because they are easier and cheaper to create or unintentionally because attempts to replicate hydrology, vegetation, and soil types fail (e.g., Brown and Veneman 1998; Minkin and Ladd 2003). Some wetland types, such as bogs, are difficult or impossible to replicate owing to their unique chemistry and deep organic soils (Tiner 1995). For other wetland types, replication requires very long spans of time. For instance, it takes many decades for a created or restored forested wetland to achieve maturity; in the interim, functions lost to permitted alterations are not completely replaced. As bogs, fens, and swamps give way to ponds and marshes, biodiversity is lost, regardless of replacement ratios. There has been a shift at regional and landscape scales from complex wetlands to simpler habitats (Kentula 1993), with associated shifts in overall functionality and biodiversity.

Additional issues are associated with wetland mitigation. Mitigation efforts are sometimes sited outside the watershed in which the impact occurred. In such cases, even successful mitigation will result in local changes in hydrology and habitat availability. In addition, improvement of an existing degraded wetland (i.e., a wetland with impaired functions, such as one with invasive plant species) is sometimes accepted as mitigation for filling wetlands. Changes are made to an existing wetland to offset the outright loss of another wetland. This practice, called *enhancement mitigation*, results in a net loss of wetland area. Enhancement efforts may exacerbate impacts. For example, artificial flooding of a forested swamp to create marshland to improve habitat for ducks will result in loss of habitat for a diverse suite of forested wetland–associated species.

Uplands that surround wetlands are often completely unprotected. Under some regulatory programs, these adjacent uplands receive limited protection in the form of narrow "buffer" zones, or "setbacks," that extend, in general, up to 100 feet (30 meters) beyond wetland boundaries. These buffer zones can be effective in reducing pollutants from runoff and can serve as a screen for wetland wildlife. However, many wetland wildlife species respond to changes in surrounding uplands at a scale much broader than the narrow strip encompassed within these zones. Unfortunately, urbanization at the scale of landscapes and regions is beyond the scope of wetlands regulations (Miller 1999; Calhoun and Klemens 2002).

Land-use regulations have been successful in slowing the pace of wetland loss and degradation. They provide a strong and essential foundation for wetland conservation. But regulations alone are insufficient to ensure the long-term maintenance of wetlands and wetland biodiversity. Comprehensive wetland conservation methods should include several approaches, including strong regulations supplemented by proactive (i.e., nonregulatory) wetland restoration attempts and innovative alternatives, such as incorporating wetland protection into land-use planning efforts.

WETLAND RESTORATION

As described in the previous section, wetland restoration and creation in a regulatory context (i.e., through compensatory mitigation) cannot adequately offset the loss of wetlands to sprawl and urbanization. Furthermore, although strong regulations are essential, wetland acreage continues to decline because of unauthorized alterations and the cumulative effect of wetland alterations permitted through regulatory channels. Proactive, nonregulatory attempts to restore wetlands may help to address this problem. A number of states, including Washington, Rhode Island, Massachusetts, and North Carolina, have recognized this potential and have developed strategies to identify and prioritize restoration opportunities at statewide or watershed scales (Miller and Golet 2001). Although wetland restoration has many potential benefits, it is an imperfect science and has limitations. The protection of existing wetland resources is the cornerstone of any successful wetland management strategy (Golet et al. 2002).

Although restorability of certain wetland types (e.g., bogs) and certain wetland functions (e.g., habitat for particular species) may be difficult or even unattainable, *any* degree of restoration success in a nonregulatory context will result in a net gain of wetland acreage and functions (Miller and Golet 2001). The restoration of former wetlands that have been converted to upland through filling or draining is particularly effective; wetland habitats and biodiversity are reinstated where they formerly existed. Restorations in these settings are also likely to be more successful than creation of wetland from upland habitats because in restoration it is easier to re-create the appropriate hydrology, which is key to restoration success (Tiner 1995). In addition, the uplands that are being replaced may provide important habitat in their own right; that is, there may be ecological costs where uplands are converted to wetlands. Restoration of degraded wetlands—those sites that are still wetlands but with impaired functions—produces less, in terms of functional gain, than restoration of sites converted to upland. In addition, restoration activities within degraded wetlands may put existing wetland functions at risk.

In urban and suburban landscapes, vegetation along the edges of wetlands is often removed to expand residential lawns or to improve views. These impacted areas present some of the most promising opportunities for effective, affordable restoration (Miller and Golet 2001). Restoring vegetation along wetland edges can provide screens for wildlife within wetlands and can provide nesting, roosting, and foraging habitat for other wildlife. Vegetation can also clean water by removing sediments from overland flow before it reaches wetlands (Lowrance 1998). Because heavy and specialized equipment is not required for restoring vegetation, as with restorations that involve the removal of fill or reestablishment of wetland hydrology, costs are lower and there is less risk of causing further damage to fragile wetland systems. Purchasing and planting native species is within the realm of possibility for many entities, including agencies, conservation organizations, watershed associations, citizens' groups, and even individuals. By revegetating uplands surrounding wetlands, it is possible to protect and reinstate key wetland functions within urbanized areas.

NEW APPROACHES AND RECOMMENDATIONS

Land-use regulations alone clearly cannot address all the impacts of sprawl on wetland systems. Landscape-scale wetland issues are often better addressed through integration into land-use planning efforts. In the United States, the majority of land-use decisions are made at the local level (Theobald et al. 2000) by county or municipal governments. Local decision-making activities include zoning, creating master plans, and reviewing development proposals. Unfortunately, most decisions made during the land-use planning process are not founded on impartial, scientifically credible information. Local officials and planning staff are rarely well versed in the wetland sciences, and such information is not readily available in a usable format. During the review of development proposals, decision makers often rely solely on information and analyses provided by the project sponsors. However, many land-use decision makers recognize the limitations of current practices and are eager to incorporate independently generated information into their planning processes to protect the public interest better. An opportunity exists for wetland and conservation scientists to provide and interpret this information.

Best management practices (BMPs) can identify specific impacts and provide solutions or alternatives to reduce those impacts, based on the best available science. However, to date there has been a lack of such manuals that focus specifically on wetland biodiversity. An exception, a manual entitled *Best Development Practices: Conserving Pool-Breeding Amphibians in Residential and Commercial Developments in the Northeastern United States* (Calhoun and Klemens 2002), provides guidelines for determining the biodiversity potential of specific vernal pools and offers planning and development recommendations based on those determinations. It gives local decision makers the power to make their own assessment of a pool's functions and relative importance and to integrate those data with specific design standards and practices. Such science-based planning tools, design standards, and recommendations are powerful mechanisms for conserving wetlands, complementing and adding ecological value to traditional regulatory protection.

As discussed in previous sections, conventional stormwater management regulations and practices can be detrimental to wetland biodiversity. New approaches to stormwater management and water quality are being developed and applied in various regions. A program called Nonpoint Education for Municipal Officials (NEMO) addresses water-quality issues through improved land-use practices within municipalities (e.g., by determining where to protect land and where to site development). The Low Impact Development (LID) Center in Maryland has pioneered new approaches to stormwater management through innovative site design techniques that replicate the preexisting hydrologic conditions of a site. In addition to maintaining and restoring water quality and hydrologic flow at landscape scales, both of these new approaches potentially will lead to increases in the quantity and quality of habitats in both wetlands and uplands. These techniques can also reduce costs of development by eliminating hard infrastructure.

A variety of steps can be taken to protect and preserve wetlands and wetland functions at the local level. Following are some guidelines for local land-use decision makers, conservation groups, concerned citizens, and others.

1. Many local decision-making bodies create open-space plans to guide the protection of areas considered important for recreation and natural resources. Open-space plans provide an excellent opportunity to protect wetlands and wetland-rich landscapes. Wetlands are the logical choice for preservation efforts because they provide many important services to communities: recreational opportunities, aesthetic values, reduction of flooding, water-quality improvement, and habitat for plants and animals. Through preservation, it is possible to extend wetland protection beyond regulatory boundaries so that upland habitats critical for wetland biodiversity can also be preserved. A diverse portfolio of preservation tools should be used to maximize acreage protected, including conservation easements, transfer of development rights, and traditional fee simple purchase.

2. A major tool for land-use planners at the local level is the Comprehensive Plan (known also as the Master Plan, Plan of Conservation and Development, and other names, depending on location). This document can be prepared or revised to address wetland biodiversity issues. To be effective, it must provide not only planning goals but also steps to achieve those goals.

3. Local governments can adopt stricter wetland regulations to compensate for the shortcomings of state and federal wetland laws. For example, state and federal laws establish lower size limits, leaving vernal pools and other small wetlands unprotected. Defining small wetlands according to function rather than size would help to protect these valuable resources. Buffer zones, primarily established to protect water quality, can be expanded to better protect wetland wildlife.

4. Wetland regulations that are unenforced are for the most part ineffective. The enforcement of regulations should be a major focus of communities attempting to preserve their wetland resources. Enforcement can be expensive and time consuming; communities with limited funds and time should consider hiring a wetlands enforcement officer on a cost-share and time-share basis with a neighboring community.

5. Existing stormwater management systems should receive regular maintenance. For example, road culverts should be kept open to avoid unintentional damming, and sediments traps should be cleaned out to maintain their effectiveness.

6. Residential housing density yields are typically calculated by dividing total property acreage by lot size, as established in zoning codes. However, this method does not account for areas within properties that are not buildable because of environmental constraints and associated regulations. Density yield should be calculated only after subtracting wetland area and other nonbuildable acres from the total property acreage. Zoning regulations should stipulate this procedure (for further details, see Arendt 1999).

7. To protect wetland biodiversity, it is very helpful to understand the extent and location of wetland habitats. Wetland maps are useful for understanding the land-use context of wetlands, for tracking changes in wetland distribution, and for proactive planning purposes. Some agencies also use them as regulatory documents, but this practice is not recommended because maps often underestimate wetland extent, which can be difficult to determine remotely (Miller, Golet, and August 2001). If possible, counties and municipalities should consider creating their own wetland maps because federal and state maps are typically created at scales too coarse for local planning efforts.

8. ISDSs can be the source of major threats to public and ecological health if they are not properly sited or maintained. Local regulations should require that ISDS units be sited in suitable soils, that they be set back from wetlands and water bodies, and that they be properly maintained to prevent failure. Where no public sewage lines are available near wetlands and public water supplies, housing densities must be controlled to minimize ISDS impacts.

9. The construction of new roads and highways should be minimized in and near wetlands because they have a major impact on wetland biodiversity. The damage caused by roads in these settings can be reduced through careful design (Calhoun and Klemens 2002; for further discussion of the environmental impacts of roads and potential solutions, see Forman et al. 2003).

10. Land-use planning and review procedures are often fraught with tension and mistrust, leading to decisions that satisfy few or none. All interested parties should be consulted and included as early as possible in this process to incor-

porate the needs and goals of developers, landowners, local governments, agencies, environmental advocates, and private citizens. Through inclusiveness and transparency in land-use decisions, irresolvable differences can be avoided, and acceptable solutions can be achieved.

11. Cluster developments, or conservation subdivisions, should be encouraged, particularly in wetland-rich landscapes. As noted earlier, however, housing densities should be controlled near wetlands where ISDS units are necessary. By clustering housing, land-use planners can reduce the overall "footprint" of developments and the amount and impact of associated infrastructure, such as roads. To maximize the ecological benefits of clustering, individual clusters should be sited with regard to greater landscape context, including the presence of wetlands and wildlife and the locations of other developments (for further ecological and design considerations for cluster developments, see Arendt 1999).

12. Wetlands are complex ecosystems with functions and values that are difficult and sometimes impossible to replicate. Compensatory mitigation efforts have not in general proved to be successful, so preservation of wetlands and wetland functions should always be the primary goal. Boards and commissions reviewing projects that propose wetland alterations should always require, in sequence:

- Complete avoidance of impacts
- Minimization of impacts where avoidance is not feasible
- Compensatory mitigation, only after the first two steps have been observed

13. Based on lessons learned from mitigation failures, numerous recommendations have been made for improving the success of compensatory wetland mitigations, where impacts are unavoidable. The following list of recommendations for conservation commissions, planning boards, and other decision-making or permit-granting bodies has been adapted, in part, from Brown and Veneman (1998) and Zedler and Shabman (2001):

- Increase monitoring of compliance.
- Supervise wetland construction or replication.
- Require completion of the wetland compensation *before* the development project can begin or before a certificate of occupancy is issued.
- Require a two-year bond (minimum) to ensure that the compensation is established.
- Do not allow stormwater detention ponds to qualify as wetland replication.

- Require rapid stabilization of soils, followed by removal of silt fencing, immediately after construction.
- Ensure that conditions of approval concerning wetland protection and mitigation are deed restricted and that reference is made to the restriction on the survey and subdivision plat.
- Require in-kind replacement wherever possible. Permittees should locate mitigation sites in hydrogeomorphic and landscape settings that maximize replication of functions and values.
- Require preservation of large buffers around mitigation sites and connectivity to other wetlands.
- Require applicants to support monitoring of the mitigation project, which can help to manage adaptively if problems are detected.
- Encourage self-maintaining wetland designs that do not rely on overengineered structures.
- Encourage restoration of former wetlands destroyed by filling or drainage, rather than the creation of wetlands from uplands or the "enhancement" of degraded wetlands.

14. Scientists from agencies, conservation organizations, and universities should create BMP (or best development practice) manuals to bring the latest research results to land-use decision makers. There is a gulf between the study of sprawl's impacts by scientists and the application of potential solutions by land-use practitioners. It is imperative that research results be distilled into the vernacular of land-use planners and decision makers. Manuals that have a better chance of being applied incorporate developers and builders' concerns in addition to environmental concerns.

15. Land-use planners and practitioners should seek out science-based information—including expert advice, peer-reviewed journal articles, and BMP manuals—and base their decisions on this information.

16. Concerned citizens can make a difference by becoming involved in community processes, such as attending meetings of municipal boards and committees. By doing so, they can understand local issues and advocate for improved wetland regulations, better enforcement of existing regulations, larger wetland buffers, and better land-use planning. Individuals' concerns can also be incorporated into the review of development proposals.

17. Citizen groups, conservation organizations, and watershed associations can organize cleanup days to remove trash from wetlands. Not only will this result in improved wetland habitats, but it will also help to raise awareness about wetland biodiversity and related issues.

18. Individuals, groups, and agencies can restore vegetation along wetland edges. Such restoration can be particularly effective in maintaining wetland biodiversity in urban areas.

CONCLUSION

Although wetland habitats have been destroyed and degraded at an alarming rate in the past, regulation of land-use activities in wetlands has helped to slow that rate. By combining regulatory protection with proactive restoration efforts, improved land-use planning, better dissemination and interpretation of wetland science, and citizen education and volunteerism, we may be able to slow further or even to stop this downward trend. Given the rapid spread of sprawl, a careful orchestration of all these mechanisms and activities is absolutely necessary if we hope to keep our wetlands diverse and functional.

REFERENCES

Andrle, R. F., and J. R. Carroll. 1988. *The Atlas of Breeding Birds in New York State.* Ithaca, N.Y.: Cornell University Press.

Angold, P. G. 1997. The impact of road upon adjacent heathland vegetation: Effects on plant species composition. *Journal of Applied Ecology* 34:409–417.

Arendt, R. 1999. *Growing Greener: Putting Conservation into Local Plans and Ordinances.* Washington, D.C.: Island Press.

Benoit, L. K., and R. A. Askins. 1999. Impact of the spread of Phragmites on the distribution of birds in Connecticut tidal marshes. *Wetlands* 19:194–208.

Berven, K. A., and T. A. Grudzien. 1990. Dispersal in the wood frog (*Rana sylvatica*): Implications for genetic population structure. *Evolution* 44:2047–2056.

Booth, D. 1990. Stream channel incision following drainage basin urbanization. *Water Resources Bulletin* 26:407–417.

Brookes, A. 1988. *Channelized Rivers: Perspectives for Environmental Management.* Chichester, England: Wiley.

Brown, S., and P. Veneman. 1998. *Compensatory Wetland Mitigation in Massachusetts.* Massachusetts Agricultural Experiment Station Research Bulletin, no. 746. Amherst: University of Massachusetts.

Calhoun, A. J. K., and M. W. Klemens. 2002. *Best Development Practices: Conserving Pool-Breeding Amphibians in Residential and Commercial Developments in the Northeastern United States.* Metropolitan Conservation Alliance Technical Paper, no. 5. Bronx, N.Y.: Wildlife Conservation Society.

Cowardin, L. M., V. Carter, F. C. Golet, and E. T. LaRoe. 1979. *Classification of Wetlands and Deepwater Habitats of the United States.* Fish and Wildlife Service, Biological Services Program FWS-OBS 79/31. Washington, D.C.: Department of the Interior, Fish and Wildlife Service.

Dahl, T. E. 1990. *Wetlands Losses in the United States 1780s to 1980s.* Washington, D.C.: Department of the Interior, Fish and Wildlife Service.

———. 2000. *Status and Trends of Wetlands in the Conterminous United States 1986 to 1997.* Washington, D.C.: Department of the Interior, Fish and Wildlife Service.

deMaynadier, P. G., and M. L. Hunter Jr. 1995. The relationship between forest management and amphibian ecology: A review of the North American literature. *Environmental Reviews* 3:230–261.

DiMauro, D. 1998. Reproduction of amphibians in natural and anthropogenic seasonal pools in managed forests. M.S. thesis, University of Maine.

Egan, R.S. 2001. Within-pond and landscape-level factors influencing the breeding effort of *Rana sylvatica* and *Ambystoma maculatum*. M.S. thesis, University of Rhode Island.

Ehrenfeld, J.G., H.B. Cutway, R. Hamilton, and E. Stander. 2003. Hydrologic description of forested wetlands in northeastern New Jersey, USA—An urban/suburban region. *Wetlands* 23:685–700.

Ferguson, B.K. 1994. *Stormwater Infiltration*. New York: Lewis.

Findlay, C.S., and J. Bourdage. 2000. Response time of wetland biodiversity to road construction on adjacent lands. *Conservation Biology* 14:86–94.

Findlay, C.S., and J. Houlahan. 1997. Anthropogenic correlates of species richness in southeastern Ontario wetlands. *Conservation Biology* 11:1000–1009.

Flather, C.H., and J.R. Sauer. 1996. Using landscape ecology to test hypotheses about large-scale abundance patterns in migratory birds. *Ecology* 77:28–35.

Forman, R.T.T, D. Sperling, J.A. Bissonette, A.P. Clevenger, C.D. Cutshall, V.H. Dale, L. Fahrig, R. France, C.R. Goldman, K. Heanue, J.A. Jones, F.J. Swanson, T. Turrentine, and T.C. Winter. 2003. *Road Ecology: Science and Solutions*. Washington, D.C.: Island Press.

Galatowitsch, S.M., N.O. Anderson, and P.D. Ascher. 1999. Invasiveness in wetland plants in temperate North America. *Wetlands* 19:733–755.

Galatowitsch, S.M., and A.G. van der Valk. 1994. *Restoring Prairie Wetlands: An Ecological Approach*. Ames: Iowa State University Press.

Gibbs, J.P. 1993. Importance of small wetlands for the persistence of local populations of wetland-associated animals. *Wetlands* 13:25–31.

Golet, F.C., A.J.K. Calhoun, W.R. DeRagon, D.J. Lowry, and A.J. Gold. 1993. *Ecology of Red Maple Swamps in the Glaciated Northeast: A Community Profile*. Fish and Wildlife Service Biological Report, no. 12. Washington, D.C.: Department of the Interior, Fish and Wildlife Service.

Golet, F.G., D.H.A. Myshrall, N.A. Miller, and M.P. Bradley. 2002. *Wetland Restoration Plan for the Woonasquatucket River Watershed, Rhode Island*. Final research report prepared for the Rhode Island Department of Environmental Management and U.S. Environmental Protection Agency, Region 1. Kingston: University of Rhode Island.

Gosselink, J.G., G.P. Shaffer, L.C. Lee, D.M. Burdick, D.L. Childers, N.C. Leibowitz, S.C. Hamilton, R. Boumans, D. Cushman, S. Fields, M. Koch, and J.M. Visser. 1990. Landscape conservation in a forested wetland watershed: Can we manage cumulative impacts? *BioScience* 40:588–600.

Hager, H.A., and K.D. McCoy. 1998. The implications of accepting untested hypotheses: A review of the effects of purple loosestrife (*Lythrum salicaria*) in North America. *Biodiversity and Conservation* 7:1069–1079.

Heinz Center. 2002. *The State of the Nation's Ecosystems: Measuring the Lands, Waters, and Living Resources of the United States*. Cambridge: Cambridge University Press.

Holland, M.M., and P.G. Risser. 1991. The role of landscape boundaries in the management and restoration of changing environments: Introduction. In M.M. Holland, P.G. Risser, and R.J. Naiman, eds., *Ecotones: The Role of Landscape Boundaries in the Management and Restoration of Changing Environments*, 1–7. New York: Chapman and Hall.

Horner, R. R., J. J. Skupien, E. H. Livingstone, and H. E. Shaver. 1994. *Fundamentals of Urban Runoff: Technical and Institutional Issues.* Washington, D.C.: Terrene Institute.

Keddy, P. A. 2000. *Wetland Ecology: Principles and Conservation.* Cambridge: Cambridge University Press.

Kentula, M. E. 1994. The status of restoration science: Wetlands ecosystems. In *Symposium on Ecological Restoration: Proceedings of a Conference, March 1993,* 21–24. EPA 841-B94-003. Washington, D.C.: Environmental Protection Agency, Office of Water.

Kiviat, E. 2001. Invasive wetland plants in the New York City region. Manuscript.

Klemens, M. W. 1993. *Amphibians and Reptiles of Connecticut and Adjacent Regions.* State Geological and Natural History Survey of Connecticut, bulletin no. 112. Hartford: Connecticut Department of Environmental Protection.

———. 2000. *Amphibians and Reptiles in Connecticut: A Checklist with Notes on Conservation Status, Identification, and Distribution.* Connecticut Department of Environmental Protection Bulletin, no. 32. Hartford: Connecticut Department of Environmental Protection.

———. 2001. *Bog Turtle* (Clemmys muhlenbergii), *Northern Population, Recovery Plan.* Washington, D.C.: Department of the Interior, Fish and Wildlife Service.

Knutson, M. G., J. R. Sauer, D. A. Olsen, M. J. Mossman, L. M. Hemesath, and M. J. Lannoo. 1999. Effects of landscape composition and wetland fragmentation on frog and toad abundance and species richness in Iowa and Wisconsin, U.S.A. *Conservation Biology* 13:1437–1446.

Lannoo, M. J., ed. 1998. *Status and Conservation of Midwestern Amphibians.* Iowa City: University of Iowa Press.

Lehtinen, R. M., S. M. Galatowitsch, and J. R. Tester. 1999. Consequences of habitat loss and fragmentation for wetland amphibian assemblages. *Wetlands* 19:1–12.

Lowrance, R. 1998. Riparian forest ecosystems as filters for nonpoint-source pollution. In M. L. Pace and P. M. Groffman, eds., *Successes, Limitations, and Frontiers in Ecosystem Science,* 113–141. New York: Springer.

Marsh, D. M., and P. C. Trenham. 2001. Metapopulation dynamics and amphibian conservation. *Conservation Biology* 15:40–49.

Meffe, G. K., and C. R. Carroll. 1994. *Principles of Conservation Biology.* Sunderland, Mass.: Sinauer.

Miller, N. A. 1999. Landscape and habitat predictors of Canada warbler (*Wilsonia canadensis*) and northern waterthrush (*Seiurus noveboracensis*) occurrence in Rhode Island swamps. M.S. thesis, University of Rhode Island, Kingston.

Miller, N. A., and F. C. Golet. 2001. *Development of a Statewide Freshwater Wetland Restoration Strategy: Site Identification and Prioritization Methods.* Final research report prepared for the Rhode Island Department of Environmental Management and the U.S. Environmental Protection Agency, Region 1. Kingston: University of Rhode Island.

Miller, N. A., F. C. Golet, and P. V. August. 2001. *Options for Mapping Rhode Island's Wetlands: Recommendations Based on User Needs and Technical, Logistical, and Fiscal Considerations.* Final research report prepared for the Rhode Island Department of Environmental Management and the U.S. Environmental Protection Agency, Region 1. Kingston: University of Rhode Island.

Minkin, P., and R. Ladd. 2003. *Success of Corps-Required Wetland Mitigation in New England.* Washington, D.C.: Army Corps of Engineers, New England District.

Mitchell, J.C., and M.W. Klemens. 2000. Primary and secondary effects of habitat alteration. In M.W. Klemens, ed., *Turtle Conservation*, 5–32. Washington, D.C.: Smithsonian Institution Press.

Mitsch, W.J., and J.G. Gosselink. 2000. *Wetlands*. 3rd ed. New York: Van Nostrand Reinhold.

National Research Council. 1995. *Wetlands: Characteristics and Boundaries*. Washington, D.C.: National Academy Press.

——. 2001. *Compensating for Wetland Losses under the Clean Water Act*. Washington, D.C.: National Academy Press.

Niering, W.A. 1988. Endangered, threatened, and rare wetland plants and animals of the continental United States. In D.D. Hook, W.H. McKee Jr., H.K. Smith, J. Gregory, V.G. Burrell Jr., M.R. Devoe, R.E. Sojka, S. Gilbert, R. Banks, L.H. Stolzy, C. Brooks, T.D. Matthews, and T.H. Shear, eds., *The Ecology and Management of Wetlands*. Vol. 1, *Ecology of Wetlands*, 227–238. Portland, Ore.: Timber Press.

Owen, C.R. 1995. Water budget and flow patterns in an urban wetland. *Journal of Hydrology* 169:171–187.

Pechmann, J.H.K., D.E. Scott, R.D. Semlitsch, J.P. Caldwell, L.J. Vitt, and J.W. Gibbons. 1991. Declining amphibian populations: The problem of separating human impacts from natural fluctuations. *Science* 253:892–895.

Richter, K.O., and A.L. Azous. 2001. Bird distribution, abundance, and habitat use. In A.L. Azous and R.R. Horner, eds., *Wetlands and Urbanization: Implications for the Future*, 167–199. Boca Raton, Fla.: Lewis.

Saunders, D.A., R.J. Hobbs, and C.R. Margules. 1991. Biological consequences of fragmentation: A review. *Conservation Biology* 5:18–32.

Schueler, T. 1995. *Site Planning for Urban Stream Protection*. Ellicott City, Md.: Center for Watershed Protection.

Semlitsch, R.D. 1981. Terrestrial activity and summer home range of the mole salamander, *Ambystoma talpoideum*. *Canadian Journal of Zoology* 59:315–322.

——. 1998. Biological delineation of terrestrial buffer zones for pond-breeding amphibians. *Conservation Biology* 12:1113–1119.

——. 2000. Principles for management of aquatic-breeding amphibians. *Journal of Wildlife Management* 64:615–631.

Semlitsch, R.D., and J.R. Bodie. 1998. Are small, isolated wetlands expendable? *Conservation Biology* 12:1129–1133.

Semlitsch, R.D., and J.B. Jensen. 2001. Core habitat, not buffer zone. *National Wetlands Newsletter* 23:5–6, 11.

Skelly, D.K., E.E. Werner, and S.A. Cortwright. 1999. Long-term distributional dynamics of a Michigan amphibian assemblage. *Ecology* 80:2326–2337.

Smith, R.D., A. Ammann, C. Bartoldus, and M.M. Brinson. 1995. *An Approach for Assessing Wetland Functions Using Hydrogeomorphic Classification, Reference Wetlands, and Functional Indices*. Washington, D.C.: Army Corps of Engineers.

Stromberg, J.C., R. Tiller, and B. Richter. 1996. Effects of groundwater decline on riparian vegetation of semiarid regions: The San Pedro, Arizona. *Ecological Applications* 6:113–131.

Theobald, D.M., N.T. Hobbs, T. Bearly, J. Zack, T. Shenk, and W.E. Riebsame. 2000. Incorporating biological information into local land use decision-making: Designing a system for conservation planning. *Landscape Ecology* 15:35–45.

Thompson, D. Q., R. L. Stuckey, and E. B. Thompson. 1987. *Spread, Impact, and Control of Purple Loosestrife* (Lythrum salicaria) *in North American Wetlands*. Fish and Wildlife Service Research Report, no. 2. Washington, D.C.: Department of the Interior, Fish and Wildlife Service.

Tiner, R. W. 1984. *Wetlands of the United States: Current Status and Recent Trends*. Newton Corner, Mass.: Fish and Wildlife Service, National Wetlands Inventory.

——. 1995. Wetland restoration and creation. In W. A. Nierenberg, ed., *Encyclopedia of Environmental Biology*, 3: 517–534. New York: Academic Press.

Turner, R. E., A. M. Redmond, and J. B. Zedler. 2001. Count it by acre or function—Mitigation adds up to net loss of wetlands. *National Wetlands Newsletter* 23:5–6, 14–16.

Windmiller, B. S. 1996. The pond, the forest, and the city: Spotted salamander ecology and conservation in a human-dominated landscape. Ph.D. diss., Tufts University.

Zedler, J., and L. Shabman. 2001. Compensatory mitigation needs improvement, panel says. *National Wetlands Newsletter* 23:1, 12–14.

4

■ ■

ECOSYSTEMS, DISTURBANCE, AND
THE IMPACT OF SPRAWL

Seth R. Reice

Ecologists now recognize that natural events such as fires, floods, and hurricanes are fundamental to ecosystem integrity. These processes can be predictable disruptive events, such as annual flooding and fires that cycle through a forest with relative frequency, or unpredictable and infrequent large-scale disturbances, such as earthquakes and volcano eruptions. All are critical to the maintenance of ecosystems and the species these systems support. Sprawling development interferes with these natural disturbance regimes by suppressing or altering them. In addition, sprawl fosters other novel anthropogenic disturbances, such as clearing for home construction, trampling of soil and vegetation, dumping, or vandalism, which in turn may impact ecosystems. This chapter focuses on how sprawl alters large-scale natural disturbance processes (for a discussion on smaller-scale, anthropogenic disturbances, see Johnson and Klemens, chapter 2, this volume).

WHAT IS A DISTURBANCE?

The most widely accepted definition of *disturbance* is "any relatively discrete event in time that disrupts ecosystem, community or population structure, and changes resources, availability of substratum, or the physical environment" (White and Pickett 1985:7). Thus defined, a disturbance is a physical event, not the result of that event. Disturbances are physical forces—including fires, floods, earthquakes, tornados, and hurricanes—that alter ecosystems. Sousa (1984) and other authors, notably Pickett, Wu, and Cadenasso (1999), include biologically driven changes as examples of disturbance—for example, insect outbreaks or the actions of disease organisms or predators. In this chapter, the definition of *disturbance* is expanded to include biologically driven per-turbations.

DISTURBANCES VARY IN SCALE AND INTENSITY

Disturbances vary in *extent*, their size or the area they cover, and in *magnitude*, their severity or degree of destructiveness. A tornado, for instance, can destroy one house or a mile-long swath of houses. Disturbances can also produce a cascade of secondary disturbances. Coastal flooding caused by a hurricane in turn causes shoreline erosion in some areas and buildup of the beaches in others. River flooding may cause bank slumping and erosion. Forest fires that remove trees on hill slopes make the hillside much more vulnerable to land-slides because the tree roots no longer hold the soil in place.

Drought in the southeastern United States has been linked to outbreaks of the southern pine bark beetle, mainly *Dendroctonus frontalis*. Five major spe-cies of pine bark beetles can be found in the Southeast: the small southern pine engraver (*Ips avulsus*), the southern pine engraver (*I. grandicollis*), the coarse writing engraver (*I. calligraphus*), the southern pine beetle (*D. frontalis*), and the black turpentine beetle (*D. terebrans*). Trees under stress are much more susceptible to infestation, so trees weakened by the drought have less resistance to the beetle. All southern yellow pines are affected, including short leaf, lob-lolly, and Virginia pines. Eastern white and Scotch pine can also be attacked. Young trees less than 10 feet (3 meters) tall (less than 3 inches [8 centimeters] in diameter) are generally not infested.

Whether a large earthquake or a single tree falling in the forest, every dis-turbance creates patchiness in the environment, resulting in the availability of new habitats. The removal of organisms through a disturbance allows other species to colonize and exploit new habitat. Although some species are removed from an ecosystem or area by the disturbance itself, subsequent colonization can bring in new species and enhance biodiversity. Thus a disturbance can be a positive force that maintains and often increases biodiversity, benefiting the overall health of the ecosystem.

DISTURBANCES ARE NORMAL BUT UNPREDICTABLE

Disturbances are unpredictable events (Resh et al. 1988), and because they occur with great suddenness, species cannot adapt to them. This issue of pre-dictability differentiates a disturbance from a regularly predictable destructive event, such as a winter freeze. The local environment often defines whether or not a certain event is predictable. Periodic flooding of a river occurs when the stream's discharge (the total volume of flow through a stream channel) exceeds the capacity of the channel and flows over the banks, often with great force (Dunne and Leopold 1978). As the air temperature warms, spring snow-melt floods are predictable in northern or mountainous areas with lots of snow. Because the exact date of these spring floods varies by just a few weeks each year, these floods are part of the structure of the stream community. The life histories of stream-dwelling species have evolved to cope with the "expected" spring flood. For example, some insects deposit resting eggs (ephipia) that survive the flood, whereas other insects emerge as adults in their terrestrial phase just prior to the flood. Such events are stressors and exert strong selective pressure on the species, but because they are predictable, many organisms have adapted to them over time, and they are not considered disturbances. Floods are much less predict-able, however, in regions without much snow. In these areas, floods are caused by heavy rains in which the resulting runoff produces a discharge that exceeds a stream's capacity. These unpredictable events can occur in any season and wash away or kill many individuals, from algae to aquatic insects to fishes. Species in these stream communities therefore cannot evolve successful strategies to pre-pare for or resist these unpredictable floods. As a result, the fauna is often devas-tated. In these systems, the flood is considered a disturbance (as defined in this chapter).

Fires are frequent occurrences—especially in certain fire-prone ecosystems. They generally occur when there are dry conditions, sufficient fuel, and a spark. In ecosystems such as the western U.S. chaparral and the South African *renosterveld*, these conditions occur with great regularity. In these communi-ties, fires are frequent, almost predictable, and essential to ecosystem survival. Some particular forest communities are also highly flammable. Many of the trees within them are so well adapted to fire that they actually require fire to reproduce. These communities include the jack pine (*Pinus banksiana*) forests of the upper midwestern United States and southern Canada, the longleaf pine (*Pinus palustris*) forests of the southeastern United States (figure 4.1), and the *Eucalyptus* forests of Australia. Many of these species' cones are serotinous, meaning that heat is required for them to open and release seeds. In these examples, fires are not disturbances, but rather predictable disruptive events. Regardless of their definition, they are an integral part of the ecological rhythm in these ecosystems, a necessary part of life.

Different communities have different fire cycles. Fire cycles are determined by climate, fuel, and chance events such as lightning strike ignitions. The return interval varies among different forest types. At the infrequent end of the spectrum, the return interval for fires in Yellowstone National Park has been estimated to be 350 years. Therefore, even the massive 1988 fires were normal, but unpredictable. In other forests not so well adapted to fires, such

FIGURE 4.1. The persistence of the longleaf pine (*Pinus palustris*) and wiregrass (*Aristida* spp.) clay hill communities of the Florida panhandle depends on periodic fire. (Photo by Keith Hackbarth)

as beech–maple and oak–hickory, fires are also frequent but unpredictable disturbances.

Some disturbances, such as thunderstorms, happen frequently enough for us to consider them a regular part of life. Hurricanes, storms of far greater magnitude, are normal, too, although they may not seem so when threatening our homes. From the perspective of the natural communities, however, these disturbances are ordinary, if uncommon, parts of life. Hurricanes may be typical, but they are still unpredictable events from the perspective of the beach fauna and flora, so they are truly disturbances. Wind frequently acts as a small-scale disturbance in the forest by felling single trees that are already weak or dead. It occasionally acts as a larger-scale disturbance, felling trees across a wide area during violent storms. As the size of the disturbance increases, the event becomes less common, but is still natural. In fact, the normal state of a community is to be recovering from the most recent disturbance (Reice 1994).

Earthquakes and volcanic eruptions are less common and less predictable. In earthquake-prone zones, tremors do occur, although without much warning. Near volcanoes, eruptions are often anticipated but are rarely forecast. These events can be catastrophic for people, but they are part of the normal geology and ecology of those regions.

SPECIES' AND COMMUNITIES' RESPONSES TO DISTURBANCES AND PREDICTABLE DISRUPTIVE EVENTS

A community's fundamental response to the disturbance or disruptive event is colonization. Such events initiate the process of *succession*—or the sequence of community change. The size and shape of the event determines the source of new colonists into the disturbed area. The colonists may come from adjacent areas by migratory movements across the edge (*migration*) or by long-distance transport methods (*recruitment*) (Reice 1994, 2001). Recruitment includes flying (e.g., birds or insects) or being carried by the wind (e.g., dandelions or maple seeds). It can also include aquatic transport (e.g., stream animals drifting with the current, long-shore and onshore transport of tiny molluscan or crustacean larvae in coastal waters, and deposit of pelagic marine animals and plants on the beach by waves and storms).

In small disturbances and disruptive events, the ratio of edge to interior of the disturbed area is large, such that migration of species is common, and it is likely that the colonists will be similar to those removed by the disturbance. Consequently, there is little or no change in *species richness,* or the total number of different species in an area. If recruitment dominates, however, as in disturbances of great extent, then there is a high probability that the species recolonizing the area will be different from the ones destroyed by the disturbance. Subsequent recruitment therefore may increase species richness. However, in many cases, such larger-scale disturbances tend to favor the establishment of introduced or very common species, which can lead to significant negative impacts to native flora and fauna (S. Reice, personal observation).

If a disturbance or another ecosystem-altering event is not too severe, then many organisms can be damaged but survive. The severity of a disturbance is a species-specific issue. A wind that topples an oak tree may not disturb the herbs nearby. Some organisms can regrow in place. Because most animals cannot regenerate, with the exception of corals and other hydroids, regrowth is typically limited to plants such as algae and clonal plants. Some trees, including oaks, elms, and maples, can occasionally sprout from their stumps. Therefore, a cooler ground fire can allow many species to survive. A very hot crown fire often kills the trees and cooks the roots, leaving little opportunity for regrowth. A bank full flood—that is, one that fills the stream channel but does not overflow its banks—often allows encrusting algae and mosses to regrow, but a more massive event scours all boulder surfaces clean with the efficiency of sandblasting. Large enough disturbances such as mudslides and volcanic eruptions are able to transform entire ecosystems.

All species have the capacity to increase exponentially, given favorable environmental conditions. Because more individuals may be produced than can survive in an area, surplus organisms usually remain available to recolonize disturbed areas after an event. Annual plants that are especially effective colonizers are often called weeds. This recolonization is familiar to any gardeners who, after tilling their garden and leaving it for a few days, return to find crabgrass growing there. In mountain streams, blackfly larvae (Simuliidae) are often the first colonizers. In piedmont and coastal plain streams, midge larvae (Chironomidae) are usually the first species to appear. In standing water, from ponds to puddles to dog water bowls and water-filled old tires, mosquitoes colonize rapidly. Along the banks of tropical rivers in the Amazonian rain forest, after floodwaters recede, the *Cecropia* trees invade and grow quickly. Poppies (*Papaver*) spring up in dry lands in Mediterranean climates, from California to Israel. Pine trees are often the first trees to colonize disturbed land, such as abandoned farmland.

In every ecosystem, certain species are very well adapted for colonization by being good dispersers and fast growers. Early colonists initiate the process of succession by spreading quickly into disturbed areas and becoming established. Colonizers also tend to have shorter generation times or life spans than other species of their approximate size. They reproduce rapidly and establish the first stage of the new community. The very adaptations that ensure their success as colonists typically mean that they are not very good competitors. They lack the characteristics required to hold and defend the space they occupy.

Every ecosystem also has a suite of species that are very good competitors and that consequently become dominant and persistent space holders. In old fields, pines give way to oaks and hickories. In rain forests, the *Cecropia* trees give way to *Ficus* and many other large rain forest trees. In streams, blackflies and chironomids are displaced by net-spinning caddisflies. These species, being such good competitors, eventually dominate the community. When the dominant space-holding species are removed after a natural disturbance, other colonizing species then have an opportunity to exploit the newly available space and resources.

Building on previous work, Joseph Connell transformed ecological thinking in 1978 with the publication of the *intermediate disturbance hypothesis*. He showed that in rain forests and coral reefs there is a tradeoff between disturbance and diversity. If disturbances are too infrequent or too mild, then diversity will decrease because of the space holders' predominance. If disturbances are too frequent or too severe, then the dominant space holders are constrained or killed off, and only colonists will exist in the system. In either case, species diversity is limited. Under conditions of intermediate disturbance frequency and severity, some competitive dominants persist along with an assortment of colonizing species. Intermediate levels of disturbance contribute to maximal species biodiversity.

BIODIVERSITY AND ECOSYSTEM SERVICES

There is a critical link between species diversity and ecosystem services. Ecosystems conduct many functions that are essential to life on Earth. When these functions benefit humanity, economists refer to them as *ecosystem servic-es* (Daily and Reichart 1997; Farber, chapter 12, this volume). In primary production, the growth of plants produces food (e.g., corn, rice, soybeans) or fibers (cotton) that we use for clothing or building materials or fuel (wood). Stream ecosystems purify water for drinking. Livestock feed on the primary producers and provide people with meat and fiber. Decomposition processes recycle nutrients and break down dead organic matter. Ecosystem services are essential for the continued health of ecosystems and the survival of humanity. In addition, these services, which ecosystems provide for free, would be costly to replicate. In most cases, man-made substitution for ecosystem services is either prohibitively expensive or impossible.

Increased biodiversity tends to increase the level and efficiency of ecosystem functions, such as productivity. Species diversity, one aspect of biodiversity, has two components—richness and *evenness*. Species richness is simply the total number of species present in an area. Species evenness refers to a similar representation of most species as opposed to an overwhelming dominance of just a few species. Increased species diversity (i.e., both species richness and species evenness) results in improved ecosystem function. Several mechanisms are involved, including *niche complementarity* (Tilman et al. 2001). Differing species possess different niches that include varying ecological roles in the community. Niche complementarity is the hypothesis that with increased numbers of species present, the ecosystem function is achieved in a greater number of ways. A second mechanism is that high species diversity increases the likelihood that the most efficient species will be present (Chapin et al. 1997). These mechanisms confer stability to the processes and improve their efficiency. The specific relationships among plant diversity, plant production, and nutrient cycling are currently the subject of intensive research and debate among ecologists. Biodiversity is regarded as a critical measure of ecosystem or community health. Higher levels of biodiversity can be viewed as nature's insurance for the stability, diversity, and continuity of ecosystem services on which humans depend. Therefore, it is in our own self-interest to preserve biodiversity.

The preceding discussion has illustrated the important connection between disturbances and enhanced biodiversity. Yet people fear disturbances and try to minimize them. Dams and levees are built to prevent floods; forest fires are suppressed. We must change our attitudes toward disturbances, whether fires or floods, and embrace them, for they are critical for healthy ecosystems and, ultimately, for our own survival.

HUMAN ATTITUDES AND BEHAVIORS TOWARD DISTURBANCES AND DISRUPTIVE EVENTS

It is unquestionable that a raging flood or forest fire is a dangerous and fearsome event that threatens human life and property. Although we fear disasters, we often fail to recognize the risks that we take when building our homes and workplaces in disaster-prone areas. The appeal of a dramatic landscape often clouds perceptions of inherent risks at such locales. The disturbances themselves are often responsible for what we perceive as beautiful in these ecosystems. The openness of the chaparral, the biodiversity of second-growth forests, and the floodplain with a clear view of the river indicate these ecosystems' dynamic nature. Too often we ignore these warnings.

DISTURBANCE ECOLOGY AND THE THREAT OF SPRAWL

Sprawl results from decisions and incentives made by government policy compounded by individual desires. Moving beyond city limits brings people and their homes in closer contact with nature. Although this contact is what many people seek, it also brings them into potential conflict with the natural cycle of disturbances. What are the long-term consequences of this movement of people from urban areas, as viewed from the perspective of natural disturbances? The relationship between sprawl and disturbance has three major aspects:

1. Sprawl brings people into conflict with large-scale natural disturbance processes, leading to suppression of these processes.
2. Sprawl can increase the frequency and severity of some disturbances.
3. Sprawl introduces novel disturbances into ecosystems.

The remainder of the chapter focuses on the first two categories, the ways in which sprawl affects natural processes and other disruptive ecosystem events by suppression or by enhancement. In chapter 2 of this volume, Johnson and Klemens address the impacts of novel and small-scale disturbances such as trampling, dumping, and recreational activities (see also Byers and Mitchell, chapter 8, this volume).

SPRAWL-INDUCED CONFLICT WITH NATURAL DISTURBANCE PROCESSES: SUPPRESSION

The same disturbance or disruptive event, whether fire or flood, that can be so beneficial to the natural ecosystem is often a direct threat to human property and life. It is an understandable response for people to increase their security by imposing limits on the natural cycles of fires and floods.

SPRAWL AND FIRE SUPPRESSION The dramatic chaparral landscape outside Los Angeles, California, has been developed with houses in spite of the known threat of recurrent wildfire. The return interval for fire (i.e., the average time between fires) in the chaparral is approximately 15 years (Christensen and Mueller 1975). The chaparral is a fire-dependent system because its health depends on frequent fire (Fuller 1991). The chaparral vegetation has evolved to facilitate fire. Snowbush (*Ceanothus* spp.), a common chaparral plant, has leaves coated in a flammable resin. For its seeds to germinate, they must be heated to 113°F for at least eight minutes. Typical chaparral shrubs, such as manzanita (*Arctostaphylos* spp.) and chamise (*Adenostoma fasciculatum*), have waxy sheaths on their leaves to reduce evaporative water loss in the dry climate. When they are water stressed, their branches die, and strips of bark fall off. In a mature plant, often as much as half of its tissue is dead and poised to burn. These plants catch fire readily and burn easily. The chaparral ecosystem is practically a fire waiting to happen. Yet chaparral fires are not really destructive for these fire-adapted plants. Underground parts of the plants escape the fire. Fire releases the nutrients that were bound up in the plant's dead tissues and makes them available in mineral form for the plant to reabsorb. This is a key phase of the nutrient recycling. When the plants sprout from their roots, they grow much more quickly than they did before the fire. Without fire, the chaparral would disappear, yielding to the inexorable competition from scrub oaks. The fires kill the oaks, while the chaparral plants thrive. The new tender growth on the chaparral shrubs enhances the food for browsing elk and deer (Wright and Bailey 1982). Therefore, in the chaparral, fire is both normal and necessary for the survival of the entire ecosystem.

When people build homes in the chaparral or other fire-prone systems, they create a great demand for fire suppression; yet to have a chaparral, there must be frequent fires. Short of not building in the chaparral, an alternative is to enforce strict fireproof building codes, specifying building materials (brick versus wood, metal roofs), land clearing of flammable materials 328 feet (100 meters) around the house. In this way, people can let the fires burn, protect the vitality of the chaparral, *and* protect their homes. Fire suppression in the chaparral means the loss of the chaparral ecosystem itself. Sprawl is therefore a threat to the very survival of the chaparral ecosystem.

An analogous but less dramatic example of the conflict between sprawl and fires occurs in forests in the southeastern United States. Longleaf pine forests are fire dependent, and the loblolly pine (*Pinus taeda*) forests are very tolerant of fires. Longleaf pines have tough, fire-resistant bark to survive ground fires;

they also have serotinous cones and require fire to open to release seeds. Fires also suppress the encroaching oaks and other competitors. In the presettlement condition, longleaf pine savannas covered nearly all of the southeastern United States, stretching from southeastern Virginia to eastern Texas. Now, because of logging, conversion of land to agriculture and loblolly pine plantations, and especially fire suppression, longleaf pine savannas cover just 3 percent of their ancestral range. The red-cockaded woodpecker (*Picoides borealis*), a federally listed endangered species, is dependent for its survival on the longleaf pine savanna. It requires isolated old-growth longleaf pines to build its nests and to reproduce. In longleaf pine savannas, oaks outcompete and displace longleaf pines in the absence of fire. Sprawling development and expanding agriculture are major factors in the destruction of these savannas. The predictable synergism then plays out. As more people live in or near the forest, the demand for fire protection increases. With fire suppression comes the replacement of the more open longleaf pine savanna with the successional oaks. The loss of the longleaf pine savanna threatens the survival of the red-cockaded woodpecker.

Fires renew and reinvigorate most forests and are critical in nutrient cycling. They release the nutrients bound up in dead wood and leaves. The free nitrogen, phosphorus, and other nutrients in the ash become available for uptake by the remaining plants, stimulating their growth. Fires open up the canopy, letting in essential light for the growth of understory trees and shrubs. Many fire-intolerant species, such as red maple (*Acer rubrum*), can outcompete the fire-tolerant species in the absence of fire. Fire-dependent and fire-tolerant trees will be eliminated without the aid of fire. Even in the Great Smoky Mountains National Park, red maple is crowding out other species as a direct result of fire suppression (Harrod 1999).

Fire, with its associated processes such as nutrient cycling, is also essential for the survival of fire-driven systems in other areas of the world, such as the heathlands of southern Australia and the *renosterveld* habitats of South Africa, which contain 8,500 plant species, of which 68 percent are indigenous and found nowhere else on Earth. For this reason, South Africa is considered by many botanists to have its own floral kingdom, the Cape Flora. In addition to forests, natural communities such as prairie grasslands and savannas also depend on specific fire regimes for the health of these ecosystems.

Both fire frequency and fire suppression vary with suburban population density. As people move out from urban areas into the forest, the probability of fires being ignited by people increases. What began as simple appreciation and enjoyment of wildness becomes fearfulness when natural fires occur. That fearfulness translates into public pressure for fire suppression. The demand for fire suppression likewise increases with population density. If people suppress natural fires, then the entire character of the forest ecosystem changes. The cost to humanity is the loss of unique fire-dependent ecosystems, their biodiversity, and the ecosystem services they provide.

COASTAL ZONE DEVELOPMENT, DISTURBANCES, AND ECOLOGICAL PROCESSES A boom in coastal zone development and population has occurred over the past two decades. This growth compounds the established waterfront development occurring along oceanfront cities from Miami to Boston and lakefront cities like Chicago and Milwaukee. Pacific Coast sprawl extends from Los Angeles to Vancouver, British Columbia. The development of vacation communities in areas along the Outer Banks of North Carolina, the New Jersey shore, and the Florida coastline is a major shift in land-use patterns in these fragile, disturbance-prone ecosystems. The desire to live close to the ocean is powerful. So whether it is in primary residences for commuters to the cities or in vacation property, more people are living close to the oceans and the Great Lakes.

Hurricanes cause the most dramatic disturbances in the coastal zone. The destructive power of hurricanes is obvious. Sprawl into the coastal zone does not alter the frequency or severity of hurricanes, but as population in the coastal zones continues to increase, the threat to life and property from hurricanes increases as well. Hurricanes and other storms cause coastal erosion. Powerful storms on the mid-Atlantic coast blow in from the northeast Atlantic Ocean, with high tides and strong waves, which commonly strip sand from the northern beaches and deposit it farther south. This is how barrier islands are formed and function (Kaufman and Pilkey 1983). The beaches are constantly in a state of flux, which is fundamental to the dynamics of the coastline. Ironically, the processes and disturbances that we fear are the same disturbances that built the beaches in the first place. The features that we value, from the sandy beaches to the low windswept maritime forests, are the direct result of the powerful storms and wave action associated with the ocean. Without these "disasters," the inland forests would encroach and the very nature of the beaches would be lost. The salt-intolerant ornamental trees we plant, such as crabapple (*Malea* spp.) and Japanese yew (*Taxus* spp.), stand dead after being soaked with salt spray from high winds, whereas beach plum (*Prunus maritima*) and bayberry (*Myrica pennsylvanica*) are adapted to conditions of higher salinity and can survive sculpting by salt-laden winds. The beaches' biological communities are initially battered by storms, but then are ultimately enhanced. The sands are replaced, and new sources of food are available. The cycle of growth, disturbance, renewal, and regrowth is as natural on the beach as it is in the forest. As the beach communities' human population increases, however, the demand to stabilize the beach increases, too. Humans seem unable to reconcile their desire for permanence and security with the natural rhythms of storms, erosion, and replenishment.

People build jetties in order to prevent the scouring away of the sand in front of a development. A jetty is essentially a sea wall that projects into the ocean, sometimes for hundreds of feet. The jetty, often built out of boulders or concrete, blocks the flow and diverts it away from the beach beside the jetty. Ocean waves, which scour sand away from the beach typically in the winter storms, also transport sand back to the beach in the summer. By blocking the waves with the jetty, the adjacent beach becomes static. Such armoring does not stop erosion, but displaces it farther down the beach. Animals and plants that depend on the shifting sand are affected. For example, the piping plover (*Charadrius melodus*), a federally endangered species, requires the unvegetated beach created by recently deposited sand for nesting.

The other major intervention, designed to protect the beachfront homes from erosion, is beach "renourishment." This practice involves dredging and pumping sand from offshore onto the beach. Although designed to mitigate the effects of natural disturbance, "renourishment" is a massive man-made disturbance, causing disruption to the offshore communities. The clouds of sand stirred up during pumping operations bury sea grass and coral reef communities. It changes the sandy beach, too, because the grain size of the sand being pumped up is different from that of the sand on the beach. Often the "renourished" beach develops too high a proportion of shell fragments. The hardened beach becomes impossible for shore birds to peck through. The beach-dwelling invertebrates are unable to live there. Burrowing clams (e.g., *Donax variabilis* and *D. parvula*) and crabs (ghost crab [*Ocypode quadrata*]; mole crab [*Emerita talpoidia*]; portunid crabs [*Arenaeus cribarius* and *Ovalipes ocellatus*]) can no longer burrow through the shell layer as they seek the sand that is their home. The new habitat on the beach is unsuitable for the native beach residents. The decline in these populations from dredge and fill operations and beach "renourishment" is well documented and can reach 100 percent loss (Peterson, Hickerson, and Johnson 2000). The nests of endangered sea turtles (including loggerhead, leatherback, and green turtles) are often buried and destroyed. The shell-laden dredge spoil is too hard for many turtles to dig through to build their nests. It takes many tidal cycles to re-sort the sand grains and re-create normal beach sand particle distributions so that the beach fauna can recolonize it. This is another illustration of how human sprawl into a fragile habitat creates a biological and ecological dilemma. It indirectly conflicts with the beach's natural ebb and flow and its disturbance regime.

The newly pumped sand is a temporary fix that creates an economic and geologic problem. The forces that eroded the original beach continue to operate. The newly "renourished" beach is still subject to erosion and will ultimately erode away again. Then the process begins anew. Once a community commits itself to beach renourishment, it becomes dependent on this so-called solution to beach erosion. The community incurs repeated costs of millions of dollars every few years. The Army Corps of Engineers (1994) has spent more than $2 billion in the past 30 years on beach renourishment projects on the Atlantic coastline. Most coastal erosion occurs during major storms that are inevitable. During Hurricane Isabel in 2003, the recently completed $30 million beach renourishment project in Virginia Beach was nearly washed away entirely. It has been estimated that the sand that is pumped onto beaches erodes up to 10 times faster than the natural beach sand. The rebuilt beach rarely lasts more than 5 to 10 years. The demand for new sand and beach renourishment will thus rise again. As long as there is population pressure on the oceanfront, the conflicts with nature will continue. It is an endless, losing battle against a most primal force of nature, the power of the sea (Kaufman and Pilkey 1983).

We are caught in a self-made dilemma. Our desire to live on the seashore places us in direct conflict with the natural disturbance regime of storms and beach erosion. Renourishing beaches and building jetties and seawalls are temporary and costly fixes that are contrary to environmental protection, conservation, and healthy, functioning beach ecosystems. Imposing zoning restrictions on beachfront construction is the best solution we have available at this time.

SPRAWL INCREASES DISTURBANCE FREQUENCY

As people press farther into the natural environment, their behavior and building patterns can actually increase disturbance frequency beyond the environment's normal rhythm. This is particularly obvious with river flooding, but also extends to frequency of fires. The wildfires near Los Angeles, California, in the fall of 2003 were attributed to arsonists in the woods near the new (sprawl) settlements in San Bernadino Canyon and surrounding hillsides.

RIVER FLOODING AND RIPARIAN DEVELOPMENT Sprawl leads to conflict with the natural process of river flooding, as mentioned earlier in this chapter. The streamside forest is adapted to and dependent on periodic flooding of a river or stream. The flat, periodically flooded area extending outward from a river or stream is called the *floodplain*. The riparian zone forest is populated with "bottomland" hardwood trees; in the southeastern United States, it is a mixture of beech, maple, ironwood, sycamore, and oak. The bottomland hardwood forest provides critical habitat for wood ducks (*Aix sponsa*) and dozens of other wetland animal and plant species that are well adapted to the natural disturbance regime. Recent work on urbanizing watersheds by Geraci (2002) shows that as the proportion of forest in the riparian zone and the entire watershed increases, so increases the biodiversity of the stream community. Riparian wetlands also provide a wide range of ecosystem services. They remove excess nutrients from the water; support a great diversity of wildlife, from lush vegetation to waterfowl; and, ultimately, clean and renew our air. Given these ecosystem services, riparian zones are clearly important for stream and human health. The disturbance regime of flooding and drying in the riparian zone is essential to the maintenance of wetland habitats and biodiversity. The floods bring nutrients from the stream water to the forest and replenish the stream food chain with detritus (dead leaves and branches) from the riparian zone. They are vital to the interactions between forest and stream and are fundamental to the healthy dynamics of both ecosystems (Bayley 1995).

Problems arise when people build homes and businesses in the floodplain. In the United States, this encroachment is largely a consequence of sprawl. As more favorable home sites are built on, pressure to build in the floodplain increases. In eastern North Carolina, many of the homes built in floodplains are owned by people who cannot afford more desirable and safer upland home sites. In the fall of 1999, in the aftermath of Hurricane Floyd, the Tar River in eastern North Carolina flooded out many poor families. This scenario has been played out again and again all over the United States (recall the great Mississippi River flood of 1993 or the Red River flood in Minnesota in 1998). It is often the poorest people who are most vulnerable to displacement or death caused by river flooding.

The relationship among poverty, overcrowding, and exposure to the risk of flooding is exemplified in Bangladesh. Millions of the poorest people live in the floodplains of the Ganges River and along the coastline. Although they are aware of the risks, they are too poor to live anywhere else. They farm the fertile floodplains and hope for the best. When the monsoon rains come and the river rises and floods, hundreds, often thousands, of lives are lost. Yet when the waters recede, the floodplains are soon inhabited once again. The choice these people face is either to live on the streets of overcrowded cities or to take a chance at raising crops and families in the floodplain.

SPRAWL, THE SHIFTING FLOODPLAIN, AND INCREASED FLOOD FREQUENCY AND SEVERITY Recognition of the risk of flood damage has caused many communities to ban all development in the floodplain. A common benchmark for the location of the floodplain is the 100-year flood zone. This zone is the elevation above the river or stream that is estimated to flood once every 100 years. However, this idealized demarcation is often woefully inaccurate. During Hurricanes Dennis and Floyd in the fall of 1999, many communities in eastern North Carolina experienced three "100-year floods" in a two-week period. How is this possible? As urban sprawl proceeds, more and more roads, houses, driveways, and businesses are being built. These structures increase the amount of impervious surface in the watershed (catchment) and act as barriers to the infiltration of water into the soil, which in turn increases the amount of water that runs off into streams and the speed with which it travels. Consequently, the frequency and severity of flooding are increased.

When the land is covered in natural vegetation, rainfall can be readily absorbed into the soil and taken up by plants (trees, shrubs, herbs, and natural grasslands) during the growing season. In the winter, most plants are dormant, so the same amount of rainfall in winter will generate up to five times the volume of runoff into the streams or rivers than in the summertime. Rooftops and pavement create impervious surfaces across the landscape, which prevent the absorption of water from rain or snowmelt. Consequently, more water runs overland and into storm drains, storm sewers, or small intermittent stream channels and ultimately flows into the streams and rivers. This is what is known as *stormwater*, and it is a major environmental problem in urban areas. The elevated levels of stormwater runoff caused by the lack of absorption, generated by man-made structures, increases flood frequency.

If one-third of the watershed becomes impervious as a result of sprawling development, then the 100-year flood stage is moved much farther away from the stream bank. The old 100-year floodplain may now flood every 30 years or every 10 years or perhaps even more frequently, depending on the nature of the development, the amount of impervious surface, the proportion of vegetated land cover, the slope of the land, and so on (figure 4.2). There is a direct relationship among sprawl, degree of the landscape's imperviousness, and frequency and severity of flooding. Note that the equally negative flip side of flooding as a consequence of imperviousness is the lack of percolation of water into the ground. The movement of water into the groundwater to recharge the subterranean aquifers (the groundwater) is necessary to maintain water supplies in many communities. The paving of the environment diverts water from the aquifers into the streams, which poses a serious long-term problem in communities dependent on groundwater supplies (including much of eastern North Carolina and central Texas) for freshwater. Increasing urbanization may lower the water table, turning permanently flowing steams into intermittent streams (Hopkinson and Vallino 1995). Wahl, McKellar, and Williams (1997) found that an urbanized stream produced 72 percent greater stream volume, 66 percent higher sediment load, and twice the dissolved inorganic nitrogen than a forested watershed three times the size! Sedimentation lowers stream biodiversity. High discharge scours organisms and food resources from substrates; sedimentation lowers biodiversity by degrading habitat; and high loading of inorganic nitrogen degrades water quality. It is well established that urban stream reaches have dramatically lower biodiversity than rural reaches (Benke et al. 1981; Lenat and Eagleson 1981; Jones and Clark 1987; Lenat and Crawford 1994). Schueler (1995) has argued that 15 percent imperious surface is the damage threshold

FIGURE 4.2. Widespread development and loss of wetlands throughout the upper Mississippi River basin led to extreme flooding in 1993, costing an estimated $20 billion in damages. (Photo by Michael Reuter)

for urbanized streams. Above this level of riparian development, we begin to see the loss of the most sensitive benthic invertebrates and fishes. Sprawl is a threat to the survival of these stream communities.

As the population builds up in the flood hazard zones, people's demand for protection from flooding also increases. An ecologically uninformed government agency may well yield to this political pressure. Flood control is typically imposed in the form of dams to create flood control reservoirs or levees to contain the floodwaters in an artificially raised bank. Both approaches have significant ecological costs because natural floods are essential for the creation and maintenance of the biodiversity of healthy streams and wetlands.

Dams impede the river's flow and back up water into artificial reservoirs. The community of organisms changes from a stream community into a lake community. The biodiversity of streams is greater than that of reservoirs, and the subsequent loss of riverine fauna and flora and their ecosystem services is inevitable. The stream community's water-purifying characteristics are lost when the lake formed behind the dam becomes essentially stagnant. The dam that holds back floodwaters can also exacerbate future flooding. If rainfall and runoff continue and exceed the reservoir and dam's capacity to hold back the waters, then the ensuing flood will be of much greater magnitude than a flood in a free-flowing, undammed river. The damage to property can thus be far more devastating, as was illustrated by the Neuse River in eastern North Carolina after Hurricane Fran in 1996. Another major ecological problem is the fragmentation of the river into segments separated by reservoirs, which makes the upstream spawning migrations of many fishes impossible, with consequent loss of fish stocks and even extinction of some species. Riverine turtle species from Turkey to Bangladesh are also affected by the impounding of river systems (IUCN 1991). The loss of salmon stocks in the Pacific Northwest of the United States is a classic example of this process. The native fishes of the Colorado River are endangered or extinct because of the dams there. Levees act similarly, except they cut the stream off from its floodplain, rather than from upstream or downstream segments. A berm 6 to 10 feet (2–3 meters) high means that the riparian wetlands will dry out and result in a loss of biodiversity and ecosystem services. These riparian wetlands are important nursery grounds for fishes during spring floods. Severing the fishes from their spawning grounds in this way has severely endangered many native Mississippi River fishes (Sparks, Nelson, and Yin 1998). The key point is that flooding is an integral part of how stream ecosystems work.

An important solution to these problems is prevention. Zoning ordinances to prevent building in floodplains are now being developed and implemented. As the degree of impervious surface in the watershed increases, floodplain maps need to be updated in order to reflect the reality of changing runoff amounts and potential flood patterns and the increasing size of the floodplain.

CONCLUSION

Overpopulation and the nature of development drive sprawl. People's desire to live in a single-family home with a yard lures them out from the cities so that they are pressing farther and farther into the natural environment. Fires, floods, hurricanes, tornadoes, earthquakes, and volcanoes are part of the natural cycle of disturbance and renewal that exists in all ecosystems. As sprawl continues, the safe places to build are used up, and development spreads into areas with increasing ecological risk from natural disasters. Yet some areas are far more hazardous than others. People make the choices to live on the coastline in hurricane zones or in the fire-prone chaparral or forests or in flood hazard zones along rivers. As we seek to protect ourselves from these disturbances, we damage our vital ecosystems. By using our knowledge of disturbance frequency and severity, we can make wiser and more informed decisions about where to build and live. Zoning, supported by economic incentives—that is, differential tax structures based on ecological risk—is one solution. One key step in protecting ourselves is to replace sprawl with well-informed planning that takes these ecological concerns into account. If we make our cities more livable, we will relieve the pressure on our natural ecosystems, which will benefit us all.

REFERENCES

Army Corps of Engineers. 1994. *Ocean City, Maryland, and Vicinity Water Resources Study Reconnaissance Report, Baltimore District.* Washington, D.C.: Army Corps of Engineers.

Bayley, P. 1995. The flood-pulse concept. *BioScience* 45:153–158.

Benke, A.C., G.E. Wilkins, F.K. Parrish, and D.L. Stiles. 1981. *Effects of Urbanization on Stream Ecosystems.* Georgia Institute of Technology ERC 07–81. Atlanta: Georgia Institute of Technology.

Chapin, F.S., B.H. Walker, R.J. Hobbs, D.U. Hooper, J.H. Lawton, O.E. Sala, and D.H. Tilman. 1997. Biotic control over the functioning of ecosystems. *Science* 277:500–504.

Christensen, N.L., and C.H. Mueller. 1975. Effects of fire on factors controlling plant growth in *Adenostoma* chaparral. *Ecological Monographs* 45:29–55.

Connell, J.H. 1978. Diversity in tropical rainforests and coral reefs. *Science* 199:1302–1310.

Daily, G.C., and J.S. Reichart, eds. 1997. *Natures Services: Societal Dependence on Natural Ecosystems.* Washington, D.C.: Island Press.

Dunne, T., and L.B. Leopold. 1978. *Water in Environmental Planning.* San Francisco: Freeman.

Fuller, M. 1991. *Forest Fires: An Introduction to Wildfire Behavior, Management, Firefighting, and Prevention.* New York: Wiley.

Geraci, C.J. 2002. The influence of land cover on the benthic macroinvertebrate communities of the Little Creek and Morgan Creek Watersheds. Master's thesis, University of North Carolina.

Harrod, J. 1999. Disturbance history and ecological change in a southern Appalachian landscape: Western Great Smoky Mountains National Park, 1936–1996. Ph.D. diss., University of North Carolina.

Hopkinson, C.S., Jr., and J.J. Vallino. 1995. The relationships among man's activities in watersheds and estuaries: A model of runoff effects on patterns of estuarine community metabolism. *Estuaries* 18:598–561.

International Union for Conservation of Nature and Natural Resources (IUCN). 1991. *Tortoises and Freshwater Turtles: An Action Plan for Their Conservation.* 2d ed. Gland, Switzerland: IUCN, Species Survival Commission, Tortoise and Freshwater Turtle Specialist Group.

Jones, R.C., and C.C. Clark. 1987. Impact of watershed urbanization on stream insect communities. *Water Resources Bulletin* 23:1047–1055.

Kaufman, W., and O.H. Pilkey. 1983. *The Beaches Are Moving: The Drowning of America's Shoreline.* Durham, N.C.: Duke University Press.

Lenat, D.R., and J.K. Crawford. 1994. Effects of land use on water quality and aquatic biota of three North Carolina Piedmont streams. *Hydrobiologia* 294:185–199.

Lenat, D.R., and K.W. Eagleston. 1981. *Ecological Effects of Urban Runoff on North Carolina Streams.* North Carolina Division of Environmental Management Biological Series, no. 104. Raleigh: North Carolina Division of Environmental Management.

Peterson, C. H., D. H. M. Hickerson, and G. Johnson. 2000. Short-term consequences of nourishment and bulldozing on the dominant large invertebrates of a sandy beach. *Journal of Coastal Research* 16:368–378.

Pickett, S. T. A., J. Wu, and M. L. Cadenasso. 1999. Patch dynamics and the ecology of disturbed ground: A framework for synthesis. In L. R. Walker, ed., *Ecosystems of Disturbed Ground*, 707–722. New York: Elsevier.

Reice, S. R. 1994. Nonequilibrium determinants of biological community structure. *American Scientist* 82:424–435.

——. 2001. *The Silver Lining: The Benefits of Natural Disasters*. Princeton, N.J.: Princeton University Press.

Resh, V. H., A. V. Brown, A. P. Covich, M. E. Gurtz, H. W. Li, G. W. Minshall, S. R. Reice, A. L. Sheldon, J. B. Wallace, and R. C. Wissmar. 1988. The role of disturbance in stream ecology. *Journal of the North American Benthological Society* 7:433–455.

Schueler, T. 1995. *Environmental Land Planning Series: Site Planning for Urban Stream Protection*. Center for Watershed Protection Publication, no. 95708. Ellicott City, Md.: Center for Watershed Protection.

Sousa, W. P. 1984. The role of disturbance in natural communities. *Annual Review of Ecology and Systematics* 15:353–391.

Sparks, R. C., J. C. Nelson, and Y. Yin. 1998. Naturalization of the flood regime in regulated rivers. *BioScience* 48:706–720.

Tilman, D., J. P. B. Reich, J. Knops, T. Mielke, and C. Lehman. 2001. Diversity and productivity in a long-term grassland experiment. *Science* 294:843–845.

Wahl, M. H., H. N. McKellar, and T. M. Williams. 1997. Patterns of nutrient loading in forested and urbanized coastal streams. *Journal of Experimental Marine Biology and Ecology* 213:111–131.

White, P. S., and S. T. A. Pickett. 1985. Natural disturbance and patch dynamics: An Introduction. In P. S. White and S. T. A. Pickett, eds., *The Ecology of Natural Disturbance and Patch Dynamics*, 3–13. New York: Academic Press.

Wright, H. A., and A. W. Bailey. 1982. *Fire Ecology, United States and Canada*. New York: Wiley.

BEES, POLLINATION, AND THE CHALLENGES
OF SPRAWL

James H. Cane

ollination, broadly defined, is the transfer of pollen within and between compatible flowers. Pollen carries the male nuclei, so pollination is a key step for sexual reproduction by seed plants, the group that dominates Earth's terrestrial flora. Primary agents of pollination include wind, some birds and bats, and insects, especially bees, but also some kinds of beetles, flies, wasps, moths, and butterflies. Too little is known to generalize about links among sprawl, pollination, and seed set overall, but urban and suburban sprawl does alter ecological features important to pollinators, such as plant community composition and reproductive opportunities. This chapter focuses on our predominant pollinator group, the bees, and the impact of urbanization and sprawl on their survival. Three of bees' needs require consideration: floral resources, nesting opportunities, and condition of the urban matrix. Resultant changes in pollinator communities can have consequences for pollination of native plant communities.

Bees are essential pollinators in many agricultural contexts and all wild areas. Bees have value in and around urban areas, too. Their pollination activities yield vegetables and fruits for home and market gardeners alike, fruits and seeds for resident and migratory songbirds, and successful perpetuation of revegetated wasteland (e.g., landfills) and parkland floras. Because of their importance and prevalence, native bees also provide good educational opportunities for city dwellers to observe nature and learn about some of the interrelationships between plants and animals.

But how well and for how long do bees persist in and around our cities and suburbs? The question has received little focused attention. Do any bee species long withstand urban conditions, are any of them native, which ones, what are their attributes, and do they matter? How does urban and suburban sprawl perturb bee communities, and can we apply this knowledge to their stewardship in cities and suburbs? Amid urban areas, do green spaces (e.g., small reserves, gardens, parks, and mixed agricultural land uses) provide suitable habitat for native bees, and are bees' responses at all predictable? This chapter addresses these questions and provides an illustrative example that highlights how bees' needs and vulnerabilities play out in a landscape increasingly dominated by sprawl.

THE BENEFITS OF BEES

The primary ecological and agricultural benefit derived from bees is pollination. As foraging bees fly from flower to flower in search of pollen and nectar to feed their progeny, they inadvertently shuttle pollen between receptive flowers of the same species. This simple act of pollen transfer is pollination. Ensuing fertilization of the flower's ovules yields fertile seeds that are often imbedded in a developing fruit. Every year, bee pollination is essential for $14 billion of U.S. agricultural production (Morse and Calderone 2000). The crops include seed for alfalfa (*Medicago sativa*) hay (which feeds the dairy industry), many tree fruits (apples [*Malus* spp.], plums [*Prunus* spp.], cherries [*Prunus* spp.], pears [*Pyrus* spp.], almonds [*Prunus* spp.]), oilseed crops (sunflower [*Helianthus* spp.], hybrid canola [*Brassica* spp.]), small fruits (blueberries and cranberries [*Vaccinium* spp.], raspberries [*Rubus* spp.]), and some vegetables (squashes, melons, pumpkins [Family Cucurbitaceae], cucumbers [*Cucumis sativus*], greenhouse tomatoes [*Lycopersicon esculentum*]). Bees pollinate seed crops for many other vegetables (e.g., onion [*Allium* spp.], carrots [Family Apiaceae]). Together, wind or bees pollinate most of the flowering plants in North America, Europe, and northern Asia, with lesser contributions from flower-visiting flies, beetles, moths, butterflies, wasps, and specialized birds. In our cities and towns, pollinating insects, especially bees, provide four underappreciated services.

HOME AND MARKET GARDENS

The seeds that we sow are typically the products of commercial pollination on distant farms, but bees are nonetheless essential for pollinating a subset of our local garden produce. Some well-loved vegetables and orchard fruits require bees in order to bear fruit, as noted earlier, whether grown in our home gardens or in urban market farmers' orchards and fields. These latter growers typically farm around the peripheries of many cities and towns, where their highly valued lands are especially vulnerable to sprawl. More than 19,000 growers sell produce solely through the 3,100 farmers' markets around the United States; many more sell through other markets or farm stands as well.[1] Gross sales in California farmers' markets alone exceed $140 million annually (Feenstra and Lewis 1999). Native bees' pollination contributions at these farms are often significant but underappreciated (Cane and Payne 1993; Roulston, Sampson, and Cane 1996; Kremen, Williams, and Thorp 2002).

SONGBIRDS

Humans are not the only beneficiaries of bees' pollination services in our towns and cities. Many songbirds of the Northern Hemisphere depend on seeds and fruits to power their southward fall migration (e.g., vireos [Family Vireonidae], flycatchers [Family Tyrannidae], warblers [Family Parulidae], robins and thrushes [Family Turdidae]). For others that remain behind, seeds and fruits sustain them during our frosty winters (e.g., waxwings [Family Bombycillidae], goldfinches [*Carduelis* spp.], cardinals [*Cardinalis* spp.], thrashers [*Toxostoma* spp.], finches [Family Fringillidae]). Some of these birds, resident and migratory alike, can be found in urban and suburban areas. A portion of their food plants are wind pollinated, as urban hay fever sufferers well know (e.g., birches [*Betula* spp.], grasses [Family Gramineae], conifers [Division Pinophyta]), but many are insect pollinated, often by bees, including blueberries (*Vaccinium* spp.), magnolias (*Magnolia* spp.), elderberries (*Sambucus* spp.), crabapples (*Malus* spp.), viburnums (*Viburnum* spp.), sumacs (*Rhus* spp.), honeysuckles (*Lonicera* spp.), sunflowers (Family Asteraceae, mostly *Helianthus*), and thistles (Family Asteraceae), to name but a few.

HABITATS PRESERVED OR RESTORED

Certain wildflowers and trees set seed only when they are cross-pollinated (wherein flowers receive pollen from a different individual); such outcrossing benefits even self-fertile species, yielding more vigorous and diverse progeny. Bees pollinate many wildflowers, including desirable nitrogen-fixing legumes, plants such as clovers whose associated bacteria convert nitrogen into a usable form for the plant. Pollination by insects, especially bees, helps maintain self-perpetuating urban and suburban meadows and understory wildflower communities, which may be found in more natural corners of our reserves, parks, and gardens. Bees can be essential for pollinating wildflowers used to revegetate degraded urban lands, too, such as capped landfills and toxic-cleanup sites. Divorced of their pollinators, urban insect-pollinated plants suffer poor fruit and seed set and, without cross-pollination, inbreeding and the loss of valuable genetic diversity (Washitani 1996).

---

1. Information is available at www.ams.usda.gov/farmersmarkets/.

EDUCATION

Bees are the most accessible and engaging of the beneficial insect groups for urban residents, revealing ecological links between species critical in both nature and agriculture. The lives of urban and suburban dwellers are largely removed from the natural world: the few insects they do notice—cockroaches, mosquitoes, ants, wasps—are viewed as adversaries. Workers of large-bodied social bees (e.g., honeybees [*Apis* spp.] and bumblebees [*Bombus* spp.]) and their social relatives (ants, hornets, yellow jackets) defend their nests by painful stings. Their potent venoms are indeed unpleasant. But most native bees are not social, so they have little venom and little inclination to sting unless strongly provoked. Children (but too few adults) are captivated by the foraging and nesting activities of bustling bees. Urban reserves rarely feature in bee conservation, but bees have a critical mission nonetheless. Urban and suburban bees are engaging educational ambassadors, revealing their ecological value as pollinators to a public unfamiliar with farms and wildlands.

THE NEEDS OF BEES

Bees require both suitable floral resources and nesting substrates. Floral resources invariably include nectar and pollen, but not necessarily from the same plant species. Nectar sugars fuel bees' flight and sweetly moisten the mass of pollen gathered by each mother bee to feed her progeny.[2] Pollen supplies the proteins, fats, minerals, and vitamins in larval diets. An individual bee can exploit many flowering species for nectar. Social bees, such as bumblebees and honeybees, utilize diverse plant species for pollen, as do many solitary species, which endows them with foraging versatility when confronting change. Females of other solitary species specialize on one or a few related flowering species for all their pollen needs (a practice termed *oligolecty*) (Wcislo and Cane 1996). Some bee species additionally gather materials to line, partition, seal, or cap their nests using leaf or petal clippings, plant hairs, resins, mud, or fine pebbles (O'Toole and Raw 1991). The amassed resources in bee nests invite exploitation, so among bees there exist many *cleptoparasitic* species. Instead of making their own nests, cleptoparasites slip their eggs into a host bee's nest, and their larvae then devour the larder provided by their host (Wcislo and Cane 1996). The rich bee faunas of some botanical and community gardens attest to the link between bee and floral diversity (table 5.1).

---

2. Bees have four distinct life stages: egg, larva, pupa, and adult. Bee larvae are helpless white grubs, the same life stage as a caterpillar.

TABLE 5.1. Results of Faunistic Surveys of Urban Bees from Around the World

COUNTRY	CITY	PARK OR OTHER URBAN SITES	AREA (HA)[1]	NUMBER OF BEE SPECIES[2]	CITED REFERENCE
Belgium	Liège	Sites within city	—	(54) 93	Jacob-Remacle 1984, citations therein
Germany	Berlin	Tierpark Friedrichsfelde	160	72	H. H. Dathe, cited in Saure 1996
Germany	Berlin	Sites within city	—	262	Saure 1996
Germany	Bochum	University botanical garden	13	69	Küpper 1999
Germany	Bonn	Bonn University Botanic Garden	6	74	Bischoff 1996
Germany	Bremen	Bürgerpark	136	57	Riemann 1995
Poland	Wroclaw	Zoological Garden	100?	52	J. Noskiewicz, cited in Banaszak 1982
Poland	Warsaw	Sites within city	—	(52)	Banaszak 1982
Russia	Moscow	Sites within city	—	17[3]	Berezin, Beiko, and Berezina 1995
Japan	Sapporo	Hokkaido University Botanical Garden	9	85	Sakagami and Fukuda 1973
Japan	Kagoshima City	Shiroyama Park	—	40	Ikudome 1992
United States	New York City	Parks of northern Bronx	—	50[4]	Parker Gambino, personal communication, 2002
United States	Albany, California	Peralta Community Garden	0.25	22	Frankie et al. 2002
Brazil	Ribeirão Preto	University of São Paulo branch campus	569	212[5]	Camargo and Mazucato 1984
Brazil	Curitiba	Passeio Publico park	5.7	74	Laroca, Cure, and Bortoli 1982
Brazil	São Paulo	University of São Paulo campus	10	133	Knoll, Bego, and Imperatriz-Fonseca 1993

[1]Actual vegetated area may be less because this measure often includes buildings and pavement.

[2]Species totals in parentheses were sampled using pan trapping, which underrepresents some groups of bees but allows for more extensive sampling (Cane, Minckley, and Kervin 2000).

[3]Only reports bumblebees (*Bombus*).

[4]Does not include cleptoparasitic species.

[5]Does not include highly social species, in particular the numerous species of stingless bees (Meliponini).

Bees' nesting habits are even more species specific and diverse than their foraging activities (Westrich 1989; O'Toole and Raw 1991; Michener 2000). Many of the more than 17,000 nonsocial bee species dig their own subterranean nests, sometimes grouped in populous aggregations. Soil preferences range from loose sands and dunes to loams and clays, with varying degrees of specificity in their requirements. Some bees like friable (loose, crumbly) soils, whereas others prefer compacted soils. Some prefer banks to flat ground. Few can handle dense turf or waterlogged soils during active nesting, both often characteristic of developed areas. Others nest aboveground. The large carpenter bees (*Xylocopa* spp.) bore tunnels in dead wood. Others excavate softer substrates, like pithy plant stems. Many *Megachile* (e.g., leaf-cutting bees), *Osmia*, and other Megachilidae adopt tunnels left in deadwood by the larvae of wood-boring beetles. Some specialists use peculiar substrates (plant galls, snail shells); a few others construct free-standing nests from mud, pebbles, or resins, or all three. Habitats offering a diverse mix of these nesting substrates and materials clearly favor bee diversity.

Bees are "central place foragers," a concept that is key to appreciating their limits for a spatial mosaic of nesting and foraging sites. Females venture forth from a nest to collect resources, but they must then navigate their return, often many times daily. In this respect, they resemble ants and wasps, but contrast with the other flower-visiting insects (e.g., butterflies, flies), which do not make nests. Hence, the specific nesting and provisioning needs of a bee species must be met within flight range of one another, typically less than 2,300 feet (700 meters) apart (Gathmann and Tscharntke 2002). One species may nest in deep friable sands and provision with willow pollen; another may nest in beetle-riddled wood, her nest sealed with collected pine resin and provisioned with sunflower pollen. Achievable flight ranges between these resource islands varies with body size. Some larger-bodied social and solitary species can readily navigate 0.5 to1.5 miles (1–2 kilometers) or more from nest site to flower patch. Foraging ranges of smaller bees are unknown, but probably do not exceed a few hundred feet. These smaller bees compose most of the individuals and species in local faunas, including cities (table 5.1).

Bees are clearly adapted to shifting landscape mosaics of patchy nesting and foraging resources. However, should specific forage and nesting habitats become too widely isolated from one another, then the remaining habitat of just flowers or just nesting substrate will not fulfill bees' needs. These habitats are dubbed "partial habitats" (Westrich 1996). The mosaic of sprawl development that is inhospitable to bees can swell to an extensive, coarse spatial scale that exceeds bees' flight ranges, effectively severing links in the network of remnant nesting sites and floral patches and so curtailing bees' service as pollinators. Local population extinction soon follows, for which no recourse is known. Even if a habitat patch satisfies a bee species' nesting and foraging needs, it may prove to be so isolated as to preclude discovery by new colonists. Inbreeding inevitably ensues and, eventually, local extinction. Unfortunately, bees' extinction, immigration, and colonization dynamics are poorly known. But knowing bees' needs and the constraints on their habitat flexibility aids our interpretation of their responses to urbanization, fragmentation, and sprawl. Understanding the suitability and spatial dimensions of the urban habitat mosaic will be essential for integrating pollinator conservation into planned growth of our cities and towns.

URBAN BEE FAUNAS

Published surveys of urban bee faunas come mostly from European cities. These reports are sparsely scattered through regional natural-history journals. Some selected examples are summarized in table 5.1. The surveyed cities are in northern Europe, Japan, Brazil, and the United States. Bee taxonomists made the surveys, seeking bees in scattered parks, public squares, cemeteries, botanical and zoological gardens, and neglected places (e.g., levees, abandoned railroads). Hence, the bee faunas reported from these green urban islands might be largely restricted to them, imprisoned by the surrounding matrix of pavement and buildings.

Rich communities of native bees have been found foraging and nesting in the municipal parks and gardens of even the most populous older cities (table 5.1). Bee species in these city faunas were invariably a substantial subset of the regional fauna, even though some of these parks and gardens have been isolated in their cities for more than a century. Thus Shiroyama Park in Japan hosted half the bee species found in Kagoshima Prefecture. A tiny park in downtown Curitiba, Brazil (sampled when the human population was 1.3 million), hosted half the bee species of a 494-acre (200-hectare) area of mixed land use beyond that city's margins. Each of two tiny community gardens in Berkeley and Albany, California, each hosted 20 of the 72 native bee species found scattered through the greater residential community. Bremen's Bürgerpark was home to nearly one-fifth of northwestern Germany's bee species. Half of Germany's entire bee fauna was represented in Berlin. Obviously, these botanical gardens were floristically rich. Nonetheless, fewer urban species were oligolectic (16 percent in Bochum, 30 percent in Bonn, Germany) compared with those in rural areas; most of the few floral specialists persisting in European cities took their pollen from willow or a weedy native *Campanula*. Those bee genera of the Northern Hemisphere that contain numerous and often abundant or ubiquitous species were the ones most commonly represented in the surveyed cities.[3] More than 90 percent of the individual bees (other than honeybees) collected in each urban survey belonged to just these dozen ubiquitous genera.[4] Like wildland bee faunas (reviewed in Williams, Minckley, and Silveira 2001), a few species numerically dominated the urban bee faunas, with many rarities. Most of these city bees were natives, in contrast with the common exotics among our communities of urban birds, mammals, pestiferous insects, and plants. Where exotic bees were present, they did not dominate. This observation holds true for bee faunas generally, at least in North America (Cane 2003). In the case study of urban desert bees in Tucson, Arizona, reported in the box "The Responses of a Desert Bee Fauna," the only common nonnative bee found at *Larrea* (creosote bush) was the European honeybee, constituting less than 10 percent of the bee fauna in any one urban habitat fragment. Thus floristically diverse green oases even in an otherwise hostile urban matrix can support substantial numbers of native, mostly generalist native bee species that represent a subset of the regional fauna. Because these surveys are not replicated locally, however, they provide little insight into the factors and mechanisms that act as filters of regional bee faunas once urbanization and fragmentation ensue. "The Responses of a Desert Bee Fauna" extends these insights to include the effects of fragment size, fragment age, and bees' life history attributes for community responses to urban habitat fragmentation.

Can we extrapolate from the city bee surveys and the study of the urban desert bees of Tucson, Arizona, to the general effects of urbanization and sprawl for native bee communities? The dearth of focused studies necessitates some speculation, especially for the many indirect factors that still have to be investigated in this context. The discussion in the next section has a North American perspective; Westrich (1989, 1996) provides an insightful European perspective.

ALTERNATIVES TO SPRAWL

URBAN OASES AND BEES

Thoughtful urban and suburban planning holds great promise for bee conservation and its companion benefits. Properly managed parks, campuses, and public and private gardens, if they offer a diverse flora attractive to bees and

---

3. The dozen dominant urban bee genera in these studies were *Colletes* and *Hylaeus* (Colletidae); *Andrena* (Andrenidae); *Lasioglossum, Dialictus, Halictus,* and *Sphecodes* (Halictidae); *Megachile* and *Osmia* (Megachilidae); and *Anthophora, Nomada,* and *Bombus* (Apidae).

4. The European honeybee (*Apis mellifera*) is often present but rarely dominant; its frequent management in hives and distinctive ecology make its presence difficult to assess.

THE RESPONSES OF A DESERT BEE FAUNA TO URBAN HABITAT FRAGMENTATION IN TUCSON, ARIZONA

We studied the guild of bees that visit creosote bush (*Larrea tridentata*), a shrub that dominates the basin floras of North America's warm deserts. We systematically surveyed for bees at flowering creosote bushes in habitat fragments scattered through mostly older residential sections of Tucson and at 2.5-acre (1-hectare) plots in the surrounding scrub desert. Fragment size ranged from four bushes to 5 acres (2 hectares). Fragment age ranged from 20 to 70 years old. Bee species were classified by nesting (or parasitic) habits, floral associations, and body size. We analyzed patterns of abundance (bees sampled per hour) and incidence (proportion of sampled sites inhabited by a given species). In all, 59 fragments were sampled, yielding 2,500 individual native bees belonging to 62 species and 31 genera that visit flowers of creosote bush.

Two aerial photographs of the Arizona Inn of Tucson and its environs: 1942 (*left*) and 1998 (*right*). The white arrows point to a sampled habitat fragment dominated by creosote bushes just west of the inn. The conversion of scrub desert to residential neighborhoods during the half century is evident, as is the great increase in landscape trees and structures. (Photos courtesy of Gene Magee [Glinski 1996] and James Glinski)

Bee faunal composition differed dramatically among fragment classes varying in size and age. Habitat loss and disruption, not fragmentation per se, accounted for the absence of a few species expected in the city. Cleptoparasitic species were largely absent, too, perhaps because they need reliable large host populations to persist. Dramatically fewer species and numbers of ground-nesting *Larrea* specialists were found in progressively smaller or older fragments. Scarcity and prolonged isolation typify populations facing extinction. Bee species with additional dependencies (such as cleptoparasites or floral specialists) proved to be especially vulnerable to urban fragmentation in this study.

To our surprise, some floral generalists and most cavity-nesting species were proliferating in the smaller fragments. Their increased abundances at *Larrea* bushes in smaller fragments balanced the diminished numbers of ground nesters. For example, the sole cavity-nesting *Larrea* specialist was 30 times more abundant at urban *Larrea* bushes than in the surrounding desert scrub. Why this seemingly contrasting response to apparent habitat fragmentation? The explanation does not lie in body size; *Larrea* growing in smaller and older fragments hosted as many small-bodied bee species as it hosted in larger, more recent fragments. Causal explanation lies in part within the individual fragments, but additional reasons are to be found beyond the fragments themselves, in nesting opportunities afforded by the urban matrix.

Bees' susceptibility to Tucson's habitat fragmentation has entailed at least three

(continued)

key factors: nesting habits, floral predilections, and the condition of the urban matrix surrounding fragments. Most important, Tucson represents in some ways a best-case scenario. The city has been expanding into existing desert rather than into abandoned agricultural land (see figure), plus homesite development of older neighborhoods did not include scraping of intervening lots.

NESTING

Urban sprawl eliminates or alters nesting habitats for ground-nesting bees. Pavement, buildings, and turf are clear culprits in the loss of nest sites. In desert cities, the elimination of washes and riparian boundaries, whose sand deposits and vertical banks are favored nesting sites for many bees, is also a problem. In Tucson, surface runoff and erosion have been hastened by streets set below grade, by storm drains, and by ditching. Formerly suitable nesting soils have thereby been transformed into shallow parched soils overlying impenetrable caliche (a stratum cemented by calcium carbonate).

HOST ASSOCIATION

Floral specialists face considerable risk. Their paucity where noted in the city surveys supports this contention. Specialists cannot use alternative floral hosts in the urban matrix either as supplemental forage within fragments or as stepping-stones to recolonize from neighboring populations. The fates of floral specialists follow those of their floral hosts: if sprawl extirpates the floral hosts, their specialist bees are doomed. In Tucson, *Larrea* is a particularly resilient element of the native flora, responding to even marginal rainfall with a prolific, reliable bloom. The bees most susceptible to fragmentation in Tucson are native species with multiple specialized needs (e.g., for both floral host and ground-nesting substrate).

FRAGMENT MATRIX

The proliferation of cavity-nesting bees was unexpected in Tucson; we were too focused on fragment attributes to notice the surrounding urban matrix. Compared with undeveloped scrub desert, Tucson's parks and older neighborhoods have far more trees and wooden structures, a kind of man-made oasis for the needs of cavity-nesting desert species. For cavity nesters in particular, individual fragments need supply only desert floral hosts, within flight range, if the neighboring urban matrix supplies nesting substrate.* The problem with urban sprawl for bees may not be so much the fragmentation of habitats per se as the inevitable degradation of the surrounding urban matrix, even if that matrix remains undeveloped.

---

*Tucson's older residential properties may benefit bees in another way. They are often lightly managed xeriscapes that probably receive few, if any, regular applications of insecticides.

Source: Cane et al. (2006).

are of at least modest size, can fulfill the nesting and foraging needs of some native bees, in particular the more common floral generalists. This assertion is broadly supported by the city bee surveys. Even tiny Peralta Community Garden in Berkeley, California, although only the size of a house lot, hosts at least 20 species of native bees (table 5.1; see also Frankie et al. 2002). The value of such small urban oases is illustrated by the study conducted in Tucson as well. Species in these minutely fragmented faunas undoubtedly nest and forage amid suitable habitats in the surrounding residential matrix. Although generalist foragers predominate, some specialist species can also be retained if their specific floral hosts are available, as seen in some German botanical gardens and in the Tucson study. Those studies also show that some specialists are inevitably lost with fragmentation. Hence, these urban native bee communities will be only a subset of their larger regional faunas. Nonetheless, in many cases they will continue to pollinate forbs, shrubs, and trees whose fruits and seeds feed people, songbirds, and other wildlife in parks and gardens. Another important benefit of these urban bee communities lies in their education of urban residents about bees and pollination and about the role of interdependencies and mutualisms in ecological processes and in the food we eat.

NEIGHBORING FARMLAND AND BEES

The working agricultural landscapes that surround cities and towns are more favorable to bee faunas than the undeveloped weedy interstices (or scarified edge habitats) of urban sprawl (although Berlin's rich bee fauna seems to be an enigmatic exception). Farmland around Carlinville in southern Illinois was home to 297 bee species a century ago; nearly all could still be found there in the 1970s (Marlin and LaBerge 2001). Marlin and LaBerge surmise that this rich bee fauna has benefited from the persistence of hedgerows, riparian corridors, and other uncultivated habitats, as well as from a patchwork mix of row crops, orchards, woodlots, and pasture. Farms growing produce for nearby urban markets can profit from the free pollination services of such largely intact rural bee faunas (Cane and Payne 1993; Roulston et al. 1996; Kremen, Williams, and Thorp 2002), provided that spatial scales do not exceed bees' commuting distances from nest site to forage patch and that pesticides, if used, have been judiciously applied. Obviously, the economic productivity and employment created by farms adjoining cities and towns are superior alternatives to the unproductive land-use inefficiencies created by urban sprawl: native bees can contribute to the profitability of some of these farms on the fringes of cities and towns.

CONSEQUENCES OF SPRAWL: DISTURBED FLORAS AND BEES

EXOTIC PLANT ADDITION

Native bees are not averse to exotic plants per se. Any observant gardener can watch native bees foraging at exotic garden flowers, an observation confirmed in botanical garden studies (Bischoff 1996). Native bees visited 50 of

600 exotic urban plants surveyed in Berkeley, California, although a greater proportion of native flowers were found to be attractive to the bees (Frankie et al. 2002). Weedy species such as alfalfa and sweet clover have Old World origins and occupy disturbed sites in the western United States. Nonetheless, their bloom is popular with many New World bees. But when invasive exotics displace native plant communities, specialist bees that rely on these natives are doomed. Urban sprawl favors invasion by exotic plants and the accompanying displacement of native plants (Roy, Hill, and Rothery 1999; Johnson and Klemens, chapter 2, this volume). By this indirect effect, urban sprawl may deplete native bee communities of their floral specialists, severing mutualistic relationships that are currently impossible to restore.

NATIVE PLANT SUBTRACTION

By subsidizing burgeoning populations of some common herbivorous mammals that devour critical floral hosts, urban sprawl can harm native plant communities and thereby hurt native bee communities. These mammals' intense browsing can denude the understory shrub and herb layers, whose flowers are essential to many native bee communities. Two scenarios are illustrative. In hardwood forests of the eastern United States, a community of early spring wildflowers blooms before canopy leaf flush (Schemske et al. 1978). Diverse native bees, both generalists and floral specialists, rely on the flowers of these understory herbs. Spring beauty (*Claytonia virginica*) alone attracts 58 bee species (Marlin and LaBerge 2001). Burgeoning populations of white-tailed deer intensively browse in the suburbs, parks, and rural developments of the region, however, devastating these communities of understory wildflowers (Rooney and Dress 1997), on which so many spring bees depend. In Tucson, Arizona, rabbits seemed vastly more abundant in the vacant city lots sampled for bees than in the outlying desert scrub, perhaps as a result of diminished predation pressures. Their voracious grazing would explain the sparse understory layer of blooming annual forbs found in the urban fragments. The dozens of bee species that depend on those desert wildflowers for pollen and nectar were, of course, absent as well. City-smart herbivores subsidized by urban sprawl likely exacerbate the forage limitations and habitat loss experienced by native bees, although the problem with white-tailed deer, at least, extends into rural areas, too (Rooney and Dress 1997).

PERTURBED ECOLOGICAL PROCESSES

In the undeveloped matrix, urban sprawl disrupts and sometimes cancels ecological processes that are critical to maintenance of the native plant community. For instance, California's fire-prone chaparral contains rich bee diversity. Homeowners demand wildfire suppression, however. Wildfire suppression has been widely blamed for impoverishing wildland plant and animal communities by unintentionally favoring the spread of aggressive, fire-intolerant plant species at the expense of fire-adapted ones (e.g., Recher and Serventy 1991). In recent years, wildfire-suppression activities have increasingly revolved around protecting human settlement, including secondary recreational homes in rural areas, through both firefighting and proactively removing woody fuel (Reice, chapter 4, this volume). In California, the targeted fire-prone shrubs include those that provide significant bee forage (e.g., manzanita [*Arctostaphylos* spp.]).

In wetter biomes, damming and channelization for urban floodplain development disrupts annual flooding regimes (Reice, chapter 4, this volume). Flood-adapted plant communities shrink, and sand deposition cycles cease. In floodplains, sand- and bank-nesting bees lose nest sites to stream channelization (Westrich 1996). Local extinction of flood-adapted floral hosts dooms the oligolectic bees that depend on them.

A concluding example illustrates the interplay of these direct and indirect ecological perturbations that accompany sprawl and the consequences for a native bee new to science (Cane et al. 1996). Along the margins of the northern Gulf of Mexico, coastal backdunes host suites of bees and plants derived from desert relatives. Beachfront recreational development there (condominiums, summer homes, and attending commercial sprawl) typically flattens these backdunes. The specialist coastal bee (*Hesperapis oraria*) is absent wherever beachfront development has intruded because it apparently requires those dune sands to nest. It is also restricted to a single sand-loving floral host, yellow buttons (*Balduina angustifolia*). Where this plant is missing, the bee is absent. The bee has remained populous in those coastal Florida parks and military bases that have retained intact dunes plus this floral host. The bees' formerly continuous coastal habitat is therefore now fragmented by sprawl, severing recolonization routes that no doubt formerly rescued this bee's populations following natural disturbances, such as hurricanes (Cane 1997). In one park, the floral host abounded, but the bee was unexpectedly absent. Inquiry revealed that beach-goers and residents had demanded broad-spectrum insecticides for biting fly control during this bee's brief flight season, no doubt to the bee's detriment. Because sprawl has now fragmented neighboring habitat, cessation of the insecticide sprays will not guarantee recolonization by the bee because patches of suitable habitat and host are now too widely separated for colonists to traverse.

This combination of factors, fragmentation and extensive use of broad-spectrum insecticides, is a threat to bee populations in areas of development and human use. Many suburban homeowners use insecticides, often imprudently. In order to prevent unnecessary harm to native pollinators, the use of poisons around home and garden should be minimized. And by taking simple measures—such as following label warnings, avoiding blooming plants, using spot applications, spraying near dusk, and skipping unnecessary sprays—we can also lessen the impacts of insecticides on bees.

CONCLUSION

The fragmented bee fauna of Tucson, Arizona, illustrates the trio of bees' needs: (1) suitable nest substrates, (2) appropriate and sometimes specific floral hosts (in the case of specialists) within flight range of nesting sites, and (3) favorable condition of the landscape matrix. In Tucson, creosote bushes flourished where lots had not been scraped for development. Ground-nesting bee species persisted where surface soils were intact. Cavity-nesting species were favored by the proliferation of woody substrates in the neighboring matrix of residential yards.

In the example of the specialist coastal bee, the species persisted where the floral host was present and its nesting dunes remained intact. The bee was absent from one coastal park despite suitable bloom and dunes. There, broad-spectrum insecticides had been aerially applied for fly control at a time that coincided with bloom and adult activity. As with birds, bees may fly, nest, and forage in the developed matrix surrounding parks and gardens; what we do in these places may be either beneficial or calamitous for their survival. As with the coastal bee, long-term persistence of isolated bee populations additionally requires connectivity with sources of colonists to offset periodic population crashes (see Byers and Mitchell, chapter 8, and Sanjayan and Crooks, chapter 11, this volume). Land-use planning that accommodates these requirements should retain more diverse and functional native bee communities. Conversely, we do not know how to reestablish bee communities extinguished by sprawl. Mitigation and restoration may appear to offset habitat lost to sprawl by creating greenery, but current methods fail to re-create displaced bee communities. We can plant seeds and saplings, but not yet their pollinators.

REFERENCES

Banaszak, J. 1982. Apoidea (Hymenoptera) of Warsaw and Mazovia. *Polish Academy of Sciences Memorabilia Zoologica* 36:129–142.

Berezin, M. V., V. B. Beiko, and N. V. Berezina. 1995. Bumble bees of the Moscow region. *Entomologist's Monthly Magazine* 131 (November 27): 259–268.

Bischoff, I. 1996. Die Bedeutung städischer Grünflächen für Wildbienen (Hymenoptera, Apidae) untersucht am Beispiel des Botanischen Gartens und weiteren Grünflächen in Bonner Stadtgebiet. *Dechenlana* 149:162–178.

Camargo, J. M. F., and M. Mazucato. 1984. Inventário de apifauna e flora apícola de Ribeirao Preto, Sp, Brasil. *Dusenia* 14:55–87.

Cane, J. H. 1997. Violent weather and bees: Populations of the barrier island endemic *Hesperapis oraria* (Hymenoptera: Melittidae) survive a category 3 hurricane. *Journal of the Kansas Entomological Society* 70:73–75.

———. 2003. Exotic non-social bees (Hymenoptera: Apoidea) in North America: Ecological implications. In K. V. Strickler and J. H. Cane, eds., *For Non-native Crops, Whence Pollinators of the Future?* 113–126. Lanham, Md.: Thomas Say Publications in Entomology, Entomological Society of America.

Cane, J. H., R. L. Minckley, and L. J. Kervin. 2000. Sampling bees (Hymenoptera: Apiformes) for pollinator community studies: Pitfalls of pan-trapping. *Journal of the Kansas Entomological Society* 73:225–231.

Cane, J. H., R. L. Minckley, L. J. Kervin, T. H. Roulston, and N. M. Williams. 2006. Multiple responses of a desert bee guild (Hymenoptera: Apiformes) to urban habitat fragmentation. *Ecological Applications.*

Cane, J. H., and J. A. Payne. 1993. Regional, annual, and seasonal variation in pollinator guilds: Intrinsic traits of bees (Hymenoptera: Apoidea) underlie their patterns of abundance at *Vaccinium ashei* (Ericaceae). *Annals of the Entomological Society of America* 86:577–588.

Cane, J. H., R. R. Snelling, L. J. Kervin, and G. C. Eickwort. 1996. A new monolectic coastal bee, *Hesperapis oraria* Snelling and Stage (Hymenoptera: Melittidae), with a review of desert and neotropical disjunctives in the southeastern U.S. *Journal of the Kansas Entomological Society* 69:238–247.

Feenstra, G., and C. Lewis. 1999. Farmers markets offer new business opportunities for farmers. *California Agriculture* 53:27.

Frankie, G. W., R. W. Thorp, M. H. Schindler, B. Ertter, and M. Przybylski. 2002. Bees in Berkeley? *Fremontia* 30:50–58.

Gathmann, A., and T. Tscharntke. 2002. Foraging ranges of solitary bees. *Journal of Animal Ecology* 71:757–764.

Glinski, J. T. 1996. *Above Tucson Then and Now*. Tucson, Ariz.: JTG Enterprise.

Ikudome, S. 1992. The environment and the wild bee fauna of natural park in a city, with the result taken at Shiroyama Park in Kagoshima City, Japan, and with the appendix of a revised bee list recorded from the mainland of Kagoshima Prefecture (Hymenoptera, Apoidea). *Bulletin of Kagoshima Women's Junior College* 27:99–135.

Jacob-Remacle, A. 1984. Etude écologique du peuplement d'Hyménoptères Aculéates survivant dans la zone la plus urbanisée de la ville de Liège. *Bulletin et Annales de la Société Royale d'Entomologie de Belgique* 120:241–262.

Knoll, F. R. N., L. R. Bego, and V. L. Imperatriz-Fonseca. 1993. As abelhas em áreas urbanas. In J. R. Pirani and M. Cortopassi-Laurino, eds., *Flores e abelhas em São Paulo*, 31–41. São Paulo: EDUSP/FAPESPl.

Kremen, C., N. M. Williams, and R. W. Thorp. 2002. Crop pollination from native bees at risk from agricultural intensification. *Proceedings of the National Academy of Sciences* (United States) 99:16812–16816.

Küpper, G. 1999. Wildbienen (Hymenoptera, Apidae) im Siedlungsbereich: Eine Untersuchung der Bienenfauna im Botanische Garten der Ruhr-Universität Bochum. *Natur und Hiemat* 59:45–52.

Laroca, S., J. R. Cure, and C. Bortoli. 1982. A associaçao de abelhas silvestres

(Hymenoptera, Apoidea) de uma área restrita no interior de cidade de Curitiba (Brasil): Uma abordagem biocenótica. *Dusenia* 13:93–117.

Marlin, J. C., and W. E. LaBerge. 2001. The native bee fauna of Carlinville, Illinois, revisited after 75 years: A case for persistence. *Conservation Ecology* 5:87–89. Also available at: www.consecol.org/vol5/iss1/art3.

Michener, C. D. 2000. *The Bees of the World*. Baltimore: Johns Hopkins University Press.

Morse, R. A., and N. W. Calderone. 2000. The value of honey bees as pollinators of U.S. crops in 2000. *Bee Culture* 128:1–15.

O'Toole, C., and A. Raw. 1991. *Bees of the World*. New York: Facts on File.

Recher, H. F., and D. L. Serventy. 1991. Long-term changes in the relative abundances of birds in Kings Park, Perth, Western Australia. *Conservation Biology* 5:90–102.

Riemann, H. 1995. Zur Stechimmenfauna des Bremer Bürgerparks (Hymenoptera: Aculeata). *Abhandlungen des Naturwissenschaftlichen Vereins Bremen* 43:45–72.

Rooney, T. P., and W. J. Dress. 1997. Species loss over sixty-six years in the ground-layer vegetation of Heart's Content, an old-growth forest in Pennsylvania USA. *Natural Areas Journal* 17:297–305.

Roulston, T., B. Sampson, and J. Cane. 1996. Squash and pumpkin pollinators plentiful in Alabama. *Alabama Agricultural Experiment Station* 43:19–20.

Roy, D. B., M. O. Hill, and P. Rothery. 1999. Effects of urban land cover on the local species pool in Britain. *Ecography* 22:507–515.

Sakagami, S. F., and H. Fukuda. 1973. Wild bee survey at the campus of Hokkaido University. *Journal of the Faculty of Science, Hokkaido University, Series VI: Zoology* 19:190–250.

Saure, C. 1996. Urban habitats for bees: The example of the city of Berlin. In A. Matheson, S. L. Buchmann, C. O'Toole, P. Westrich, and I. H. Williams, eds., *The Conservation of Bees*, 47–54. New York: Academic Press.

Schemske, D. W., M. F. Willson, M. N. Melampy, L. J. Miller, L. Verner, K. M. Schemske, and L. B. Best. 1978. Flowering ecology of some spring woodland herbs. *Ecology* 59:351–366.

Washitani, I. 1996. Predicted genetic consequences of strong fertility selection due to pollinator loss in an isolated population of *Primula sieboldii*. *Conservation Biology* 10:59–64.

Wcislo, W. T., and J. H. Cane. 1996. Floral resource utilization by solitary bees (Hymenoptera: Apoidea) and exploitation of their stored foods by natural enemies. *Annual Review of Entomology* 41:195–224.

Westrich, P. 1989. *Die Wildbienen Baden-Württembergs. Allgemeiner Teil: Lebensräume, Verhalten, Ökologie und Schutz*. Stuttgart: Eugen Ulmer.

———. 1996. Habitat requirements of central European bees and the problems of partial habitats. In A. Matheson, S. L. Buchmann, C. O'Toole, P. Westrich, and I. H. Williams, eds., *The Conservation of Bees*, 1–16. New York: Academic Press.

Williams, N. M., R. L. Minckley, and F. A. Silveira. 2001. Variation in native bee faunas and its implications for detecting community changes. *Conservation Ecology* 5:57–86. Also available at: www.consecol.org/vol5/iss1/art3.

6

EFFECTS OF URBANIZATION ON DECOMPOSER COMMUNITIES AND SOIL PROCESSES IN FOREST REMNANTS

Margaret M. Carreiro

The past 50 years have witnessed the accelerating spread of cities and suburbs at the expense of agricultural land and natural ecosystems in the
contiguous United States. Between 1960 and 1997, 42 million acres (17.1
million hectares) of rural land were converted to urban and suburban land use
(Dougherty 1992; Department of Agriculture 2000). The states that have experienced the greatest population growth per unit land area between 1990 and
1996 are in the East, where human settlement is expanding primarily into forested land (Dwyer et al. 2000). Birch, Rachel, and Kern (1997) estimated that
as a consequence 25 percent of the urban areas in New York and Pennsylvania
were currently forested, defined by the Department of Agriculture Forest
Service as being at least 1 acre (0.4 hectare) in size and 10 percent stocked
with trees. This estimate considered only remnant forests and did not include
street trees, city parks, or trees in commercial, institutional, and residential
locations. Therefore, urban and suburban conditions affect the long-term sustainability of not only street trees but many forest remnants, where successional
forces influenced by urban land use and sprawl determine future species composition and health.

Awareness of the social, economic, and environmental benefits provided by
forest remnants is increasing. People value forest remnants created by urban
sprawl for several reasons, including the economic value they confer on residential areas; the recreational and educational opportunities they offer; the
ecosystem services they provide, such as filtering pollutants from air and water,
and recharging local aquifers; and the critical role they play in conserving local
biotic heritage, a role that contributes to our cultural sense of identity with a
particular landscape. Therefore, it is especially important and challenging to
develop land-use policies and adaptive management strategies that can accommodate both the needs of people and the needs of species composing these for-

est "islands." Although the effects of development on the "aboveground forest" (trees, understory plant communities, and associated vertebrates) are commonly considered, there is less awareness of the "underground forest," the soil infrastructure and decomposer communities on which the plant community's vigor and species composition depends. The intent of this chapter is to provide ecological background about forest soil organisms for natural-areas managers and municipal planners who want to understand better how to preserve and sustain their town woodlands and forests. This overview provides information on the types and abundance of decomposer organisms that inhabit forest soils and the roles they play in forest ecosystems. It then focuses on the effects that cities and sprawl are known to have or are likely to have on decomposers and their activities. Consideration of soils as *living* rather than inert systems should make it more apparent that their conservation and maintenance must be integrated into planning, management, and restoration activities if native plant communities in and near cities and sprawling developments are to be sustained.

DECOMPOSER COMMUNITIES: ORGANISMS AND ECOLOGICAL ROLES

ORGANISMS

Soil decomposer communities are often more species rich than the plants and vertebrate animals with which they interact. A temperate deciduous forest may contain as many as 1,000 species of soil invertebrates (Swift, Heal, and Anderson 1979). One square yard of forest soil may contain 300 species of fungi and an even greater number of bacterial species. This number makes detailed accounting of the species composition of decomposer communities exceedingly labor intensive. As a consequence, very few comprehensive studies have been made of the effects of habitat size on the species number or abundance of bacteria, fungi, or soil invertebrates in remnant natural habitats created by urbanization (Faeth and Kane 1978). This paucity is in stark contrast to a number of studies conducted in cities and suburbs that examine relationships between patch size and species number of plants, birds, reptiles, amphibians, or mammals. In general, the latter studies have shown that species number decreases with diminishing size of the forest remnant (Butcher et al. 1981; Hobbs 1988; Corlett and Turner 1997). Such "island biogeographic" studies have served to highlight the negative impact that fragmentation of forest ecosystems has had on biodiversity. However, studies of urban effects on microbial or invertebrate communities or species composition are rare (Faeth and Kane

1976; Garay and Nataf 1982; Santas 1986; Korsós et al. 2002; Niemalä et al. 2002). Therefore, ecological understanding of the effects of urban sprawl on decomposer community diversity has lagged behind understanding of organisms that are easier to count and identify. A greater number of studies have focused on the processes that these microbial and invertebrate organisms regulate collectively—decomposition and nutrient cycling.

Some of the more important groups of organisms that inhabit forest soils and decompose dead organic material include bacteria, microfungi and macrofungi, nematode worms, arthropods (e.g., mites, collembola, millipedes, insects), earthworms, slugs, and snails (figure 6.1). Most of these organisms occur in the organic matter–rich, upper soil horizons. Bacteria can attain densities of 1 billion cells per gram of forest soil. In fact, bacteria are so numerous that 1 square yard of a temperate forest soil down to approximately 1.2 inches (3 centimeters) depth can contain as much as 1.10 pounds (0.5 kilogram) of bacterial cells (M. M. Carreiro, unpublished data). Both microfungi (smaller microscopic molds) and macrofungi (e.g., mushrooms, puffballs, shelf fungi) occur in decaying leaves, wood, and mineral soil. In forests, fungi are typically the most abundant decomposers, composing from 60 to 80 percent of the living decomposer

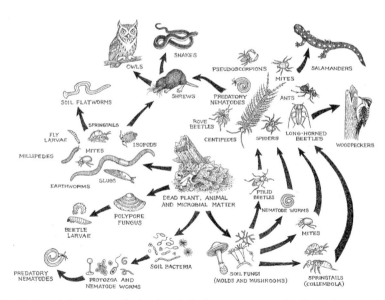

FIGURE 6.1. A decomposer food web typical of many temperate deciduous forests includes dead organic matter, microbes (bacteria, fungi, protozoa), invertebrates, and vertebrates. (Artwork by Patricia Wynne)

biomass (Dighton and Boddy 1989). In the upper 1.2 inches (3 centimeters) of temperate forest soil, their threadlike hyphae can attain total lengths of 930 to 5,580 miles per square yard (1,500–9,000 kilometers per square meter) (M. M. Carreiro, unpublished data). Smaller soil invertebrates—such as nematode worms (0.008–0.08 inch [0.2–2 millimeters] long), Collembola (springtails, 0.008–0.195 inch [0.2–5 millimeters] long), and mites (0.008–0.098 inch [0.2–2.5 millimeters] long)—are also abundant in forest soils and have respective densities per square yard of up to 20 million and 400,000 (for Collembola and mites combined) (Swift, Heal, and Anderson 1979). Many species in these three invertebrate groups selectively eat bacteria and fungi. Larger invertebrates (e.g., earthworms, millipedes, slugs) ingest the organic detritus, including colonizing microbes, and release nutrients into the soil after partially digested material passes through their gut.

ECOLOGICAL ROLES OF THE DECOMPOSER COMMUNITY

NUTRIENT CYCLING Decomposer organisms rely on carbon-rich, dead organic matter as their source of energy and nutrients. The abundance of bacterial and fungal cells in soils results in their extensive contact with a variety of organic materials. Thus these microbes have evolved the ability to break down many complex molecules and chemically transform them during their metabolic activities. Microbes accomplish these decomposition processes by exporting enzymes into their surroundings, each targeting specific organic molecules, such as cellulose, lignin, and proteins. Without bacteria and fungi to decompose them, these and other organic materials would accumulate in ecosystems, preventing their constituent molecules from becoming available for continued plant growth. The greatest amount of dead organic material in forests is of plant, not animal, origin. Hence, ecosystem studies of decomposition in forests focus primarily on the decay of plant matter. During decay, microbes convert dead organic matter into carbon dioxide (CO_2) gas, causing the plant material to "disappear" as it decomposes. Decomposers must extract nourishment from materials (leaves, stems, and roots) that are high in carbon (mostly cellulose and lignin), but very low in the nitrogen and phosphorus they need to make their own cell proteins. Consequently, during decomposition, fungi and bacteria sequester much of the dead plant nitrogen and phosphorus in their growing cells, making those elements temporarily unavailable to plants. By grazing on fungi and bacteria, the smaller invertebrates cause this nitrogen and phosphorus to be released more rapidly into the soil in inorganic mineral forms that plants can take up (ammonium, nitrate, phosphate). Larger invertebrates, such as worms, fragment and ingest some of the organic material and thereby accelerate the release of CO_2 and inorganic forms of nitrogen and phosphorus from organic matter, including the living microbes they ingest. This decomposer-mediated release of inorganic nitrogen is particularly important because nitrogen is the nutrient that most limits plant growth in terrestrial ecosystems (Vitousek and Howarth 1991). Decomposers provide from 60 to 80 percent of a temperate forest's annual growth requirement for nitrogen, with the remaining 20 to 40 percent of a forest's nitrogen needs entering from outside the system in wet (rain and snow) and dry (particles and gases) precipitation (Waring and Schlesinger 1985). In summary, the coupled microbial–invertebrate system behaves to transform organic carbon, nitrogen, and phosphorus into inorganic forms (CO_2, ammonium [NH_4^+], nitrate [NO_3^-], and phosphate [PO_4^{+3}]) that plants require for growth and reproduction.

MEMBERS OF THE DETRITIVORE FOOD WEB Unlike grasslands and aquatic ecosystems, where at least half of all plant or algal biomass is grazed by animals, forest ecosystems contribute only 10 to 20 percent of living plant tissue to a grazer food web (e.g., herbivorous insects and mammals) (Aber and Melillo 1991). The remaining forest plant biomass (80–90 percent) sustains a complex detritivore food web consisting of decomposer organisms and the amphibians, reptiles, mammals, and birds that in turn consume them. Many vertebrates prey on invertebrates that depend on microbes or decaying plant matter for food (figure 6.1). For example, woodpeckers eat invertebrates in decaying logs or standing dead trees, and other animals (e.g., birds, toads, shrews) consume invertebrates in leaf litter. Therefore, many forest vertebrates ultimately rely on dead organic matter and its microbial colonizers as their energy and matter base.

EFFECTS OF URBAN SPRAWL ON FOREST SOIL COMMUNITIES AND THEIR ECOLOGICAL FUNCTIONS

Sprawl reduces the size of forests and isolates remnants; it also interposes an environment that is often hostile to species dispersal among forest fragments. As forests become smaller, their edge-to-interior ratios increase, thereby exposing them to proportionately greater inputs of energy, matter, and species from their altered surroundings (Saunders, Hobbs, and Margules 1991). This may be especially true for forest remnants that become enveloped by cities and suburbs because urban land cover properties (e.g., impervious surfaces, roads) and activities (e.g., fossil-fuel combustion) are distinctly different from those of forests. Enhanced external inputs to urban and suburban forests include warmer temperatures from the urban heat island effect (Oke 1995); injurious pollutants and beneficial nutrients (Turner et al. 1990; Lovett et al. 2000); and nonforest species, including exotics (Rebele 1994) and human visitors (Matlack

1993). Fragmentation also isolates formerly connected species populations and can therefore hasten local species extinctions in the greater landscape. In the remainder of this chapter, I consider the effects of high-density human settlements on soil organisms and their ecological functions from two perspectives that I consider important for long-term management of forests surrounded by cities and sprawl: the integrity of the forest-floor litter layer and the persistence and dispersal of two ecologically important, but often overlooked groups of forest organisms—decomposer macrofungi and ectomycorrhizal fungi.

URBAN EFFECTS ON FOREST LITTER-LAYER DEPTH

The rate at which leaf litter decays determines the *average* litter depth in a forest. Climate, the abundance and species composition of the decomposer community, the chemical composition of dead plant tissues, and the availability of inorganic nutrients contribute to the rate at which organic materials such as leaves and wood decay (Swift, Heal, and Anderson 1979) (figure 6.2). By affecting the composition and activity of decomposer communities, these factors alter the thickness and integrity of the forest-floor leaf litter and humus layers that protect the mineral soil from erosion, provide habitat for many small vertebrates, and selectively affect the future forest's seed germination and therefore its plant species composition (Facelli and Pickett 1991). As explained later, urban and suburban land uses can change all the factors that control litter-layer depth.

URBAN CLIMATE EFFECTS As long as moisture is not limiting, warmer temperatures increase the metabolic rate of microbes and invertebrates, thus increasing decomposition (figure 6.2). The urban heat island (Oke 1995) may extend decomposers' activity in forests for a greater portion of the year relative to nearby rural areas. Therefore, one would predict that forests in many urban areas should have faster decomposition rates and thinner leaf litter layers than their suburban and rural counterparts. In an experiment conducted in oak stands along an urban–rural land-use gradient in metropolitan New York City, Pouyat, McDonnell, and Pickett (1997) found that after six months sugar maple leaf litter decomposed nearly twice as fast in the Bronx, New York (urban forests, 76 percent weight loss), as in Litchfield County, Connecticut (rural forests, 40 percent weight loss). Sugar maple (*Acer saccharum*) litter in suburban Westchester County, New York, decayed nearly as rapidly as the same litter in the Bronx (68 percent weight loss). Forests in New York City were on average 5.4°F (3°C) warmer year round than rural forests (McDonnell, Pickett, and Pouyat 1993). In a subsequent study, Kostel-Hughes, Young, and Carreiro (1998) found that

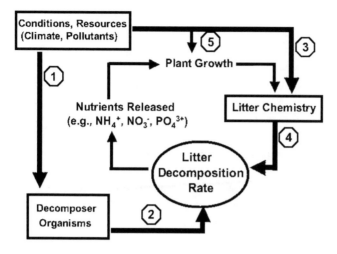

FIGURE 6.2. The three main factors (conditions and resources, decomposer organisms, litter chemistry) that control the decomposition rate of organic plant litter (dead leaves, roots, wood). Cities and suburban environments can alter all three of these main factors and hence the rate at which litter decays. Pavement and buildings warm local surroundings through the heat island effect, and fossil-fuel combustion and industrial processes produce air pollutants that settle onto soil. Heat and pollutants (such as heavy metals, nitrogen, and sulfur) can affect the types, numbers, and activity levels of decomposer organisms (*arrow 1*) that break down organic materials (*arrow 2*) into nutrients that plants use to grow. Urban conditions and pollutants, such as ozone, can also directly affect the chemistry of plant foliage and subsequent leaf litter (*arrow 3*). Decomposers respond to these chemical changes by either accelerating or decelerating litter breakdown (*arrow 4*). Urban environments can also change the way plants grow and incorporate nutrients into their cells (*arrow 5*), such that their foliage, wood, or roots become chemically altered. Again, decomposers can react to such changes in chemical quality by becoming more or less abundant and thereby either speeding up or slowing down litter decay. These processes combined can alter the average depth of the forest-floor organic layer with potential ecological consequences for forest species and functions. At this time, not enough research has been done in a large number of cities to determine whether there is a generalized urban sprawl effect on forest-floor litter depth, and patterns have to be assessed on a city-by-city basis.

forest-floor litter mass (weight) in the same forests was almost three times greater in the rural stands (mean of 23 ounces per square yard [653 grams per square meter]) than in the urban stands (mean of 8 ounces per square yard [228 grams per square meter]), with suburban stands intermediate (14 ounces per square yard [405 grams per square meter]). Although not the only cause of this pattern in New York City–area forests, the urban heat island likely contributed to these differences in leaf litter decay rates.

URBAN EFFECTS ON DECOMPOSER COMMUNITY COMPOSITION The composition and numbers of decomposer organisms also affect forest-floor thickness (figure 6.2). Pouyat, Parmelee, and Carreiro (1994) found that urban stands in New York City contained nematode and microinvertebrate densities that were 34 percent and 43 percent lower than those in rural stands. They also found that densities of fungal filaments developing on oak litter in the urban forests were half those in the rural forests. Because the trends in fungal and microinvertebrate densities were not consistent with the more rapid litter decay rates observed in these urban stands compared with rural ones (lower decomposer abundance should result in slower decomposition rates), a survey of macroinvertebrate abundance was made. High numbers of exotic earthworms, mostly Asian species in the genus *Amynthas*, were found in the urban and suburban forests in and near New York City, but not in the rural stands (Steinberg et al. 1997). This urban-to-rural trend in worm abundance was thought to be important in explaining the trends in litter-layer thickness in these forests, as described earlier. This pattern of exotic macroinvertebrate species dominance in urban forests has also been reported for Baltimore, Maryland, and for many European cities (Korsós et al. 2002; Hornung and Szlávecz 2003). In Baltimore's urban and suburban forests, exotic species from Europe and Asia composed 79 percent, 100 percent, and 33 percent of the Oligochaete (e.g., earthworms), Isopod (e.g., pillbugs), and Diplopod (e.g., millipedes) assemblages, respectively (K. Szlávecz, unpublished data). Forests with large numbers of macroinvertebrates should have thinner litter layers than those with low macroinvertebrate densities because many of these organisms consume leaf litter.

URBAN EFFECTS ON CHEMICAL QUALITY OF PLANT LITTER The chemical composition of dead plant material can also affect the rate at which microbes and invertebrates process litter (Cadisch and Giller 1997) (figure 6.2). Lower lignin (a compound that makes plant tissues "woody") and greater nitrogen concentrations in litter generally increase litter decay rates. Therefore, the decomposition rate occurring in a forest is closely related to its plant species composition as a result of species-specific lignin and nitrogen compositions. Compared with reference forests in nearby rural areas, forests embedded in cities and suburbs may differ in their plant species composition because of land-use history, successional age, an altered physical environment (warmer temperatures) and chemical environment (pollutant and excess nutrient inputs), and greater probability of colonization by invasive exotic plant species (Hobbs 1988).

Altered plant species composition is not the only mechanism by which litter quality can vary among urban, suburban, and rural forests. Urban and suburban environments may also change the leaf litter chemistry of a single species. Altered patterns of soil nutrient uptake by plants or modifications of plant metabolism caused by abiotic and biotic factors in cities can affect leaf litter chemistry (Smith 1990). In addition, air pollutants such as sulfur dioxide, ozone, nitrogen dioxide, ammonium, nitrate, and acid precipitation can directly change the chemical and physical properties of leaves of a single plant species (Constantinidou and Kozlowski 1979; Garten and Hanson 1990; Latus, Forstel, and Fuhr 1990; Jordon et al. 1991). In some cases, alterations of living leaf chemistry caused by such pollutants persist after leaf senescence and result in either accelerated or decelerated rates of decay of fallen leaves (Prescott and Parkinson 1985; Garden and Davies 1988; Findlay et al. 1996). This outcome implies that the air pollution affecting living foliage during the plant growing season may continue to affect ecosystem processes even if pollutant levels decline temporarily. Carreiro and colleagues (1999) demonstrated that the decomposability of red oak leaf litter varied predictably along an urban–rural gradient in the New York City area (rural litter greater than suburban litter greater than urban litter) and that the decay results were correlated with greater lignin content and decreased labile material in urban litter.

DIRECT POLLUTANT DEPOSITION TO THE FOREST FLOOR Air pollutants can also affect the abundance and activities of decomposers directly once these chemicals are deposited on the forest floor (figure 6.2). A large literature exists on the effects of heavy-metal, sulfur, and acid deposition on decomposer communities and microbial processes in forest soils at varying distances from urban-industrial centers (Bååth 1989; Francis 1989; Smith 1990). Most studies have demonstrated that these pollutants cause both short-term and long-term reductions in the abundance of soil organisms, rates of litter decay, and soil nutrient return. In several cases, pollutant deposition has resulted in increasing the depth of the litter layer in these forests by reducing decay rates.

Recently, however, there has been great interest in quantifying the amounts of inorganic nitrogen (e.g., as nitrogen oxide [NO_x] gases, nitrate [NO_3^-], ammonium [NH_4^+]) entering forests via atmospheric deposition. Such knowledge is important because (1) trends in the production of NO_x gases (precursors of nitric acid and nitrate) from automobile exhaust and other combustion sources are rising in the United States and worldwide (Vitousek 1994; EPA 2000); (2) NO_2 gas, NO_3^-, and NH_4^+ are not only pollutants, but also important nutrients for plants and microbes and hence can differentially affect ecosystem processes of primary production and decomposition; and (3) despite its being a nutrient, excessive amounts of inorganic nitrogen entering a forest may result in saturation of the ecosystem with this resource and initiate eventual forest decline in part through its effects on soil (Aber et al. 1998). Urban and suburban atmospheres contain high concentrations of nitrogenous compounds in gaseous, soluble, and particulate form. Despite the availability of nitrogen-concentration data in city air and precipitation (Gatz 1991), there is little information on actual deposition rates of nitrogen to vegetated areas in and near metropolitan areas. However, Lovett and colleagues (2000) found that the combined amount of NO_3^--N and NH_4^+-N in dry particulate form deposited on the forest floor during the plant growing season was 17 times greater in New York City oak forests than in outlying suburban and rural oak forests. Not only may such increased inputs of nitrogen be promoting plant growth in cities, but they may also be affecting leaf litter decomposition rates because nitrogen is also a nutrient for fungi and bacteria. Carreiro and colleagues (2000) found that ammonium nitrate (NH_4NO_3) both stimulated and slowed litter decay rates, depending on the litter's relative lignin and cellulose content. Leaf litter high in lignin (such as oak) decayed more slowly when NH_4NO_3 was added, whereas leaf litter low in lignin (such as dogwood) decayed more rapidly. Therefore, the net effect of added inorganic nitrogen on forest-floor thickness will likely depend on the relative forest dominance by particular tree species and the amount of lignin in their litter.

DIRECT HUMAN EFFECTS ON FOREST-FLOOR INTEGRITY Recreational use of natural areas has been increasing rapidly throughout the United States in the past two decades (Flather and Cordell 1995), and forested parks close to cities are intensely visited. As human traffic (hikers, bicyclists, motor bikers, horse riders) increases in urban and suburban forest patches, the amount of exposed soil also increases, particularly on slopes where people and animals enlarge trail width and depth while seeking improved footing (Liddle 1975; Weaver and Dale 1978). In addition, people on foot, vehicle, or horseback have a tendency not to stay on paths and to create "desire trails" when established trails are rutted or blocked by fallen trees or if shortcuts are perceived. This results in loss of the litter layer and in increased soil compaction (Cole and Marion 1988). These changes affect soil invertebrate communities (Garay and Nataf 1982) and result in greater erosional loss of the organic matter–rich, upper soil horizon where the highest concentration of decomposer organisms and nutrients exists. Loss of litter-layer integrity and increased soil compaction ultimately affect vegetation cover detrimentally and cause plant species to decline, which in turn accelerates further loss of litter and soil (Kuss and Hall 1991). Therefore, trail placement and management in small forest parks in cities and suburbs is critical for minimizing long-term damage to both plant and decomposer communities.

Forests next to suburban developments are also exposed to numerous small-scale disturbances caused by residential and commercial activity along their boundaries that can affect decomposer communities. For example, Matlack (1993) found that most suburban activities penetrated more deeply into the forest than did natural microclimatic edge effects. These sociological edge-effect phenomena included trash dumps, piles of building rubble, campsites, wood-piles, and piles of lawn clippings. He also found that most small forest patches (1.7–49.4 acres [0.7–20 hectares]) possessed numerous leaf litter–free paths and that residential lawns often penetrated beneath the tree canopy. These disturbances affect soil organisms and processes in ways similar to those described earlier for recreational activities. In addition, the probability of introducing both exotic plant and decomposer species such as earthworms from gardens and lawns into forests is increased.

Many factors interact to affect the decay rate of plant litter. Some factors accelerate litter decomposition, whereas others slow it. Therefore, different levels and combinations of these factors, which can differ among cities, may intensify or even counteract one another in terms of their effects on soils and soil nutrient release to plants. Until soil processes in urban and suburban forest remnants receive greater study in more cities across the United States, few generalizations can be made yet about the *net* effects of urbanization on average litter-layer depth in forest remnants. However, although environmental managers cannot directly control factors such as the urban heat island or air-pollutant inputs, they do have the ability to reduce the extent of human trampling and sociological edge-effect activities that have large and well-known detrimental impacts on soils and soil organisms.

FRAGMENTATION EFFECTS ON MACROFUNGAL POPULATIONS

Reduced forest size and increased isolation may also affect decomposer populations by changing their dispersal dynamics within and among remnants in the landscape. To maintain population size and genetic variation, all species, including fungi, must reproduce and disperse. However, as sprawl proceeds across a landscape, it leaves behind habitat remnants that become not only smaller but more isolated from other like habitats. As a once freely interbreeding population becomes spatially separated into subpopulations, decreased gene flow and increased rates of local species extinction often follow (Wilcove 1987). Many studies have been made of metapopulation dispersal dynamics of animals and plants (both pollen and seed dispersal) among wooded remnants in agricultural landscapes (Mader 1984; Henderson, Merriam, and Wegner 1985; Foré et al. 1992), but few, if any, studies have focused on metropolitan areas. This lack of information on dispersal dynamics of species in cities and suburbs is even more extreme for decomposer invertebrates and fungi. Because many of these genera or species have a broad geographic distribution, it is often assumed that decomposers are being adequately dispersed by abiotic and biotic vectors. However, this assumption may not be warranted for some of these organisms. In the remainder of this chapter, I call attention to two microbial groups that deserve more attention from the management community because of their critical ecological roles in forests. These groups are decomposer macrofungi and ectomycorrhizal fungi.

Decomposer macrofungi decay primarily wood and leaf litter, whereas *ectomycorrhizal fungi* are obligate mutualistic symbionts of trees, colonizing tree roots. Most decomposer macrofungi and ectomycorrhizal fungi produce large reproductive bodies (e.g., gilled mushrooms, saclike puffballs, polypores and boletes with pores instead of gills) where spore production occurs. In an ectomycorrhizal symbiosis, the fungi receive carbohydrates from the photosynthesizing trees, and the trees benefit through improved nutrient (especially phosphorus and nitrogen) and water status as well as through increased resistance to root diseases and to heavy-metal toxicity (Smith and Read 1997). Most individual trees can be colonized simultaneously by many species of ectomycorrhizal fungi, and for some trees the particular species of fungi change as a tree ages or as an entire forest stand matures (Last et al. 1983; Last, Dighton, and Mason 1987). In some forests, the late-successional ectomycorrhizal species have a tendency to be more specific to the tree host (Dighton, Poskitt, and Howard 1986). Within a forest stand, some macrofungi and ectomycorrhizal fungi can disperse several feet over and through the soil by means of hyphal cords or even thicker (approximately 0.39 inch [1 centimeter] wide) rhizomorphs (Dix and Webster 1995). But long-range dispersal of the type needed to reach isolated forest patches requires colonization by spores. After acquiring enough mass (which can take years) and following periods that meet specific temperature and rainfall requirements (Dix and Webster 1995), these fungi produce fruiting bodies from which billions of haploid spores are dispersed. The fruiting bodies of both leaf litter fungi and many ectomycorrhizal fungi erupt through the soil and are therefore at ground level. However, certain ectomycorrhizal fruiting bodies (e.g., truffles) develop belowground. Vertebrate animals can disperse decomposer and ectomycorrhizal fungal spores after eating aboveground or belowground fruiting bodies, and some of these fungal species depend heavily on animal dispersal (Johnson 1996). Because reproductive bodies of wood decay fungi emerge through fallen and standing dead trees at various heights within the forest, they may send spores quite a distance. These microscopic spores are capable of long-distance dispersal if they escape through various atmospheric boundary layers, but most spores will settle out of the air within 66 to 328 feet (20–100 meters) of their source (Wolfenbarger 1946; Lacey 1996).

We have little direct understanding of how urban or suburban environments surrounding a forest can affect macrofungal spore dispersal and species viability in complex fragmented landscapes such as those in urban and suburban areas. Dispersal at this landscape scale may be important for the long-term survival of a species in a small forest remnant because suitable substrate or plant hosts may be limited over time owing to succession or to excessive removal of standing dead trees or fallen logs by forest managers. Local extinctions of animals and restriction of animal movement between forest remnants in urban and suburban areas will likely have strong effects on the spread of some fungal species, in particular those that fruit belowground.

Based on studies of species–area relationships with plants and animals, it is believed to be very possible that macrofungal species richness may decline with decreasing forest size and increasing forest isolation. Because certain macrofungi (both decomposers and ectomycorrhizal species) have varying degrees of stringency for specific substrates or hosts (Molina and Trappe 1982; Boddy, Bardsley, and Gibbon 1987), fungal species shifts can track changes caused by aging trees (Last et al. 1983), tree community succession (Last, Dighton, and Mason 1987), or past management decisions affecting tree species composition (e.g., tree planting, controlled burns). In addition, macrofungal species composition and diversity in urban and suburban forests may be differentially affected by atmospheric deposition of pollutants and nutrients such as nitrogen (Arnolds 1988; Shaw et al. 1992). For example, Baxter and colleagues (1999) found that the number of ectomycorrhizal types on roots of mature oak trees was greater in rural areas than in urban forests (26 types in rural areas, 16 in urban) along the New York City urban–rural gradient. Therefore, the long-term presence of a macrofungal species in a landscape mosaic might well be determined by its ability to escape one forest patch and colonize another with more suitable conditions for growth. In the case of ectomycorrhizal fungi, maintenance of high species diversity in forest remnants may be a particularly desirable management goal. The specific suite of mycorrhizal symbionts that can colonize a tree's roots may be important for tree nutrition, and the diversity of fungal symbionts may confer varying degrees of benefit to a tree under different environmental conditions (Baxter and Dighton 2001).

Management practices can also introduce or spread ectomycorrhizal species among forest remnants. Urban forest managers have recently become interested in planting seedlings and saplings of native tree species into forest patches where they are no longer numerous. To increase the probability of survival, tree seedlings and saplings have been intentionally infected with species of ectomycorrhizal fungi grown in laboratories. Although the intent here is commendable, great care should be taken to choose species of ectomycorrhizal fungi that are native to a particular habitat. The fungi (e.g., *Pisolithus arhizus* [= *P. tinctorius*] or *Cenococcum* spp.) with which the trees are inoculated may grow well under greenhouse conditions, but they may not confer the benefits sought for the tree under field conditions. Also, because the scientific community has not yet evaluated whether the introduced fungal species may have a detrimental impact on the native ectomycorrhizal community, caution should be used when introducing greenhouse variety ectomycorrhizal species into habitats where they are not native. As an alternative to this practice, seedlings can be started in soil cores removed beneath the canopy of the desired tree species growing in nearby habitats to allow colonization with ectomycorrhizal fungi specific to that location. Doing otherwise can introduce exotic fungi into the forest and may do more harm than good to the system in the long term.

CONCLUSION

Urban and suburban lands are expanding rapidly, creating numerous natural-habitat remnants that will require active management to maintain their biodiversity and function. For forest remnants in particular, this management will require strategies based on knowledge of the interdependence of both aboveground and belowground components. Decomposer organisms create humus, make inorganic nutrients available to plants, detoxify and aerate soils, and form the base of a complex food web that includes familiar aboveground vertebrates of conservation importance. Ectomycorrhizal fungi provide trees with improved nutrition and water status as well as resistance to some root diseases. Other ecological services rendered by trees and intact soil communities include flood control, pollutant removal from air (which promotes human respiratory health), and detoxification and immobilization of some pollutants in soil so that water entering our aquatic systems (potentially for drinking) is cleansed. These soil organisms and the ecosystem services they provide are affected by the heat, chemicals, and species that enter forests from surrounding urban and suburban land. Forest managers can control or mitigate some, but not all, of these factors. Restriction of human access as a means of controlling direct harmful disturbance to soil and vegetation has long been recognized as important to maintaining the integrity of forest parks. These restrictions have additional benefits, such as reducing the invasion potential of exotic plant, animal, and microbial species into natural-habitat remnants. Land-use planners of newly suburbanizing developments can incorporate land buffers around forest remnants to prevent or reduce the probability of sociological edge effects that erode long-term forest viability.

Management practices driven by the desire to maintain or restore a particular plant community type should also take into consideration the needs of organisms living in soil and dead wood. It is often assumed that these small organisms will "take care of themselves" and colonize new areas "naturally." This may not always be the case, particularly for species such as decomposer macrofungi and ectomycorrhizal fungi. However, once brought into a habitat, many small species such as microbes and invertebrates usually cannot be controlled. Therefore, the active importation of such species by managers should be done thoughtfully, with scientific advice, and from local sources. The impacts of such management practices should also be evaluated through scientific experimentation, preferably before implementation. Partnerships and dialogue between scientists and practitioners will increase understanding of the behavior of plant–soil systems in urban and suburban forest remnants, focus scientific awareness on the special needs of these remnant communities, and help managers prioritize strategies that will promote the long-term viability of native species in these culturally and ecologically important habitats.

Regional planners should be encouraged to regard the landscape holistically, without political boundaries, when they assess the value of retaining the intactness of forest remnants that straddle different municipal jurisdictions. Planning recommendations that will provide greater habitat connectivity in the landscape for both aboveground and belowground organisms may promote longer viability of forests and consequently the cost-free ecosystem services they provide to our human communities. Integrating both the natural and built environments in cities and suburbs so that they function as a whole should promote not only regional biodiversity, but also more sustainable and resilient human communities as our future global environment changes.

REFERENCES

Aber, J. D., W. McDowell, K. Nadelhoffer, A. Magill, G. Berntson, M. Kamakea, S. McNulty, W. Currie, L. Rustad, and I. Fernandez. 1998. Nitrogen saturation in temperate forest ecosystems: Hypotheses revisited. *BioScience* 48:921–934.

Aber, J.D., and J.M. Melillo. 1991. *Terrestrial Ecosystems*. Orlando, Fla.: Saunders College.

Arnolds, E. 1988. The changing macromycete flora in the Netherlands. *Transactions of the British Mycological Society* 90:391–406.

Bååth, E. 1989. Effects of heavy metals in soil on microbial processes and populations (a review). *Water, Air, and Soil Pollution* 47:335–379.

Baxter, J.W., and J. Dighton. 2001. Ectomycorrhizal diversity alters growth and nutrient acquisition of grey birch (*Betula populifolia*) seedlings in host-symbiont culture conditions. *New Phytologist* 152:139–149.

Baxter, J.W., S.T.A. Pickett, M.M. Carreiro, and J. Dighton. 1999. Ectomycorrhizal diversity and community structure in oak forest stands exposed to contrasting anthropogenic impacts. *Canadian Journal of Botany* 77:771–782.

Birch, T.W., R. Rachel, and P. Kern. 1997. Identifying forest lands in urban areas in the Central Hardwood Region. In S.G. Pallardy, R. A. Cecich, E. H. Garrett, and P. S. Johnson, eds., *Proceedings of the 11th Central Hardwood Forest Conference*, 98–116. General Technical Report GTR-NC-188. Washington, D.C.: Department of Agriculture, Forest Service.

Boddy, L., D.W. Bardsley, and O.M. Gibbon. 1987. Fungal communities in attached ash branches. *New Phytologist* 107:143–154.

Butcher, G.S., W.A. Niering, W.J. Barry, and R.H. Goodwin. 1981. Equilibrium biogeography and the size of nature preserves: An avian case study. *Oecologia* 49: 29–37.

Cadisch, G., and K.E. Giller, eds. 1997. *Driven by Nature: Plant Litter Quality and Decomposition.* Wallingford, England: CAB International.

Carreiro, M.M., K. Howe, D. F. Parkhurst, and R. V. Pouyat. 1999. Variations in quality and decomposability of oak leaf litter along an urban–rural gradient. *Biology and Fertility of Soils* 30:258–268.

Carreiro, M., R. Sinsabaugh, D. Repert, and D. Parkhurst. 2000. Microbial enzyme shifts explain litter decay responses to simulated nitrogen deposition. *Ecology* 81:2359–2365.

Cole, D.N., and J.L. Marion. 1988. Recreation impacts in some riparian forests of the eastern United States. *Environmental Management* 12:99–107.

Constantinidou, H.A., and T.T. Kozlowski. 1979. Effects of sulfur dioxide and ozone on *Ulmus americana* seedlings. II. Carbohydrates, proteins, and lipids. *Canadian Journal of Botany* 57:176–184.

Corlett, R.T., and I.M. Turner. 1997. Long-term survival in tropical forest remnants in Singapore and Hong Kong. In W.F. Laurance and R.O. Biierregaard Jr., eds., *Tropical Forest Remnants: Ecology, Management, and Conservation of Fragmented Communities,* 333–345. Chicago: University of Chicago Press.

Department of Agriculture. 2000. *Summary Report: 1997 National Resources Inventory.* Rev. ed. Washington, D.C., and Ames: Natural Resources Conservation Service and Statistical Laboratory, Iowa State University.

Dighton, J., and L. Boddy. 1989. Role of fungi in nitrogen, phosphorus, and sulphur cycling in temperate forest ecosystems. In L. Boddy, R. Marchant, D.J. Read, eds., *Nitrogen Phosphorus and Sulphur Utilization by Fungi,* 269–298. New York: Cambridge University Press.

Dighton, J., J.M. Poskitt, and D.M. Howard. 1986. Changes in occurrence of basidiomycete fruit bodies during forest stand development: With specific reference to mycorrhizal species. *Transactions of the British Mycological Society* 87:163–171.

Dix, N.J., and J. Webster. 1995. *Fungal Ecology.* New York: Chapman and Hall.

Dougherty, A.B. 1992. *Major Uses of Land in the United States.* Agricultural Economics Report, no. 723. Washington, D.C.: Department of Agriculture, Natural Resources and Environment Division, Economic Research Service.

Dwyer, J.F., D.J. Nowak, M.H. Noble, and S.M. Sisinni. 2000. *Connecting People with Ecosystems in the 21st Century: An Assessment of Our Nation's Urban Forests.* Department of Agriculture Forest Service Technical Report PNW-GTR-490. Washington, D.C.: Department of Agriculture, Forest Service.

Environmental Protection Agency (EPA). 2000. *National Air Quality Trends 2000.* Washington, D.C.: EPA. Also available at: www.epa.gov/oar/aqtrnd00/.

Facelli, J.M., and S.T.A. Pickett. 1991. Plant litter: Its dynamics and effects on plant community structure. *Botanical Review* 57:1–32.

Faeth, S.H., and T.C. Kane. 1978. Urban biogeography: City parks as islands for Diptera and Coleoptera. *Oecologia* 32:127–133.

Findlay S., M.M. Carreiro, V. Krischik, and C.G. Jones 1996. Effects of damage to living plants on leaf litter quality. *Ecological Applications* 6:269–275.

Flather, C.H., and H.K. Cordell. 1995. Outdoor recreation: Historical and anticipated trends. In R.L. Knight and K.J. Gutzwiller, eds., *Wildlife and Recreationists:*

Coexistence Through Research and Management, 3–16. Covelo, Calif.: Island Press.

Foré, S.A., R.J. Hickey, J.L. Vankat, S.I. Guttman, and R.L. Schaefer. 1992. Genetic structure after forest fragmentation: A landscape ecology perspective on Acer saccharum. Canadian Journal of Botany 70:1659–1668.

Francis, A.J. 1989. Effects of acidic precipitation on soil microorganisms. In D. C. Adriano and A.H. Johnson, eds., Acidic Precipitation. Vol. 2, Biological and Ecological Effects, 305–326. New York: Springer.

Garay, I., and L. Nataf. 1982. Microarthropods as indicators of human trampling in suburban forests. In R. Bornkamm, J.A. Lee, and M.R.D. Seaward, eds., Urban Ecology, 201–207. Oxford: Blackwell.

Garden, A., and R.W. Davies. 1988. The effects of a simulated acid precipitation on leaf litter quality and the growth of a detritivore in a buffered lotic system. Environmental Pollution 52:303–313.

Garten, C. T., Jr., and P.J. Hanson. 1990. Foliar retention of ^{15}N-nitrate and ^{15}N-ammonium by red maple (Acer rubrum) and white oak (Quercus alba) leaves from simulated rain. Environmental and Experimental Botany 30:333–342.

Gatz, D.F. 1991. Urban precipitation chemistry: A review and synthesis. Atmospheric Environment 25B:1–15.

Henderson, M.T., G. Merriam, and J. Wegner. 1985. Patchy environments and species survival: Chipmunks in an agricultural mosaic. Biological Conservation 31:95–105.

Hobbs, E. 1988. Species richness of urban forest patches and implications for urban landscape diversity. Landscape Ecology 1:141–152.

Hornung, E., and K. Szlávecz. 2003. Establishment of a Mediterranean isopod (Chaetophiloscia sicula Verhoeff, 1908) in a North American temperate forest. Crustaceana Monographs 2:181–189.

Johnson, C.N. 1996. Interactions between mammals and ectomycorrhizal fungi. Trends in Ecology and Evolution 11:503–507.

Jordan, D.N., T.H. Green, A.H. Chappelka, B.G. Lockaby, R.S. Meldahl, and D.H. Gjerstad. 1991. Response of total tannins and phenolics in loblolly pine foliage exposed to ozone and acid rain. Journal of Chemical Ecology 17:505–513.

Korsós, Z., E. Hornung, K. Szlávecz, and J. Kontschán. 2002. Isopoda and Diplopoda of urban habitats: New data to the fauna of Budapest. Annales Historico-naturales Musei Nationalis Hungarici 94:193–208.

Kostel-Hughes, F., T. Young, and M.M. Carreiro. 1998. Leaf litter traits and seedling occurrence in forests along an urban–rural gradient. Urban Ecosystems 2:263–278.

Kuss, F.R., and C.N. Hall. 1991. Ground flora trampling studies: Five years after closure. Environmental Management 15:715–727.

Lacey, J. 1996. Spore dispersal—Its role in ecology and disease: The British contribution to fungal aerobiology. Mycological Research 100:641–660.

Last, F.T., J. Dighton, and P.A. Mason. 1987. Successions of sheathing mycorrhizal fungi. Trends in Ecology and Evolution 2:159–161.

Last, F. T., P. A. Mason, J. Wilson, and J. W. Deacon. 1983. Fine roots and sheathing mycorrhizas: Their formation, function, and dynamics. Plant and Soil 71:9–21.

Latus, C., H. Forstel, and F. Fuhr. 1990. Quantitative measurement of NO_2 uptake and metabolism by sunflower plants. Naturwissenschaften 77:283–285.

Liddle, M. 1975. A selective review of the ecological effects of human trampling on natural ecosystems. Biological Conservation 7:17–36.

Lovett, G. M., M. M. Traynor, R. V. Pouyat, M. M. Carreiro, W. Zhu, and J. W. Baxter. 2000. Atmospheric deposition to oak forests along an urban–rural gradient. *Environmental Science and Technology* 34:4294–4300.

Mader, H. J. 1984. Animal habitat isolation by roads and agricultural fields. *Biological Conservation* 29:81–96.

Matlack, G. R. 1993. Sociological edge effects: Spatial distribution of human impact in suburban forest fragments. *Environmental Management* 17:829–835.

McDonnell, M. J., S. T. A. Pickett, and R. V. Pouyat. 1993. The application of the ecological gradient paradigm to the study of urban effects. In M. J. McDonnell and S. T. A. Pickett, eds., *Humans as Components of Ecosystems: Subtle Human Effects and the Ecology of Populated Areas*, 175–189. New York: Springer.

Molina, R., and J. M. Trappe. 1982. Patterns of ectomycorrhizal specificity and potential among Pacific Northwest conifers and fungi. *Forest Science* 28:423–458.

Niemalä, J., D. J. Kotze, S. Venn, L. Penev, I. Stoyanov, J. Spence, D. Hartley, and E. Montes de Oca. 2002. Carabid beetle assemblages (Coleoptera, Carabidae) across urban–rural gradients: An international comparison. *Landscape Ecology* 17:387–401.

Oke, T. R. 1995. The heat island characteristics of the urban boundary layer: Characteristics, causes, and effects. In J. E. Cermak, A. G. Davenport, E. J. Plate, and D. X. Viegas, eds., *Wind Climate in Cities*, 81–107. Dordrecht, Netherlands: Kluwer Academic.

Pouyat, R. V., M. J. McDonnell, and S. T. A. Pickett. 1997. Litter decomposition and nitrogen mineralization in oak stands along an urban–rural land use gradient. *Urban Ecosystems* 1:117–131.

Pouyat, R. V., R. W. Parmelee, and M. M. Carreiro. 1994. Environmental effects on forest soil invertebrate and fungal densities in oak stands along an urban–rural land use gradient. *Pedobiologia* 38:385–399.

Prescott, C. E., and D. Parkinson. 1985. Effects of sulphur pollution on rates of litter decomposition in a pine forest. *Canadian Journal of Botany* 63:1436–1443.

Rebele, F. 1994. Urban ecology and special features of urban ecosystems. *Global Ecology and Biogeography Letters* 4:173–187.

Santas, P. 1986. Soil communities along a gradient of urbanization. *Revue d'Ecologie et Biologie du Sol* 23:367–380.

Saunders, D. A., R. J. Hobbs, and C. R. Margules. 1991. Biological consequences of ecosystem fragmentation: A review. *Conservation Biology* 5:18–32.

Shaw, P. J. A., J. Dighton, J. Poskitt, and A. R. McLeod. 1992. The effects of sulphur dioxide and ozone on the mycorrhizas of Scots pine and Norway spruce in a field fumigation system. *Mycological Research* 96:785–791.

Smith, S. E., and D. J. Read. 1997. *Mycorrhizal Symbiosis*. 2d ed.. San Diego: Academic Press.

Smith, W. H. 1990. *Air Pollution and Forests: Interactions Between Air Contaminants and Forest Ecosystems*. 2d ed. New York: Springer.

Steinberg, D. A., R. V. Pouyat, R. W. Parmelee, and P. M. Groffman. 1997. Earthworm abundance and nitrogen mineralization rates along an urban-rural land use gradient. *Soil Biology and Biochemistry* 29:427–430.

Swift, M. J., O. W. Heal, and J. M. Anderson. 1979. *Decomposition in Terrestrial Ecosystems*. Studies in Ecology, vol. 5. Berkeley: University of California Press.

Turner, B. L., II, W. C. Clark, R. W. Kates, J. F. Richards, J. T. Mathews, and W. B. Meyer, eds. 1990. *The Earth as Transformed by Human Action: Global and Regional*

Changes in the Biosphere over the Past 300 Years. New York: Cambridge University Press.

Vitousek, P. M. 1994. Beyond global warming: Ecology and global change. *Ecology* 75:1861–1876.

Vitousek, P. M., and R. W. Howarth. 1991. Nitrogen limitation on land and sea: How can it occur? *Biogeochemistry* 13:87–115.

Waring, R. H., and W. H. Schlesinger. 1985. *Forest Ecosystems: Concepts and Management.* San Diego: Academic Press.

Weaver, T., and D. Dale. 1978. Trampling effects of hikers, motorcycles, and horses in meadows and forests. *Journal of Applied Ecology* 15:451–457.

Wilcove, D. S. 1987. From fragmentation to extinction. *Natural Areas Journal* 7:23–29.

Wolfenbarger, D. O. 1946. Dispersion of small organisms. *American Midland Naturalist* 35:1–152.

7

■ ■

SPRAWL AND DISEASE

Fred W. Koontz and Peter Daszak

It is becoming increasingly clear that demographic and anthropogenic environmental changes play a central role in disease ecology in social-ecological systems (Aron and Patz 2001; Daszak, Cunningham, and Hyatt 2001). Urbanization and the inevitable degradation of the environment that ensues disrupt ecosystem processes and ultimately threaten human health and the well-being of all species of animals and plants (Grifo and Rosenthal 1997; Vitousek et al. 1997; Aguirre et al. 2002; Chivian 2002). The link between health and the environment was first described in Hippocrates's "Air, Water, Places," in which he discussed the influence of climate, water supply, and sanitation on human health (cited in McCally 2002). The connections between disease and the environment became readily apparent to ancient civilizations when thousands of city dwellers died during outbreaks of smallpox, tuberculosis, and measles. Since these early times, scientists and health practitioners have often focused their research on how disease transmission is linked to environmental degradation, health practices, and public policies. Today's urban areas and sprawling metropolises also provide examples of the connections between the environment and ecological health. For example, the incidence of cholera, hemorrhagic dengue, malaria, rabies, West Nile virus, and yellow fever have increased in urban centers in recent years. A growing number of ecologists, veterinarians, and public-health physicians are focusing on unraveling the subtle, complex, and often overlooked interactions between health and human-induced environmental change, including the diseases of people, animals, and plants that are facilitated by urban sprawl and its collateral human activities (Daszak, Cunningham, and Hyatt 2000; Aguirre et al. 2002; Tabor 2002). Urban-planning efforts would benefit greatly from the integration of the lessons learned by these researchers and the ecological health guidelines they are setting forth.

ANTHROPOGENIC CHANGE AND EMERGING DISEASES

From the early stages of urbanization to contemporary urban sprawl, disease agents have taken advantage of empty niches and new opportunities, including climate change, made available in landscapes disturbed by humans and their activities (Aron and Patz 2001). As humans modify their surrounding environments, increase their population density, and encroach into new areas, predator–parasite–prey interactions, competitive dynamics, community structure, and other ecological processes are perturbed. This perturbation opens up novel microbial niches, drastically alters the dynamics of hosts and pathogens, and increases the host contact rate within or between populations and species. Because of the diversity of pathogen types and strains and their ability to move into new host species or to evolve rapidly or both, strains of known or previously unknown pathogens quickly fill new niches, leading to emerging diseases.

Emerging infectious diseases (EIDs) are defined as diseases that have recently expanded in geographic or host range, recently infected new host species, recently evolved or been discovered, or recently increased in pathogenicity or impact on host populations (Lederberg, Shope, and Oaks 1992; Morse 1993). The process of emergence is essentially a form of anthropogenically driven natural selection, and the key factor that links all EIDs known to science is that they are driven by human-induced environmental changes (Morse 1993; Daszak, Cunningham, and Hyatt 2001). Using the criteria that define EIDs, recent investigators have shown that domestic animals, wildlife, and plants are also affected by emerging diseases (Anderson and Morales 1994; Brown and Bolin 2000; Daszak, Cunningham, and Hyatt 2000). In all these categories, emergence is driven by anthropogenic change, including cases fueled by sprawl—for example, introduction of alien species, encroachment of human populations into natural areas, and agricultural intensification (Daszak, Cunningham, and Hyatt 2000, 2001).

Lederberg, Shope, and Oakes (1992), Morse (1993), and Daszak, Cunningham, and Hyatt (2000) have listed the key drivers of disease emergence as human travel; transport of domestic animals, wildlife, and animal products; agricultural changes (e.g., intensification); changes to medical and veterinary practices (e.g., increased use of antibiotic drugs); and encroachment of people into wildlife habitat and other forms of urbanization. We focus here on the role of modern urban sprawl and habitat encroachment in driving emerging diseases that threaten human, animal, and plant health in social-ecological systems (e.g., metropolitan regions). Ever since the first cities were built, emerging diseases have plagued people—the link between environmental degradation and human health is not new. What is new is a greater appreciation of the links between environmental degradation and the health of all species, not just humans.

In cities, humans and their domesticated animals began to dwell together at high population densities, leading to the first recorded cases of emerging diseases. The close contact between humans and domestic cattle allowed cattle viruses (e.g., rinderpest and cowpox virus) to shift hosts and to evolve into new, devastating infections in humans (measles and smallpox, respectively). The unprecedented dense human populations produced enough susceptible hosts each year to sustain these viruses continuously. Dobson and Carper (1996) noted that repeated outbreaks of these and other novel pathogens occurred simultaneously with reports of the biblical plagues. These pathogens were supremely preadapted to urban ecology so that repeated cycles of measles outbreaks persisted until the advent of vaccination in the twentieth century.

In the past few decades, antimicrobials and vaccines had all but halted the impact of infectious diseases on urban populations in developed countries. However, a new phase of disease emergence recently began, associated with antibiotic resistance, air travel, and previously unknown pathogens, causing new diseases such as Lyme disease, hantavirus pulmonary syndrome, acquired immunodeficiency syndrome (AIDS), and severe acute respiratory syndrome (SARS). Although urban populations in northern countries are dealing with these threats, accelerating urbanization in the tropics has led to the emergence of different diseases. Here, shanty towns and slums with dense populations, poor water supplies, and inadequate sanitation create ideal habitat for vector-borne diseases such as dengue, filariasis, and malaria (Knudsen and Slooff 1992; Rodhain 1996). Dengue hemorrhagic fever, a new disease caused when multiple strains of dengue flavivirus continually circulate within a population, is an especially serious public-health threat. Increased human migrations into cities, the expansions of tropical urban centers, and alterations to sanitation and climate have led to the emergence of dengue hemorrhagic fever as a public-health issue. Dengue currently threatens 2.5 billion people and causes illness in 60 million people, of which 30,000 die each year (Rodhain 1996). Control of these infections relies heavily on environmental management and education because drugs and vaccines are either unavailable or too costly (Knudsen and Slooff 1992).

URBAN SPRAWL AND DISEASE

Late-twentieth-century sprawl has provided yet another series of niches for microbes to exploit. From a microbial viewpoint, sprawl is a complex form of landscape modification that fosters closer connections among wildlife, domestic animals, and humans; fragmentation of habitat; pollution; agricultural changes; and deforestation. Making the links between sprawl and disease requires understanding how these complex environmental changes alter transmission rates between and within populations. Recent work on Lyme disease in the northeastern United States has revealed such complexity and shown a definitive connection among sprawl, reduction of species richness, and disease emergence (Ostfeld and Keesing 2000a, 2000b; Johnson and Klemens, chapter 2, this volume).

One of the key features of sprawl is habitat fragmentation as blocks of habitat are replaced with agricultural and built environments (Main, Roka, and Noss 1999). Fragmentation reduces the biodiversity of woodland avian and rodent species in the northeastern United States. LoGiudice and colleagues (2003) and Allan, Keesing, and Ostfeld (2003) have demonstrated a clear link among habitat fragmentation, reduced mammalian biodiversity, increased density of white-footed mice (an important reservoir of the Lyme disease pathogen), and increased incidence of Lyme disease in human populations. A more direct association between sprawl and disease risk occurs where expansion of suburban development brings humans in close proximity to new *zoonotic reservoirs* (animal species that act as the natural host for human pathogens). This association has serious conservation consequences, even when zoonotic transmission is rare. For example, the same disease known as the Black Death in Europe in the fourteenth century, the plague, is still emerging in some parts of the United States. The causative agent, the bacterium *Yersinia pestis*, was introduced into North America via San Francisco in 1899/1900. As it spread eastward, regular outbreaks in prairie dog colonies served as a reservoir for the pathogen (Cully et al. 1997). For unknown reasons, it has not crossed the hundredth meridian, but human population expansion in the intermountain west and the Rocky Mountain front has led to an increasing number of human cases of pneumonic and bubonic plague. In places such as Boulder, Colorado, developers and farmers cull or relocate prairie dogs at great expense. Ironically, this relocation has led to another form of disease emergence: two recent human cases of a fungal disease (blastomycosis) are thought to have been acquired from soil-dwelling spores during relocation programs ("Blastomycosis" 1999). Despite these incidences, human plague cases in the United States amount to little more than a handful annually.

The health effects of sprawl on wildlife and plant populations are poorly understood. It is certain that expanding human populations always bring domestic animals and ornamental plants with them; therefore, it is likely that these companions make contact with wild species and affect ecological health in areas of sprawl. For example, increased contact with domestic animals allows transmission of diseases such as bovine TB, canine distemper, and toxoplasmosis to a diverse array of wildlife species (Daszak, Cunningham, and Hyatt 2000). This form of anthropogenic introduction of alien parasites (*pathogen pollution*) is the most commonly cited driver of disease emergence in wildlife (Dobson and Foufopoulos 2001) and is a significant cause of wildlife mortality and population decline (Daszak, Cunningham, and Hyatt 2000).

Pathogen pollution from ornamental plants and the invasive spread of the exotic plants themselves undoubtedly affect wild plants and the natural ecological communities they form. The disease agent of "sudden oak death" (which is infecting many oaks in the western United States) is also found in laurel and rhododendrons, which are popular plant choices for new homes and are used to make Christmas wreaths; it is suspected that shipments of these plants from California was the route for sudden oak death to spread to Oregon. When the decorative evergreen ornamental hemlock is shipped, it unfortunately sometimes carries and spreads the hemlock woolly adelgid (*Adelges tsugae*), an invasive sap-sucking insect originally from Asia that is destroying much of the hemlock forests in the eastern United States.

Infectious diseases are just one manifestation of the impact of sprawl on health. For example, with sprawl comes road construction and heavy dependence on automobile travel. Air pollution, asthma, automobile crashes, and pedestrian injury increase significantly in sprawl regions (Frumkin 2002). Also, somewhat ironically, car-loving suburbanites appear to get less exercise than city dwellers, which some posit has led to increased obesity and a variety of other detrimental health consequences. Car, truck, boat, and train strikes of wildlife also can be significant, even threatening some endangered species (e.g., Florida panther [*Puma concolor coryii*] and Florida manatee [*Trichechus manatus latirostris*]) with extinction. The nutritional effects and health consequences that anthropogenic food sources (e.g., trash, pet food, and wild bird feed) are having on wild animals has been little studied, but it is likely to be detrimental in many cases. Other unhealthy by-products of sprawl that can weaken immune systems and lead to disease include compromised water quality and increased toxic burdens from lawn and agricultural pesticides.

SPRAWL, HABITAT ENCROACHMENT, AND DISEASE EMERGENCE

Sprawl inevitably involves encroachment of humans into natural areas. This encroachment brings people, domesticated animals, and urban-adapted species (e.g., pigeons, cockroaches, Canada geese) in closer contact with known and unknown pathogens harbored by wild species (figure 7.1). For example, encroachment effectively underpinned the emergence of AIDS. Analysis of the phylogeny of the AIDS-causing viruses HIV 1 and 2 suggests that they evolved from two separate progenitor viruses that moved into human hosts dur-

FIGURE 7.1. An increased amount of grass from suburban lawns has led to an overabundance of Canada geese (*Branta canadensis*) in the northeastern United States, which in turn has threatened water reservoirs and humans with *E. coli* infection. (Photo by Fred W. Koontz)

ing the early twentieth century: simian immunodeficiency virus (SIV) from the chimpanzee (*Pan troglodytes*) for HIV 1, and an SIV from the sooty mangabey (*Cercocebus torquatus*) for HIV 2 (Hahn et al. 2000). Socioeconomic factors, changes in human migration, and human social behavior have been implicated in the emergence of the AIDS pandemic. However, central to these implications is extensive road building in West Africa, an increased volume of the bushmeat trade, and other consequences of human expansion into wildlife habitat (Hahn et al. 2000; Wolfe et al. 2000).

A series of novel zoonotic viruses have recently emerged from fruit bat reservoirs in Australia and Malaysia (Mackenzie 1999). The most significant of these is Nipah virus, which emerged in 1999 to kill more than 100 people in Malaysia and Singapore (Chua et al. 2000). This virus is a particular threat because of its high fatality rate (greater than 40 percent) and the lack of an adequate treatment or a vaccine. Initial investigations showed that almost all human cases were in people associated with the pork industry in Malaysia, workers either on pig farms or in slaughterhouses. Pig farms have become more intensified over the past few decades, and the first farm identified with this emerging disease in Malaysia, for example, housed 30,000 pigs. This farm was situated on the edge of a rapidly expanding industrial town in primary forest habitat for fruit bats, the reservoir for Nipah virus.

Encroachment and the "spillover" of domestic animals' pathogens into wildlife populations may have devastating consequences for wildlife. In some situations, for example, domestic animal hosts outnumber native wildlife hosts (e.g., canine distemper and rabies in African wild dogs). These domestic surrogates act as hosts, enabling the pathogen to avoid being regulated by relatively low numbers of natural hosts; consequently, the disease can drive the smaller populations of wild animals to virtual extinction (Cleaveland and Dye 1995). In the urban sprawl setting, new infections of birds, such as mycoplasmal conjunctivitis in house finches in the United States and salmonellosis in passerines in the United Kingdom, have emerged apparently as a product of the artificially high density and rate of interspecies contact that backyard feeders foster (Fischer et al. 1997; Kirkwood 1998).

CONCLUSION

Sprawl influences diseases of humans, animals, and plants in ways similar to other forms of urbanization and anthropogenic environmental change. A research priority is to understand disease responses that are specific to sprawl regions (areas with low to moderate numbers of people, who are distributed in spatially discontinuous patterns across mixed land-use landscapes). It seems likely that in sprawl landscapes, the juxtaposition of human habitation, agricultural areas, and natural areas makes these regions especially prone to emerging diseases. Also, it will be important to investigate more thoroughly the effects of habitat fragmentation on vector biology and disease ecology (Allan, Keesing, and Ostfeld 2003). Knowledge of disease ecology and ecosystem interrelationships in sprawl landscapes ought to be integrated into metropolitan and suburban regional planning activities, public-health policies, and wildlife conservation strategies.

In order to study disease ecology and to apply the results to biodiversity conservation in urban sprawl areas, transdisciplinary and integrative approaches are required. The importance of understanding the physical, human, and biological dimensions of the social-ecological systems that encompass sprawl regions has to be emphasized for regional planners, public-health officials, and conservation biologists. *Conservation medicine* is a new discipline that offers a methodological approach for such studies (for a review, see Aguirre et al. 2002). Conservation medicine strives to understand the links among anthropogenic environmental change; the health of all species, including humans; and the conservation of biodiversity. Practitioners conduct collaborative scientific

research in these fields and use the outcomes to inform policy, develop cur-
ricula, and formulate practical solutions to environmental threats that affect
these links.

A conceptual framework that uses many ideas of conservation medicine and
that is recommended here for studying ecological health in urban sprawl regions
is the *bioscape paradigm*. Koontz (2004) defines a *bioscape* as "a social-ecological
landscape whose geographic boundary is set by a common sphere of human influence, and it serves as a regional unit for integrating the natural and built environments through science, natural resource management, public health policy,
local values, and other activities required to ensure ecological health and sustainability." A bioscape is both a way to describe a particular place and a framework
to integrate the components necessary for its ecological health. Geographically, a
bioscape is a region bounded by a common sphere of human influence and composed of a mosaic of areas with varying levels of human disturbance. A bioscape
also serves as a human-oriented ecosystem for regional management and care
of both the natural and built environments. Successful bioscapes are marked
by a strong local sense of place linked to an understanding of the connections
among biodiversity, health, ecosystem function, and sustainability. In successful
bioscapes, policies exist to protect biodiversity, maintain ecosystems, and safeguard public health. Bioscapes can vary in geographic scale (e.g., towns, metropolitan regions, states, recreational regions) and can be hierarchically nested and
overlapping. The idea behind setting boundaries by a "common sphere of human
influence," as opposed to by natural boundaries (e.g., watersheds or ecoregions),
is to increase the ease of connecting human decision making to ecological stewardship and public-health policy.

Urban planners, especially those designing strategic plans at regional scales
(Leccese and McCormick 2000), would benefit by incorporating design features that protect nature and its ecological functions *across landscapes.* We posit
that in human-dominated regions, such design elements are essential to ensure
the long-term health of all species, including humans. This realization gets at
the core of the bioscape approach and at the need for both conservation medicine and more ecologically integrated, regional planning strategies.

The traditional zoning approach of compartmentalizing land use into human
built areas (e.g., residential, light commercial, heavy industry) and more natural
open space is unlikely to shelter adequate amounts of biodiversity to generate
sufficient ecological services required to ensure health. The problem is that not
enough open space is being designated in urbanized city regions (usually less
than 5–10 percent of land area), and urbanized parks are often further degraded
by multiple demands and habitat fragmentation. This is not surprising because
open space in both urban and sprawling suburban areas is created primarily for
recreation and human relaxation. Only recently have some planners realized

the essential connections among biodiversity, health, ecological function, and ecoservices (Grifo and Rosenthal 1997; Vitousek et al. 1997; Aguirre et al. 2002; Chivian 2002), all of which parks and other open lands potentially contribute.

Unfortunately from a health perspective, in most cases it appears that insufficient open space is being set aside. Although most contemporary urban and suburban park systems do save representative examples of species and habitats, we believe that they do not protect enough individual animals and plants specimens to provide for ecologically functional landscapes. In other words, from an ecological health perspective, not only is the number of species important, but the number of individuals as well. Ecoservices are a function of biodiversity and biomass.

Urban planners, health professionals, and environmental scientists can work together to safeguard the health of all species, including humans, by devising strategies across metropolitan regions to protect biodiversity, ecological function, and ecoservices. Although, of course, traditional park systems are beneficial for many reasons, we also recommend an equally shared focus on saving ecological processes "between the parks." One new design principle, for example, will be the need to blur the boundaries between the natural and human-built environments (e.g., "green rooftop projects" and "backyard sanctuary programs"). To protect health and to manage disease in sprawling metropolitan regions, humans ultimately must find improved ways to redesign anthropogenic habitats so that their use is compatible with a broad array of species and individuals. A new science that explores the mutual survival of people and all species in shared habitats is required; Rosenzweig (2003) calls this approach "reconciliation ecology."

REFERENCES

Aguirre, A. A., R. S. Ostfeld, G. M. Tabor, C. House, and M. C. Pearl, eds. 2002. *Conservation Medicine: Ecological Health in Practice*. New York: Oxford University Press.

Allan, B. F., F. Keesing, and R. S. Ostfeld. 2003. Effect of forest fragmentation on Lyme disease risk. *Conservation Biology* 17:267–272.

Anderson, P. K., and F. J. Morales. 1994. The emergence of new plant diseases—The case of insect-transmitted plant viruses. *Annals of the New York Academy of Sciences* 740:181–194.

Aron, J. L., and J. A. Patz, eds. 2001. *Ecosystem Change and Public Health*. Baltimore: Johns Hopkins University Press.

Blastomycosis acquired occupationally during prairie dog relocation—Colorado, 1998. 1999. *Morbidity and Mortality Weekly Report* 48:98–100.

Brown, C. C., and C. Bolin. 2000. *Emerging Diseases of Animals*. Washington, D.C.: American Society for Microbiology Press.

Chivian, E. 2002. Species loss and ecosystem disruption. In M. McCally, ed., *Life*

Support: The Environment and Human Health, 119–133. Cambridge, Mass.: MIT Press.

Chua, K. B., W. J. Bellini, P. A. Rota, B. H. Harcourt, A. Tamin, S. K. Lam, T. G. Ksiazek, P. E. Rollin, S. R. Zaki, W. J. Shieh, C. S. Goldsmith, D. Gubler, J. T. Roehrig, B. T. Eaton, A. R. Gould, J. Olson, H. Field, P. Daniels P, A. E. Ling, C. J. Peters, L. J. Anderson, and B. J. Mahy. 2000. Nipah virus: A recently emergent deadly Paramyxovirus. *Science* 288:1432–1435.

Cleaveland, S., and C. Dye. 1995. Maintenance of a microparasite infecting several host species: Rabies in the Serengeti. *Parasitology* 111:S33–S47.

Cully, J. F., A. M. Barnes, T. J. Quan, and G. Maupin. 1997. Dynamics of plague in a Gunnison's prairie dog colony complex from New Mexico. *Journal of Wildlife Diseases* 33:706–719.

Daszak P., A. A. Cunningham, and A. D. Hyatt. 2000. Emerging infectious diseases of wildlife—Threats to biodiversity and human health. *Science* 287:443–449.

———. 2001. Anthropogenic environmental change and the emergence of infectious diseases in wildlife. *Acta Tropica* 78:103–116.

Dobson, A. P., and E. R. Carper. 1996. Infectious diseases and human population history. *BioScience* 46:115–126.

Dobson, A., and J. Foufopoulos. 2001. Emerging infectious pathogens of wildlife. *Philosophical Transactions of the Royal Society of London, Series B, Biological Sciences* 356:1001–1012.

Fischer, J. R., D. E. Stallknecht, M. P. Luttrell, A. A. Dhondt, and K. A. Converse. 1997. Mycoplasmal conjunctivitis in wild songbirds: The spread of a new contagious disease in a mobile host population. *Emerging Infectious Diseases* 3:69–72.

Frumkin, H. 2002. Urban sprawl and public health. *Public Health Reports* 117:201–217.

Grifo, F., and J. Rosenthal, eds. 1997. *Biodiversity and Human Health*. Washington, D.C.: Island Press.

Hahn, B. H., G. M. Shaw, K. M. de Cock, and P. M. Sharp. 2000. AIDS as a zoonosis: Scientific and public health implications. *Science* 287:607–614.

Kirkwood, J. K. 1998. Population density and infectious disease at bird tables. *Veterinary Record* 142:468.

Knudsen, A. B., and R. Slooff. 1992. Vector-borne disease problems in rapid urbanization—New approaches to vector control. *Bulletin of the World Health Organization* 70:1–6.

Koontz, F. 2004. What is a bioscape? Available at: www.nybioscape.org/about/concepts. htm (accessed December 16, 2004)

Leccese, M., and K. McCormick, eds. 2000. *Charter of the New Urbanism*. New York: McGraw-Hill.

Lederberg, J., R. E. Shope, and S. C. Oakes Jr. 1992. *Emerging Infections: Microbial Threats to Health in the United States*. Washington, D.C.: Institute of Medicine, National Academy Press.

LoGiudice, K., R. S. Ostfeld, K. A. Schmidt, and F. Keesing. 2003. The ecology of infectious disease: Effects of host diversity and community composition on Lyme disease risk. *Proceedings of the National Academy of Sciences* (United States) 100:567–571.

Mackenzie, J. S. 1999. Emerging viral diseases: An Australian perspective. *Emerging Infectious Diseases* 5:1–8.

Main, M. B., F. M. Roka, and R. F. Noss. 1999. Evaluating costs of conservation. *Conservation Biology* 13:1262–1272.

McCally, M. 2002. Environment, health, and risk. In M. McCally, ed., *Life Support: The Environment and Human Health*, 1–14. Cambridge, Mass.: MIT Press.

Morse, S. S. 1993. Examining the origins of emerging viruses. In S. S. Morse, ed., *Emerging Viruses*, 10–28. New York: Oxford University Press.

Ostfeld, R. S., and F. Keesing. 2000a. Biodiversity and disease risk: The case of Lyme disease. *Conservation Biology* 14:722–728.

——. 2000b. The role of biodiversity in the ecology of vector-borne zoonotic diseases. *Canadian Journal of Zoology* 78:2061–2078.

Rodhain, F. 1996. Worldwide situation of dengue. *Bulletin de la Société de Pathologie Exotique* 89:87–90.

Rosenzweig, M. L. 2003. Reconciliation ecology and the future of species diversity. *Oryx* 37:194–205.

Tabor, G. M. 2002. Defining conservation medicine. In A. A. Aguirre, R. S. Ostfeld, G. M. Tabor, C. House, and M. C. Pearl, eds., *Conservation Medicine: Ecological Health in Practice*, 8–16. New York: Oxford University Press.

Vitousek, P. M., H. A. Mooney, J. Lubchenco, and J. M. Meillo. 1997. Human domination of earth's ecosystems. *Science* 277:494–499.

Wolfe, N. D., N. E. Mpoudi, J. Gockowski, P. K. Muchaal, C. Nolte, T. A. Prosser, J. N. Torimiro, S. F. Weise, and D. S. Burke. 2000. Deforestation, hunting, and the ecology of microbial emergence. *Global Change and Human Health* 1:10–25.

PART III
SPRAWL AND SPECIES

8

■ ■

SPRAWL AND SPECIES
WITH LIMITED DISPERSAL ABILITIES

Diane L. Byers and Joseph C. Mitchell

Many plants and animals have life history strategies that include limited dispersal abilities of adults and offspring. Among plants, many species produce propagules that are dispersed by gravity, and others have their seeds dispersed by animals that may have limited mobility. Such plants may be limited in their geographic distribution because they cannot easily disperse across the landscape, whereas wind-dispersed plant species, which may disperse for greater distances, tend to be more widely distributed. Unlike birds, large mammals, bats, or flying insects, many animals cannot travel long distances. Those with limited ability to disperse include many amphibians, reptiles, small mammals, and invertebrates. Populations of these less-mobile plant and animal species risk decline or local extinction in urban and suburban landscapes in part because they cannot escape the impacts of local sprawl. Many species occur in nature as *metapopulations* (a network of populations connected by movements across the landscape) where the viability of each individual population depends on the exchange of individuals among them (Hanski 1999). However, when habitat fragments are surrounded by barriers and inhospitable habitats, migration is limited or completely prevented. Such landscapes characterize urban and suburban areas where natural habitats are interspersed with human settlement, creating a patchwork of isolated and usually small fragments of suitable habitat.

Urban and suburban development involves a two-step process, with the first being the destruction of natural systems or habitats and the second being the replacement of those natural systems with artificial ones that favor the welfare or wealth of humans (Soulé 1991). Species with limited dispersal abilities are dependent on the quantity and quality of these natural systems. As development occurs, the rate of loss of interior forest habitat and the increased amount of habitat edge (known as the *edge effect*; Johnson and Klemens, chapter 2, this volume) have impacts as great as the complete loss of natural areas (Swenson and Franklin 2000). Further contributing to the edge effect is the varying size of many fragments, which also may be subjected to trampling and collecting of native species (Bhuju and Ohsawa 1998; Young and Jarvis 2001). If natural-habitat fragments are isolated from others, then populations within them are likely to be isolated. Such a scenario leads to unstable populations with low survivorship, low reproductive success, reduced genetic diversity, and declining populations. Environments with reduced native species diversity also are more susceptible to encroachment by invasive species (Knops et al. 1999). Species with limited dispersal abilities are among the first to disappear from the landscape during urbanization and as a result may become endangered and threatened (Dodd 1997; Duncan and Young 2000).

The aim of this chapter is to review the effects of sprawl on plants and animals with limited dispersal abilities. First, we discuss the primary effects of initial habitat loss and fragmentation and a concomitant decrease in connectivity among habitat patches. We show that these topics are best understood conceptually as landscape-level effects that include the nature of the large-scale environment between patches (the matrix). Second, we discuss the consequences of such changes for populations living in isolated fragments. We focus on environmental, demographic, and genetic dynamics that determine the viability within a patch of populations of species with limited dispersal ability. Given the low quality of the matrix environment and the limited potential for dispersal among fragments, most of these species will be confined to remnant patches; thus an understanding of the dynamics within a patch is most critical for their conservation. Third, we discuss the secondary effects of problems such as introduced species, subsidized predators, and direct human interactions (for further discussion of these topics, see Mitchell and Klemens 2000; Johnson and Klemens, chapter 2, this volume). Primary and secondary effects of sprawl integrate over a wide range of landscape and habitat scales to create environments that hinder many native species' survival and population viability. Plant and animal interactions are dynamic and reflect normal ecological processes of communities if such interactions are intact. We point out that species with limitations to dispersal are particularly vulnerable to a wide array of forces associated with sprawl. Last, we suggest some ways of managing populations, their habitats, and the landscape in order to lessen the impacts of sprawl on poorly dispersed species.

LANDSCAPE-SCALE EFFECTS OF HABITAT LOSS AND FRAGMENTATION

The complete loss of habitat as a result of development causes the elimination of populations of native plants and animals. Many, if not all, of these plants and animals are killed on site because they do not have the ability to relocate out of harm's way. Those that remain are located in the patches or fragments of habitat that may be left by the development process. A variety of effects occur in and on the landscape following such changes. These effects include the degradation of the physical quality of the environment, development of unsuitable areas between fragments for human use, and inhospitable nature of the landscape between the fragments that can limit dispersal between them (figure 8.1). Indeed, the species and individuals remaining in the fragments resulting from urbanization and suburbanization are often those that by chance were present in those patches of habitat left intact.

LUCK OF THE DRAW

Because many species are limited in their ability to disperse and do not occur widely, the diversity of species remaining in a habitat fragment will depend initially on which plants and animals happened to live in that patch of land before isolation. This resulting assemblage of native species will be a subset of those that occurred in the area historically. Species with specialized ecological requirements and those that were not widespread are usually underrepresented in isolated fragments. Furthermore, species that have limited dispersal abilities will be underrepresented in the pool of potential migrants to any isolated fragment.

Inherent rarity, as termed by Maina and Howe (2000), refers to species whose populations occurred infrequently in communities even before fragmentation. Such species are likely to become rare in habitat patches following fragmentation and are often most vulnerable to extinction. Fragmentation, particularly if the patches are small, favors only the more mobile and more common species (Maina and Howe 2000). For example, after European settlement and urbanization in New Zealand, rare plants were more likely to become extirpated than those that occupied a broader range of habitats (Duncan and Young 2000). Gopher frogs (*Rana capito*) were not found among amphibians studied in a Florida suburban area because the fragment lacked the sandhill habitat and the gopher tortoise (*Gopherus polyphemus*) burrows used by this rare frog species (Delis, Mushinsky, and McCoy 1996). Rare species or populations in very small isolated areas often occur in small populations. Such units are subject to random fluctuations in environmental quality, survivorship, reproduction, and genetic diversity in addition to habitat loss and edge effects. These fluctuations contribute to rare species' being especially sensitive to extinction during and after habitat loss and fragmentation.

CHANGES IN ENVIRONMENTAL QUALITY

Urbanization and suburbanization result in habitat patches that differ in size, environmental quality, and degree of isolation from one another (Young and

 (a)

(b)

FIGURE 8.1. Effects of urban
sprawl on natural ecosystems
in Henrico County, Virginia.
(*a*) Note the loss of habitat;
fragmentation; potential habitat
degradation from chemicals
(oils, fertilizers, herbicides, pesticides); barriers to dispersal of
frogs, turtles, snakes, and small
mammals; density of roads;
and likely changes in thermal
characteristics of the area. (*b*) A
population of pink lady slippers
(*Cyperipedium acaule*) existed
in the 1970s and 1980s but is
now locally extirpated. (Photos
by Joseph C. Mitchell: [*a*] 2001;
[*b*] May 1973)

Jarvis 2001). The nature of the environment between habitat fragments (the *matrix*) and size and type of natural connections between them, if they exist at all, are highly variable. The loss of intact interior habitats within patches and the amount of increased edge around them may occur more quickly than the direct loss of habitat owing to fragmentation and urban development (Swenson and Franklin 2000). Hence, with increased edge habitat, the landscape becomes dominated by the type and quality of the surrounding matrix environment. As urbanization of areas with forests and other natural habitats proceeds, changes in thermal dynamics occur because of decreases in the size of patches and increases in the amount of impervious surfaces and distance from forests (Fuller 2001). Such changes usually lead to higher temperatures, which may alter daily and seasonal activity patterns and survivorship of species remaining in the area. Simply reducing forest cover causes local extinctions of some amphibians. Wood frogs (*Rana sylvatica*), spotted salamanders (*Ambystoma maculatum*), and red-spotted newts (*Notophthalmus viridescens*) were absent from forest tracts with less than 30 percent and 50 percent cover in urban and suburban gradients in southern Connecticut (Gibbs 1998).

Other environmental-quality changes include nitrogen runoff from fertilizers on lawns, golf courses, and landscaped areas and trampling of natural habitats from increased rate of human visitation per area (Bhuju and Ohsawa 1998; Brown and Valiela 2001). The number of species of fishes, amphibians, and reptiles were substantially lower in urban Maryland than in rural areas owing to degraded environments, especially those with greater than 25 percent impervious surface (Broward et al. 1999). Fertilizers and household herbicides applied to lawns and golf courses have been shown to cause amphibian malformations, individual mortality, and sublethal effects (Cowman and Mazanti 2000; Sparling, Fellers, and McConnell 2001). Based on an abundance of recent literature, we can reasonably conclude that historic and modern uses of numerous chemicals have caused declines in populations of vertebrates and invertebrates in urban and suburban areas worldwide.

LIMITATIONS ON DISPERSAL IN FRAGMENTED HABITATS

The stability of populations depends on the ability of plants and animals to migrate, usually via corridors of natural habitat suitable to each species's needs. Only fragmented landscapes with connected natural areas that allowed for dispersal stabilized these populations and communities, as was found with beetles and mice in field experiments (Coffman, Nichols, and Pollock 2001; Davies, Melbourne, and Margules 2001). Immigration to and emigration from isolated fragments of natural habitats can be difficult, if not impossible, in urbanized and suburbanized environments. This is especially true of species that do not disperse easily or widely or that have limited abilities to negotiate obstacles.

Barriers to dispersal of small animals at the ground level are abundant in urban and suburban systems. These barriers include curbs, culverts, concrete ditches, large asphalt and concrete surfaces, fences, walls, window wells, buildings, house foundations, silt fencing, lawns, railroads, and swimming pools. Roads are effective dispersal barriers for some species of small mammals that will not cross paved surfaces and open areas 295 feet (90 meters) or more in width (Oxley, Fenton, and Carmody 1974). The threatened bog turtle (*Clemmys muhlenbergii*) in the northeastern United States is unable to negotiate roadside curbs during dispersal between wetlands (Mitchell and Klemens 2000). Barriers at the scale perceived by small animals are much more complex than they are to us.

Numerous papers have documented the negative effects of vehicular traffic and road density on amphibian and reptile populations in urban and suburban areas (e.g., Fahrig et al. 1995; Spellerberg 1998). The full impact of road construction on species inhabiting adjacent wetlands may go undetected for decades because of the periodic but continued loss of individual amphibians, reptiles, birds, mammals, and plants over time (Findlay and Bourdages 2000). Aquatic breeding sites may be located away from upland habitats where some species spend most of their time. Dispersal to and from these required habitats may be difficult, if not impossible. For example, spotted salamanders, red-spotted newts, and other amphibians that migrate annually from forested areas to vernal pools and back are vulnerable to mortality from vehicles on roads (Mitchell 2000; Calhoun and Klemens 2002; Johnson and Klemens, chapter 2, this volume).

IMPORTANCE OF CONNECTIVITY OF FRAGMENTS IN URBAN AND SUBURBAN LANDSCAPES

Isolation of populations can lead to local extinctions. Small populations of species are often unable to persist in the long term without immigration from other populations (Hanski 1999). For example, local extinctions of the plant bog swertia (*Swertia perennis*) resulted from small population size, isolation owing to decline of habitat quality from intensive mowing, and habitat fragmentation (Lienert, Fischer, and Diemer 2002). Long-term persistence of the dingy skipper butterfly (*Erynnis tages*) depends on migration from other populations for survival (Gutiérrez, Thomas, and León-Cortés 1999). Amphibian species richness in urban wetlands in Minnesota declined with increasing isolation and with the proportion of urban land use (Lehtinen, Galatowitsch, and Tester 1999). A review of 20 experimental fragmentation studies suggested that movement between fragments is essential for preserving species diversity, particularly for species with limited mobility (Debinski and Holt 2000). Even with movement among fragments, populations in very small patches are likely to be unstable because all the movement may be out of the patch (Andreassen and Ims 2001).

Locally isolated populations may decline in numbers but may be "rescued" by migration of individuals from other populations in the area (Hanski 1999). Hence, a metapopulation structure in a fragmented landscape allows some species to persist despite the seeming isolation of populations (Holsinger 2000). Dispersal corridors allow for maintenance of metapopulations and therefore play important roles in conservation and management of native species. Intense fragmentation of once continuous habitat or a landscape with metapopulations that cannot interact can, however, completely isolate individual populations of species with limited dispersal. Dispersal abilities depend on the quality of the matrix environment. Such fragmentation and isolation is a common result of urban and suburban sprawl and conversion of wild areas to agricultural land.

The composition and dimensions of corridors of habitat between fragments directly influence a species's ability to disperse. The presence of corridors influenced the movement of insects in experimentally fragmented grasslands and resulted in a slight increase in species richness; however, the corridors' usefulness depended on the particular species, size of fragments, and characteristics of the landscape (Collinge 2000). Corridors may also reveal a sex-specific response. Male root voles (*Microtus oeconomus*) in southeastern Norway moved among fragments with or without corridors, but the females' movement depended on corridors (Aar and Ims 1999). Root vole dispersal was also dependent on the number of individuals in each patch, and corridors in these studies did not always rescue small fragments from loss of species diversity. Thus knowledge of how the landscape matrix is used by different segments of the population is necessary for effective management and long-term persistence of plants and animals living in fragmented habitats (for additional discussion of connectivity, see Sanjayan and Crooks, chapter 11, this volume).

LIVING IN HABITAT FRAGMENTS

Species that cannot disperse or migrate to another habitat fragment will be entirely dependent on the quality of their local environment for food, reproduction, and shelter. However, the quality and diversity of habitats found in the suburban environment may be poor. In this section, we briefly discuss some of the consequences of living in fragments of a formerly widespread habitat. These consequences include the impacts of living in less environmentally diverse patches that lack historical disturbance regimes and the demographic and evolutionary effects that can affect population viability.

LIMITED DIVERSITY OF THE LOCAL HABITATS

Habitat diversity usually correlates with the size of the fragment, with small fragments generally having less diversity than larger fragments (Schwartz 1997). Many species require different types of habitats during their life cycles. For example, frogs and dragonflies require both aquatic and upland habitats; thus successful populations must be located in a rich mosaic of environments. Such mosaics are often not found within isolated fragments, especially if the fragments are small. A higher abundance of small mammals is associated with forest areas that have high diversity and complex structure (Schmid-Holmes and Drickamer 2001); other species require the characteristics of an older forest, such as large hollow trees that maintain beetle diversity and other wildlife. As these older trees disappear, there is a loss of beetle species, food for predators, and the predators themselves (Ranius 2002).

THE ROLE OF DISTURBANCE TO THE LOCAL PATCH

Urbanization, suburbanization, and fragmentation of natural habitats result in loss of natural disturbance regimes, such as periodic fire and windthrows. Humans sometimes introduce new disturbance regimes—for example, by mowing and using herbicides—to control unwanted vegetation, but they create other problems in the process. Such changes in the local environment usually result in a loss of species if native plants and animals have a limited ability to disperse or cannot adapt to the new environmental conditions. For example, snake diversity in New Hampshire was found to decline with a loss of natural habitat and early-successional environments (Kjoss and Litvaitis 2001). Seasonal variability in timing of fires was found to be important for successful reproduction of the diverse community of legumes in longleaf pine (*Pinus palustris*) savannas of the southeastern United States (Hiers, Wyatt, and Mitchell 2000). Periodic fire in this rare ecosystem maintains quality habitat for several increasingly rare vertebrates (e.g., gopher frogs, gopher tortoises) (Dodd 1995). Fire suppression in prairies in midwestern North America has contributed to a decline of population growth rate of the royal catchfly (*Silene regia*), an endangered prairie plant (Menges and Dolan 1998). Changes in the historical human disturbance regime reduced reproductive rates in marsh gentian (*Gentiana pneumonanthe*), a rare plant adapted to early-successional grassy meadows (Oostermeijer 2000). Thus maintenance of species diversity and viable populations in urbanized and fragmented habitats requires knowl-

FIGURE 8.2. A gravel prairie (Harlem Hills Natural Preserve) surrounded by suburbia associated with Rockford, Illinois. To maintain viable populations of several rare prairie species, the management of this preserve includes regular burning of the prairie. The burning preserves the historical disturbance associated with this environment. (Photo by Diane L. Byers)

edge of both the role of natural disturbances in habitat maintenance and species responses to these disturbances (figure 8.2) (for additional discussion on disturbance, see Reice, chapter 4, this volume).

DEMOGRAPHIC CONSEQUENCES OF LIVING IN ISOLATION

Demographic characteristics of a population include patterns of survivorship and reproduction among individuals of different ages. For conservation and management purposes, they are a measurement of a population's viability. Surviving and leaving offspring in isolated populations is a "numbers game" where the basic number is the population size (Holsinger 2000). Species-specific life history parameters (e.g., survivorship, age at first reproduction, number of offspring) will determine if the population size increases or decreases. Deterministic factors, such as loss of suitable habitat, and stochastic effects, such as variation in survivorship rates, also influence these life history parameters. Variation in life history parameters that results in a decrease in population growth is particularly problematic for smaller populations because they are prone to extinction (Holsinger 2000).

For a population of a species to remain viable within an isolated fragment without immigration, adults must be able to survive and leave enough offspring to maintain that population. Ecological, behavioral, and genetic factors may be the underlying causes of poor survivorship and reproduction. Studies of basic demographic parameters help to determine if a population currently is viable (i.e., has potential for positive growth rate). These studies can also elucidate the life history characteristics that may be problematic to successful population growth and can isolate stages to investigate the underlying causes of population decline (Schemske et al. 1994; Byers and Meagher 1997; Oostermeijer 2000). Demographic data can be particularly important for use in population viability analysis and other models that predict population growth under current life history parameters or under modifications of these parameters (Menges and Dolan 1998; see chapters in Young and Clarke 2000).

The presence of a species in a habitat fragment does not necessarily mean that the population is healthy and that it is successfully leaving genetically diverse offspring for future generations. The presence of some long-lived species may give the illusion that the habitat patch is high quality. However, populations of long-lived plants and animals may consist entirely of old individuals that are just barely surviving on the remaining few resources. For example, many prairie plants are very long-lived (to 100 years), but without successful recruitment during their lives, the populations will decline. This is especially true of those species whose individuals reproduce on irregular schedules. Some animals, such as long-lived box turtles (*Terrapene carolina*), may occur in small forest patches and, indeed, in some cases are commonly encountered. However, their populations are not viable because the remaining turtles are old adults that have little to no successful reproduction (Klemens 1989, 1993). Size and genetic diversity of these populations decrease over time in isolated habitat fragments.

DEMOGRAPHIC CONSEQUENCES: EFFECTS ON REPRODUCTIVE SUCCESS

Many aspects of urban systems can affect the reproductive ability and the quality and success of plants and animals in small isolated fragments. For example, sizes of moor frog (*Rana arvalis*) eggs in urban environments in Russia were smaller than in rural areas; although the cause of the decreased egg size is unknown, these smaller eggs resulted in smaller juveniles and lower survival, resulting in poor reproductive success (Vershinin and Gatiyatullina 1994).

Many species require particular population densities for behavioral interactions, which may not be achievable in small natural fragments if populations are small (Courchamp, Clutton-Brock, and Grenfell 1999; Stephens and Sutherland 1999). In low-density populations, limited reproduction because of the inability to find a mate is termed the *Allee effect*. Plants with a deceptive pollination life history (no reward for the pollinator) are often avoided by individual insects after the insects learn that there is no reward. Models of this learning process showed that low plant density resulted in limited pollination success (Ferdy et al. 1999).

Small and isolated populations, typical of species of limited dispersal ability in fragmented environments, may experience substantial variation in sex ratios as a result of genetic drift or behavioral changes. Alteration of sex ratios can result in lower reproductive success. In species of plants that have separate female and hermaphroditic (both sexes in a flower) individual plants, small population size can lead to populations with female-biased sex ratios. Seed set and germination in bladder campion (*Silene vulgaris*) were found to decrease as the proportion of females increased in the population (McCauley et al. 2000). In many bird species, natal dispersal is female biased with very limited male dispersal, which in small fragments can lead to male-biased populations and unpaired mates, potentially contributing to local species extinction (Dale 2001). In extremely fragmented landscapes, species that are seemingly widely dispersed at the mating stage, such as wind-pollinated species, have a very limited number of mates. For example, reduction in the number of pollen-producing individuals of wind-pollinated blue oak (*Quercus douglasii*) by fragmentation reduced acorn production, with some trees of this California endemic producing no acorns at all (Knapp, Goedde, and Rice 2001).

DEMOGRAPHIC CONSEQUENCES:
EFFECTS ON POLLINATORS AND ON SEED AND FRUIT DISPERSAL

Many species of plants depend on animals for successful pollination and dispersal of their seeds (Kearns, Inouye, and Waser 1998). Plants have evolved to attract various animals by offering sufficient rewards, but in changing modern landscapes the pollinators and dispersers may no longer be available, or the numbers of pollinators may have declined owing to changes in the quality of the environment. The rewards now offered by the plants in a landscape affected by urban and suburban sprawl will be diminished because of decreased population size and increased distance between populations. Thus many plants in urban habitat fragments may not be able to attract pollinators or dispersers effectively (Spira 2001). Loss of suitable environment for nest sites used by pollinators will lead to declines and losses of these species (Buchmann and Nabhan 1996). Decline of such plant–animal interactions can directly affect plant reproductive success and cause a loss of food sources for many species of animals. Ensuring the survival of these interactions will have to be context specific because there is typically a web of interactions that shift in time and space rather than a set of species-specific interactions (Buchmann and Nabhan 1996; Kearns, Inouye, and Waser 1998).

Many examples show the effects of habitat fragmentation and small populations on interactions between plants and their pollinators and dispersers (see references in Kearns, Inouye, and Waser 1998). Here, we discuss briefly a few of these studies and focus on species interactions without long-distance gene flow. Species richness and number of bees in small experimental fragments of wild mustard (*Sinapis arvensis*) and wild radish (*Raphanus sativus*) in Germany, for example, declined with degree of isolation from the nearest grassland; bees had to travel greater distances, and the isolated plants had lower seed set (Steffan-Dewenter and Tscharntke 1999). Two common species, grey wattle (*Acacia brachybotrya*) and emu bush (*Eremophila glabra*), in New South Wales, Australia, had lower pollinator visitation and less pollen deposited on the plants in fragmented habitat than in larger preserves; the result was decreased seed set (Cunningham 2000). Characteristics of pollinator behavior may not always lead to decreased visitation in smaller fragments. Some individual plant characteristics (e.g., large size) may allow for a greater increased visitation by pollinators and reproductive success when individuals are found in a sparse population than when such individuals are found in larger habitat fragments (or in larger populations) (Mustajärvi et al. 2001). However, most of the offspring in these smaller fragments will be produced by just a few individuals through self-pollination, thus causing a decline in genetic diversity and potentially increased inbreeding depression (lower survivorship and reproduction owing to matings among relatives). As habitats decline in quality, in very fragmented landscapes, the local pollinator composition is likely to change to a community of stronger fliers, as suitable areas become more dispersed (Steffan-Dewenter and Tscharntke 1999). Although results from individual studies vary, overall there is often a decrease in pollinator abundance and activity as the local environment becomes fragmented and degraded (Kearns, Inouye, and Waser 1998; Cane, chapter 5, this volume).

In small, isolated populations, plants may escape their herbivores, but the trade-off in losing pollinators and the resulting decrease in reproductive success and growth rate of populations has larger consequences. Results of two studies on red ribbons (*Clarkia concinna concinna*) in northern California (Groom 2001) and cross-leaved gentian (*Gentiana cruciata*) in Switzerland (Kéry, Matthies, and Spillman 2000) suggest the decrease in pollination is more critical.

GENETIC CONSEQUENCES OF LIVING IN ISOLATION

Small populations in urban and suburban areas that are isolated with limited or nonexistent migration will lose genetic diversity, have increased inbreeding, and have potentially increased inbreeding depression (lower reproductive success from mating among relatives) (Crow and Kimura 1970). Loss of genetic diversity in small populations results from limited numbers of individuals in each generation possessing the full range of genetic variation. Genetic diversity has been shown to decrease with decreasing population size and increased isolation, as would be found in species with limited dispersal in areas with urban sprawl (Frankham 1996). These populations with lower genetic diversity are of concern because they are at greater risk of extinction (Lynch 1996; Newman and Pilson 1997; Saccheri et al. 1998).

The amount of genetic diversity in populations in highly fragmented urban and suburban habitats can be revealed through analysis of genetic markers (e.g., differences in DNA sequences). Populations of the common toad (*Bufo bufo*) in an urban fragmented landscape versus a rural area in England have lower levels of genetic diversity, in addition to lower survivorship and higher levels of developmental abnormalities (Hitchings and Beebee 1998). The increase of roads and railroads in association with sprawl is associated with a decline in the genetic diversity of the moor frog in the Netherlands (Vos et al. 2001) and the common frog (*Rana temporaria*) in Germany (Reh and Seitz 1990). Analysis of genetic markers in small and large isolated populations of a rare perennial plant, creeping spearwort (*Ranunculus reptans*), a buttercup, in Germany, Austria, and Switzerland, revealed that smaller populations are less diverse (Fischer et al. 2000; Fischer, van Kleunen, and Schmid 2000). Thus populations of these widely different types of species are at greater risk of extinction owing to a limited potential to adapt to the environment.

Another genetic approach, quantitative genetics, directly assesses the extent of genetic variation in traits such as survivorship, growth rate, and reproduction that directly influence the viability and demographic characteristics of populations and the potential for the species to adapt (Lynch 1996). Analysis of the genetic variation in critical traits of a species with limited dispersal living in fragmented habitats can determine if isolated populations have sufficient variation to adapt to the changing quality of the environment. Cowslip (*Primula veris*) seedlings from small populations in Switzerland were less competitive and less able to respond to increased nutrient conditions than seedlings from larger populations (Kéry, Matthies, and Spillman 2000). Smaller isolated populations of creeping spearwort, described previously, had less adaptive genetic variation for competitive ability than genetic lines from larger populations (Fischer, van Kleunen, and Schmid 2000). These studies illustrate that demographic characteristics such as survivorship are adversely affected in isolated populations with low genetic diversity.

The range of genetic variation for traits needed to maintain viable populations is unknown, but models predict that this critical diversity will decline with fragmentation, increasing isolation, and global climate change (Lynch

1996; Etterson and Shaw 2001). This situation is ominous for species occurring in habitats fragmented by urbanization and suburbanization, where they will be subject to strong selection pressures as the environment declines. Many likely will have little to no genetic variation in critical traits to respond to the changes.

INBREEDING DEPRESSION AND GENETIC LOAD

The measurement of traits important to survivorship and reproduction in individuals that differ in the extent of inbreeding can illustrate the extent of deleterious genes in a population (Lynch 1991; Waller 1993). The number of deleterious genes (forms of a gene that have a negative effect on the individual's survivorship and reproduction) in a population is referred to as the *genetic load*. Some researchers have suggested that genetic loads in small isolated populations should be removed or purged because the deleterious alleles will be increasingly expressed by the increased inbreeding and be exposed to selection (Lande and Schemske 1985). However, removal of genetic loads in small isolated populations may not be feasible because small populations are more influenced by random processes than by natural selection (Byers and Waller 1999; Hedrick and Kalinowski 2000). In comparisons of less and more isolated populations of red ribbons in California, where the more isolated populations are small with a great extent of inbreeding, the expected corresponding decrease in expression of inbreeding depression was not found (Groom and Preuninger 2000). For small populations of scarlet gilia (*Ipomopsis aggregeta*) in Arizona, pollen from another population of this species increased seed set and germination, suggesting that the small populations have substantial genetic load (Heschel and Paige 1995). Therefore, the viability of small, isolated populations in areas fragmented by sprawl is likely to be affected by inbreeding depression. If gene flow is increased among isolated small populations, then the negative effects of inbreeding depression may be ameliorated.

THE LINK BETWEEN GENETICS AND DEMOGRAPHY

Although demographic dynamics and genetic diversity of populations are typically treated as separate issues, they are usually linked. Only by considering both at once can the impact of isolation and small population size (as is common with species of limited dispersal abilities) on population viability be fully realized (Young and Clarke 2000). Lack of genetic diversity or fixation of deleterious alleles can influence populations through demographic parameters such as lower survivorship and thus can lead to population extinction (see chapters in Young and Clarke 2000). As discussed in the previous section, the genetic diversity of demographic parameters such as survivorship and reproduction can be studied directly to determine if populations of species with limited dispersal can successfully adapt to changes owing to sprawl.

Another example is in plants that have "self-incompatible" breeding systems, where the genetic diversity for mating types determines the number of potential mates for each individual in a population. In this very common type of breeding system, successful seed production can occur only where mating takes place between different mating types. If the genetic diversity for mating types is low, then the number of potential mates will be limited, which may be reflected directly in the amount of seed set (reproductive success). This joint effect of reduced genetic variation and lower reproductive success has been found in several rare species of plants that occur in small and isolated populations (DeMauro 1993; Byers 1995). This consideration is important for conservation of plants with limited mobility because approximately half of all plant species, the angiosperms, have self-incompatible breeding systems (Richards 1986).

The genetic effects of inbreeding depression have a direct negative impact on survivorship and reproductive success, which in turn may jeopardize local populations' viability and a species's existence. This point is nicely illustrated by marsh gentian, whose increased related matings have led to inbreeding depression expressed as lower reproduction and inability of populations to maintain their current size (Oostermeijer 2000).

DIRECT AND INDIRECT HUMAN EFFECTS

Humans directly affect natural areas in urban and suburban systems in a variety of ways, either by direct interactions or by indirect effects through human subsidy of bird and mammal predators or changes of the local environment (see also Johnson and Klemens, chapter 2, this volume). Direct impacts include trampling by foot, mountain bikes, and off-road vehicles; collecting plant species for gardens (e.g., orchids), culinary uses (wild leeks), and medical uses (American ginseng [*Panax quinquefolium*] and *Echinacea* spp.); collecting animals for pets (turtles); and killing of unwanted animals (snakes and lizards). Populations of many of these species have been lost because of direct human interactions, and the closer local populations are to urban areas, the more likely they will go extinct.

Humans living in urban and suburban areas often cause declines of native species. Two populations of wood turtles (*Clemmys insculpta*) in Connecticut were stable until the areas were opened for recreation (hiking and fishing), but both were extirpated through collection of adults, roadkills, and disturbance by humans and dogs (Garber and Burger 1995). Placement of housing developments in Maryland in areas supporting snake populations (e.g., copperheads [*Agkistrodon contortrix*] and timber rattlesnakes [*Crotalus horridus*]) has resulted in the killing of many of these long-lived animals, causing populations to decline (T. Akre, personal communication, March 2001).

As urban and suburban development affects the natural landscape, we intentionally or unintentionally introduce nonnative species into the region. Introductions of exotic plants and animals create many problems for the remaining native species in these fragments. As the diversity of native species declines, these fragments will be more susceptible to invasion from exotic species and to outbreaks of disease (Deem, Karesh, and Weisman 2001). Fires are typically suppressed in human inhabited areas, which can lead to establishment of invasive plants (Smith and Knapp 2001). Even if fire is part of the management regime of an area, many exotic species' greater dispersal abilities into isolated fragments can still overwhelm the native species. Urban and suburban landscapes provide abundant habitat for many nonnative species living in the matrix environment (Rebele 1994), and these species have easy access to native habitat fragments.

Numerous examples indicate the negative impact of introduced and invasive species on poorly dispersed native species. Feral and free-ranging housecats (*Felis catus*) kill thousands, if not millions, of birds, mammals, amphibians, and reptiles annually in urban areas (Churcher and Lawton 1987; Mitchell and Beck 1992). Red fire ants (*Solenopsis invicta*) in the southern United States are known to kill many species of wildlife, including fawns, quail, hatchling turtles, snakes, and many invertebrates, especially native ant species (Allen, Demarias, and Lutz 1994; Forys et al. 2001). Introduction of nonnative races of the red-eared slider turtle (*Trachemys scripta elegans*) into wetlands historically occupied by yellow-bellied sliders (*T. scripta scripta*) in urbanized southeastern Virginia has caused the erosion of the genetic integrity of native populations (Mitchell 1994). Two species of native shrews (*Notiosorex crawfordi* and *Sorex ornatus*) in southern California were not negatively impacted by habitat fragmentation directly, but increased urbanization resulted in invasions of Argentine ants (*Linepithema humile*), which in turn caused population declines of both shrew species (Laakkonen, Fisher, and Case 2001).

Populations of some native vertebrates that prey on other native species are enhanced by human subsidy. Mammalian and avian predators (e.g., raccoons [*Procyon lotor*], striped skunks [*Mephitis mephitis*], crows and ravens [*Corvus* spp.]) occur in large numbers in urban and suburban systems. These and other subsidized predators kill many species of native animals (Campbell 1977; Mitchell and Klemens 2000). Mojave Desert populations of the desert tortoise (*Gopherus agassizii*) were emergency listed because of high levels of predation by ravens that colonized landfills (Fish and Wildlife Service 1994). Subsidized

predators acting as agents of native species decline have received little management attention in urban areas and offer a ripe field for exploration (DeStefano
and Johnson, chapter 10, this volume).

The worst case of direct impacts by humans is the complete loss of species when the habitat fragment is destroyed by urban development. Extirpation
of native amphibian populations resulting from urban sprawl has been documented, for example, in Florida (Delis, Mushinsky, and McCoy 1996), Indiana
(Minton 1968), Oklahoma (Bragg 1960), and Virginia (Mitchell 1996). Paton
and Egan (2001) determined that urban areas in Rhode Island have three primary effects on amphibians: (1) reduction in number and quality of ephemeral
wetlands; (2) reduction in forested habitat for aquatic-breeding and terrestrial
species; and (3) dispersal barriers created by roads.

CONCLUSIONS AND RECOMMENDATIONS

The list of effects of sprawl on native species with low or limited dispersal
abilities is longer than we can adequately review in our limited space in this
chapter. The negative effects are many; the positive effects are few, if any.
However, the opportunities for research, management, and conservation of
plants and animals in urban and suburban systems around the world abound.
Humans have the opportunity in many areas, especially in suburban zones, to
rectify at least some of the historic losses. Habitat restoration and urban ecology are growing fields that can provide ways to stabilize or even enhance native
populations, although these restorations must be done with a clear knowledge
of the potential negative ecological and genetic effects. Education of public
citizens of all ages and especially of local planning boards and commissions
should also be used to create an understanding of how urban sprawl affects
these ecologically important and often charismatic flora and fauna. Thus the
story is not "all is bad" for urban plants and animals, but it means that we
must do something about the problems soon or lose more species.

The presence of long-lived species of plants and animals in urban and suburban
habitat fragments may give the appearance that populations are doing well, yet
the reality may be just the opposite. Such populations are usually in trouble, and
we may not recognize this fact until it is too late to remedy the situation. Management of habitat, subsidized predators, and resources may be necessary to ensure
that such populations survive in habitat fragments in developed areas. It may be
appropriate to look for populations of short-lived species with low dispersal abilities
and for populations of long-lived species to gain an accurate picture of the health
of the plants and animals in habitat fragments. Population viability analysis models
with demographic data will assist in predictions for longer-lived species.

Elucidation of the genetic status of plant and animal populations in developed and developing areas is possible through several genetic methods (genetic markers to determine degree of isolation, genetic variation of critical traits, estimates of genetic load). Analysis of the demographic structure of populations (e.g., distribution of age classes) also provides insight into the status of populations in urban habitat fragments. Integration of results from such studies reveals ways to reduce the likelihood of local extinctions and population declines. Realistic management and conservation strategies will derive directly from such insights. Of course, the best management of our natural areas is not to fragment the unique or more sensitive places in the first place, which requires careful and bold land-use planning.

Humans can reduce the impacts of sprawl on native species in many ways. We list only a few ways here because there is a growing and robust literature on these topics. Indeed, our brief review of the effects of sprawl on plants and animals with limited dispersal abilities belies the abundant literature on this subject. There can be no excuse based on lack of reliable information for avoiding realistic landscape planning from an ecological perspective. Landscape designs can include greenways that may serve as dispersal corridors for plants and animals with limited dispersal abilities. Ecopassages under roads and highways have been used in Massachusetts to aid salamander migrations; in Florida to reduce vehicular mortality of alligators, snakes, turtles, frogs, and mammals; and in Spain to support a wide variety of species (Yanes, Velasco, and Suarez 1995; Department of Transportation 2000). Opportunities for habitat restoration abound and are limited by only human creativity. Engaging the services of knowledgeable ecologists early in the planning process, not after decisions have been made and development contracts have been signed, will result in a variety of creative and realistic ways to reduce the impacts of urban sprawl on many native species.

We offer several management recommendations to stimulate creative thinking about how to reduce the impacts of sprawl on plants and animals characterized by limited dispersal abilities.

1. Consider the quality of the landscape matrix between the habitat fragments in land-use planning and conservation efforts. Furthermore, remember that the spatial distribution of fragments in the landscape is as important as the amount of land that is undeveloped. Include ecopassages as part of the land-use planning process when necessary.

2. Citizen involvement and response to the development of connections between fragmented habitats of targeted species should be obtained before management strategies are put into effect.

3. Management practices that maintain genetic variation of critical traits for targeted species should be implemented—for example, human assistance

with pollen transfer between fragments for those self-incompatible plant species with low reproductive success.

4. Increased ecological knowledge to understand the causes of species decline and loss has to be sought for species with poor reproduction in small, isolated fragments compared with larger sites. Understanding the quality of the environment (abiotic and biotic factors), genetic variation and genetic load, and demographic structure of populations will lead to valuable insights for management.

5. The importance of genetic considerations should be understood, especially when managing isolated populations. The use of genetic markers to determine the historical connections among populations will aid in making informed decisions about the construction of corridors or movements of individuals in order to decrease population isolation.

6. Control of subsidized and introduced species in urban and suburban areas can greatly enhance the viability of many native species populations.

7. Conservation and management of wetlands for wildlife must take into consideration the use and size of the adjacent terrestrial habitat because narrow buffer zones will not provide adequate protection of local biodiversity.

8. Restoration of native habitat in urban and suburban areas can have positive impacts on native plants and animals; however, all restoration projects, in particular wetland restoration or creation designs, should consider all aspects of the local landscape and habitat and the target species' dispersal abilities.

REFERENCES

Aar, J., and R.A. Ims. 1999. The effect of habitat corridors on rates of transfer and interbreeding between vole demes. *Ecology* 80:1648–1655.

Allen, C.R., S. Demarias, and R.S. Lutz. 1994. Red imported fire ant impact on wildlife: An overview. *Texas Journal of Science* 46:51–59.

Andreassen, H.P., and R.A. Ims. 2001. Dispersal in patchy vole populations: Role of patch configuration, density dependence, and demography. *Ecology* 82:2911–2926.

Bhuju, D.R., and M. Ohsawa. 1998. Effects of nature trails on ground vegetation and understory colonization of a patchy remnant forest in an urban domain. *Biological Conservation* 85:123–135.

Bragg, A.N. 1960. Population fluctuation in the amphibian fauna of Cleveland County, Oklahoma, during the past twenty-five years. *Southwestern Naturalist* 5:165–169.

Broward, D.M., P.F. Kazyak, S.A. Stranko, M.K. Hurd, and T.P. Prochaska. 1999. *From the Mountains to the Sea: The State of Maryland's Freshwater Streams.* Environmental Protection Agency report, no. EPA-903-R-99–023. Annapolis: Maryland Department of Natural Resources, Monitoring and Nontidal Assessment Division.

Brown, J.L., and L. Valiela. 2001. The ecological effects of urbanization of coastal watersheds: Historical increases in nitrogen loads and eutrophication of Waquoit Bay estuaries. *Canadian Journal of Fisheries and Aquatic Sciences* 58:1489–1500.

Buchmann, S. L., and G. P. Nabhan. 1996. *The Forgotten Pollinators.* Washington, D.C.: Island Press.

Byers, D. L. 1995. Pollen quantity and quality as explanations for low seed set in small populations. *American Journal of Botany* 82:1000–1006.

Byers, D. L., and T. R. Meagher. 1997. A comparison of demographic characteristics in a rare and common species of *Eupatorium. Ecological Applications* 7:519–530.

Byers, D. L., and D. M. Waller. 1999. Do plant populations purge their genetic load? Effects of population size and mating history on inbreeding depression. *Annual Review of Ecology and Systematics* 30:479–513.

Calhoun, A. J. K., and M. W. Klemens. 2002. *Best Development Practices: Conserving Pool-Breeding Amphibians in Residential and Commercial Developments in the Northeastern United States.* Metropolitan Conservation Alliance Technical Paper, no. 5. Bronx, N.Y.: Wildlife Conservation Society.

Campbell, C. A. 1977. Survival of reptiles and amphibians in urban environments. In J. H. Noyes and D. R. Progulske, eds., *Symposium: Wildlife in an Urbanizing Environment,* 61–66. Amherst: University of Massachusetts Cooperative Extension Service.

Churcher, P. B., and J. H. Lawton. 1987. Predation by domestic cats in an English village. *Journal of Zoology* (London) 212:439–455.

Coffman, C. J., J. D. Nichols, and K. H. Pollock. 2001. Population dynamics of *Microtus pennsylvanicus* in corridor-linked patches. *Oikos* 93:3–21.

Collinge, S. K. 2000. Effects of grassland fragmentation on insect species loss, colonization, and movement patterns. *Ecology* 81:2211–2226.

Courchamp, F., T. Clutton-Brock, and B. Grenfell. 1999. Inverse density dependence and the Allee effect. *Trends in Ecology and Evolution* 14:405–410.

Cowman, D. F., and L. E. Mazanti. 2000. Ecotoxicology of "new generation" pesticides to amphibians. In D. W. Sparling, G. Linder, and C. A. Bishop, eds., *Ecotoxicology of Amphibians and Reptiles,* 233–268. Pensacola, Fla.: SETAC Press.

Crow, J. F., and M. Kimura. 1970. *An Introduction to Population Genetics Theory.* Minneapolis: Burgess.

Cunningham, S. A. 2000. Depressed pollination in habitat fragments causes low fruit set. *Proceedings of the Royal Society of London, Series B, Biological Sciences* 267:1149–1152.

Dale, S. 2001. Female-biased dispersal, low female recruitment, unpaired males, and the extinction of small and isolated bird populations. *Oikos* 92:344–356.

Davies, K. F., B. A. Melbourne, and C. R. Margules. 2001. Effects of within- and between-patch processes on community dynamics in a fragmentation experiment. *Ecology* 82:1830–1846.

Debinski, D. M., and R. D. Holt. 2000. A survey and overview of habitat fragmentation experiments. *Conservation Biology* 14:342–355.

Deem, S. L., W. B. Karesh, and W. Weisman. 2001. Putting theory into practice: Wildlife health in conservation. *Conservation Biology* 15:1224–1233.

Delis, P. R., H. R. Mushinsky, and E. D. McCoy. 1996. Decline of some west-central Florida anuran populations in response to habitat degradation. *Biodiversity and Conservation* 5:1579–1595.

DeMauro, M. M. 1993. Relationship of breeding system to rarity in the lakeside daisy (*Hymenoxys acaulis* var. *glabra*). *Conservation Biology* 7:542–550.

Department of Transportation. 2000. *Critter Crossings: Linking Habitats and Reducing Roadkill.* Washington, D.C.: Federal Highway Commission.

Dodd, C.K., Jr. 1995. Reptiles and amphibians in the endangered longleaf pine ecosystem. In E.T. LaRoe, G.S. Ferris, C.E. Puckett, P.D. Doran, and M.J. Mac, eds., *Our Living Resources: A Report to the Nation on the Distribution, Abundance, and Health of U.S. Plants, Animals, and Ecosystems,* 129–131. Washington, D.C.: National Biological Survey.

———. 1997. Imperiled amphibians: A historical perspective. In G.W. Benz and D.E. Collins, eds., *Aquatic Fauna in Peril: The Southeastern Perspective,* 165–200. Southeast Aquatic Research Institute Special Publication, no. 1. Decatur, Ga.: Lenz Design and Communications.

Duncan, R.P., and J.R. Young. 2000. Determinants of plant extinction and rarity 145 years after European settlement of Auckland, New Zealand. *Ecology* 81:3048–3061.

Etterson, J.R., and R.G. Shaw. 2001. Constraints to adaptive evolution in response to global warming. *Science* 294:151–154.

Fahrig, L, J.H. Pedlar, S.E. Pope, P.D. Taylor, and J.F. Wegner. 1995. Effect of road traffic on amphibian density. *Biological Conservation* 73:177–182.

Ferdy, J.-B., F. Austerlitz, J. Moret, P.-H. Gouyon, and B. Godelle. 1999. Pollinator-induced density dependence in deceptive species. *Oikos* 87:549–560.

Findlay, C.S., and J. Bourdages. 2000. Response time of wetland biodiversity to road construction on adjacent lands. *Conservation Biology* 14:86–91.

Fischer, M., R. Husi, D. Prati, M. Peintenger, M. van Kleunen, and B. Schmid. 2000. RAPD variation among and within small and large populations of the rare clonal plant *Ranunculus reptans* (Ranunculaceae). *American Journal of Botany* 87:1128–1137.

Fischer, M., M. van Kleunen, and B. Schmid. 2000. Genetic Allee effects on performance, plasticity, and developmental stability in a clonal plant. *Ecology Letters* 3:530–539.

Fish and Wildlife Service. 1994. *Desert Tortoise (Mojave Populations) Recovery Plan.* Washington, D.C.: Fish and Wildlife Service.

Forys, E.A., A. Quisorff, C.R. Allen, and D.P. Wojcik. 2001. The likely cause of extinction of the tree snail *Orthalicus reses reses* (Say). *Journal of Molluscan Studies* 67:369–376.

Frankham, R. 1996. Relationship of genetic variation to population size in wildlife. *Conservation Biology* 10:1500–1508.

Fuller, D.O. 2001. Forest fragmentation in Loudoun County, Virginia, USA, evaluated with multitemporal Landsat imagery. *Landscape Ecology* 16:527–642.

Garber, S.D., and J. Burger. 1995. A 20-year study documenting the relationship between turtle decline and human recreation. *Ecological Applications* 5:1151–1162.

Gibbs, J.P. 1998. Distribution of woodland amphibians along a forest fragmentation gradient. *Landscape Ecology* 13:263–268.

Groom, M.J. 2001. Consequences of subpopulation isolation for pollination, herbivory, and population growth in *Clarkia concinna concinna* (Onagraceae). *Biological Conservation* 100:55–63.

Groom, M.J., and T.E. Preuninger. 2000. Population type can influence the magnitude of inbreeding depression in *Clarkia concinna* (Onagraceae). *Evolutionary Ecology* 14:155–180.

Gutiérrez, D., C.D. Thomas, and J.L. León-Cortés. 1999. Dispersal, distribution, patch network, and metapopulation dynamics of the dingy skipper butterfly (*Erynnis tages*). *Oecologia* 121:506–517.

Hanski, I. 1999. *Metapopulation Ecology*. Oxford: Oxford University Press.

Hedrick, P. W., and S. T. Kalinowski. 2000. Inbreeding depression in conservation biology. *Annual Review of Ecology and Systematics* 31:139–162.

Heschel, M. S., and K. N. Paige. 1995. Inbreeding depression, environmental stress, and population size variation in scarlet gilia (*Ipomopsis aggregata*). *Conservation Biology* 9:126–133.

Hiers, J. K., R. Wyatt, and R. J. Mitchell. 2000. The effects of fire regime on legume reproduction in longleaf pine savannas: Is a season selective? *Oecologia* 125:521–530.

Hitchings, S. P., and T. J. C. Beebee. 1998. Loss of genetic diversity and fitness in common toad (*Bufo bufo*) populations isolated by inimical habitat. *Journal of Evolutionary Biology* 11:269–283.

Holsinger, K. E. 2000. Demography and extinction in small populations. In A. G. Young and G. M. Clarke, eds., *Genetics, Demography, and Viability of Fragmented Populations*, 55–74. Cambridge: Cambridge University Press.

Kearns, C. A., D. W. Inouye, and N. M. Waser. 1998. Endangered mutualisms: The conservation of plant–pollinator interactions. *Annual Review of Ecology and Systematics* 29:83–112.

Kéry, M., D. Matthies, and H.-H. Spillman. 2000. Reduced fecundity and offspring performance in small populations of the declining grassland plants *Primula veris* and *Gentiana lutea*. *Journal of Ecology* 88:17–30.

Kjoss, V. A., and J. A. Litvaitis. 2001. Community structure of snakes in a human-dominated landscape. *Biological Conservation* 98:285–292.

Klemens, M. W. 1989. The methodology of conservation. In I. R. Swingland and M. W. Klemens, eds., *The Conservation Biology of Tortoises*, 1–4. International Union for Conservation of Nature and Natural Resources (IUCN), Species Survival Commission (SSC), Occasional Paper no. 5. Gland, Switzerland: IUCN/SSC.

——. 1993. *Amphibians and Reptiles of Connecticut and Adjacent Regions*. State Geological and Natural History Survey of Connecticut, bulletin no. 112. Hartford: Connecticut Department of Environmental Protection.

Knapp, E. E., M. A. Goedde, and K. J. Rice. 2001. Pollen-limited reproduction in blue oak: Implications for wind pollination in fragmented populations. *Oecologia* 128:48–55.

Knops, J. M. H., D. Tilman, N. M. Haddad, S. Naeem, C. E. Mitchell, J. Haarstad, M. E. Ritchie, K. M. Howe, P. B. Reich, E. Siemann, and J. Groth. 1999. Effects of plant species richness on invasion dynamics, disease outbreaks, insect abundances, and diversity. *Ecology Letters* 2:286–293.

Laakkonen, A., R. N. Fisher, and T. J. Case. 2001. Effect of land cover, habitat fragmentation, and ant colonies on the distribution and abundance of shrews in southern California. *Journal of Animal Ecology* 70:776–788.

Lande, R., and D. W. Schemske. 1985. The evolution of self-fertilization and inbreeding depression in plants. I. Genetic models. *Evolution* 39: 24–40.

Lehtinen, R. M., S. M. Galatowitsch, and J. R. Tester. 1999. Consequences of habitat loss and fragmentation for wetland amphibian assemblages. *Wetlands* 19:1–12.

Lienert, J., M. Fischer, and M. Diemer. 2002. Local extinctions of the wetland specialist *Swertia perennis* L. (Gentianaceae) in Switzerland: A revisitation study based on herbarium records. *Biological Conservation* 103:65–76.

Lynch, M. 1991. The genetic interpretation of inbreeding depression and outbreeding depression. *Evolution* 45:622–629.

———. 1996. A quantitative-genetic perspective on conservation issues. In J. C. Avise and J. L. Hamrick, eds., *Conservation Genetics: Case Histories from Nature,* 471–501. New York: Chapman and Hall.

Maina, G. G., and H. F. Howe. 2000. Inherent rarity in community restoration. *Conservation Biology* 14:1335–1340.

McCauley, D. E., M. S. Olson, S. N. Emery, and D. R. Taylor. 2000. Population structure influences sex ratio evolution in a gynodioecious plant. *American Naturalist* 155:814–819.

Menges, E. S., and R. W. Dolan. 1998. Demographic viability of populations of *Silene regia* in midwestern prairies: Relationships with fire management, genetic variation, geographic location, population size, and isolation. *Journal of Ecology* 86:63–78.

Minton, S. A., Jr. 1968. The fate of amphibians and reptiles in a suburban area. *Journal of Herpetology* 2:113–116.

Mitchell, J. C. 1994. *The Reptiles of Virginia.* Washington, D.C.: Smithsonian Institution Press.

———. 1996. Natural history notes on the amphibians of a recently extirpated suburban wetland in central Virginia. *Banisteria* 7:41–48.

———. 2000. Mass mortality of red-spotted newts (*Notophthalmus viridescens viridescens* Rafinesque) on a central Virginia road. *Banisteria* 15:44–46.

Mitchell, J. C., and R. A. Beck. 1992. Free-ranging domestic cat predation on native vertebrates in rural and urban Virginia. *Virginia Journal of Science* 43:197–207.

Mitchell, J. C., and M. W. Klemens. 2000. Primary and secondary effects of habitat alteration. In M. W. Klemens, ed., *Turtle Conservation,* 5–32. Washington, D.C.: Smithsonian Institution Press.

Mustajärvi, K., P. Siikamäki, S. Rytkönen, and A. Lammi. 2001. Consequences of plant population size and density for plant–pollinator interactions and plant performance. *Journal of Ecology* 89:80–87.

Newman, D., and D. Pilson. 1997. Increased probability of extinction due to decreased genetic effective population size: Experimental populations of *Clarkia pulchella.* *Evolution* 51:354–362.

Oostermeijer, J. G. B. 2000. Population viability analysis of the rare *Gentiana pneumonanthe:* The importance of genetics, demography, and reproductive biology. In A. G. Young and G. M. Clarke, eds., *Genetics, Demography, and Viability of Fragmented Populations,* 313–334. Cambridge: Cambridge University Press.

Oxley, D. J., M. B. Fenton, and G. R. Carmody. 1974. The effects of roads on populations of small mammals. *Journal of Applied Ecology* 11:51–59.

Paton, P., and S. Egan. 2001. *Effects of Roads on Amphibian Community Structure at Breeding Ponds in Rhode Island.* Report to the Transactions of Environment Research Program. Baltimore: Federal Highway Administration.

Ranius, T. 2002. Influence of stand size and quality of tree hollow on saproxylic beetles in Sweden. *Biological Conservation* 103:85–91.

Rebele, F. 1994. Urban ecology and special features of urban ecosystems. *Global Ecology and Biogeography Letters* 4:173–187.

Reh, W., and A. Seitz. 1990. The influence of land use on the genetic structure of populations of the common frog *Rana temporaria*. *Biological Conservation* 54:239–249.

Richards, J. J. 1986. *Plant Breeding Systems*. London: George Allen and Unwin.

Saccheri, I. J., M. Kuussaari, M. Kankare, P. Viman, W. Forteliu, and I. Hanski. 1998. Inbreeding and extinction in a butterfly metapopulation. *Nature* 392:491–494.

Schemske, D. W., B. C. Husband, M. H. Ruckelshaus, C. Goodwillie, I. M. Parker, and J. G. Bishop. 1994. Evaluating approaches to the conservation of rare and endangered plants. *Ecology* 75:584–606.

Schmid-Holmes, S., and L. C. Drickamer. 2001. Impact of forest patch characteristics on small mammal communities: A multivariate approach. *Biological Conservation* 99:293–305.

Schwartz, M. W. 1997. *Conservation in Highly Fragmented Landscapes*. New York: Chapman and Hall.

Smith, M. D., and A. K. Knapp. 2001. Size of the local species pool determines invisibility of a C-4-dominated grassland. *Oikos* 92:55–61.

Soulé, M. E. 1991. Land use planning and wildlife maintenance. *Journal of the American Planning Association* 57:313–323.

Sparling, D. W., G. M. Fellers, and L. L. McConnell. 2001. Pesticides and amphibian declines in California, USA. *Environmental Toxicology and Chemistry* 20:1591–1595.

Spellerberg, I. F. 1998. Ecological effects of roads and traffic: A literature review. *Global Ecology and Biogeography Letters* 7:317–333.

Spira, T. P. 2001. Plant–pollinator interactions: A threatened mutualism with implications for the ecology and management of rare plants. *Natural Areas Journal* 21:78–88.

Steffan-Dewenter, I., and T. Tscharntke. 1999. Effects of habitat isolation on pollinator communities and seed set. *Oecologia* 121:432–440.

Stephens, P. A., and W. J. Sutherland. 1999. Consequences of the Allee effect for behavior, ecology, and conservation. *Trends in Ecology and Evolution* 14:401–405.

Swenson, J. J., and J. Franklin. 2000. The effects of future urban development on habitat fragmentation in the Santa Monica Mountains. *Landscape Ecology* 15:713–730.

Vershinin, V. L., and E. Z. Gatiyatullina. 1994. Population viability of egg size for moor frog depending on the level of urbanization. *Russian Journal of Ecology* 25:391–395.

Vos, C. C., A. G. Antonisse-De Jong, P. W. Goedhart, and M. J. M. Smulders. 2001. Genetic similarity as a measure for connectivity between fragmented populations of the moor frog (*Rana arvalis*). *Heredity* 86:598–608.

Waller, D. 1993. The statics and dynamics of mating system evolution. In N. W. Thornhill, ed., *Natural History of Inbreeding and Outbreeding Depression*, 97–117. Chicago: University of Chicago Press.

Yanes, M., J. M. Velasco, and F. Suarez. 1995. Permeability of roads and railways to vertebrates: The importance of culverts. *Biological Conservation* 73:217–222.

Young, A. G., and G. M. Clarke, eds. 2000. *Genetics, Demography, and Viability of Fragmented Population*. Cambridge: Cambridge University Press.

Young, C. H., and P. J. Jarvis. 2001. Measuring urban habitat fragmentation: An example from the Black Country, UK. *Landscape Ecology* 16:643–658.

■ ■

SPRAWL AND HIGHLY MOBILE OR
WIDE-RANGING SPECIES

Justina C. Ray

H abitat destruction, through its fragmentation, degradation, or outright loss, is the root cause of species imperilment throughout North America (Wilcove et al. 1998). Since large-scale land clearing began in earnest on the continent around 150 years ago, human-caused habitat loss has been attributed mostly to processes such as agricultural clearing and industrial resource extraction. More recently, human settlement itself has become a culprit as urban and suburban sprawl affects natural areas in even larger concentric rings around cities and towns (National Wildlife Federation 2001). Of interest to wildlife managers and land-use planners alike are the impacts to wildlife communities of this relatively novel agent of landscape transformation.

Because of differing area requirements for various species, ecologists have classified many wildlife species based on their sensitivity to reduction in available habitat, including impacts from urban development. Highly mobile or wide-ranging species fall under this category of area-sensitive species because they often require a wide variety of habitat types to provide necessary food or shelter resources or, because of their large size or prey selectivity, require great acreage to meet minimum food requirements (Noss and Csuti 1997). Such species typically range widely over relatively large areas in order to fulfill their daily or seasonal requirements; they need a certain minimum habitat quality that is not easily maintained in the face of direct or indirect habitat degradation that occurs close to edges with anthropogenic habitats (Faaborg et al. 1995; Noss et al. 1996; Bosakowski and Smith 1997; Crooks 2002). Ironically, highly mobile or space-demanding species are similar to those with poor dispersal abilities (Byers and Mitchell, chapter 8, this volume) in that they often need relatively large and contiguous blocks of natural habitat in order for populations to persist.

To illustrate the dynamic interaction between wildlife populations and urban or suburban land use, this chapter focuses on three groups of wide-ranging or mobile species that exhibit area sensitivity: mammalian carnivores, raptors, and migrant songbirds. For many of the species that fall into these groups, populations consistently diminish or disappear when their once continuous natural habitats are carved up into smaller pieces. Not all species within these groups respond negatively to sprawl, nor are they by any means the only organisms whose wide-ranging tendencies (e.g., large ungulates) make them particularly vulnerable in the face of human-induced fragmentation. Nevertheless, the different degrees of sensitivity to sprawl-induced fragmentation among species within these three groups provide insight into the nature of community change in the face of human perturbations. The emphasis of this chapter is on forest-dwelling fauna; however, in many cases, the principles examined apply to other ecosystem types, such as grasslands and shrublands.

An understanding of how sprawl affects the most vulnerable components of biodiversity is essential for predicting likely future impacts of development and for redesigning growth so that the negative effects associated with the spatial characteristics of the landscape transformation are minimized (Collinge 1996). If we are able to satisfy these species' needs, we will be an important step closer to the ultimate goal of retaining all components of natural biodiversity in the landscape. Moreover, in the provision of the appropriate large habitat blocks many of these taxa require, there may be a coattail or an umbrella effect for other components of biodiversity that use the same areas. Carnivores, raptors, and songbirds generally attract attention and enjoy a prominent place in the public imagination, and they often are a factor in strategies for influencing land-use policy and natural-resource conservation. Hence, they are potentially useful conservation tools (Ray 2005) from both biological and social perspectives.

Most habitat evaluation has traditionally occurred at local scales. In order to develop an understanding of what it means to be an area-sensitive species, one has to take a much broader perspective. What may constitute perfectly good habitat at a local scale may be severely compromised by the nature of the surrounding habitat or by the distance to nearby habitat of similar quality. This landscape perspective is a relatively recent phenomenon in wildlife ecology (Forman and Godron 1986) and requires an appreciation of how individual pieces fit into a giant puzzle that may be best perceived, for example, from an airplane or a mountain top. In this chapter, I focus on studies that have considered this larger scale, and I compare and contrast the particular process associated with sprawl against those processes typical of other large-scale anthropogenic disturbances.

CARNIVORES, RAPTORS, AND MIGRANT SONGBIRDS AS AREA-SENSITIVE SPECIES

Mammalian carnivores (hereafter, *carnivores*) and raptors share a number of traits that put them at risk in the face of human development. By virtue of their position at the top of the food chain, they typically live at low population densities, resulting in individuals being widely distributed across a landscape. Carnivores, in particular males, often maintain exclusive territories and can make long-distance movements when searching for new territories or when foraging or exploring (Sunquist and Sunquist 2001). Nesting raptors likewise show relatively wide spacing, with average distances between nests measuring several miles for many species, and are often territorial (Johnsgard 1990). The relatively low reproductive output of species high in the food chain often makes their populations less capable of rebounding in the face of high natural or human-caused mortality (Weaver, Paquet, and Ruggiero 1996).

Defining wide-ranging species depends on the locality in question. For example, in northeastern North America, where all the top carnivores were extirpated by the beginning of the twentieth century, the area requirements of the remaining carnivores fall at the bottom end of the requirements spectrum when compared with those inhabiting intact ecosystems such as the northern Rockies (figure 9.1). Although truly large-bodied carnivores were already gone from most areas throughout the continent long before sprawl became a dominant agent of

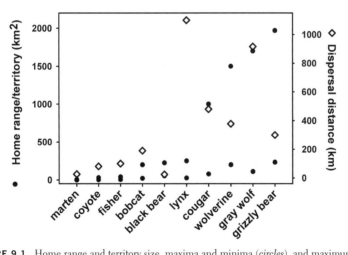

FIGURE 9.1. Home range and territory size, maxima and minima (*circles*), and maximum dispersal distances (*diamonds*) of male mammalian carnivores. All 10 species can be found today in the Greater Yellowstone Ecosystem, whereas only the first 6 survive in viable populations in the northeastern United States.

TABLE 9.1. Examples of Songbirds in North America Whose Populations Have Been Shown in Selected Studies to Be Area Sensitive and Hence Negatively Affected by Residential Development

LOCALE (SOURCE)	SPECIES
Southeastern Connecticut (Askins, Philbrick, and Sugeno 1987)	Black-throated green warbler, blue-gray gnat-catcher, brown creeper, cerulean warbler, worm-eating warbler, yellow-throated vireo
Central California (Blair 1996)	Ash-throated flycatcher, blue-gray gnatcatcher, dark-eyed junco, Hutton's vireo, western wood-pewee, wrentit
Southwestern Ontario (Friesen, Eagles, and MacKay 1995)	Eastern wood-pewee, northern oriole, ovenbird, rose-breasted grosbeak, scarlet tanager, wood thrush
Western Massachusetts (Kluza, Griffin, and DeGraaf 2000)	Ovenbird, veery, wood thrush
Central Missouri (Nilon, Long, and Zipperer 1995)	Black-and-white warbler, Kentucky warbler, northern parula, ovenbird, red-eyed vireo, scarlet tanager
Midwestern United States (Robinson, Thompson et al. 1995)	Hooded warbler, indigo bunting, Kentucky warbler, ovenbird, wood thrush, worm-eating warbler
Central Maryland (Wilcove 1985)	Veery, yellow-throated vireo, northern parula, black-and-white warbler, worm-eating warbler, ovenbird, Kentucky warbler, hooded warbler, scarlet tanager
Western Colorado (Odell and Knight 2001)	Blue-gray gnatcatcher, black-headed grosbeak, dusky flycatcher, orange-crowned warbler, spotted towhee

Source: Updated and modified from Craighead, Gilpin, and Vyse (1999).

land transformation, some populations still survive in several places in North America in the direct line of sprawl. The Greater Yellowstone Ecosystem is one example, as the southeasternmost point on the continent where an intact large carnivore suite (including gray wolves [*Canis lupus*], grizzly bears [*Ursus arctos*], cougars [*Puma concolor*], and wolverines [*Gulo gulo*]) still exists (Clark et al. 1999). Sprawl is increasingly becoming an issue impacting their movements: the Mountain West experienced the most rapid human population growth rates in the United States in the 1990s, with counties neighboring protected areas in the Greater Yellowstone Ecosystem experiencing some of the most rapid population increases (Hansen et al. 2002). Cougars still roam on the outskirts of densely settled areas in southern California and Florida (Beier 1993; Maehr 1997).

Individual songbirds have minuscule area requirements compared with raptors; however, many species are area sensitive, requiring relatively large tracts of natural habitat to breed successfully (Faaborg et al. 1995) (table 9.1). Most area-sensitive passerines tend to be migratory birds that spend most of the year in the southern United States (short-distance migrants) or the New World tropics (*neotropics*) and migrate to temperate and boreal forests or grasslands to breed in spring (April–June). During the breeding season, many neotropical migrants (warblers, vireos, flycatchers, tanagers, and thrushes) are obligatory forest dwellers that thrive best in large, forest interior habitats, whereas other groups of long-distance migrants (meadowlarks [*Sturnella* spp.], bobolinks [*Dolichonyx oryzivorus*], upland sandpipers [*Bartramia longicauda*], prairie-chickens [*Tympanuchus* spp.], and savannah sparrows [*Passerculus sandwichensis*]) seek out grassland areas for their breeding territories. All have evolved the habit of migration to temperate and boreal regions to exploit abundant food resources (insects and other invertebrates), enjoy reduced competition and lower predation rates, and have higher production rates of young than in tropical and subtropical regions (DeGraaf and Rappole 1995). Not having adapted to overwintering in temperate and boreal regions, most long-distance migrants are more specialized in their habitat and area requirements than resident species. Furthermore, most breeding birds guard territories and compete for coveted nest sites, a condition that limits the number of individuals able to inhabit a given area. Because migrant songbirds have only a small window of opportunity in which to breed and lay their eggs, they are generally only single brooded, in contrast to permanent resident species (DeGraaf and Rappole 1995).

ECOLOGICAL CONSEQUENCES OF SPRAWL

Impacts of disturbances on resident fauna have been most intensively studied in logged and farmed landscapes; the unique conditions of sprawl as they relate to area-sensitive species' responses have received relatively little attention (Kluza, Griffin, and DeGraaf 2000). Habitat fragmentation brought about by sprawl differs fundamentally from that arising from the land clearing carried out earlier in the twentieth century. First, houses and associated pavement are relatively permanent in comparison with the temporary reduction in wildlife habitat characterized by fields and forest clearings. In the latter, vegetation has the potential to regrow quickly following the original disturbance (depending on its scale of disturbance). Large clearings generated by forestry or agriculture, however, often result in the eventual elimination of large-diameter trees, perches, or even food resources, whereas urbanized landscapes can still contain significant numbers of large trees and enhanced food resources through human subsidization.

Therefore, although many lessons can be gleaned from research on the effects of clear-cutting and agriculture on wide-ranging species, extending these conclusions to landscapes affected by urbanized sprawl must be undertaken with some caution. Sometimes, however, such studies are all we have available, and the ability to draw inferences from this work depends on the extent to which we are able to appreciate the ecological differences between the different forms of land use. In principle, impacts to carnivores, raptors, and migrant songbirds from sprawl fall under categories similar to those of any agent of fragmentation: habitat loss, isolation and barriers to movement, edge effects, nest predation and parasitism, interspecific competition, and conflict with humans.

HABITAT LOSS AND THE EFFECTS OF PATCH SIZE WITHIN FRAGMENTED LANDSCAPES

When habitats of wide-ranging species are fragmented, the population's long-term survival depends on its members' ability to reconnoiter this new and foreign landscape (Sweanor, Logan, and Hornocker 2000). Wide-ranging species may be affected simply because the amount of natural habitat is no longer large enough to meet the needs of a viable population. The Florida panther (*Puma concolor coryi*), for example, is a top predator with sizable home range requirements (males' home ranges average approximately 193 square miles (400 square kilometers]) whose natural habitat is being carved up by sprawl and citrus development (Maehr 1997). Unlike other representatives of the same species, cougars in Florida rely on forest cover for many aspects of life history, including foraging, denning, and resting. Viable Florida panther home ranges must, therefore, contain some minimal amount of forest to ensure survival (Maehr, Hoctor, and Harris 2001). Although a wide-ranging animal's natural response to poor habitat quality will be to increase the size of its home range, there is an upper physiological limit beyond which it becomes impossible for the animal to utilize and defend the range. For Florida panthers in areas of sprawl, the fact that suitable habitat exists only in relatively small patches means that individuals must range over inordinately large geographic areas to move through enough forested hunting grounds to meet basic caloric intake needs. The net effect can be high mortality rates as the panthers are confronted in all directions by hostility, whether from conspecifics defending their territories or from adverse interactions with humans (Maehr, Hoctor, and Harris 2001).

For migrant songbirds and raptors, the area of remnant forest patches within fragmented landscapes also appears to be critical, with many species disappearing from forest or grassland patches as these patches decrease in size (Askins, Philbrick, and Sugeno 1987; Bosakowski and Smith 1997; Helzer and Jeliniski

1999). In fact, many interior habitat–specialist songbirds tend to disappear from fragments that are quite a bit larger than individuals' area requirements (Askins, Philbrick, and Sugeno 1987; Robbins et al. 1989; Vickery, Hunter, and Melvin 1994; Faaborg et al. 1995). Although habitat patch area is a strong predictor of relative abundance or even extirpation of many songbirds, numerous correlating factors relevant to habitat quality likely account for this relationship (Faaborg et al. 1995). In many cases, for example, unsuitability of a small fragment relates to more subtle, but still critical factors, such as the absence of specific microhabitats or habitat heterogeneity, or perhaps enhanced vulnerability to predation and parasitism, among others.

ISOLATION AND BARRIERS TO MOVEMENT AND DISPERSAL

The landscape matrix in which natural-habitat islands are embedded can be viewed as a filter through which some (but not all) species will be able to move. In general, the greater the distance between fragments or the more hostile the matrix, or both, the more the matrix will act as a barrier for a given species. Even without human-caused fragmentation, individuals will exhibit faster rates of transit through certain types of habitats than through others; however, the distance between fragments also is important because of its influence on the probability of successful movement between fragments. The key to long-term survival of subpopulations is often to maintain their movement between geographically separated units (Wiens 1996). Individuals may undertake many different types of movements in the course of their lives, including general ranging, migration, and dispersal. Whereas dispersal and movement abilities are inherent traits, variation in habitat types and landscape structure influences the expression of these traits (Fahrig 2001).

Dispersal from natal territories represents a critical period in an organism's life history. In the case of many male yearling carnivores, these movements are generally the longest observed movements during their lives and can take several months to complete (Sweanor, Logan, and Hornocker 2000). The fewer options that remain once habitats have become fragmented, the longer are the distances that must be traversed. The longer the period of travel, the less likely an individual will survive to reproductive age. In areas where the best habitats have already been occupied, individuals will have to settle for suboptimal habitat or return to natal areas after frustrated attempts or suffer high rates of mortality in a continued quest (Beier 1995; Maehr 1997; Palomares et al. 2000). They often will exhibit higher tolerances for unfavorable areas en route, but establishment will be successful only in high-quality habitat (Mladenoff et al. 1995; Palomares et al. 2000). Movements across wide expanses of inhospitable habitat while in dispersal mode are generally rapid and unidirectional (Sweanor,

Logan, and Hornocker 2000). Cougars dispersing through fragmented habitats in southern California used corridors for travel that were characterized by relatively high cover, low housing density, and no artificial outdoor lighting. Nevertheless, seven of nine individuals died before establishing home ranges (Beier 1995). Dispersing individuals can be the most visible members of the population because they are the most likely to spend time in unsuitable (i.e., human-dominated) areas. In extreme cases, they may even end up in city centers ("Bear Shot" 2000). Unfortunately, such incidents can generate misconception among the public that these species can coexist with humans or are at least adaptable to human development. Established individuals tend to inhabit areas relatively far from human settlements and thus are seldom encountered by humans. Such a scenario can also exacerbate conflicts, which in turn can affect human attitudes toward all members of the population.

The relationship between dispersal and extent of isolation of forest fragments remains relatively unexplored for birds (Faaborg et al. 1995; Burke and Nol 2000). Not only are such studies difficult to undertake, but there is also the perception that birds have excellent dispersal capabilities because they are expected to be able to fly over potential barriers. Some evidence from studies of migrant songbirds suggests, however, that a greater degree of isolation makes it less likely for a patch to be occupied or recolonized (Faaborg et al. 1995). Several studies have shown, for example, that some songbird species' long-distance (nonmigratory) movements are more likely to occur through forested areas rather than over open areas (Haas 1995) and that forested routes will be taken when given a choice (Desrochers and Hannon 1997). Proximity and connectivity of forest patches, therefore, facilitate movement.

Human-made structures constitute additional barriers, particularly during the long-distance migrations of passerine birds. Collisions with television and radio towers, support wires, and buildings—many of which carry beacons, strobe lights, or flood lights—are frequent mortality sources for these birds that travel mainly at night. With approximately 5,000 new communication towers being built in the United States each year, this phenomenon represents an additional (and often overlooked) challenge to the maintenance of biodiversity in human-modified landscapes (Lopez 2001). Power lines, which are often associated with roads, can be a significant source of mortality for raptors as well, especially for eagles, hawks, and owls (Harness and Wilson 2001).

Roads acting as barriers through direct mortality are an additional concern, particularly for animal populations that are already at low numbers or exist at naturally low densities. Research on carnivores has shown that some species will simply avoid roads—for example, bobcats (*Lynx rufus*) (Lovallo and Anderson 1996), cougars (Sweanor, Logan, and Hornocker 2000), and black bears (*Ursus americanus*) (Brody and Pelton 1989). However, their large range sizes mean that even at low road densities, crossings will be inevitable, particularly when these species attempt to reach critical habitats. Once road densities reach high enough levels, they become difficult or impossible to avoid, and there may be little room to shift territories or movements (Brody and Pelton 1989).

EDGE EFFECTS AND THE LOSS OF INTERIOR HABITATS

The individual elements within a landscape mosaic do not merely abut one another; rather, features of one will extend into the other, resulting in an area of *edge* habitat that shows characteristics typical of neither habitat. These influences include differences in microclimate, vegetation structure, and species composition, as well as shifts in processes such as predation, competition, and parasitism (Forman and Godron 1986). In spite of an increase in forest cover in the past eight decades in northeastern North America, most of today's forests are near edges (Matlack 1997). The greater the structural contrast between adjacent patches, the more intense the edge effects, although there is no general rule for the extent of the permeation into a patch (Collinge 1996). Hence, a stretch of asphalt or a mowed lawn adjacent to a forested habitat will impose a stronger edge effect than will the proximity of another forest type. Because the contrasts between converted and natural habitat can be so pronounced and severe, edge effects are a key issue in areas of suburban sprawl.

Depending on the depth to which such edge effects extend into the forest, habitat patches below a certain size may lack any true interior habitat. In general, because of the greater perimeter-to-area ratio, smaller patches contain a larger proportion of edge habitat than do larger fragments. This phenomenon also depends on shape, with a square habitat fragment, for example, able to maintain a greater proportion of interior habitat than a rectangle of the same area (Collinge 1996). Circular habitats evoke the lowest perimeter-to-area ratio of any potential polygon. Although the actual decrease in total habitat area may be small when continuous habitat is converted into disjunct pieces, the overall amount of edge habitat inevitably increases, thereby seriously affecting the quality of the remaining habitat (Vogelmann 1995; Collinge 1996).

Extensive research in such fragmented environments has repeatedly demonstrated that the associated losses of interior-forest or grassland habitat result in negative impacts for several species of songbirds. Fragmentation of continuous forest into patches can result in reduced breeding success even in fairly heavily forested landscapes (reviewed in Askins 1994; Faaborg et al. 1995; Burke and Nol 2000). For example, changes brought about near the border of the remnant patches result in an absence of suitable microhabitats for nesting. In rural Ontario, Burke and Nol (1998) found that the ovenbird (*Seiurus aurocapillus*)—a ground-nesting, insectivorous songbird—generally chose nest sites that were more than

820 feet (250 meters) from forest edges, thereby eliminating the suitability of small forest fragments. Nest choice appeared to be related to leaf litter depth and insect biomass, both of which were many times higher within the largest fragments. In a forested landscape in the southern Appalachians, abundance and richness of the soil macroinvertebrate fauna and leaf litter depth were significantly lower close to forest roads than elsewhere (Haskell 2000).

In heavily settled areas, "natural" edge effects may be dwarfed by impacts of pedestrian traffic (Matlack 1993). Trampling of vegetation and disposing of garbage, for example, reach the farthest distances into a forest patch when roads are present, and most damage generally emanates from the nearest house (Matlack 1997). Forman and Deblinger (2000) identified a "road-effect zone" that extends outward from the road itself, at a distance that depends on the species in question. Although the actual road area may be small, when this road-effect zone is taken into account, the area of habitat directly affected by the road environment may become quite large. In a suburban–rural landscape near Boston, Forman, Reineking, and Hersperger (2002) discovered that traffic volume had a negative impact on grassland birds' presence and breeding activity; for roads with the heaviest volume (multilane highways), this impact stretched 3,937 feet (1,200 meters) from the highway. Likewise, roads have been shown to compromise habitat quality for forest-interior birds through traffic noise. In one European study (Reijnen et al. 1995), avian diversity was reduced and total bird density was one-third lower at distances from roads reaching out to 2,133 feet (650 meters). The authors found that traffic noise was a more important factor affecting bird densities than visual disturbance, the amount of air pollutants, or even the extent of predation, and they hypothesized that noise interfered with bird communication during the breeding period.

NEST PREDATION AND PARASITISM

Nest predation has been found to account for the largest proportion of nest failures of migrant songbirds, with landscape change factoring prominently in the problem (Burke and Nol 2000; Heske, Robinson, and Brawn 2001). The juxtaposition of natural and anthropogenic environments within rural and suburban landscapes often results in population increases of edge-loving species across many taxa that are largely opportunistic in nature, such as raccoons (*Procyon lotor*), coyotes (*Canis latrans*), red foxes (*Vulpes vulpes*), red-tailed hawks (*Buteo jamaicensis*), American robins (*Turdus migratorius*), and corvids (Oehler and Litvaitis 1996; Danielson, DeGraaf, and Fuller 1997; Heske, Robinson, and Brawn 1999). These and other species that flourish in open agriculture or suburban areas enter neighboring forest fragments to forage and in the process encounter bird eggs, among other prey items. In a similar vein, ground-nesting birds in grassland habitat patches are most vulnerable to nest predation near woody edges.

Nest predation rates are generally higher in small woodlots than in large forested tracts (Wilcove 1985; Burke and Nol 2000). Patterns suggest that predators are not selecting habitats on the basis of songbird nest density; instead, predation events are incidental and opportunistic (Danielson, DeGraaf, and Fuller 1997; Heske, Robinson, and Brawn 1999). Which species will be the dominant nest predators at a given site will depend on the region and on the nature of the local landscape (Danielson, DeGraaf, and Fuller 1997; Heske, Robinson, and Brawn 2001). Species with particularly high susceptibility to predation—including many area-sensitive migrant warblers, thrushes, vireos, and flycatchers—are open-cup nesters that nest close to the ground (Böhning-Gaese, Taper, and Brown 1993; Kluza, Griffin, and DeGraaf 2000; O'Connell, Jackson, and Brooks 2000). Many of these species are showing continental decreases in population sizes (Wilcove 1985; Böhning-Gaese, Taper, and Brown 1993). However, in at least one study, concealment of nests was found to have little impact on the extent of predation, probably because olfactory cues are more important for mammalian predators than are visual cues (Bayne and Hobson 1997). Although it is often assumed that nest predation itself is an edge phenomenon, closer scrutiny of research results shows that they do not support a universal axiom of higher nest predation near habitat edges, although there is a positive correlation between incidence of nest predation at edges and degree of landscape fragmentation (Lahti 2001).

Nest or brood parasites are bird species that lay their eggs in nests belonging to other species, leaving their young to be tended by them. The brood parasites typically have shorter incubation periods than their hosts, and nestlings are often able to outcompete the host's nestlings for food and parental attention. The best-studied nest parasite and a great example of a species that has benefited from forest fragmentation in North America is the brown-headed cowbird (*Molothrus ater*). Originally native to midwestern prairie habitats, cowbirds expanded their range both eastward and westward in response to the clearing of forests and other habitats for agriculture, in the process encountering many new potential host species (Robinson, Rothstein et al. 1995). Increases in cowbird populations in forested areas have coincided with declines in migrant bird species in many places in North America (Böhning-Gaese, Taper, and Brown 1993), and nest parasitism has indeed been shown to act in concert with nest predation as an important cause of nest failure and local extirpation of species in forest fragments (Robinson, Thompson et al. 1995).

As with predation, nest parasitism is not necessarily an edge effect; patterns of cowbird density and resulting rates of parasitism are not always associated with local edges (Faaborg et al. 1995). The same species may experience differential impacts from one locale to another. At the local level, the density of cowbirds may respond to the density of potential hosts, whereas at the landscape scale the amount of nonforest area or perimeter-to-area ratio may be more important (Faaborg et al. 1995; Robinson, Thompson et al. 1995). Geographic variation in parasitism levels is also apparent at a continental scale, with the highest levels of parasitism in North America evident in the Midwest, the stronghold of cowbird distribution (Robinson, Rothstein et al. 1995). Parasitism rate often does not display a relationship to forest fragment size or forest cover that is similar in kind to the relationship held by nest predation. Nest parasitism also does not have as large an impact as nest predation by virtue of the fact that even if a nest is parasitized, one or more young may fledge, whereas few eggs are spared during predation events (Burke and Nol 2000). In addition, some hosts have evolved mechanisms of escaping parasitism by ejecting eggs from their nests or by deserting their nests and renesting (Robinson, Rothstein et al. 1995).

INTERSPECIFIC COMPETITION

Shifts in the composition and structure of wildlife communities have taken place along with changes in human-induced habitat configuration and fragmentation, such that some species have been forced to share their ranges with a new suite of potential competitors, often over a short period on an evolutionary timescale. Species that are more specialized in their resource requirements tend to be the most vulnerable in the face of such change because they have a limited ability to take immediate advantage of alternative food sources that become available (Ray 2000; Litvaitis 2001).

Even if an animal is able to tolerate the habitat changes brought about by fragmentation of continuous forest, it may be unable to persist because of competition from another species. Raptors provide excellent examples of this phenomenon. Regional population declines of red-shouldered hawks (*Buteo lineatus*) have occurred simultaneously with increases in population of the more aggressive and opportunistic red-tailed hawks (which are generally able to take better advantage of early-successional habitats), leading many researchers to conclude that interrelationships between these species have played an important role in population declines of red-shouldered hawks (Crocoll 1994). Similarly, open-country raptors—such as great horned owls (*Bubo virginianus*), long-eared owls (*Asio otus*), and red-tailed hawks—normally steer clear of northern goshawk (*Accipiter gentilis*) territories in continuously forested areas. Once forests become fragmented, however, the competitive balance may shift, with such species able to invade goshawk territories in what has become degraded habitat for goshawks (Crocker-Bedford 1990). In the Northeast, bobcats appear to be experiencing a similar fate, with more opportunistic coyotes able to exploit rabbits more effectively than the relatively specialized cats, reducing such prey densities to a point where bobcats cannot efficiently prey on them except in the most productive habitats. Litvaitis (2001) thus speculates that coyotes are indirectly contributing to the regional decline of bobcat populations. It should be noted that these relationships between coexisting species are largely speculative; little or no research has convincingly demonstrated cause and effect in the wild. Owing to the daunting nature of the research task, the evidence thus far has been largely indirect, although it is compelling.

CONFLICT WITH HUMANS

The antagonistic relationship between humans and many carnivores makes it very challenging to separate the habitat effects of fragmentation per se from the increased adverse behavioral interaction with humans that development brings (Wilcove 1988). By contrast, conflict with humans does not play a role in influencing songbird responses to fragmentation and sprawl discussed previously, which relate almost exclusively to the manner in which such processes affect the amount, distribution, and quality of habitats. Species such as cougars, wolves, and black bears are actually quite flexible with respect to habitat requirements, but often avoid human settlements even though suitable habitat appears to exist (Weaver, Paquet, and Ruggiero 1996). It is usually conflict with humans that hastens the demise of large carnivores in settled areas or prevents their colonization of such areas. For example, gray wolves and mountain lions are quite capable of living in relatively open habitats; however, they tend to restrict themselves to forested landscapes in areas with heavy human presence (Mladenoff et al. 1995; Maehr 1997). The current range of black bear in eastern North America suggests that the species is forest dependent. Yet one study conducted in intensively farmed landscape recorded among the highest black bear density in the world (Anderson 1997, cited in Sunquist and Sunquist 2001), offering the possibility that as long as the intervening habitat between forest patches is free of human conflict, bear populations may survive substantial levels of forest fragmentation.

Conflict with humans has been the primary cause of historical carnivore population declines (Treves and Karanth 2003), and humans today are directly responsible for most mortality of adult large carnivores (Weaver, Paquet, and Ruggiero 1996; Woodroffe 2001; Treves and Karanth 2003), even though persecution is not as common as it once was. As a result, some large carnivores are able to persist only inside protected areas because of conflicts with humans outside the protected area boundaries (Woodroffe 2001). Species that range widely come frequently into contact with people, particularly in high-settlement areas (Woodroffe and Ginsberg 2000). This problem is sobering in light of the fact that no protected area in North America is currently large enough to support viable populations of large carnivores (Noss et al. 1996). Even smaller carnivores, such as canids, are not well liked and are subject to high human-caused mortality.

Numerous studies have demonstrated a negative relationship between carnivores and road densities (e.g., Van Dyke, Brocke, and Shaw 1986; Mladenoff et al. 1995). Roads not only contribute to fragmentation and, through edge effects, reduce habitat quality, but also provide access for humans. Road density is generally directly proportional to human population density (Brocke, O'Pezio, and Gustafson 1988), and road systems are notorious for increasing the efficiency of hunters (Brody and Pelton 1989). When avoidance of roads by individual carnivores can be demonstrated, it is likely learned behavior linked to costs and benefits perceived by individuals (Brody and Pelton 1989).

Like carnivores, many raptors are also habitat generalists. However, because they generally do not suffer the same conflict issues with humans, they are often in a better position to take advantage of the increased food resources sometimes associated with urbanization. Great-horned owls respond favorably, for example, to greater complexity of habitats available in an urban landscape, resulting in higher degree of selectivity for nests than in rural areas (Smith, Bosakowski, and Devine 1999). Even some raptors considered sensitive to forest fragmentation induced by clear-cut logging have been shown to nest successfully in urban and suburban areas provided that suitable habitat components are available (Love and Bird 2000). For example, the availability of perches to hunt from is an important factor influencing the quality of raptor habitats; the lack of this factor (as in many logged areas) will impede many species' ability to exploit prey resources, even if prey are abundant (Widen 1994). Likewise, many reports indicate successful nesting on human-made structures in suburban and urban areas throughout the world (Love and Bird 2000). In the case of Cooper's hawks (*Accipiter cooperii*), for example, suitable habitat components may come in the form of tall and large-diameter trees, such as ornamental shade trees. Nesting pairs have been shown to select trees with these characteristics even in busy residential and recreational areas, which may attract the birds because of high localized availability of food and water resources (Boal and Mannan 1998). Even though a raptor pair may not depend on a large area for nesting, the ranges required for foraging are often substantial, and because of low prey density such ranges may be perhaps prohibitively large in some areas of sprawl. Raptors are particularly vulnerable to disturbance during the fledgling stage, so nest site locations need protection from harassment by both humans and their pets (Cade et al. 1996). A host of dangers are posed by vehicles, buildings, utility lines, and refuse dumps (Love and Bird 2000). In spite of the lure of suitable structures and the sometimes elevated prey densities found in human-modified environments, urban living has numerous drawbacks (Love and Bird 2000).

THE LANDSCAPE CONTEXT

The composition and spatial configuration of a landscape can do much to off-set the negative influences of patch size and edge effects (Heske, Robinson, and Brawn 2001; Rodewald and Yahner 2001). For example, interior-forest bird species are more abundant in small forest fragments if these fragments are located within a larger landscape that contains a high proportion of forest cover (Villard, Trzcinski, and Merriam 1999; Austen et al. 2001). The configuration of local habitats determines the type and severity of nest predators as well as the intensity of cowbird parasitism and hence can be expected to affect processes within forest patches (Robinson, Thompson et al. 1995; Danielson, DeGraaf, and Fuller 1997; Lahti 2001). The importance of landscape context is clearly demonstrated when the songbird communities of agricultural landscapes and of industrial-forestry landscapes are compared. Invariably, the former, which are characterized by more abrupt edges and higher densities of subsidized predators, will yield more species loss (Askins 1994; Bayne and Hobson 1997; Heske, Robinson, and Brawn 1999; Rodewald and Yahner 2001). The forest patches left behind in sprawl-impacted landscapes can be expected to have edge effects that reach above and beyond "natural" edge effects (Matlack 1993). Within such areas, the context provided by housing density appears to exert an influence on songbird abundance and diversity patterns (Nilon, Long, and Zipperer 1995; Kluza, Griffin, and DeGraaf 2000; Odell and Knight 2001). Friesen, Eagles, and MacKay (1995) found lower abundances of neotropical migrant songbirds in forest patches surrounded by housing than in patches of the same size not surrounded by housing development. This factor was so important that even 9.88-acre (4-hectare) woodlots without nearby houses had higher abundances of songbirds than 61.75-acre (25-hectare) urban woodlots.

HOMOGENIZATION: A WORLD CHARACTERIZED BY SPRAWL BECOMES A LESS INTERESTING PLACE

Opportunistic species with generalized habitat requirements are often in the best position to take advantage of the new environments created by sprawl, whereas specialized members of a given animal community tend to disappear beyond some threshold of disruption. Although the initial effect of development may be to increase local diversity, the end point is often impoverished habitats and communities. Even worse, no matter where one lives in North America, the same players show up again and again in highly disturbed areas.

Mammalian carnivores typify this pattern, with certain species—such as raccoons, skunks, domestic cats, and some foxes—becoming dominant community members as patches of the original habitat become smaller and more isolated (Oehler and Litvaitis 1996; Crooks 2002). As one of the most highly urbanized regions in eastern Canada, Prince Edward Island provides an excellent illustration. Although the island never supported populations of large carnivores such as cougar, wolves, or wolverines, medium-size carnivores such as lynx (*Lynx canadensis*), marten (*Martes americana*), bobcat, fisher (*Martes pennanti*), and river otters (*Lontra canadensis*) were originally present (Ray 2000). All were extirpated by the 1890s; in their stead, striped skunks (*Mephitis mephitis*) and raccoons became established from fur farm escapees, and coyotes invaded from the mainland. Although the species richness of today's carnivore community is not that much different from the species richness of the nineteenth century, one would be well placed to argue that the community has become impoverished, having been replaced by the same suite of generalized predators that typify urban and suburban areas through northeastern North America (Ray 2000).

In examining the distribution and abundance of bird species across a gradient from relatively undisturbed to highly developed landscapes, shifts in composition can be detected. Passerines that thrive at the human-dominated end of the spectrum tend not to be area sensitive and are better adapted to disturbed habitats. Species diversity, however, will peak at moderately disturbed sites, where representatives of both area-sensitive and area-nonsensitive groups are present. Moderate levels of development may actually enhance diversity and abundance of available resources; however, the species that remain in the resulting landscape will be those that are the most equipped to co-opt novel resources (Blair 1996; O'Connell, Jackson, and Brooks 2000). O'Connell, Jackson, and Brooks (2000) argue that forest bird communities begin to lose their integrity when they are no longer dominated by species that are dependent on attributes of native ecosystems.

Raptor researchers have likewise found evidence of shifts in community composition, but not necessarily in diversity, with increasing human disturbance. For example, as red-shouldered hawks, northern goshawks, and barred owls (*Strix varia*) dropped out of suburban landscapes in New Jersey with increasing fragmentation, less sensitive and more opportunistic species such as great horned owls, red-tailed hawks, eastern screech-owls (*Otus asio*), and broad-winged hawks (*Buteo platypterus*) became more abundant. By the same token, such species became less abundant and eventually disappeared from increasing large wilderness areas (Bosakowski and Smith 1997). The hawks and owls in a study undertaken in Tucson, Arizona, were predictably found along a development gradient. Where a species occurred on the continuum was apparently a function of species-specific hunting strategies and prey preferences (Mannan et al. 2000).

ARE THERE THRESHOLDS TO SPRAWL-INDUCED LANDSCAPE CHANGE?

The threshold when landscape connectivity becomes disrupted is defined as the "transition range across which small changes in spatial pattern provide abrupt shifts in ecological responses" (With and Crist 1995:2446). When the remaining habitat patches are too small to allow persistence of subpopulations or are too far apart for frequent recolonization, a species may rapidly disappear from the landscape. For animals with large ranges, this threshold becomes the point at which movement options become severely limited because individuals are unable to move through the obstacles that have materialized (Sunquist and Sunquist 2001). Using computer models, With and King (2001) identified different habitat thresholds for different species in the landscape, ranging from 5 to 90 percent of the original habitat. The large range resulted from the unique responses exhibited by each species toward habitat fragmentation and landscape pattern.

Unfortunately, empirical data are sparse, although we do understand enough to know that common threshold values cannot be applied across species or across landscape types or configurations. As a result, single "cookbook" conservation targets can be wildly unrealistic (With and Crist 1995; Fahrig 2001). The degree to which area-sensitive species are influenced by habitat fragmentation may depend on both the abundance and the spatial configuration of habitat. It may also depend on the species' habitat specificity and movement abilities (With and Crist 1995), characteristics that can change from one locale to another. The factors determining the threshold may also vary across species and localities and may include the proportion of original habitat remaining (Vogelmann 1995; Fahrig 1998), fragment size (Bosakowski and Smith 1997; Burke and Nol 2000), road density (Mladenoff et al. 1995), or edge effects (Matlack 1993). Some authors have precisely identified thresholds of forest fragment area or percent forest cover (Askins, Philbrick, and Sugeno 1987; O'Connell, Jackson, and Brooks 2000). However, observed thresholds may in part be a function of study design, of size of landscape window and study area, and of the size and dispersion of study plots.

PROSPECTUS: ARE WE CLOSE TO ACHIEVING AN ACCURATE UNDERSTANDING OF IMPACTS OF URBAN SPRAWL ON AREA-SENSITIVE SPECIES?

The challenges to understanding wildlife responses to landscape change are legion and include the way in which impacts are measured, the evolution and time course of the change, the particularities of locations and species, and our knowledge of the mechanisms that drive the change. One danger is being unable to detect a problem with a population until long after the habitat has been reduced below some threshold (Fahrig 2001). Early effects of fragmentation can provide a potentially misleading picture, as has been demonstrated in the case of songbirds, when densities were at first observed to increase above normal levels owing to crowding (Hagan, Van der Haegen, and McKinley 1996). Individuals of many area-sensitive species may persist in a landscape several years after it is subjected to fragmentation, either because they are long-lived or because they exhibit fidelity to the breeding range (Crocker-Bedford 1990).

These results point to the importance of gathering data on mating and breeding success rather than just on presence or absence or even abundance because the latter characteristics are not necessarily indicative of a thriving population. This point has been borne out many times in studies of songbirds (Faaborg et al. 1995; Burke and Nol 2000). Only measures of breeding productivity can provide information as to whether a given habitat patch is acting as a source or a sink for the population—that is, whether it is contributing to or detracting from the population at large. Does a given subpopulation contribute enough such that the population's losses through mortality are at least compensated for? However, even in the case where a fragment is determined to be a sink, our limited knowledge of the phenomenon of dispersal in birds prohibits us from understanding the extent to which the fragment may be colonized even when production is low or nonexistent (Faaborg et al. 1995). Some human-created habitats may even function as "ecological traps" in that wildlife populations are attracted to them, but are subjected to higher rates of mortality than might otherwise occur in their natural habitats (Schlaepfer, Runge, and Sherman 2002). For example, burrowing owls (*Athene cunicularia*) in Florida apparently responded positively to increased prey densities around homes, but in areas that are the most heavily developed, they demonstrated an increase in human-caused nest failures and declines in the number of young fledged (Millsap and Bear 2000). Cooper's hawks in urban areas may have higher nesting densities than outside the cities, but nesting success is significantly lower (Boal and Mannan 1998).

Finally, the precise causes and effects of observed impacts on wildlife communities following human perturbations are not always obvious, particularly in the case where a site has a long and complicated history. Northeastern North America—the first area on the continent to be colonized by European settlers—has been subjected to intensive land-modification activities for at least 350 years (Foster 1992; Matlack 1997). Most of the natural region surrounding and extending south of the Canadian border was altered extensively through the processes of farming, fuelwood gathering, timbering, and even reforestation long before sprawl became the force of change we know today. The forests that have rebounded since the beginning of the twentieth century bear little resemblance to the forests of three centuries ago, and faunal communities have been extensively altered. Under such circumstances, therefore, interpretation of current patterns of change is by no means straightforward. Migratory songbirds and raptors add an extra dimension of ambiguity because it is not easy to surmise whether the ultimate root of population decline of a certain species is forces at work in the breeding grounds or in southern stopover or wintering ranges, including tropical forests (DeGraaf and Rappole 1995).

CONCLUSION: TAKE-HOME MESSAGES FOR LAND-USE PLANNERS

An inevitable result of increasing human populations and development activities in North America has been the damaging effects on wildlands and wildlife. Since World War II, these pressures have increasingly extended to land clearing to meet housing, commercial, and transportation needs. It is ironic that the resulting sprawl has at its root so many people's desire to move closer to nature and away from the confines of the urban quagmire; in the process of this movement, however, the very essence of what is natural is being erased or eroded. Although native species exhibit varying degrees of tolerance to such changes, it is typically the area-sensitive species—sensitive to habitat fragmentation by definition—that are among the first to disappear.

Citizens have frequently voiced concerns about paying such a steep price for development and often express the desire to retain biodiversity in as intact a condition as possible. Not surprisingly, land-use planners involved at the interface between wildlands and human communities have become increasingly sensitive to these issues. It is clear that biodiversity conservation in such areas requires an approach that goes beyond the mere "defensive," such as setting aside reserves (Terris 2002). Planners will instead have to be more proactive with respect to managing growth. In so doing, they will need to be alert to the actions that can have the greatest negative impact and to the ways in which negative effects might be realistically mitigated. Even a rudimentary understanding of the ecological basis of habitat fragmentation and destruction goes a long way toward making informed decisions regarding urbanization threats to wildlife populations and taking appropriate actions.

A few guiding principles can help ensure the persistence of populations of area-sensitive songbirds, raptors, and carnivores in sprawl-impacted environments:

1. Retain large blocks of natural habitat in the landscape (Matlack 1993; Burke and Nol 2000). (Unfortunately, published minimum critical sizes of fragments can vary considerably between regions or even between species [Faaborg et al. 1995].)
2. Cluster development (Odell and Knight 2001).
3. Maximize the amount of interior within habitat patches by minimizing area-to-perimeter ratios (Faaborg et al. 1995; Vogelmann 1995).
4. Minimize disturbance within large habitat blocks (Matlack 1993; Faaborg et al. 1995).
5. Avoid segmentation of large patches by roads or power lines (Matlack 1993; Askins 1994).
6. Make every effort to consolidate new roads and power lines into single corridors, preferably on the peripheries of natural-habitat blocks (Askins 1994; Faaborg et al. 1995).
7. Ensure connectivity between natural areas to facilitate movement between patches (Sanjayan and Crooks, chapter 11, this volume).
8. Apply buffers between houses and forest blocks, similar in nature to protective measures that are required for wetland habitats (Friesen, Eagles, and MacKay 1995).

We currently lack the precision that will make land-use planners and other decision makers comfortable with predicting impacts on wildlife from many activities common to suburban areas. There are no precise rules of thumb to follow regarding fragment size, number of fragments, area of remnant natural habitat, degree of isolation, and so on. Nevertheless, scientific research has provided a common objective frame of reference that can enable local communities, planners, developers, and landowners to work out among themselves the compromises necessary to forge lasting informed agreements about complex land-use issues that affect the most vulnerable components of the natural environment.

REFERENCES

Anderson, D. R.. 1997. Corridor use, feeding ecology, and habitat relationships of black bears in a fragmented landscape in Louisiana. M.S. thesis, University of Tennessee.

Askins, R.A. 1994. Open corridors in a heavily forested landscape: Impacts on shrubland and forest-interior birds. *Wildlife Society Bulletin* 22:339–347.

Askins, R.A., M.J. Philbrick, and D.S. Sugeno. 1987. Relationship between the regional abundance of forest and the composition of forest bird communities. *Biological Conservation* 39:129–152.

Austen, M.J.W., C.M. Francis, D.M. Burke, and M. S. W. Bradsteet. 2001. Landscape context and fragmentation effects on forest birds in southern Ontario. *Condor* 103:701–714.

Bayne, E.M., and K.A. Hobson. 1997. Comparing the effects of landscape fragmentation by forestry and agriculture on predation of artificial nests. *Conservation Biology* 11:1418–1429.

Bear shot in New York: Wayward bear was wandering state capital. 2000. Reuters, June 16.

Beier, P. 1993. Determining minimum habitat areas and habitat corridors for cougars. *Conservation Biology* 7:94–108.

———. 1995. Dispersal of juvenile cougars in fragmented habitat. *Journal of Wildlife Management* 59:228–237.

Blair, R.B. 1996. Land use and avian species diversity along an urban gradient. *Ecological Applications* 6:506–519.

Boal, C.W., and R.W. Mannan. 1998. Nest-site selection by Cooper's hawks in an urban environment. *Journal of Wildlife Management* 62:864–871.

Böhning-Gaese, K., M.I. Taper, and J.H. Brown. 1993. Are declines in North American insectivorous songbirds due to causes on the breeding range? *Conservation Biology* 7:76–86.

Bosakowski, T., and D.G. Smith. 1997. Distribution and species richness of a forest raptor community in relation to urbanization. *Journal of Raptor Research* 31:26–33.

Brocke, R.H., J.P. O'Pezio, and K.A. Gustafson. 1988. A forest management scheme mitigating impact of road networks on sensitive wildlife species. In R. M. DeGraaf and W. M. Healy, eds., *Is Forest Fragmentation a Management Issue in the Northeast?* 13–17. Northeastern Forest Experiment Station General Technical Report NE-140. Washington, D.C.: Department of Agriculture, Forest Service.

Brody, A.J., and M.R. Pelton. 1989. Effects of roads on black bear movements in western North Carolina. *Wildlife Society Bulletin* 17:5–10.

Burke, D.M., and E. Nol. 1998. Influence of food abundance, nest-site habitat, and forest fragmentation on breeding ovenbirds. *The Auk* 115:96–104.

———. 2000. Landscape and fragment size effects on reproductive success of forest-breeding birds in Ontario. *Ecological Applications* 10:1749–1761.

Cade, T.J., M. Martell, P. Redig, and G. Septon. 1996. Peregrine falcons in urban North America. In D.M. Bird, D. Varland, and J.J. Negro, eds., *Raptors in Human Landscapes: Adaptations to Built and Cultivated Environments*, 3–13. London: Academic Press.

Clark, T.W., S.C. Minta, A.P. Curlee, and P. M. Kareiva. 1999. A model ecosystem for carnivores in Greater Yellowstone. In T.W. Clark, A. P. Curlee, S.C. Minta, and P. M. Kareiva, eds., *Carnivores in Ecosystems: The Yellowstone Experience*, 1–9. New Haven, Conn.: Yale University Press.

Collinge, S.K. 1996. Ecological consequences of habitat fragmentation: Implications for landscape architecture and planning. *Landscape and Urban Planning* 36:59–77.

Craighead, F. L., M. E. Gilpin, and E. R. Vyse. 1999. Genetic considerations for carnivore conservation in the Greater Yellowstone Ecosystem. In T. W. Clark, A. P. Curlee, S. C. Minta, and P. M. Kareiva, eds., *Carnivores in Ecosystems: The Yellowstone Experience*, 285–322. New Haven, Conn.: Yale University Press.

Crocker-Bedford, D. C. 1990. Goshawk reproduction and forest management. *Wildlife Society Bulletin* 18:262–269.

Crocoll, S. T. 1994. Red shouldered hawk (*Buteo lineatus*). In A. Poole and F. Gill, eds., *The Birds of North America*, 1–20. Academy of Natural Sciences Bulletin, no. 107. Philadelphia: Academy of Natural Sciences.

Crooks, K. R. 2002. Relative sensitivities of mammalian carnivores to habitat fragmentation. *Conservation Biology* 16:488–502.

Danielson, W. R., R. M. DeGraaf, and T. K. Fuller. 1997. Rural and surburban forest edges: Effect on egg predators and nest predation rates. *Landscape and Urban Planning* 38:25–36.

DeGraaf, R. M., and J. H. Rappole. 1995. *Neotropical Migratory Birds: Natural History, Distribution, and Population Change*. Ithaca, N.Y.: Comstock.

Desrochers, A., and S. J. Hannon. 1997. Gap crossing decisions by forest songbirds during post-fledgling period. *Conservation Biology* 11:1204–1210.

Faaborg, J., M. Brittingham, T. Donovan, and J. Blake. 1995. Habitat fragmentation in the temperate zone. In T. E. Martin and D. M. Finch, eds., *Ecology and Management of Neotropical Migratory Birds: A Synthesis and Review of Critical Issues*, 357–380. New York: Oxford University Press.

Fahrig, L. 1998. When does fragmentation of breeding habitat affect population survival? *Ecological Modelling* 105:273–292.

———. 2001. How much habitat is enough? *Biological Conservation* 100:65–74.

Forman, R. T. T., and R. D. Deblinger. 2000. The ecological road-effect zone of a Massachusetts (U.S.A.) suburban highway. *Conservation Biology* 14:36–46.

Forman, R. T. T., and M. Godron. 1986. *Landscape Ecology*. New York: Wiley.

Forman, R. T. T., B. Reineking, and A. M. Hersperger. 2002. Road traffic and nearby grassland bird patterns in a suburbanizing landscape. *Environmental Management* 29:782–800.

Foster, D. R. 1992. Land use and vegetation dynamics in central Massachusetts: An historical perspective. *Journal of Ecology* 80:753–772.

Friesen, L. E., P. F. J. Eagles, and R. J. MacKay. 1995. Effects of residential development on forest-dwelling neotropical migrant songbirds. *Conservation Biology* 9:1408–1414.

Haas, C. A. 1995. Dispersal and use of corridors by birds in wooded patches on an agricultural landscape. *Conservation Biology* 9:845–854.

Hagan, J. M., W. M. Van der Haegen, and P. S. McKinley. 1996. The early development of forest fragmentation effects on birds. *Conservation Biology* 10:188–202.

Hansen, A. J., R. Rasker, B. Maxwell, J. J. Rotella, J. D. Johnson, A. W. Parmenter, L. Langner, W. B. Cohen, R. L. Lawrence, and M. P. V. Kraska. 2002. Ecological causes and consequences of demographic change in the New West. *BioScience* 52:151–162.

Harness, R. E., and K. R. Wilson. 2001. Electric-utility structures associated with raptor electrocutions in rural areas. *Wildlife Society Bulletin* 29:612–623.

Haskell, D. G. 2000. Effects of forest roads on macroinvertebrate soil fauna of the southern Appalachian mountains. *Conservation Biology* 14:57–63.

Helzer, C. J., and D. E. Jelinski. 1999. The relative importance of patch-area and perimeter-area ratio to grassland breeding birds. *Ecological Applications* 9:1448–1458.

Heske, E. J., S. K. Robinson, and J. D. Brawn. 1999. Predator activity and predation on song-bird nests on forest-field edges in east-central Illinois. *Landscape Ecology* 14:345–354.

———. 2001. Nest predation and neotropical migrant songbirds: Piecing together the fragments. *Wildlife Society Bulletin* 29:52–61.

Johnsgard, P. A. 1990. *Hawks, Eagles, and Falcons of North America.* Washington, D.C.: Smithsonian Institution Press

Kluza, D. A., C. R. Griffin, and R. M. DeGraaf. 2000. Housing developments in rural New England: Effects on forest birds. *Animal Conservation* 3:15–26.

Lahti, D. C. 2001. The "edge effect on nest predation" hypothesis after twenty years. *Biological Conservation* 99:365–374.

Litvaitis, J. A. 2001. Importance of early successional habitats to mammals in eastern forests. *Wildlife Society Bulletin* 29:466–473.

Lopez, J. A. 2001. The impact of communication towers on neotropical songbird populations. *Endangered Species Update* 18:50–54.

Lovallo, M. J., and E. M. Anderson. 1996. Bobcat movements and home ranges relative to roads in Wisconsin. *Wildlife Society Bulletin* 24: 71–76.

Love, O. P., and D. M. Bird. 2000. Raptors in urban landscapes: A review and future concerns. In R. D. Chancellor and B.-U. Meyburg, eds., *Raptors at Risk*, 425–434. Surrey, B.C.: Hancock House.

Maehr, D. S. 1997. *The Florida Panther: Life and Death of a Vanishing Carnivore.* Washington, D.C.: Island Press.

Maehr, D. S., T. S. Hoctor, and L. D. Harris. 2001. The Florida panther: A flagship for regional restoration. In D. S. Maehr, R. F. Noss, and J. L. Larkin, eds., *Large Mammal Restoration: Ecological and Sociological Challenges in the 21st Century,* 293–312. Washington, D.C.: Island Press.

Mannan, R. W., C. W. Boal, W. J. Burroughs, J. W. Dawson, T. S. Estabrook, and W. S. Richardson. 2000. Nest sites of five raptor species along an urban gradient. In R. D. Chancellor and B.-U. Meyburg, eds., *Raptors at Risk*, 447–453. Surrey, B.C.: Hancock House.

Matlack, G. R. 1993. Sociological edge effects—Spatial-distribution of human impacts in suburban forest fragments. *Environmental Management* 17:829–835.

———. 1997. Land use and forest habitat distribution in the hinterland of a large city. *Journal of Biogeography* 24:297–307.

Millsap, B. A., and C. Bear. 2000. Density and reproduction of burrowing owls along an urban development gradient. *Journal of Wildlife Management* 64:33–41.

Mladenoff, D. J., T. A. Sickley, R. G. Haight, and A. P. Wydeven. 1995. A regional landscape analysis and prediction of favorable gray wolf habitat in the northern Great Lakes region. *Conservation Biology* 9:279–294.

National Wildlife Federation. 2001. *Paving Paradise: Sprawl's Impact on Wildlife and Wild Places in California.* Washington, D.C.: National Wildlife Federation.

Nilon, C. H., C. N. Long, and W. C. Zipperer. 1995. Effects of wildland development on forest bird communities. *Landscape and Urban Planning* 32:81–92.

Noss, R. F., and B. Csuti. 1997. Habitat fragmentation. In G. K. Meffe and C. R. Carroll, eds., *Principles of Conservation Biology*, 269–304. 2d ed. Sunderland, Mass.: Sinauer Associates.

Noss, R. F., H. B. Quigley, M. G. Hornocker, T. Merrill, and P. C. Paquet. 1996. Conservation biology and carnivore conservation in the Rocky Mountains. *Conservation Biology* 10:949–963.

O'Connell, T. J., L. E. Jackson, and R. P. Brooks. 2000. Bird guilds as indicators of ecological condition in the central Appalachians. *Ecological Applications* 10:1706–1721.

Odell, E. A., and R. L. Knight. 2001. Songbird and medium-sized mammal communities associated with exurban development in Pitkin County, Colorado. *Conservation Biology* 15:1143–1150.

Oehler, J. D., and J. A. Litvaitis. 1996. The role of spatial scale in understanding responses of medium sized carnivores to forest fragmentation. *Canadian Journal of Zoology* 74:2070–2079.

Palomares, F., M. Delibes, P. Ferreras, J. M. Fedriani, J. Calzada, and E. Revilla. 2000. Iberian lynx in a fragmented landscape: Predispersal, dispersal, and postdispersal habitats. *Conservation Biology* 14:809–818.

Ray, J. C. 2000. *Mesocarnivores of Northeastern North America: Status and Conservation Issues.* Wildlife Conservation Society Working Paper, no. 15. Bronx, N.Y.: Wildlife Conservation Society.

——. 2005. Large carnivorous animals as tools for conserving biodiversity: Assumptions and uncertainties. In J. C. Ray, K. H. Redford, R. S. Steneck, and J. Berger, eds., *Large Carnivores and the Conservation of Biodiversity*, 34–56. Washington, D.C.: Island Press.

Reijnen, R., R. Foppen, C. ter Braak, and J. Thissen. 1995. The effects of car traffic on breeding bird populations in woodland. III. Reduction of density in relation to the proximity of main roads. *Journal of Applied Ecology* 32:187–202.

Robbins, C. S., J. R. Sauer, R. S. Greenberg, and S. Droege. 1989. Population declines in North American birds that migrate to the neotropics. *Proceedings of the National Academy of Sciences* (United States) 86:7658–7662.

Robinson, S. K., S. I. Rothstein, M. C. Brittingham, L. J. Petit, and J. A. Grzybowski. 1995. Ecology and behavior of cowbirds and their impact on host populations. In T. E. Martin and D. M. Finch, eds., *Ecology and Management of Neotropical Migratory Birds: A Synthesis and Review of Critical Issues*, 428–460. New York: Oxford University Press.

Robinson, S. K., F. R. Thompson III, T. M. Donovan, D. R. Whitehead, and J. Faaborg. 1995. Regional forest fragmentation and the nesting success of migratory birds. *Science* 267:1987–1990.

Rodewald, A. D., and R. H. Yahner. 2001. Avian nesting success in forested landscapes: Influences of landscape composition, stand and nest-patch microhabitat, and biotic interactions. *The Auk* 118:1018–1028.

Schlaepfer, M.A., M. C. Runge, and P. W. Sherman. 2002. Ecological and evolutionary traps. *Trends in Ecology and Evolution* 17:474–480.

Smith, D. G., T. Bosakowski, and A. Devine. 1999. Nest site selection by urban and rural great horned owls in the northeast. *Journal of Field Ornithology* 70:535–542.

Sunquist, M. E., and F. Sunquist. 2001. Changing landscapes: Consequences for carnivores. In J. L. Gittleman, S. L. Funk, D. Macdonald, and R. K. Wayne, eds., *Carnivore Conservation*, 399–418. Cambridge: Cambridge University Press.

Sweanor, L. L., K. A. Logan, and M. G. Hornocker. 2000. Cougar dispersal patterns, metapopulation dynamics, and conservation. *Conservation Biology* 14:798–808.

Terris, J. 2002. *Unwelcome Human Neighbors: The Impacts of Sprawl on Wildlife.* Washington, D.C.: Natural Resources Defense Council.

Treves, A., and K. U. Karanth. 2003. Human–carnivore conflict and perspectives on carnivore management worldwide. *Conservation Biology* 17:1491–1499.

Van Dyke, F. G., R. H. Brocke, and H. G. Shaw. 1986. Use of road track counts as indices of mountain lion presence. *Journal of Wildlife Management* 50:102–109.

Vickery, P. D., M. L. Hunter, and S. M. Melvin. 1994. Effects of habitat area on the
distribution of grassland birds in Maine. *Conservation Biology* 8:1087–1097.

Villard, M. A., M. K. Trzcinski, and G. Merriam. 1999. Fragmentation effects on forest
birds: Relative influence of woodland cover and configuration on landscape occupancy. *Conservation Biology* 13:774–783.

Vogelmann, J. E. 1995. Assessment of forest fragmentation in southern New England
using remote sensing and geographic information systems technology. *Conservation
Biology* 9:439–449.

Weaver, J. L., P. C. Paquet, and L. F. Ruggiero. 1996. Resilience and conservation of
large carnivores in the Rocky Mountains. *Conservation Biology* 10:964–976.

Widen, P. 1994. Habitat quality for raptors—A field experiment. *Journal of Avian
Biology* 25:219–223.

Wiens, J. A. 1996. Wildlife in patchy environments: Metapopulations, mosaics,
and management. In D. R. McCullough, ed., *Metapopulations and Wildlife
Conservation*, 53–84. Washington, D.C.: Island Press.

Wilcove, D. S. 1985. Nest predation in forest tracts and the decline of migratory songbirds. *Ecology* 66:1211–1214.

———. 1988. Forest fragmentation as a wildlife management issue in the eastern
United States. In R. M. DeGraaf and W. M. Healy, eds., *Is Forest Fragmentation a
Management Issue in the Northeast?* 1–5. Northeastern Forest Experiment Station
General Technical Report NE-140. Washington, D.C.: Department of Agriculture,
Forest Service.

Wilcove, D. S., D. Rothstein, J. Dubow, A. Phillips, and E. Losos. 1998. Quantifying
threats to imperiled species in the United States. *BioScience* 48:607–615.

With, K. A., and T. O. Crist. 1995. Critical thresholds in species' responses to landscape
structure. *Ecology* 76:2446–2459.

With, K. A., and A. W. King. 2001. Analysis of landscape sources and sinks: The effect of
spatial pattern on avian demography. *Biological Conservation* 100:75–88.

Woodroffe, R. 2001. Strategies for carnivore conservation: Lessons from contemporary
extinctions. In J. L. Gittleman, S. M. Funk, D. Macdonald, and R. K. Wayne, eds.,
Carnivore Conservation, 61–92. Cambridge: Cambridge University Press.

Woodroffe, R., and J. R. Ginsberg. 2000. Ranging behaviour and vulnerability to extinction in carnivores. In L. M. Gosling and W. J. Sutherland, eds., *Behaviour and
Conservation*, 125–140. Cambridge: Cambridge University Press.

10

SPECIES THAT BENEFIT FROM SPRAWL

Stephen DeStefano and Elizabeth A. Johnson

E nvironmental conditions throughout the world have always been in a state of change. In many cases, such as the uplifting or erosion of mountains, the change is gradual. In the face of gradual change—measured over geologic time—species adapt and evolve. In the face of rapid environmental change, however, there is simply not enough time for many species to adapt. Most species either are preadapted to the conditions brought about by such changes or are extirpated and become locally extinct.

For any species or community of species to exist in a given environment, the range of environmental conditions must be within the range tolerated by that species. Biological diversity will be high where the range of conditions suits the widest number of species (e.g., a tropical forest) and low in environments that have harsher, narrow ranges of conditions (e.g., the coast of Antarctica). As conditions along environmental gradients become extreme—whether of temperature, salinity, elevation, or some other factor or combination of factors—fewer organisms are able to cope, and biodiversity declines.

Among the changes and challenges in environmental conditions faced by the Earth's species during the past several centuries, the rapid change in environmental conditions caused by the exponentially growing human population may be the greatest. It is responsible for what many ecologists feel is the latest and perhaps greatest "extinction spasm" the planet has known (Soulé and Wilcox 1980; Chapin et al. 2000). Not only does the Earth's human population continue to grow exponentially, but our demands for resources—such as energy, building materials, food, and space—continue to increase at a tremendous rate (Vitousek et al. 1997; Liu et al. 2003).

An outgrowth of rapidly increasing human populations and resource consumption is urbanization (Marzluff, Bowman, and Donnelly 2001). Sprawling environments often have cities as their epicenters, and the resulting growth that spreads out from these population centers can form a gradient, transitioning from urban to suburban to rural to natural areas (McDonnell and Pickett 1990). Change—to the landscape, to the structure of the environment, and to ecological processes—is rapid. One result is that the number of species able to cope with these conditions declines with the greater amount and degree of human development. Fewer native species of birds, mammals, amphibians, fishes, and aquatic invertebrates are found in more heavily developed areas than in less-developed areas, and cultivated plants and domestic animals tend to replace native species (Minton 1968; Limburg and Schmidt 1990; Blair 1996; Knutson et al. 1999; Marzluff 2001; Morley and Karr 2002).

Of the species that remain in developed areas, their numbers are usually high, sometimes to the point of being labeled "overabundant" by the local human residents. These species are synanthropic to varying degrees; that is, they are able to coexist with humans (Johnston 2001), some being subsidized by or relying on humans for their existence (Mitchell and Klemens 2000). These plants and animals actually benefit from urban and suburban development, sometimes to the detriment of other species and sometimes merely from the ability to exploit conditions that other species cannot.

In this chapter, we highlight representative examples of the species that can thrive in human-dominated environments. We examine their common characteristics and discuss some of the problems and benefits that can be construed from their close association with humans.

THE URBAN–SUBURBAN ENVIRONMENT

To understand how some species exploit urban and suburban developments, whereas others cannot, it is important to understand the changes to environmental conditions and processes that result from urbanization and suburbanization. In the United States and other countries experiencing rapid urbanization, land development takes at least two major courses: expansion of urban areas along the urban fringe and large-lot development (greater than 1 acre [0.4 hectare]) for single-family homes, which can take place along the urban edge or farther out into rural areas. In many countries, such as in Latin America and Asia, large cities continue to grow in both number of people and land area, which is also true for cities in the United States. But the building of homes in suburbs and rural settings, such as agricultural fields, consumes more land per unit of housing than development associated with urban expansion (Heimlich and Anderson 2001). Although cities in the United States and other countries continue to grow, it is the sprawling suburbs—consisting largely of single-family housing units, large yards, roadways, and services such as strip malls and

shopping centers—that consume large areas of land. This suburban development or sprawl alters the natural landscape and has an effect on the composition and distribution of biodiversity to a greater degree than urban growth.

Most conservation biologists would agree that the effects of sprawl are largely
negative for native flora and fauna (Marzluff 2002; DeStefano and DeGraaf
2003). As the Earth's landscapes become ever more dominated by humans, the
threat to the remaining natural world becomes larger and more pervasive. At
the same time, however, some species have a distinct suite of attributes enabling
them to occupy urban, suburban, and disturbed environments successfully. It
is important to remember several principles when examining this group of species. First, organisms respond to the environmental conditions around them.
Some species will not only be able to tolerate conditions in developed areas,
but also actually be able to exploit those conditions for their own success. The
subsidies of food, water, shelter, or other resources or conditions provided by
people often allow these species to thrive in human-dominated environments
(Mitchell and Klemens 2000). Second, there are no intrinsically "bad" species.
Introduced exotics such as kudzu (*Pueraria lobata*), zebra mussels (*Dreissena
polymorpha*), and European starlings (*Sturnus vulgaris*); nest predators such
as Australian magpies (*Gymnorhina tibicen*), American crows (*Corvus brachyrhynchos*), and common ravens (*C. corax*); mammalian predators such as coyotes (*Canis latrans*) and mongooses (Family Viverridae); and species that may
damage property, such as white-tailed deer (*Odocoileus virginianus*) and beaver
(*Castor canadensis* in North America and *C. fiber* in Europe), are merely responding to the landscape conditions caused by humans' intentional or unintentional actions. In order to understand how some species benefit from development, we need to understand the environmental elements and conditions
that exist in these areas, which form the habitat and niches suitable for urban
and suburban plants and animals.

CHARACTERISTICS OF URBAN–SUBURBAN ENVIRONMENTS

The most obvious characteristics of urbanization are the people, buildings,
and roads—all of them in high densities. The habitat or vegetative cover
that does remain tends to be fragmented into islandlike patches in a matrix
of development (Knight 1990; VanDruff, Bolen, and San Julian 1994). As
development expands, these habitat patches become smaller and more isolated. Species–area relationships dictate that as area decreases, so does the
number of species present (Kinzig and Grove 2001). Thus as urban centers
grow in size and degree of development, the amount of land available for
native wild plants and animals within the city or village declines and so
does overall biodiversity. The species that remain and thrive in these areas

are either unaffected or are favored by these patterns of habitat fragmentation.

The amount of edge between different cover types increases with the proliferation of distinct habitat patches. This increase can benefit species that favor edges, but it can also increase vulnerability to predation, especially to nests (Russo and Young 1997; Manolis, Andersen, and Cuthbert 2002). Gradual edge transitions, such as from a woodlot to a shrubby border to a field, are beneficial to a wider variety of plants and animals than, for example, the sharp edge contrasts found between a grove of trees and a vacant lot. In addition, connectivity among patches is poor in developed areas, and those species that are able to travel from one patch to another encounter new and pervasive forms of mortality, such as road traffic, curbs and catch basins, and domestic animals (Adams and Geis 1983; Barratt 1998; Crooks and Soulé 1999; Shuttleworth 2001; Calhoun and Klemens 2002; Gibbs and Shriver 2002). Most natural environments, even relatively undisturbed ones, have some level of patchiness, especially when different perspectives of scale are considered, but a high degree of patchiness, sharp edge contrasts, fragmentation, and isolation are especially characteristic of urban environments (Niemalä 1999).

Urban and suburban areas show a higher prevalence of small-scale disturbances than most (nondeveloped) areas where humans are less pervasive. Activities such as mowing, removing brush, and grading open lots down to bare soil create disturbances that promote early-successional vegetation stages that favor early-successional species (Niemelä 1999). These disturbances also occur at much more frequent time intervals in urban settings (mowing occurs weekly, brush and leaf litter removal occurs annually), and the material is removed and not allowed to recycle back through the system (grass clippings, leaves, and tree branches do not decompose in situ). At the same time, large-scale disturbances such as wildfire and floods are minimized or eliminated (Reice, chapter 4, this volume). Major disturbances, such as 100-year floods, play an important role in regional ecology, but are in conflict with the kind of stability sought by city and town residents.

The structure of habitat patches within urban–suburban environments is often simplified by human activity (Jokimäki 1999). For example, groupings of trees, such as in parks, undergo pruning and thinning to manipulate growth forms into similar sizes and shapes, removal of dead and dying standing and downed wood (snags and logs), and clearing of the understory. This grooming removes much of the structure of the habitat that provides a variety of niches for an array of organisms; for example, the brushy undercover can provide nesting cover for songbirds and escape cover for rabbits. The same is true of grassy areas; natural meadows and grasslands that are mowed infrequently (say, one to two times per year rather than weekly) have taller vegetation and a more diverse array of plants and thus have a more complex structure than suburban lawns and golf courses.

All these circumstances make urban and suburban environments more conducive to biological invasions, to native species that are adapted to these conditions, but also to many exotic species. Urbanization and the spread of exotic species are correlated, and human developments act as a source for populations of nonindigenous species (Withers et al. 1998). People knowingly or unwittingly contribute to the spread of nonnative plants and animals, and where human densities are highest, exotic biodiversity is greatest. The processes characteristic of urbanization described earlier—disturbance, the setting back of succession, simplification of the environment—often favor the spread of certain exotic species. In addition, exotic species are aided or subsidized by people either intentionally through introduction and cultivation or unintentionally through accidental transportation. The native species that do remain are in such a dramatically altered environment from the one they evolved to fit that they may have no competitive advantage over newly introduced species (Byers 2002; Johnson and Klemens, chapter 2, this volume).

Despite the dramatic changes that urbanization causes to local environments, urban and suburban areas are nonetheless ecosystems, either in and of themselves or as part of larger regional ecosystems (Zipperer et al. 2000). Ecological functions, such as energy flow, hydrologic cycles, and plant and animal community dynamics, take place within cities and towns, albeit in altered states (Pickett et al. 2001). The creation of these new ecosystems brings about new ecological relationships, even including changes in soil chemistry, leaf litter quality, and exotic invertebrates (McDonnell et al. 1997). The result has been termed a *recombinant community*—an entirely different array of plants and animals than was there historically (Soulé 1990). These organisms survive under the newly created conditions brought about by urbanization and develop new interactions and relationships. For example, house cats (*Felis catus*) are common in cities and towns, and they will prey on a variety of introduced species such as house sparrows (*Passer domesticus*), starlings, rats, and mice, but also on native songbirds and small mammals.

HABITATS AND HABITAT COMPONENTS IN
URBAN–SUBURBAN ENVIRONMENTS

Although urbanization destroys, degrades, or alters many kinds of habitats, it also creates others. These *habitats* (a term used loosely here to identify landcover types that can be used by plants and animals; for further discussion of this term, see Hall, Krausman, and Morrison 1997) are often structurally simple and exist as small, dispersed patches. Nonetheless, some species will use them. In addition, other habitat components, such as shelter and water, are often provided in urban and suburban areas, some intentionally for wildlife and some as offshoots of the developed landscape.

Parks, golf courses, greenways, and other open spaces create habitat for some species, such as eastern gray squirrels (*Sciurus carolinensis*) in North America, blackbirds (*Turdus merula*) and song thrushes (*T. philomelos*) in New Zealand, and even some species of kangaroo (Family Macropodidae) in Australia. Almost any assemblage of vegetation can provide shelter, nest sites, and food in the midst of towns and cities. Vacant lots, although usually unintended by city or town planners, are another version of open space. If these lots are surrendered to natural succession, they provide a place for plants and animals, both native and nonnative. In Tucson, Arizona, species such as creosote bush (*Larrea tridentata*) and ocotillo (*Fouquieria splendens*), several types of cactus, and many species of songbirds and lizards inhabit or frequent vacant lots (S. DeStefano, personal observation).

Lawns can provide food and resting sites for geese and prey such as earthworms and other invertebrates for starlings, robins, and flickers. Lawns are thought to be particularly important to the proliferation of starlings in urban environments (Mennechez and Clergeau 2001) and are another good example of species subsidy. Gardens (both vegetable and flower) provide food and sometimes shelter and breeding sites, but also are a source of cultivated, nonindigenous plants that often escape into the wild.

Increased availability of water and food (for animals) and nutrients (for plants) are among the chief factors that draw some species to urban and suburban environments. These resources may not only serve to establish the presence of some species, but contribute to individual fitness (i.e., the ability to remain healthy and maximize reproduction) and demographic success (i.e., high productivity and survival, resulting in increased population size).

Examples of plants and animals that benefit from abundant water and food in urban and suburban settings are not difficult to find. In the desert Southwest, urban javelina (*Tayassu tajacu*) adjusted their home ranges and activity patterns to best use available water and food (Ticer et al. 1994), and individual saguaro cactus (*Carnegiea gigantea*) plants may benefit from being inside city limits because there is a more consistent and larger supply of water (figure 10.1). Canada geese (*Branta canadensis*) are common around city parks and golf courses in the Northeast because of the availability of water and grass.

Shelter and breeding sites for wildlife can be available opportunistically or intentionally as well. Sheds, basements, porches, building foundations, culverts, fence rows, and brush piles can provide cover from both predators and weather. The opossum (*Didelphis virginiana*) has likely increased its range northward because buildings have allowed it to survive colder winter temperatures (De-

FIGURE 10.1. Individual saguaro cactus (*Carnegiea gigantea*) plants may benefit from being inside city limits because there is a more consistent and larger supply of water. The Tucson, Arizona, homeowner stated that this cactus grew rapidly and large, with many arms, at least in part aided by an underground irrigation system. (Photo by Stephen DeStefano)

Graaf and Yamasaki 2001; T. K. Fuller, personal communication, March 2003). Roadrunners (*Geococcyx californianus*) will nest in carports, on sheds, and in ornamental trees in the desert cities of the southwestern United States (Webster 2000). Bird and bat houses are common examples of intentionally provided shelter.

RESPONSES TO DEVELOPMENT

DISTURBANCE AND DIVERSITY

As mentioned previously, overall biodiversity tends to decline with increasing urbanization. Centers of metropolitan cities or large industrial parks will have fewer species than less-developed areas on the urban-suburban-rural-natural gradient. Species diversity may actually be greater, however, in lightly developed suburban areas than in less-disturbed environments. According to the *intermediate disturbance hypothesis* (Connell 1978), species richness or diversity will be greater in moderately disturbed environments than in either heavily disturbed areas (such as city centers) or lightly disturbed habitats (such as intact forestland outside the city limits). Thus it is not urbanization per se that causes an increase in biodiversity, but the moderate increase in disturbance that creates a wider array of vegetative cover types. In this case, the increase in biodiversity often comes about because more habitat generalist species occupy the area; species that specialize in interior forest usually decline or are extirpated. Research on several taxa—including birds (Jokimäki and Suhonen 1993; Blair 1999), insects (Eversham, Roy, and Telfer 1996; Blair and Launer 1997; Blair 1999), and arthropods and plants (Niemelä 1999)—supports the intermediate disturbance theory as it relates to suburban development, but the type and level of development is critical. Moderate development may create a wider array of vegetation types in some areas, thus increasing biodiversity on a local level. Extensive development, however, is characterized by a decrease in biodiversity.

DEGREES OF SYNANTHROPY

Species responses to development can be placed into several broad categories, and the responses among and within groups can vary greatly. *Urban-sensitive species* are those species that cannot cope with the rapid change and conditions of urbanization. Such species are very sensitive to human activities. For example, desert bighorn sheep (*Ovis canadensis mexicana*) (Schoenecker and Krausman 2002) require large expanses of land, as do many large carnivores, and are adversely affected by loss and fragmentation of their habitat. *Obligate* or *full synanthropes* are species that have a symbiotic relationship with humans, such as house mice (*Mus musculus*), Norway rats (*Rattus norvegicus*), house sparrows, rock pigeons (*Columba livia*), European starlings, and perhaps chimney swifts (*Chaetura pelagica*). These species have become essentially dependent on humans for at least part of their life history requirements, such as food, components of their habitat, or assistance with dispersal, and their presence in North America would be very different from what it is today without human development. *Casual synanthropes* can exploit human ecology without necessarily being dependent on it. Gulls (*Larus* spp.) are good examples, taking advantage of food at garbage dumps to supplement their diet. *Tangential synanthropes* include individuals within a species that occasionally exploit human ecology. Johnston (2001) states that these species are more difficult to classify because individuals exhibit different degrees of synanthropy. For example, individuals among certain species of raptors such as red-tailed hawks (*Buteo jamaicensis*), Cooper's hawks (*Accipiter cooperii*), peregrine falcons (*Falco peregrinus*), and great horned owls (*Bubo virginianus*) will nest on buildings, utility line poles, or neighborhood shade trees in cities and towns. These species are widely distributed across North America and are not dependent on humans to provide nest structures, but some individuals will opportunistically use anthropogenic features of the urban and suburban environment (for a full discussion of synanthropy, see Johnston 2001).

CHARACTERISTICS OF URBAN SYNANTHROPES

The response to urban sprawl will vary even among species that can exist or benefit from development, but some general trends can be identified. Because large body size usually equates to large space requirements, big animals are less likely to be present in urban or suburban environments. This is especially true of carnivores. Wolves (*Canis lupus*) and mountain lions (*Puma concolor*) are not nearly as likely to be present in and around cities and towns as are coyotes, raccoons (*Procyon lotor*), and red foxes (*Vulpes vulpes*). The fishing cat (*Prionailurus virverrinus*) is about the size of a lynx (*Lynx canadensis*) and can be found in residential areas in Colombo, the largest city in Sri Lanka (Seidensticker 2003). Moose (*Alces alces*) have some tolerance for suburbia (Schneider and Wasel 2000), but not nearly to the degree of white-tailed deer. Many species that are successful in developed areas, especially those that are casual synanthropes, are life history generalists—their diet is varied, and they can use a variety of cover types as habitat (DeStefano and DeGraaf 2003). A generalist life history strategy is helpful in an environment that is varied and changing, as in urban and suburban settings. These species also tend to be behaviorally adaptive, being able to tolerate the presence of humans.

In general, K-selected species (long-lived species with delayed breeding and low reproductive rates) are less likely to do well in disturbed environments than r-selected species (short-lived species with high reproductive rates). Gambel's quail (*Callipepla gambelii*) are common in the southwestern desert cities and suburbs of Tucson and Phoenix. These birds are good examples of r-selected species; they generally live only 1.5 years on average, but begin reproducing at an early age (before reaching one year old) and produce large clutches of eggs (usually 10–12) (Brown et al. 1998). In contrast, most turtle species, which are K-selected, do poorly in urban areas, where mortality rates of long-lived adults outpace recruitment rates (Klemens 1989; Congdon, Dunham, and Van Loben Sels 1993).

A long history of close association with humans can affect birds' life history strategies and evolutionary pathways (Johnston and Selander 1964; Johnston 2001). Martin and Clobert (1996) have shown that some European species' longevity and fecundity have changed in response to high human populations. The general trend is to favor higher fecundity but shorter lives, probably in response to increased predation by humans and other predators (Martin and Clobert 1996; Johnston 2001). Thus individuals favored in human-dominated environments are more likely to be short-lived with high reproductive rates.

Those species present in suburban areas will likely be able to cope with a patchy environment composed of early-successional-stage vegetation. A wide variety of songbirds, such as northern mockingbirds (*Mimus polyglottos*), northern cardinals (*Cardinalis cardinalis*), and song sparrows (*Melospiza melodia*), may be well adapted for the patchy environment of the suburbs of the northeastern United States, whereas other species that require large habitat tracts will not—such as ovenbirds (*Seiurus aurocapillus*) and hermit thrushes (*Catharus guttatus*) in forest and brown thrashers (*Toxostoma rufum*) in open or brushy areas (DeGraaf and Wentworth 1981, 1986).

Mobility or lack of mobility can also play a role in a species's susceptibility to urban sprawl. Species with limited movement capabilities can become isolated from conspecifics in highly disturbed, fragmented environments. Animals that do move within cities and towns often become subject to a major source of mortality or morbidity—death or injury from impacts or crushing by motor vehicles accounts for the death of many animals (Gibbs and Shriver 2002; for a more detailed discussion, see also Byers and Mitchell, chapter 8, this volume). For example, more than 90 percent of mortality or morbidity in 19 coyotes in Tucson, Arizona, was caused by humans (11 killed by vehicles, 5 hit by vehicles, 2 trapped, 1 unknown) (Grinder and Krausman 2001b).

Some animals may also change their behavior when occupying urban or suburban environments. Coyotes and red foxes change the time when they are active, becoming more nocturnal, when living in cities or towns rather than in their native habitat (Andelt and Mahan 1980; Adkins and Stott 1998; Grinder and Krausman 2001a). Individual birds of the species great tit (*Parus major*) sing at higher frequencies in noisier urban areas than individuals in more rural areas (Slabbekoorn and Peet 2003). The ability to be heard increases chances of getting and keeping territories. Because of greater high-noise levels in urban environments, the higher frequencies of the tits' songs are more likely to be heard by other birds and more likely to be copied by juveniles learning the songs.

DEMOGRAPHIC RESPONSES

As urbanization increases, biodiversity typically decreases, but the remaining species tend to be very abundant. Underlying this phenomenon is the high demographic success of those few abundant species; that is, their reproduction and survival are high. The density or abundance of a species does not necessarily mean that its population is stable or even viable (van Horne 1983). Animals can be drawn to areas that appear to have the proper cues, only to face unforeseen mortality of either adults or young or both. These so-called *population sinks* (Pulliam 1988) are important considerations for the metapopulation dynamics of urban and suburban wildlife.

The American robin (*Turdus migratorius*) is certainly one of the most recognized species in many cities and towns. Robins respond positively to the shade trees and lawns of urban parks and suburban yards. However, Howard (1974) found that robins' productivity in a suburb of Boston was too low to maintain the population. She believed that ground-level disturbance from intensive human activity, heavy predation (particularly by crows), and low food availability because of a lack of leaf litter and repeated use of pesticides made it necessary for this suburban robin population to be periodically replenished by immigration.

Gulls are also perceived to have increased in abundance because of their close association with humans and garbage dumps. However, Pierotti and Annett (2001) found that productivity of western gulls (*Larus occidentalis*) was negatively influenced by urbanization. They showed that an increase of human refuse with a concurrent decrease in fish in the gulls' diet had negative effects on fledgling nutrition and survival. They believed it is best to view gulls as not necessarily doing well in urban environments, but rather as being adaptable enough to persist under such conditions.

Boal and Mannan (1998, 1999) reported that Cooper's hawks are drawn to the city of Tucson by the presence of water, small groves of large trees (many of them exotic species such as eucalyptus [*Eucalyptus* spp.] and aleppo pine [*Pinus halepensis*]) for nesting, and high densities of prey (at least some of them exotic species, such as Inca doves [*Columbina inca*]). Nesting densities and productivity of Cooper's hawks were higher in urban versus exurban areas, but juvenile hawks suffered high mortality in the city owing to the disease trichomoniasis (Boal et al. 1998; Boal, Mannan, and Hudelson 1998). Thus Tucson may have been acting as a sink for Cooper's hawks, drawing adult birds in for breeding, but causing nestlings to suffer from high rates of mortality from urban-related disease.

MAJOR TAXA AND SPECIES

In the following paragraphs, we provide a sampling of selected species characteristic of some urban and sprawled suburban environments.

BIRDS

Birds are among the most heavily studied terrestrial vertebrates (DeStefano 2002). Early interest in urban wildlife focused on attracting birds to backyards;

American households spend millions, probably billions, of dollars annually feeding wild birds (DeGraaf and Payne 1975; DeStefano and DeGraaf 2003).

As early as the mid-seventeenth century, it was known that chimney swifts nested in the chimneys in the homes of American colonists (Josselyn [1672] 1860). Examples of close associations between birds and people, such as storks nesting on the chimneys and rooftops of houses in Europe, have a long history. In general, however, increased urbanization usually equates with fewer ground-nesting and low-nesting birds because of people's and pets' increased activities, the loss of understory cover (Preston 1946; Howard 1974), and an increase in exotics over natives (Germaine et al. 1998).

Johnston (2001) examined synanthropy in birds of North America and concluded that at least 25 percent of all avian species are either full (or obligate), casual, or tangential synanthropes. Of these 213 species, 30 percent (63) use some form of urban habitat. The chimney swift, common house sparrow, and rock pigeon are among the few truly obligate synanthropic species. These species benefit directly from a close association with humans, and their continued existence, at least locally, depends on inputs or subsidies from humans, usually in the way of food, structural habitat (such as buildings for nest sites), or assistance in dispersal.

Most of the 213 species Johnston examined are casual (39 species, 18 percent) or tangential (161 species, 76 percent) in their relations to humans. Among the casual species are the familiar house finch (*Carpodacus mexicanus*), the American robin, and several species of gulls and doves. Tangential species include the northern mockingbird, northern cardinal, dark-eyed junco (*Junco hyemalis*), blue jay (*Cyanocitta cristata*) and Stellar's jay (*C. stellari*), American crow, common raven, chickadees, nuthatches, many species of sparrows, and several species of blackbirds and orioles.

Only 13 species (6 percent) are full or obligate synanthropes. Not all of them are urban dwellers; several species of upland game birds, such as the chukar (*Alectoris chukar*) and ring-necked pheasant (*Phasianus colchicus*), owe their existence in North America to people. Of these 13 species of obligate synanthropes, 11 (85 percent) are introduced exotics from Europe or Asia. Only the chimney swift and purple martin (*Progne subis*) are native, each taking advantage of human-provided nest sites—one intentional (purple martin houses) and one not (chimneys).

WATERFOWL Among waterfowl, mallards (*Anas platyrhynchos*) and Canada geese are common urban and suburban residents (Conover and Chasko 1985; Ankney 1996). Open water, aquatic vegetation, and grass—common components of parks and golf courses—attract these birds to developed areas (Adams, Dove, and Franklin 1985; Conover 1991). Heated water from power plants and other sources that keep water free of ice allow Canada geese and mallards to remain in developed areas during some winters longer than they would normally and sometimes for the entire winter. Mute swans (*Cygnus olor*) are also common residents of urban parks, having been brought here from Europe. They are aggressive during the breeding season and sometimes prevent other waterbirds from nesting in their territories.

CORVIDS AND RAPTORS Marzluff and colleagues (2001) report that populations of corvids (crows, ravens, jays, and magpies) are increasing worldwide in response to agriculture and urbanization. American crow populations peak in urban and suburban areas probably because abundant food draws exurban crows into cities and towns and allows them to breed in higher densities (Marzluff et al. 2001; McGowan 2001).

Many species of raptors can take advantage of the nest sites and high abundance of prey that exist in cities and town. Peregrine falcons, once an icon of endangerment, now nest on the roofs and ledges of some of the highest buildings in major cities, feeding themselves and their young on the plentiful pigeons. Cooper's hawks and great horned owls are drawn into suburban environments for the same reasons (food and nest sites). Red-tailed hawks, one of the most widespread raptor species in North America, will establish territories within and on the edges of suburbia, as will Swainson's hawks (*Buteo swainsoni*) and American kestrels (*Falco sparverius*) (Berry, Bock, and Haire 1998). Many of these species are common and widespread and are adapted to a wide range of conditions and tolerant of the presence of humans if not persecuted (figure 10.2).

FIGURE 10.2. Many birds of prey take advantage of groves of trees or artificial structures near urban or suburban areas for nesting. It is not uncommon to see osprey (*Pandion haliaetus*) nests on power lines and similar structures in Florida and other states throughout the bird's range. (Photo by Stephen DeStefano)

MAMMALS

DEER Deer, in particular white-tailed deer, are very successful in suburban settings, responding favorably to the abundance of edge habitat, food, and protection from mortality, specifically hunting and predation (Gaughan 2003). White-tailed deer are so successful, in fact, that they are often labeled as "overabundant" by suburban residents and wildlife managers; some biologists consider such overabundant deer populations and the problems they create to be one of the greatest management challenges in this millennium (Garrott, White, and Vanderbilt White 1993; Warren 1997). Deer can greatly alter the structure and composition of vegetation, thus affecting biodiversity of local flora and fauna (Waller and Alverson 1997). For example, high populations of deer in Pennsylvania have suppressed or eliminated palatable seedlings and saplings, such as oaks, resulting in a slow conversion to less-palatable species, such as American beech (*Fagus grandifolia*) (Waller and Alverson 1997). Waller and Alverson (1997) also noted that in suburban areas, problems with deer browsing are compounded by invasion of woody and herbaceous exotic plants. Suburban residents are often opposed, sometimes adamantly, to lethal methods of deer population control such as firearm or archery hunting, and they favor capture and movement (not always legal) or the use of contraceptives (not always effective) (Stout, Knuth, and Curtis 1997). Deer have also been implicated in the spread of the ticks that carry Lyme disease (Deblinger et al. 1993; Johnson and Klemens, chapter 2, and Koontz and Daszak, chapter 7, this volume).

BEAVER Beaver can live in close proximity to humans if there are lakes, streams, or other adequate watercourses and an ample supply of woody vegetation and other foods. Beaver benefit from sprawl not necessarily because humans alter the landscape to make it more suitable to beaver, but because suburban dwellers are less likely to favor fur trapping, hunting, or lethal methods of animal control. In some states that have banned or limited fur trapping, beaver populations have grown exponentially (Deblinger, Woytek, and Zwick 1999). In Massachusetts, beaver populations are doing so well across the suburban–rural gradient that many people consider them pests. Recent studies show that with the reduction of fur trapping, beaver mortality is quite low in both rural and suburban landscapes (DeStefano et al. 2002), and a major source of mortality now includes problem-animal damage control and removal. Beaver impoundments create habitat for a wide variety of organisms and are usually beneficial for biodiversity, but damming of streams by and in areas with high beaver densities can reduce habitat for species that require fast-flowing water, such as some endangered mussels, or can flood vernal pools, required by some breeding amphibians.

CARNIVORES In general, many large carnivores, such as wolves and grizzly bears (*Ursus arctos*), are not likely to be present in highly developed areas. Black bears (*U. americanus*) and mountain lions can be found in regions of the country where suburban and rural areas meet, and where residences are built farther into wild country. But a host of medium-size carnivores, the so-called meso-carnivores, can do quite well in urban and suburban settings. Striped skunks (*Mephitis mephitis*), raccoons, red foxes, and coyotes are common in suburban and even some urban areas. These species are generalists in their diet and habitat. Skunks and raccoons can be found in some highly developed areas. Red foxes will tolerate the presence of people, but generally red and gray foxes (*Urocyon cinereoargenteus*) require some open country (e.g., fields) and woodlots (DeGraaf and Yamasaki 2001). They are more likely to be found in suburban than in urban settings. Even species such as fisher (*Martes pennanti*) and bobcat (*Lynx rufus*) (Tigas, Van Vuren, and Sauvajot 2002; Riley et al. 2003) can be found around light suburban development within their range, especially if developments have low-density housing and are intermixed with conservation property, wildlife management areas, protected watersheds, or other protected land.

Coyotes are adaptable canids. They are opportunistic hunters and foragers, with a broad diet and the ability to travel great distances and occupy many different types of habitat in North America, including many urban areas (Grinder and Krausman 2001a; Tigas, Van Vuren, and Sauvajot 2002; Riley et al. 2003). Coyotes will eat small mammals, birds, fruits, and berries; hunt or scavenge deer; and take advantage of garbage, pet food, and handouts from local residents (Quinn 1997). In urban settings, coyotes are most active during the night, but can be active at all times of the day, particularly when not persecuted by humans (Andelt and Mahan 1980; Atkinson and Shackleton 1991; Grinder and Krausman 2001a; Riley et al. 2003). Evidence indicates that when coyotes are present, they control the population levels of smaller predators, such as foxes and domestic cats. The absence of coyotes may thus lead to higher levels of predation on songbirds and small mammals by these smaller predators in a process called *mesopredator release* (Soulé et al. 1988; Crooks and Soulé 1999).

Some medium-size carnivores, such as mink (*Mustela vison*) and river otter (*Lontra canadensis*), may be less tolerant of development because of their reliance on undeveloped water courses and their susceptibility to water-born toxins and pollutants (DeGraaf and Yamasaki 2001).

OTHER MAMMALS The diversity of small mammals (e.g., rodents) is lower in urban settings than in natural settings (Morrison, Scott, and Tenant 1994; Bock et al. 2002). Commensal species, such as house mice and Norway rats, are abundant, especially around dwellings, sewers, and rubbish dumps. Courtney and Fenton (1976) found some native species, such as the white-footed mouse (*Peromyscus leucopus*) and eastern striped chipmunk (*Tamias striatus*), to be numerous around small rural dumps in Ontario. Omnivorous and scavenging species may attain large populations in urban areas. In Great Britain, the wood mouse (*Apodemus sylvaticus*) and, to a lesser extent, the bank vole (*Clethrionomys glareolus*) were widespread and abundant in urban centers (Dickman and Doncaster 1987, 1989). Adler and Wilson (1987) attributed generalist diet and habitat use and demographic flexibility to these species' success in urbanizing areas. However, even common native species, such as deer mice (*Peromyscus maniculatus*) and voles, are less abundant in grassland plots close to suburban edges (Bock et al. 2002). The prevalence of domestic cats and dogs (*Canis familiaris*), as well as foxes, may depress populations of small mammals, which in turn limits the distribution and abundance of specialist small carnivores such as weasels (Dickman and Doncaster 1987).

Tree squirrels, such as the eastern gray squirrel, are common in urban and suburban parks and neighborhoods where there are abundant shade and nut trees (e.g., oaks) for food and shelter (McComb 1985). In St. Louis, Missouri, fox squirrels (*Sciurus niger*) were replaced by gray squirrels with the development of a new subdivision, indicating that gray squirrels were more able to adapt to suburbanization than were fox squirrels (Sexton 1990). Eastern cottontails (*Sylvilagus floridanus*) are found in suburban areas with adequate food and cover, but the rare New England cottontail (*S. transitionalis*) is restricted in range and numbers, largely because of its dependence on early-successional-stage forest, which is increasingly less common in the northeastern United States (DeGraaf and Yamasaki 2001; Fuller and DeStefano 2003).

In Europe, one source indicates that 8 of 24 bat species are urban species and can be considered synanthropic (Redel 1995), including the common pipistrelle (*Pipistrellus pipistrellus*), serotine bat (*Eptesicus serotinus*), and common long-eared bat (*Plecotus auritus*) (Greenaway and Hutson 1990). In the United States, several species of bats are associated with urban and suburban areas, and three species—little brown myotis (*Myotis lucifugus*), big brown bat (*Eptesicus fuscus*), and Mexican free-tailed bat (*Tadarida brasiliensis*)—are among the most common to use bat houses in urban and suburban settings (Kiser and Kiser 2003).

REPTILES AND AMPHIBIANS

Many species of reptiles and amphibians are tied to specific habitat requirements. This is particularly true of amphibians and certain reptiles, such as turtles, that require water. In addition to the need for water in which to breed and survive, the kind or type of water or wetland is important. For example, several species of salamanders require seasonally available bodies of water called *vernal pools*. When these specific habitats are destroyed or altered by development, these populations of amphibians decline.

Like other groups of animals, some species of amphibians and reptiles will be more common than others in human-dominated landscapes. The bullfrog (*Rana catesbeiana*) is native to the eastern United States and resides in many urban and suburban wetlands, thriving because it can use a variety of habitats, including man-made ponds. Bullfrogs are highly aquatic, and although they spend most of their time in the water and do not have to use other habitats to complete their life cycle, they can also be quite mobile and move among wetlands, especially during wet conditions. Bullfrogs can complete life cycle requirements in a relatively small area, are relatively tolerant of high pollutant loads, and can coexist with predators such as fishes (figure 10.3). Bullfrogs have been introduced to the western United States, where they prey on native western amphibians and can have a major impact on the viability of some populations of native species.

Gibbs and Shriver (2002) have argued that the demographic characteristics and mobility of land turtles (*Terrapene, Clemmys, Emydoidea,* and *Gopherus*) and, to a lesser extent, of large-bodied pond turtles (*Chelydra*) may jeopardize population persistence in the eastern and central United States. Land turtles are highly susceptible to road mortality, and some larger turtles require bigger

FIGURE 10.3. Bullfrogs (*Rana catesbeiana*) often thrive in developed areas because they can use man-made ponds. (Photo by Elizabeth A. Johnson)

wetlands that may no longer exist within town or city limits. However, Gibbs and Shriver have also suggested that some small-bodied pond turtles (e.g., *Chrysemys*, *Pseudemys*, and *Trachemys*) would be able to survive in urban settings. In fact, Klemens (1993) found that painted turtles (*Chrysemys picta*) were able to exploit human-altered wetlands in Connecticut because they prefer open wetlands and ponds that are often more common in these built environments. The higher nutrient loads in these wetlands increase vegetation growth, also beneficial to these primarily vegetation-eating turtles. Snapping turtles (*Chelydra serpentina*) will also live in urban and suburban settings, often in ponds with high nutrient loads, but modification of the vegetation and disturbance by humans may compromise nest sites (Kolbe and Janzen 2002). In Brazil, numbers of Geoffroy's side-necked turtle (*Phrynops geoffroanus*) inhabiting an urban river were elevated probably because of abundant sewage and organic waste produced by humans, which increased the turtles' food availability, decreased the number of predators, and increased availability of nesting sites (Souza and Abe 2000).

Several species of Mediterranean house geckos (*Tarentola mauritanica*, *Hemidactylus turcicus*, and *Cyrtopodion scabrum*) are frequently found in urban and suburban areas in North America and Europe, where they inhabit buildings, can frequently be found on walls, and are attracted to lights at night to feed on insects (Vaughan, Dixon, and Cooke 1996; Luiselli and Capizzi 1999).

FISHES

Streams, rivers, and other water bodies in urban and suburban systems are often characterized by higher nutrient loads, warmer temperatures, lower levels of dissolved oxygen, and higher levels of pollution than water bodies in less-developed areas. Although it may at times be difficult to differentiate fish presence owing to fish-stocking activity from presence owing to higher tolerance levels, in general the fishes found in these urbanized areas tend to be more tolerant of these altered conditions (Limburg and Schmidt 1990). In Pennsylvania, Kemp and Spotila (1997) found creek chubs (*Semotilus atromaculatus*), green sunfish (*Lepomis cyanellus*), and sand shiners (*Notropis stramineus*) to be more common in urbanized streams than pollution-intolerant species, such as brown trout (*Salmo trutta*), tessellated darter (*Etheostoma olmstedi*), and longnose dace (*Rhinichthys cataractae*). Fishes such as mosquitofish (*Gambusia* spp.) that have short life cycles and bear live young can be more tolerant of pollution events because their population numbers can rebound quickly after the event. Other forms of pollution, such as increased sediment loads, are harmful to many fish, reducing the amount of light penetrating the water column, affecting primary productivity (and hence food supply), and often actually covering spawning sites (Adams 1994).

INVERTEBRATES

Urbanization is considered to be one of the main causes for the decline of arthropod invertebrates (Pyle, Bentzien, and Opler 1981). However, whereas many studies of urban invertebrate populations show a general increase in species diversity with increasing distance away from the inner-city environment (Jones and Clark 1987; Denys and Schmidt 1998; Blair 1999), others have shown increases in species richness in urban centers (Kozlov 1996). More research is needed to better understand the direct and indirect effects of development on invertebrates (McIntyre 2000).

The diversity of invertebrates in human-dominated landscapes is related to the diversity of vegetation, the variety of artificial niches, the amount of air pollution or other disturbance, and the extent of isolation or suitable habitat (Kendle and Forbes 1997). In urban and suburban environments in general, there is a decrease in those invertebrates with specialized life history requirements. For example, certain butterflies and their caterpillars that are dependent on a specific food plant no longer found in the urban area can no longer survive in that environment (Kendle and Forbes 1997). Thacker (2004) highlights recent work by Shapiro in California that shows there may be exceptions to this finding and that some butterflies in developed areas may actually shift host plant associations to more abundant, nonnative species; however, further study is needed. Bark-living invertebrates that feed on lichen are absent in urban areas where pollution has reduced lichen cover (Gilbert 1971). Insects and other arthropods that depend on a particular habitat structure, such as sheet web–spinning spiders that use leaf litter on which to build their webs, will also likely be less abundant in the more manicured habitats of the cities and suburbs (K. Catley, personal communication, July 1998). In fact, the most important stress factor in urban areas (which also holds true in suburban areas as they become more heavily developed and manicured) is the absence of a leaf litter layer in which invertebrates can overwinter. In the absence of litter, insects that survive best in city environments are those that instead hibernate under tree bark, in twigs, or in aboveground vegetation. Other stresses to invertebrates abound in human-dominated landscapes, including increased use of pesticides and soil trampling by city and suburban dwellers (Davis 1982; for discussion of bees in developed areas, see Cane, chapter 5, this volume).

Invertebrates that do survive in city cores are often habitat generalists, are smaller in size with a more flattened shape, and are highly vagile with high dispersal capability (Schaefer 1982). With these characteristics, they can better take advantage of the diversity of physical structures and environments created by humans. Many ant species live in more urban environments, and a variety of ant genera and species can also be found in landscaped suburban habitats, associating with ornamental shrubs in both sunny and shaded locations, lawns, wooded areas, and concrete and brick walkways, which are important nesting sites (Nuhn and Wright 1979). Invertebrate synanthropes, such as certain millipede species, take advantage of novel habitats in urban and suburban environments, thriving in compost piles. In fact, some suites of invertebrate species are associated with rubbish and gardens (Davis 1982). Other novel habitats colonized by invertebrates include discarded tires and other small containers that hold water and often harbor populations of mosquitoes, and the bags of stored food that support flour and grain beetles (Frankie and Ehler 1978).

In many cases, invertebrates commonly found in cities are nonnative species, perhaps because many urban centers, especially along coastal areas, are major ports of entry into the country, allowing for repeated introductions over the years. In California, pitfall traps set near urban edges were dominated primarily by nonnative species from three orders: pillbugs (Isopoda), earwigs (Dermaptera), and roaches (Blattaria) (Bolger et al. 2000). The exotic Argentine ant (*Linepithema humile*) is more abundant near developments, and the presence of this species suppresses populations of native ground-foraging ants, especially army ants (*Neivamyrmex* spp.) and harvester ants (*Messor* and *Pogonomyrmex*) (Suarez, Bolger, and Case 1998). In North America, native earthworm populations were pushed south as a result of the most recent period of glaciation (Gundale 2002). Since then, exotic European and Asian earthworm species have colonized northern parts of the continent and are found in greatest abundance near human population centers (Steinberg et al. 1996; Gundale 2002). Survey and restoration work in the forested areas of both Central Park in New York City and the Schuylkill Center in Philadelphia has identified only nonnative annelid worms at these locations (E. Johnson and K. Catley, unpublished data; D. Burton, personal communication, February 2004). Surveys of invertebrates in woodland patches in Baltimore indicated a predominance of nonnative lumbricid earthworm species as well (Csuzdi and Szlávecz 2003).

Most terrestrial urban invertebrates are also somewhat tolerant of pollution. Whereas many snails are absent from urban environments because their shells are sensitive to sulfur dioxide, a common atmospheric pollutant, other invertebrates such as the earthworm (*Lumbricus rubellus*) seem able to accumulate certain pollutants in localized body tissue, leaving the whole animal relatively unaffected (Kuhnelt 1982; Morgan and Morgan 1990). Pollution-tolerant aquatic invertebrates, such as amphipods, midges (Chironomidae), and a mayfly genus (*Baetis*), also dominate urban streams and rivers, whereas long-lived and intolerant taxa, such as many species of mayflies (Emphemeroptera) and most stoneflies (Plecoptera) and caddisflies (Trichoptera), decline (Morley and Karr 2002). Kemp and Spotila (1997) found isopods and oligochaetes to be more common in urbanized streams in Pennsylvania, and amphipods, mayflies, midges, stoneflies, and caddisflies were present in greater numbers in non-urbanized sites. The former presence may be the result of both tolerance to high organic pollutant loads with associated low values of dissolved oxygen and the altered hydrologic regime in place in urban and suburban environs. Pollution in the form of sedimentation clogs the filters of benthic organisms such as mussels, so they are underrepresented or absent from urban aquatic systems (Adams 1994).

PLANTS

The composition, structure, successional patterns, and community dynamics of native plants and plant communities have been immeasurably altered by human development of the landscape. Extreme cases involve the entire eradication of plant communities to bare soil for housing developments and industrial parks. Conversion of plant communities to gardens and lawns as well as vegetation management of parks, golf courses, and other open space account for much change in developed areas. Setting back of successional stages, suppression of natural disturbance regimes, removal of litter, pruning, planting of exotic ornamentals, and watering contribute to changes in regional plant communities associated with sprawl. In contrast to that of most animal groups, diversity of plants can be higher in urban and suburban environments than in the natural habitats around the cities (Kendle and Forbes 1997). The plant species that do remain in urban and suburban developments are remnants of the natural plant communities that existed before development or are subsidized heavily by people (e.g., cultivated lawns, shade trees, ornamental shrubs, backyard flower gardens) or are invaders, particularly in the early stages of plant succession, such as many so-called weeds. These weedier species typically have wide geographic and ecological ranges (Adams 1994). Although they may be poor competitors in that they are characteristic only of early-successional habitats, they grow rapidly and are excellent dispersers.

There also tends to be a higher percentage of nonnative plant species in urban and suburban areas than in less-developed areas. This greater presence is owing in part to the constant inoculation pressure from horticultural activity. Pysek (1998) found a strong correlation between city size (area and population) and richness of exotic plant species, with larger urban areas supporting more diverse floras. Clemants and Moore (2003) stressed the importance of city age and location (i.e., the presence of a seaport) in contributing to higher diversity of nonnative species in urban and suburban floras. In addition, many of these introduced plants originated in warmer climates and therefore do quite well in the warmer city and suburban environments, even if outside their natural range (Sukopp and Wurzel 2003). Once established, some exotic plants (e.g.,

Japanese barberry [*Berberis thunbergii*] and Japanese stilt grass [*Microstegeum vimineum*]) change soil properties such as pH and nitrification rates (Kourtev, Huang, and Ehrenfeld 1999) or are themselves toxic to other plants (e.g., tree of heaven [*Ailanthus altissima*]) (Heisey 1996). Such factors may not only prevent native plants from recolonizing an area, but also increase the likelihood that these exotic plant populations will persist.

Although highly altered, the anthropogenic plant communities that result provide cover, breeding sites, and food for some wildlife and insects living in these settings. In addition, these communities are important sources of propagules for the revegetation of adjacent undeveloped lots or brownfield habitats such as landfill sites (Robinson and Handel 1993). Urban and suburban vegetation also helps mitigate air pollution and the heat island effect, absorbing particulates and chemicals from the atmosphere and cooling the warmer city air via transpiration.

In some cases, human activities in urban and suburban areas that set back succession can actually benefit rare species that depend on these early-successional habitats. Certain rare wetland and pineland plant species persist on power line rights-of-way that are regularly cleared of brush (Sheridan, Orzell, and Bridges 1997). Uncommon calcium-loving plants can often be found unexpectedly in suburban and urban areas on rubble or stone walls (Gemmell 1982).

FUNGI AND LICHENS

Not much attention has been paid to the impact of development on the fungi. Fungal diversity is dependent in part on overall habitat structure and structural diversity. The manicured nature of many parks and suburban housing developments, featuring uniform rows of trees, cut lawns, and active removal of natural plant debris, creates a depauperate environment for fungal growth. As with many other taxa, there is a decline of species diversity and a shift in type of fungi found as urbanization increases. In urban areas, shorter-lived fungi with smaller fruiting bodies are more common because they have a better chance of fruiting and producing spores before being disturbed in some way. Those fungi with tougher, woody fruiting bodies that persist for any length of time are absent. There is also a preponderance of grassland saprophytes in urban and suburban areas rather than woodland fungi because of the lack of woody debris in more manicured settings (Lawrynowicz 1982).

Lichens are very sensitive to atmospheric pollution—in particular to sulfur dioxide—so they, too, exhibit a decline in species diversity in developed areas. Only those species with a high reproductive output and a strong hold on their substrate (e.g., *Lecanora muralis*) can survive and persist (Seaward 1982). In addition to higher contaminant loads, other stresses to lichens include lack of moisture in temperature extremes characteristic of human-dominated land-scapes.

CONCLUSION

Interest in and concern about the effects of urbanization and sprawl are increasing, and the scientific literature on the topic is proliferating (DeStefano and DeGraaf 2003). Although most of the examples highlighted in this chapter have been North American, related research is under way in other parts of the world. A major thrust of the research is rightly focused on threatened and endangered species and on the negative impacts that sprawl has on biodiversity (Johnson and Klemens, chapter 2, this volume). Additional work is being done on human conceptions of the common species. According to Kendle and Forbes, "People are incredibly selective in what they appreciate, or even recognize, as wildlife. Once urban animals become too common they often lose their charm and are increasingly seen as pests" (1997:62).

However, there is much to learn from those species that live among us and inhabit many of the same places that we do—the plantain (*Plantago major*) and kudzu; the house sparrow and house mouse; the Argentine ant; the bullfrog and eastern gray squirrel. By altering the composition and interrelationships of communities of organisms, our activities affect not only levels of biodiversity, but the pathways of evolution. Understanding both the species that come along with us for the ride and the species that we are and may be leaving behind will give us valuable, untold insights about our collective futures.

REFERENCES

Adams, L. W. 1994. *Urban Wildlife Habitats: A Landscape Perspective*. Minneapolis: University of Minnesota Press.

Adams, L. W., L. E. Dove, and T. M. Franklin. 1985. Mallard pair and brood use of urban stormwater-control impoundments. *Wildlife Society Bulletin* 13:46–51.

Adams, L. W., and A. D. Geis. 1983. Effects of roads on small mammals. *Journal of Applied Ecology* 20:403–415.

Adkins, C. A., and P. Stott. 1998. Home ranges, movements, and habitat associations of red foxes *Vulpes vulpes* in suburban Toronto, Canada. *Journal of Zoology* (London) 244:335–346.

Adler, G. H., and M. L. Wilson. 1987. Demography of a habitat generalist, the white-footed mouse, in a heterogeneous environment. *Ecology* 68:1785–1796.

Andelt, W. F., and B. R. Mahan. 1980. Behavior of an urban coyote. *American Midland Naturalist* 103:399–400.

Ankney, C. D. 1996. An embarrassment of riches: Too many geese. *Journal of Wildlife Management* 60:217–223.

Atkinson, K.T., and D.M. Shackleton. 1991. Coyote, *Canis latrans*, ecology in a rural urban environment. *Canadian Field-Naturalist* 105:49–54.

Barratt, D.G. 1998. Predation by house cats, *Felis catus* (L.), in Canberra, Australia. II. Factors affecting amount of prey caught and estimates of the impact on wildlife. *Wildlife Research* 25:475–487.

Berry, M.E., C.E. Bock, and S.L. Haire. 1998. Abundance of diurnal raptors on open space grasslands in an urbanized landscape. *Condor* 100:601–608.

Blair, R.B. 1996. Land use and avian species diversity along an urban gradient. *Ecological Applications* 6:506–519.

———. 1999. Birds and butterflies: Surrogate taxa for assessing biodiversity? *Ecological Applications* 9:164–170.

Blair, R.B., and A.E. Launer. 1997. Butterfly diversity and human land use: Species assemblages along an urban gradient. *Biological Conservation* 80:113–125.

Boal, C.W., K.S. Hudelson, R.W. Mannan, and T.S. Estabrook. 1998. Hematology and hematozoa of adult and nestling Cooper's hawks in Arizona. *Journal of Raptor Research* 32:281–285.

Boal, C.W., and R.W. Mannan. 1998. Nestsite selection by Cooper's hawks in an urban environment. *Journal of Wildlife Management* 62:864–871.

———. 1999. Comparative breeding ecology of Cooper's hawks in urban and exurban environments. *Journal of Wildlife Management* 63:77–84.

Boal, C.W., R.W. Mannan, and K.S. Hudelson. 1998. Trichomoniasis in Cooper's hawks from Arizona. *Journal of Wildlife Diseases* 34:590–593.

Bock, C.E., K.T. Vierling, S.L. Haire, J.D. Boone, and W.W. Merkle. 2002. Patterns of rodent abundance on openspace grasslands in relation to suburban edges. *Conservation Biology* 16:1653–1658.

Bolger, D.T., A.V. Suarez, K. Crooks, S.A. Morrison, and T.J. Case. 2000. Arthropods in habitat fragments: Effects of area, edge, and Argentine ants. *Ecological Applications* 10:1230–1248.

Brown, D.E., J.C. Hagelin, M. Taylor, and J. Galloway. 1998. *Gambel's quail* (Callipepla gambelii). Philadelphia: Birds of North America.

Byers, J.E. 2002. Impact of nonindigenous species on natives enhanced by anthropogenic alteration of selection regimes. *Oikos* 97:449–458.

Calhoun, A.J.K., and M.W. Klemens. 2002. *Best Development Practices: Conserving Pool-Breeding Amphibians in Residential and Commercial Developments in the Northeastern United States*. Metropolitan Conservation Alliance Technical Paper, no. 5: Bronx, N.Y.: Wildlife Conservation Society.

Chapin, F.S., III, E.S. Zavaleta, V.T. Eviners, R.L. Naylor, P.M. Vitousek, H.L. Reynolds, D.U. Hooper, S. Lavorel, O.E. Sala, S.E. Hobbie, M.C. Mack, and S. Diaz. 2000. Consequences of changing biodiversity. *Nature* 405:234–242.

Clemants, S., and G. Moore. 2003. Patterns of species diversity in eight northeastern United States cities. *Urban Habitats* 1. Available at: www.urbanhabitats.org/v01n01/speciesdiversity_full.html.

Congdon, J.D., A.E. Dunham, and R.C. Van Loben Sels. 1993. Delayed sexual maturity and demographies of Blanding's turtles (*Emydoidea blandingii*): Implications for conservation and management of longlived organisms. *Conservation Biology* 7:826–833.

Connell, J.H. 1978. Diversity in tropical rainforests and coral reefs. *Science* 199:1302–1310.

Conover, M.R. 1991. Herbivory by Canada geese: Diet selection and effect on lawns. *Ecological Applications* 1:231–236.

Conover, M.R., and G.G. Chasko. 1985. Nuisance Canada goose problems in the eastern United States. *Wildlife Society Bulletin* 13:228–233.

Courtney, P.A., and M.B. Fenton. 1976. The effects of a small rural garbage dump on populations of *Peromyscus leucopus* Rafinesque and other small mammals. *Journal of Applied Ecology* 13:413–422.

Crooks, K.R., and M.E. Soulé. 1999. Mesopredator release and avifaunal extinctions in a fragmented system. *Nature* 400:563–566.

Csuzdi, C., and K. Szlávecz. 2003. *Lumbricus friendi* Cognetti, 1904, a new exotic earthworm in North America. *Northeastern Naturalist* 10:77–82.

Davis, N.K. 1982. Habitat diversity and invertebrates in urban areas. In R. Borkamm and J.A. Lee, eds., *Urban Ecology*, 49–63. London: Blackwell Scientific.

Deblinger, R.D., M.L. Wilson, D.W. Rimmer, and A. Spielman. 1993. Reduced abundance of immature *Ixodes dammini* (Acari: Ixodidae) following incremental removal of deer. *Journal of Medical Entomology* 30:144–150.

Deblinger, R.D., W.A. Woytek, and R.R. Zwick. 1999. Demographics of voting on the 1996 Massachusetts ballot referendum. *Human Dimensions of Wildlife* 4:40–55.

DeGraaf, R.M., and B.R. Payne. 1975. Economic values of nongame birds and some urban wildlife research needs. *Transactions of the North American Wildlife and Natural Resources Conference* 40:281–287.

DeGraaf, R.M., and J.M. Wentworth. 1981. Urban bird communities and habitats in New England. *Transactions of the North American Wildlife and Natural Resources Conference* 46:396–413.

———. 1986. Avian guild structure and habitat associations in suburban bird communities. *Urban Ecology* 9:399–412.

DeGraaf, R.M., and M. Yamasaki. 2001. *New England Wildlife*. Hanover, N.H.: University Press of New England.

Denys, C., and H. Schmidt. 1998. Insect communities on experimental mugwort (*Artemisia vulgaris* L.) plots along an urban gradient. *Oecologia* 113:269–277.

DeStefano, S. 2002. National and regional issues for forest wildlife research and management. *Forest Science* 48:181–189.

DeStefano, S., and R.M. DeGraaf. 2003. Exploring the ecology of suburban wildlife. *Frontiers in Ecology and the Environment* 1:95–101.

DeStefano, S., K. Koenen, C.M. Henner, and R.D. Deblinger. 2002. *Demography of Beaver Populations Along an Urban Rural Gradient in Massachusetts*. Amherst: U.S. Geological Survey Massachusetts Cooperative Fish and Wildlife Research Unit, University of Massachusetts.

Dickman, C.R., and C.P. Doncaster. 1987. The ecology of small mammals in urban habitats. I. Populations in a patchy environment. *Journal of Animal Ecology* 56:629–640.

———. 1989. The ecology of small mammals in urban habitats. II. Demography and dispersal. *Journal of Animal Ecology* 58:119–127.

Eversham, B.C., D.B. Roy, and M.G. Telfer. 1996. Urban industrial and other manmade sites as analogues of natural habitats for Carabidae. *Annales Zoologici Fennici* 33:149–156.

Frankie, G.W., and L.E. Ehler. 1978. Ecology of insects in urban environments. *Annual Review of Entomology* 23:367–387.

Fuller, T. K., and S. DeStefano. 2003. Relative importance of early-successional forests and shrubland habitats to mammals in the northeastern United States. *Forest Ecology and Management* 185:75–79.

Garrott, R. A., P. J. White, and C. A. Vanderbilt White. 1993. Overabundance: An issue for conservation biologists? *Conservation Biology* 7:946–949.

Gaughan, C. 2003. Survival, cause specific mortality, and movements of white-tailed deer in rural and suburban Massachusetts. M.S. thesis. University of Massachusetts.

Gemmell, R. P. 1982. The origin and botanical importance of industrial habitats. In R. Borkamm and J. A. Lee, eds., *Urban Ecology*, 33–39. London: Blackwell Scientific.

Germaine, S. S., S. S. Rosenstock, R. E. Schweinsburg, and W. S. Richardson. 1998. Relationships among breeding birds, habitat, and residential development in greater Tucson, Arizona. *Ecological Applications* 8:680–691.

Gibbs, J. P., and W. G. Shriver. 2002. Estimating the effects of road mortality on turtle populations. *Conservation Biology* 16:1647–1652.

Gilbert, O. L. 1971. Some indirect effects of air pollution on bark living invertebrates. *Journal of Applied Ecology* 8:77–84.

Greenaway, F., and A. M. Hutson. 1990. *A Field Guide to British Bats*. London: Coleman.

Grinder, M. I., and P. R. Krausman. 2001a. Home range, habitat use, and nocturnal activity of coyotes in an urban environment. *Journal of Wildlife Management* 65:887–898.

———. 2001b. Morbidity-mortality factors and survival of an urban coyote population in Arizona. *Journal of Wildlife Diseases* 37:312–317.

Gundale, M. J. 2002. Influence of exotic earthworms on the soil organic horizon and the rare fern *Botrychium mormo*. *Conservation Biology* 16:1555–1561.

Hall, L. S., P. R. Krausman, and M. L. Morrison. 1997. The habitat concept and a plea for standard terminology. *Wildlife Society Bulletin* 25:173–182.

Heimlich, R. E., and W. D. Anderson. 2001. *Development at the Urban Fringe and Beyond: Impacts on Agriculture and Rural Land*. Washington, D.C.: Department of Agriculture.

Heisey, R. M. 1996. Identification of an allelopathic compound from *Ailanthus altissima* (Simaroubaceae) and characterization of its herbicidal activity. *American Journal of Botany* 83:192–200.

Howard, D. V. 1974. Urban robins: A population study. In J. H. Noyes and D. R. Progulske, eds., *Wildlife in an Urbanizing Environment*, 67–75. Amherst: Cooperative Extension Service, University of Massachusetts.

Johnston, R. F. 2001. Synanthropic birds of North America. In J. M. Marzluff, R. Bowman, and R. Donnelly, eds., *Avian Ecology and Conservation in an Urbanizing World*, 49–67. Boston: Kluwer Academic.

Johnston, R. F., and R. K. Selander. 1964. House sparrows: Rapid evolution of races in North America. *Science* 141:548–550.

Jokimäki, J. 1999. Occurrence of breeding bird species in urban parks: Effects of park structure and broadscale variables. *Urban Ecosystems* 3:21–34.

Jokimäki, J., and J. Suhonen. 1993. Effects of urbanization on the breeding bird species richness in Finland: A biogeographical comparison. *Ornis Fennica* 70:71–77.

Jones, R. C., and C. C. Clark. 1987. Impact of watershed urbanization on stream insect communities. *Water Resources Bulletin* 23:1047–1055.

Josselyn, J. [1672] 1860. *New-Englands Rarities Discovered: In Birds, Beasts, Fishes, Serpents, and Plants of That Country*. Boston: Veazie.

Kemp, S. J., and J. R. Spotila. 1997. Effects of urbanization on brown trout *Salmo trutta*, other fishes, and macroinvertebrates in Valley Creek, Valley Forge, Pennsylvania. *American Midland Naturalist* 138:55–68.

Kendle, T., and S. Forbes. 1997. *Urban Nature Conservation: Landscape Management in the Urban Countryside*. London: E&FN Spon.

Kinzig, A. P., and J. M. Grove. 2001. Urban suburban ecology. In S. A. Levin, ed., *Encyclopedia of Biodiversity*, 5: 733–745. San Diego: Academic Press.

Kiser, M., and S. Kiser. 2003. Tips for bat houses. *Bat Conservation International* 2:1.

Klemens, M. W. 1989. The methodology of conservation. In I. R. Swingland and M. W. Klemens, eds., *The Conservation Biology of Tortoises*, 1–4. International Union for Conservation of Nature and Natural Resources (IUCN), Species Survival Commission (SSC), Occasional Paper no. 5. Gland, Switzerland: IUCN/SSC.

——. 1993. *Amphibians and Reptiles of Connecticut and Adjacent Regions*. State Geological and Natural History Survey of Connecticut, bulletin no. 112. Hartford: Connecticut Department of Environmental Protection.

Knight, R. L. 1990. Ecological principles applicable to management of urban ecosystems. In E. A. Webb and S. Q. Foster, eds., *Perspectives in Urban Ecology*, 24–34. Denver: Denver Museum of National History.

Knutson, M. G., J. R. Sauer, D. A. Olsen, M. J. Mossman, L. M. Hemesath, and M. J. Lannoo. 1999. Effects of landscape composition and wetland fragmentation on frog and toad abundance and species richness in Iowa and Wisconsin, U.S.A. *Conservation Biology* 13:1437–1446.

Kolbe, J. J., and F. J. Janzen. 2002. Impact of nest-site selection on nest success and nest temperature in natural and disturbed habitats. *Ecology* 83:269–281.

Kozlov, M. 1996. Patterns of forest insect distribution within a large city: Microlepidoptera in St. Petersburg, Russia. *Journal of Biogeography* 23:95–103.

Kourtev, P. S., W. Z. Huang, and J. G. Ehrenfeld. 1999. Differences in earthworm densities and nitrogen dynamics in soils under exotic and native plant species. *Biological Invasions* 1:237–245.

Kuhnelt, W. 1982. Free-living invertebrates within the major ecosystems of Vienna. In R. Borkamm and J. A. Lee, eds., *Urban Ecology*, 83–87. London: Blackwell Scientific.

Lawrynowicz, M. 1982. Macro-fungal flora of Lodz. In R. Borkamm and J. A. Lee, eds., *Urban Ecology*, 41–47. London: Blackwell Scientific.

Limburg, K. E., and R. E. Schmidt. 1990. Patterns of fish spawning in Hudson River tributaries: Response to an urban gradient? *Ecology* 71:1238–1245.

Liu, J., G. C. Daily, P. R. Ehrlich, and G. W. Luck. 2003. Effects of household dynamics on resource consumption and biodiversity. *Nature* 421:530–533.

Luiselli, L., and D. Capizzi. 1999. Ecological distribution of the geckos *Tarentola mauritanica* and *Hemidactylus turcicus* in the urban area of Rome in relation to age of buildings and condition of the walls. *Journal of Herpetology* 33:316–319.

Manolis, J. C., D. E. Andersen, and F. J. Cuthbert. 2002. Edge effect on nesting success of ground nesting birds near regenerating clearcuts in a forest dominated landscape. *The Auk* 119:955–970.

Martin, T. E., and J. Clobert. 1996. Nest predation and avian life-history evolution in Europe versus North America: A possible role of humans? *American Naturalist* 147:1028–1046.

Marzluff, J.M. 2001. Worldwide urbanization and its effects on birds. In J.M. Marzluff, R. Bowman, and R. Donnelly, eds., *Avian Ecology and Conservation in an Urbanizing World*, 19–47. Boston: Kluwer Academic.

———. 2002. Fringe conservation: A call to action. *Conservation Biology* 16:1175–1176.

Marzluff, J.M., R. Bowman, and R. Donnelly. 2001. A historical perspective on urban bird research: Trends, terms, and approaches. In J.M. Marzluff, R. Bowman, and R. Donnelly, eds., *Avian Ecology and Conservation in an Urbanizing World*, 117–137. Boston: Kluwer Academic.

Marzluff, J.M., K.J. McGowan, R. Donnelly, and R.L. Knight. 2001. Causes and consequences of expanding American crow populations. In J.M. Marzluff, R. Bowman, and R. Donnelly, eds., *Avian Ecology and Conservation in an Urbanizing World*, 331–363. Boston: Kluwer Academic.

McComb, W.C. 1985. Managing urban forests to increase or decrease gray squirrel populations. *Southern Journal of Applied Forestry* 8:31–34.

McDonnell, M.J., and S.T.A. Pickett. 1990. Ecosystem structure and function along urban–rural gradients: An unexploited opportunity for ecology. *Ecology* 71:1232–1237.

McDonnell, M.J., S.T.A. Pickett, P. Groffman, P. Bohlan, R.V. Pouyat, W.C. Zipperer, R.W. Parmelee, M.M. Carreiro, and K. Medley. 1997. Ecosystem processes along an urban-to-rural gradient. *Urban Ecosystems* 1:21–36.

McGowan, K.J. 2001. Demographic and behavioral comparisons of suburban and rural American crows. In J.M. Marzluff, R. Bowman, and R. Donnelly, eds., *Avian Ecology and Conservation in an Urbanizing World*, 365–381. Boston: Kluwer Academic.

McIntyre, N.E. 2000. Ecology of urban arthropods: A review and a call to action. *Annals of the Entomological Society of America* 93:825–835.

Mennechez, G., and P. Clergeau. 2001. Settlement of breeding European starlings in urban areas: Importance of lawns vs. anthropogenic wastes. In J.M. Marzluff, R. Bowman, and R. Donnelly, eds., *Avian Ecology and Conservation in an Urbanizing World*, 275–285. Boston: Kluwer Academic.

Minton, S.A., Jr. 1968. The fate of amphibians and reptiles in a suburban area. *Journal of Herpetology* 2:113–116.

Mitchell, J.C., and M.W. Klemens. 2000. Primary and secondary effects of habitat alteration. In M.W. Klemens, ed., *Turtle Conservation*, 5–32. Washington, D.C.: Smithsonian Institution Press.

Morgan, J.E., and A.J. Morgan. 1990. The distribution of cadmium, lead, zinc, and calcium in the tissues of the earthworm *Lumbricus rubellus* sampled from one uncontaminated and four polluted soils. *Oecologia* 84:559–566.

Morley, S.A., and J.R. Karr. 2002. Assessing and restoring the health of urban streams in the Puget Sound Basin. *Conservation Biology* 16:1498–1509.

Morrison, M.L., T.A. Scott, and T. Tennant. 1994. Wildlife-habitat restoration in an urban park in southern California. *Restoration Ecology* 2:17–30.

Niemalä, J. 1999. Is there a need for a theory of urban ecology? *Urban Ecosystems* 3:57–65.

Nuhn, T.P., and C.G. Wright. 1979. An ecological survey of ants (Hymenoptera: Formicidae) in a landscaped suburban habitat. *American Midland Naturalist* 102:353–362.

Pickett, S.T.A., M.L. Cadenasso, J.M. Grove, C.H. Nilon, R.V. Pouyat, W.C. Zipperer, and R. Constanza. 2001. Urban ecological systems: Linking terrestrial ecological, physical, and socioeconomic components of metropolitan areas. *Annual Review of Ecology and Systematics* 32:127–157.

Pierotti, R., and C. Annett. 2001. The ecology of western gulls in habitats varying in degree of urban influence. In J. M. Marzluff, R. Bowman, and R. Donnelly, eds., *Avian Ecology and Conservation in an Urbanizing World*, 307–329. Boston: Kluwer Academic.

Preston, F. W. 1946. Nesting heights of birds building in shrubs. *Ecology* 27:87–91.

Pulliam, R. H. 1988. Sources, sinks, and population regulation. *American Naturalist* 132:652–661.

Pyle, R. M., M. Bentzien, and P. Opler. 1981. Insect conservation. *Annual Review of Entomology* 26:233–258.

Pysek, P. 1998. Alien and native species in central European urban floras: A quantitative comparison. *Journal of Biogeography* 25:155–163.

Quinn, T. 1997. Coyote (*Canis latrans*) food habits in three urban habitat types of western Washington. *Northwest Science* 71:15.

Redel, T. 1995. Zur Ökologie von Fledermäusen in mitteleuropäischen Städten (Ecology of bats in middle European cities). Examensarbeit am Fachbereich für Biologie der Freien Universität Berlin.

Riley, S. P. D., R. M. Sauvajot, T. K. Fuller, E. C. York, D. A. Kamradt, C. Bromley, and R. K Wayne. 2003. Effects of urbanization and habitat fragmentation on bobcats and coyotes in southern California. *Conservation Biology* 17:566–576.

Robinson, G. R., and S. N. Handel. 1993. Forest restoration in a closed landfill: Rapid addition of new species by bird dispersal. *Conservation Biology* 7:271–278.

Russo, C., and T. P. Young. 1997. Egg and seed removal at urban and suburban forest edges. *Urban Ecosystems* 1:171–178.

Schaefer, M.1982. Studies on the arthropod fauna of green urban ecosystems. In R. Borkamm and J. A. Lee, eds., *Urban Ecology*, 65–73. London: Blackwell Scientific.

Schneider, R. R., and S. Wasel. 2000. The effect of human settlement on the density of moose in northern Alberta. *Journal of Wildlife Management* 64:513–520.

Schoenecker, K. A., and P. R. Krausman. 2002. Human disturbance in bighorn sheep habitat, Pusch Ridge Wilderness, Arizona. *Journal of the Arizona–Nevada Academy of Science* 34:65–69.

Seaward, M. R. D. 1982. Lichen ecology of changing urban environments. In R. Borkamm and J. A. Lee, eds., *Urban Ecology*, 181–189. London: Blackwell Scientific.

Seidensticker, J. 2003. Fishing cats enjoy city life. Available at: http://nationalzoo.si.edu/ ConservationandScience/SpotlightOnScience/sei.

Sexton, O. J. 1990. Replacement of fox squirrels by gray squirrels in a suburban habitat. *American Midland Naturalist* 124:198–205.

Sheridan, P. M., S. L. Orzell, and E. L. Bridges. 1997. Powerline easements as refugia for state rare seepage and pineland plant taxa. In J. R. Williams, J. W. Goodrich-Mahoney, J. R. Wisniewski, and J. Wisniewski, eds., *The Sixth International Symposium on Environmental Concerns in Rights-of-Way Management*, 451–460. Oxford: Elsevier Science.

Shuttleworth, C. M. 2001. Traffic related mortality in a red squirrel (*Sciurus vulgaris*) population receiving supplemental feeding. *Urban Ecosystems* 5:109–118.

Slabbekoorn, H., and M. Peet. 2003. Birds sing at a higher pitch in urban noise. *Nature* 424:267.

Soulé, M. E. 1990. The onslaught of alien species and other challenges in the coming decades. *Conservation Biology* 4:233–239.

Soulé, M. E., D. T. Bolger, A. C. Alberts, J. Wright, M. Sorice, and S. Hill. 1988. Reconstructed dynamics of rapid extinctions of chaparral requiring birds in urban habitat islands. *Conservation Biology* 2:75–92.

Soulé, M. E., and B. A. Wilcox, eds. 1980. *Conservation Biology, an Evolutionary Ecological Approach.* Sunderland, Mass.: Sinauer.

Souza, F. L., and A. S. Abe. 2000. Feeding ecology, density, and biomass of the freshwater turtle, *Phrynops geoffroanus*, inhabiting a polluted urban river in south-eastern Brazil. *Journal of Zoology* 252:437–446.

Steinberg, D. A., R. V. Pouyat, R. W. Parmelee, and P. M. Groffman. 1996. Earthworm abundance and nitrogen mineralization rates along an urban rural land use gradient. *Soil Biology and Biochemistry* 29:427–430.

Stout, R. J., B. A. Knuth, and P. D. Curtis. 1997. Preferences of suburban landowners for deer management techniques: A step towards better communication. *Wildlife Society Bulletin* 25:348–359.

Suarez, A. V., D. T. Bolger, and T. J. Case. 1998. Effects of fragmentation and invasion on native ant communities in coastal southern California. *Ecology* 79:2041–2056.

Sukopp, H., and A. Wurzel. 2003. The effects of climate change on the vegetation of central European cities. *Urban Habitats* 1. Available at: www.urbanhabitats.org/v01n01/climatechange_full.html.

Thacker, P. D. 2004. California butterflies: At home with aliens? *BioScience* 54:182–187.

Ticer, C. L., R. A. Ockenfels, T. E. Morrell, and J. C. deVos Jr. 1994. *Habitat Use and Activity Patterns of Urban-Dwelling Javelina in Prescott, Arizona.* Arizona Game and Fish Department Technical Report, no. 14. Phoenix: Arizona Game and Fish Department.

Tigas, L. A., D. H. Van Vuren, and R. M. Sauvajot. 2002. Behavioral responses of bobcats and coyotes to habitat fragmentation and corridors in an urban environment. *Biological Conservation* 108:299–306.

VanDruff, L. W., E. G. Bolen, and G. J. San Julian. 1994. Management of urban wildlife. In T. A. Bookhout, ed., *Research and Management Techniques for Wildlife and Habitats*, 507–530. Bethesda, Md.: Wildlife Society.

Van Horne, B. 1983. Density as a misleading indicator of habitat quality. *Journal of Wildlife Management* 47:893–901.

Vaughan, R. K., J. R. Dixon, and J. L. Cooke. 1996. Behavioral interference for perch sites in two species of introduced house geckos. *Journal of Herpetology* 30:46–51.

Vitousek, P. M., H. A. Mooney, J. Lubchenco, and J. M. Melillo. 1997. Human domination of Earth's ecosystems. *Science* 277:494–499.

Waller, D. M., and W. S. Alverson. 1997. The white-tailed deer: A keystone herbivore. *Wildlife Society Bulletin* 25:217–226.

Warren, R. J. 1997. The challenge of deer overabundance in the 21st century. *Wildlife Society Bulletin* 25:213–214.

Webster, C. M. 2000. Distribution, habitat, and nests of greater roadrunners in urban and suburban environments. M.S. thesis, University of Arizona.

Withers, M. A., M. W. Palmer, G. L. Wade, P. S. White, and P. R. Neal. 1998. Changing patterns in the number of species in North American floras. In T. D. Sisk, ed., *Perspectives on the Land Use History of North America: A Context for Understanding Our Changing Environment*, 23–31. Washington, D.C.: Geological Survey.

Zipperer, W. C., J. Wu, R. V. Pouyat, and S. T. A. Pickett. 2000. The application of ecological principles to urban and urbanizing landscapes. *Ecological Applications* 10:685–688.

PART IV

■ ■ ■ ■ ■ ■ ■ ■ ■ ■ ■ ■

IDENTIFYING AND MEETING
THE CHALLENGES OF SPRAWL

11

■ ■

MAINTAINING CONNECTIVITY IN
URBANIZING LANDSCAPES

M. A. Sanjayan and Kevin R. Crooks

abitat destruction and fragmentation are principal threats to biodiversity (Wilcove et al. 1998), and fragmentation is virtually inevitable in areas with increasing sprawl (Soulé 1991b). In addition to reducing the total amount of natural habitat available, fragmentation isolates once-contiguous landscapes, thereby impeding movement between previously intermixing plant and animal populations. Small, isolated populations in fragmented systems are particularly vulnerable to extirpation through a combination of demographic, environmental, and genetic factors that interact to create a "vortex" of extinction (Gilpin and Soulé 1986). Although the best option to avoid extinction is to prevent isolation in the first place, we are in reality often confronted with areas already affected by fragmentation. In these situations, protecting or restoring linkages among otherwise isolated natural areas may be the only way to increase the size of reserves and to protect species in crisis (Crooks and Sanjayan in press). This is particularly true for urbanizing systems.

In this chapter, we review factors that disrupt movement and population continuity in nature and explore why the concept of connectivity is so important for conservation in developing landscapes. We first discuss potential benefits and costs associated with the use of corridors to mitigate fragmentation effects. We then provide an in-depth case study of how large-scale connectivity has been identified at the regional level across the urbanizing landscape of California and delve into the details of corridor planning and implementation by studying the Tenaja Corridor—a habitat linkage designed, implemented, and monitored for the sole purpose of providing connectivity to a southern California nature preserve facing isolation through sprawl. We then review several additional case studies, conducted across multiple spatial scales in a variety of ecological systems, to shed further light on the approaches to and challenges of maintaining connectivity in developing landscapes. Finally, we enunciate where we believe the new debate is leading and what frontiers in regional connectivity are yet unexplored.

REDUCING ISOLATION
THROUGH CONNECTIVITY CONSERVATION

We define *landscape connectivity* as the degree to which landscapes enhance or impede animal or plant movement and spatially sensitive ecological processes (Taylor et al. 1993), and we use the terms *corridors* and *linkages* synonymously to indicate habitat whose purpose is to facilitate connectivity and whose size and configuration is scale dependent. As discussed by Dobson and colleagues (1999), confusion about the meaning of the word *corridor* arises from multiple uses of the term in ecology, in planning, and in everyday speech. Following the lead of several recent reviews (Beier and Noss 1998; Bennett 1999; Dobson et al. 1999; Crooks and Sanjayan in press), we agree that corridors can exist on multiple spatial scales, from culverts bisecting a country road to large landscape linkages spanning entire continents. The length, width, and configuration of the most effective corridors will be determined by the primary species or ecological processes the corridor was designed to facilitate and by the permeability of the surrounding matrix. The corridor habitat may not have to be contiguous, such as "stopovers" or "stepping-stones" of suitable habitat within an unsuitable matrix, which provide resting and replenishing areas for migrant birds or for insects or bats searching for nectar or pollen sources (Moore and Simons 1992; Winker, Warner, and Weisbrod 1992; Schultz 1995; Haddad 2000).

But do corridors actually work? Criticism has been leveled at the value of corridors in adequately providing landscape connectivity, and some negative consequences of connectivity have been hypothesized (Soulé and Simberloff 1986; Noss 1987a; Simberloff and Cox 1987; Soulé 1991a; Hobbs 1992; Simberloff et al. 1992; McEuen 1993; Rosenberg, Noon, and Meslow 1997; Beier and Noss 1998; Bennett 1999; Dobson et al. 1999; Crooks and Sanjayan in press). The biological basis for the argument against corridors can be thought of as having three major components. First, do target species actually use the corridor, and is this use sufficient to improve the viability of otherwise isolated populations in the core areas connected by the corridor? Second, do corridors provide enough security or resources or both such that transient or resident individuals are not exposed to excessive risk? Third, do corridors facilitate unintended transmission of disease, weedy species, ecological disturbances, or genetic material?

Beier and Noss (1998) counteracted some of this skepticism by reviewing published studies that attempted to address empirically whether corridors enhance species' population viability in patches connected by corridors. Their review focused on both descriptive and experimental studies of corridor functionality. They found few examples of experimental studies on corridor functionality and concluded that many of these corridor studies were difficult to interpret because of poor experimental design. Mansergh and Scott's (1989) study of corridor use of the mountain pygmy-possum (*Burramys parvus*) in Australia, reviewed later in this chapter as a case study, provided the strongest experimental evidence of corridor functionality. The 17 inference studies examined by Beier and Noss's (1998) review consisted mostly of investigations of whether corridors were actually used by dispersing animals. The strongest evidence was provided by Beier (1995), who documented that five of nine juvenile dispersing mountain lions (*Puma concolor*) in southern California found and successfully used corridors, that all three potential corridors were found and traversed by at least one disperser, and that no interpatch movements occurred by way of the areas outside of the corridors within the urban matrix. Most important, the review by Beier and Noss (1998) failed to find any empirical evidence for the hypothetical negative impacts of corridors and concluded that corridors are generally beneficial.

Perhaps the most daunting obstacles to connectivity conservation may not be biological in origin, but rather the sometimes prohibitive cost of actually connecting landscapes in the real world (Morrison and Reynolds in press). Such is the case in urban areas, where potential corridors often traverse lands desirable to and thus highly valued by humans. Similarly, conserving linkages in urban systems entails inevitable political and social trade-offs, because protecting corridors through developed landscapes necessarily compels humans to alter land-use patterns. Despite debate about the conservation function of corridors, however, the concept of connectivity conservation is now so widely accepted that most land-use plans explicitly deal with the issue of connectivity, and the concept has achieved crossover status to the general public through the popular press (Crooks and Sanjayan in press).

PRESERVING REGIONAL CONNECTIVITY IN SOUTHERN CALIFORNIA: A CASE STUDY FOR MITIGATING THE IMPACTS OF SPRAWL

THE URBANIZED LANDSCAPE

Here we present a detailed case study of research aimed at protecting wildlife corridors and landscape connectivity in a system confronted with extreme sprawl: coastal southern California. We feel that its conclusions regarding the impacts of sprawl on connectivity and the possible research and conservation efforts to mitigate such impacts are broadly applicable to other urbanizing systems as well.

Coastal southern California currently exists as one of the largest megalopolitan regions in North America, stretching from Santa Barbara and Los Angeles at its northern end through San Diego (and Tijuana, Mexico) at its southern end. The six counties of coastal southern California encompass approximately 25 percent of California's land area, but as of the year 2000 contained nearly 20 million people, approximately 60 percent of the state's population. From 1990 to 2000, the population of Riverside County increased by 32 percent; San Bernardino County, by 20 percent; Orange County, by 18 percent; San Diego and Ventura Counties, by 13 percent; and Santa Barbara and Los Angeles Counties, by 7 to 8 percent (Bureau of the Census 2000).

As might be expected, the dramatic growth of human populations and the resulting sprawl has severely fragmented native habitat in coastal southern California. Development over the past century has destroyed all but 10 percent of the native Mediterranean coastal sage scrub habitat (McCaull 1994), with many of the remaining remnants of natural areas persisting as habitat islands immersed within a vast urban sea. Humans, however, are not the only residents in southern California. The coast of southern California is one of the world's "hot spots" of native biodiversity, supporting many endemic species that occur nowhere else in the world (Myers 1990; Wilson 1992). This rich biodiversity, coupled with the massive human population growth and associated environmental impacts, has helped create an epicenter of endangerment and extinction in the region (Myers 1990; Wilson 1992; Dobson et al. 1997). Indeed, San Diego County supports more threatened and endangered plant and animal species than any other county in the continental United States (Dobson et al. 1997). Despite the extensive urbanization of the natural landscape of southern California, large-scale assessments of regional connectivity have until recently been lacking; with a few exceptions—for example, in Florida, to be discussed later—this holds true for many other rapidly urbanizing regions of North America as well.

CONNECTIVITY AND CARNIVORES

The concept of focal species is a central theme in large-scale conservation planning and in regional connectivity assessments (Lambeck 1997; Miller et al. 1998; Soulé and Terborgh 1999; but see Lindenmayer et al. 2002). Mammalian carnivores can be effective focal species to evaluate the degree of landscape-level connectivity in urbanizing areas because they are particularly vulnerable to extinction in fragmented habitat given their wide ranges and resource requirements, low densities, and direct persecution by humans (Noss et al. 1996; Woodroffe and Ginsberg 1998; Crooks 2002; see also Ray, chapter 9, this volume). Because of this vulnerability, top predators may not be able to persist in landscapes that are not connected by functional movement corridors. In addition, their disappearance may generate ecological cascades that can dramatically alter ecological communities (Soulé and Terborgh 1999; Estes, Crooks, and Holt 2001). For example, in fragmented habitat in urban San Diego, Crooks and Soulé (1999) found that the extirpation of dominant predators, such as coyotes, helped contribute to increased activity (ecological release) of smaller carnivores and thus increased predation on their avian prey. Carnivores are therefore ecologically pivotal organisms whose status can be indicative of the functional connectivity of ecosystems.

In southern California, mountain lions and bobcats (*Lynx rufus*) are excellent focal species for the evaluation of connectivity across multiple spatial scales (Crooks 2000, 2002; Riley et al. 2003). Mountain lions in the Santa Ana Mountains of southern California occupy ranges that encompass up to 116 square miles (300 square kilometers), travel on average 3.7 miles (6 kilometers) per night (Beier, Choate, and Barrett 1995), and disperse distances that average 40 miles (65 kilometers), often successfully using habitat corridors during movement (Beier 1995). Indeed, a population viability analysis of cougar populations (Beier 1993) indicated that persistence of lion populations within the Santa Ana Mountains was dependent on dispersal among habitat patches and that an estimated 386 to 772 square miles (1,000–2,000 square kilometers) of habitat would be necessary to maintain a lion population with a 98 percent probability of persistence for 100 years. Similarly, in carnivore surveys conducted throughout coastal southern California, Crooks (2002) found mountain lions to persist in only the largest core wildlands with functional connections between habitat blocks (figure 11.1).

Landscape connectivity also is important to the persistence of bobcat populations in the urbanizing landscape of southern California. Compared with mountain lions, bobcats are less sensitive to fragmentation, thus occurring in smaller habitat fragments (Crooks 2002) and occupying smaller home ranges, of approximately 0.096 to 9 square miles (0.25–15 square kilometers) (Lembeck 1986; Sauvajot et al. 2000; Lyren 2001), than cougars. However, although bobcats can occur in urbanizing habitats (see also Harrison 1998), they persist only in those habitat fragments with adequate movement corridors to larger natural areas (figure 11.1). Bobcats are therefore valuable indicators of connectivity at smaller spatial scales.

CONNECTIVITY ASSESSMENTS OF SOUTHERN CALIFORNIA

Hunter, Fisher, and Crooks (2003) used mountain lions and bobcats as focal species to provide an initial assessment of the extent of landscape-level connectivity in coastal southern California. First, they generated base maps of potential mountain lion and bobcat habitat from previously derived geographic

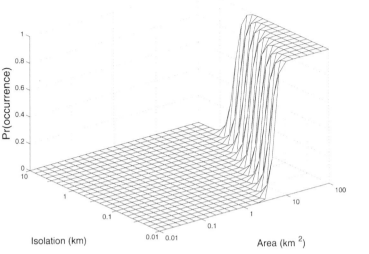

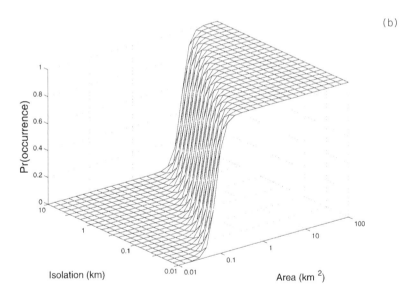

FIGURE 11.1. Multiple logistic regression models of the probability of occurrence of (*a*) mountain lions and (*b*) bobcats as a function of fragment area and isolation across 39 study sites in urban coastal southern California (modified from Crooks 2002). Probability of occurrence of both species was highest in large, less isolated sites and lowest in small and isolated habitat fragments.

information system (GIS) models of habitat relationships for the two species. Next, they evaluated the effects of roadways and urban development, which are major determinants of carnivore distribution and abundance in the southern coastal region (Beier 1993, 1995; Swift et al. 1993; Haas 2000; Sauvajot et al. 2000; Lyren 2001; Crooks 2002; Riley et al. 2003), on carnivore habitat suitability. To do so, they constructed GIS models that categorized and ranked the impacts of various road types and land-use categories on carnivore habitat suitability. These GIS models allowed for a characterization of habitat connectivity for mountain lions and bobcats in the ecoregion.

The habitat connectivity model for mountain lions suggested that the majority of high-suitability cougar habitat occurred in upland areas, including many of the mountain ranges in the region (Hunter, Fisher, and Crooks 2003). Coastal lowland areas with higher road densities and urbanization impacts represented lower-quality habitat for mountain lions, with the urban clusters of Los Angeles and San Diego yielding little to no quality habitat. The habitat connectivity model for bobcats, compared with that for mountain lions, indicated that the coastal urban areas retained relatively more suitable habitat, a result consistent with the finding that bobcats are less sensitive to urbanization impacts (Crooks 2002). Moreover, core areas of high-quality habitat in upland areas were less internally fragmented for bobcats than for mountain lions. Overall, both the suitability and the connectivity of habitat throughout coastal southern California were higher for bobcats than for mountain lions.

A particularly worrisome conclusion revealed by the connectivity models was that much of the key carnivore habitat in the southern coastal region is at risk (Hunter, Fisher, and Crooks 2003). More than 80 percent of high-suitability habitat and more than 90 percent of medium-suitability habitat for mountain lions and bobcats were found in the least-protected land-management classes—that is, in areas not managed primarily for the protection of biodiversity. Indeed, only 17 percent and 20 percent of high-suitability habitats for bobcats and mountain lions, respectively, were within the most protected lands, with permanent protection from conversion of natural land cover.

Several core habitat blocks in southern California are nearly isolated by urban development and roadways; these connectivity "choke points" are high conservation priorities to maintain landscape-level connectivity. To provide more refined evaluations of connectivity, carnivore activity in many of the primary core areas and linkages is being monitored through radiotelemetry, tracks, scat, and remotely triggered camera surveys (Haas 2000; Sauvajot et al. 2000; Lyren 2001; Crooks 2002; Riley et al. 2003). Field surveys within habitat patches have yielded predictive models of the influence of patch size and isolation on the probability of occurrence of carnivore species (Crooks 2002) (figure 11.1), and surveys (e.g., Haas 2000; Ng et al. 2004) within key linkages have quantified the dimensionality of corridors and roadway underpasses necessary to facilitate movement of wildlife.

In 2000, a meeting of experts throughout California was convened to identify the location of and threats to the most important corridors in the state (Penrod, Hunter, and Merrifield 2000; Beier et al. in press). Although using such expert opinion should be complemented with scientific analyses to ensure proper reserve design (Clevenger et al. 2002; Cowling et al. 2003), expert-based approaches can provide a quick method to identify priority areas that are of conservation concern to scientists, conservationists, resource managers, and land-use planners knowledgeable about the focal area. During the conference, participants delineated more than 230 linkages throughout the state, 60 of them in the southern coastal ecoregion. Of these 60 southern coastal linkages, 60 percent (36) were ranked by experts as severely threatened, and urbanization was overwhelmingly identified as the primary threat to connectivity in the ecoregion. Urbanization threatened 85 percent (51) of the linkages, and roads (a by-product of urban sprawl) jeopardized 40 percent (24) of the linkages, with 58 percent of these 24 corridors listed as severely threatened. In a region with such an extensive road network, underpasses and culverts have also become critical movement corridors; 35 percent of the linkages in the ecoregion were associated with roadway underpasses or culverts. As in all urbanizing systems, our ability to conserve connectivity in the face of past and present development in California will depend on a combination of sound science, advocacy, education, planning, and implementation.

THE TENAJA CORRIDOR: LESSONS FROM CONNECTIVITY PLANNING

The Nature Conservancy, through its ecoregional planning efforts, has adopted a proactive role in guiding urban development and thereby protecting large landscapes in southern California. One focal area centers on The Nature Conservancy's Santa Rosa Plateau Ecological Reserve, which covers 7,900 acres (3,200 hectares) of one of the richest and most diverse natural landscapes remaining in the lower 48 states. Unfortunately, like many regions throughout the country, the area immediately surrounding the reserve is undergoing rapid development. Both urban sprawl (through ranchettes and second homes) and agricultural development threaten to isolate the Santa Rosa Plateau permanently. To prevent isolation of this reserve, The Nature Conservancy—working with landowners; academic institutions; local, state, and federal agencies; and private foundations—is implementing a plan that attempts to maintain the reserve's connectivity by way of the Tenaja Corridor. The corridor encompasses a general zone of connectivity and habitat linkages more than 3.72 miles (6 kilometers) in length joining the western boundary of the reserve with the Santa

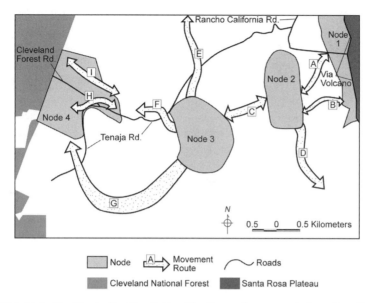

FIGURE 11.2. The Tenaja Corridor, linking The Nature Conservancy's Santa Rosa Plateau Ecological Reserve to the Cleveland National Forest (modified from Fisher and Crooks 2001). Habitat nodes and linkages among nodes are indicated on the map. Although the intervening matrix (*white areas*) is still in the early stages of urbanization, continuing development will likely cause much of the matrix to become impermeable for many species.

Ana Mountains and the mostly contiguous habitat of the 145,730-acre (59,000-hectare) Cleveland National Forest to the west (figure 11.2).

The Tenaja area is divided into almost 500 parcels, most of which are in separate private ownership. Parcels vary in size and are most dense in areas along Tenaja Road, the primary roadway along the corridor. Currently, most parcels are not yet developed, although this status changes daily. Physical factors, in particular topography, limit development options on some parcels, but regulatory limitations in the area are weak and are currently insufficient for securing adequate wildlife habitat and for maintaining the permeability of the matrix lands surrounding the reserve. Design of the Tenaja Corridor was initiated in the early 1990s to ensure that lands surrounding the reserve, particularly to the west and northwest, remain as viable movement linkages and resident habitat for local wildlife. Four possible linkage options were developed and examined originally for both biological and logistical feasibility:

- *The matrix approach.* Conservation efforts encompass landowner education, development restrictions, and conservation easements (permanent, legally binding agreements that restrict certain types of activities) to encourage compatible land development outside the reserve in order to maintain the permeability of the surrounding matrix for target species.

- *The archipelago or stepping-stone approach.* A series of habitat nodes— larger intact blocks of natural habitat—along the corridor would be fully protected in order to provide core habitat for relatively sedentary species residing within the corridor (e.g., herpetofauna and small mammals) or to provide stepping-stones for wider-ranging species traveling through the corridor.
- *The riparian approach.* A focus on riparian corridors within the area would protect the many wildlife species that reside within or travel through riparian habitat.
- *The minimal approach.* The minimum number of parcels required to pro- vide a continuous protected corridor between the reserve and the national forest would be acquired and set aside under conservation management. Lands adjacent to the minimum number of parcels would be managed as in the matrix approach. The minimum number of parcels would not nec- essarily follow riparian habitat, as would the riparian approach.

A provisional list of target species, based on their likelihood of extinction if the reserve were to become biologically isolated and on their importance for community function, was identified, and the movement requirements for these targets were evaluated against the four options (table 11.1).

A combination of these approaches was ultimately accepted as the final design of the Tenaja Corridor. The implemented design consists of an archi- pelago of four habitat nodes along the corridor (figure 11.2), with riparian areas included in the design and the surrounding matrix managed for compatible land use. Other considerations in the corridor plan included the need to allow space for periodic prescribed burns, the need to maximize representation of rare or threatened natural communities within the corridor (e.g., Englemann oak woodlands, native grasses, coastal sage scrub, and vernal pools), and the size and cost of individual parcels and their owners' attitudes. Multiple connec- tors among nodes allow for design redundancy and alternative travel routes for animals traversing the corridor (figure 11.2).

In all, a total of 1,732 acres (701 hectares) were included in the design of the Tenaja Corridor. Through fee acquisition, conservation easements, and planned developments, approximately 75 percent (1,300 acres [526 hectares]) of corridor land has been protected to date (Morrison and Reynolds in press). Nevertheless, implementation of the design is not complete, and distinct threats remain to the project's long-term viability. Functional connectivity in any corri- dor depends on the animals' ability to travel safely through the linkage from one

TABLE 11.1. Estimated Effect of Four Linkage Design Approaches on the Likelihood of Target Species Movement Through the Tenaja Area

SPECIES	LATIN NAME	MATRIX	ARCHIPELAGO	RIPARIAN	MINIMAL
Mule deer	*Odocoileus hemionus*	L	M	M	M
Badger	*Taxidea taxus*	O	L	O	L
Bobcat	*Lynx rufus*	L	M	M	M
Coyote	*Canis latrans*	M	H	H	H
Mountain lion	*Puma concolor*	L	M	M	M–L
Long-tailed weasel	*Mustela frenata*	L	M	H–M	M
Ornate shrew	*Sorex ornatus*	O	L	M	L
Striped racer	*Masticophis lateralis*	O	M	M	M
Red diamond rattlesnake	*Crotalus ruber*	O	M	M	M
Rosy boa	*Charina trivirgata roseofusca*	M	M	M	M
Granite night lizard	*Xantusia henshawi*	M	M	M	M
Western pond turtle	*Clemmys marmorata*	O	Unknown	H	Unknown
California newt	*Taricha torosa*	L	M	H	L
California thrasher	*Toxostoma redivivum*	L	M	M	L

Note: H, high; M, medium; L, low; O, none.

core area to another. As urban development progresses within and around the Tenaja Corridor, native habitats and the wildlife they support will increasingly face a suite of detrimental edge effects that will impair corridor functionality. Some private residences are necessarily permitted within the corridor to reduce the exorbitant cost of purchase outright. However, strict conservation easements are incorporated that limit the size and location of the residence, prevent out-door pets, prevent the spread of exotics, and even specify the types of fencing and outdoor lighting that may be used in order to minimize impacts on the corridor. Moreover, the right to enter the parcel for biological management is also retained, and a large public-education campaign has been directed at nearby residents in order to reduce human impacts and to minimize human–wildlife conflict. For example, the campaign helps people learn to live in mountain lion habitat and to keep domestic animals in a manner that minimizes any chance of depredation. Educational efforts, however, are not always successful; at least one mountain lion has been killed for attacking livestock kept untended near the corridor. Although the effect of such depredation on mountain lion populations in the area is unclear, this example illustrates the unfortunate fact that even the best biologically designed corridors may fail if species utilizing the linkage are not shielded from human behavior.

With a large monetary investment in the purchase and management of various parcels of land constituting the Tenaja Corridor, it becomes crucial to determine whether target species are using the corridor and to what degree. Baseline biodiversity surveys indicate that a wide variety of species is indeed utilizing the corridor (Fisher and Crooks 2001). Field surveys have detected more than 130 vertebrate species within the Tenaja Corridor, including 77 species of birds, 26 species of herpetofauna, 11 species of small mammals, 11 species of large mammals, and 10 species of bats. A variety of native species considered sensitive to habitat degradation and fragmentation have been detected in the corridor, including almost all the target species listed in table 11.1. Some of these species, such as mountain lions, were likely traversing the corridor, whereas some of the smaller species, such as the ornate shrew and coast range newt, likely have resident populations within the corridor. These results emphasize the importance of scale when considering the functionality of wildlife corridors. Corridors can provide wildlife habitat for both transient and resident animals.

Road development can be a major impediment to animal movement and a distinct threat to connectivity (Noss and Cooperrider 1994; Reed, Johnson-Barnard, and Baker 1996; Forman and Alexander 1998), and this system is no exception. Night-driving surveys revealed that roadways were considerable mortality sinks for amphibians within and around the Tenaja Corridor before, during, and after measurable rainfall events. A total of 1,114 animals were encountered during approximately one year of night-driving surveys; 44 percent of these animals were found dead on roads (Fisher and Crooks 2001). Road mortality was particularly high for amphibians, especially on wet nights when they are most active. Indeed, the overall mortality rate was 48 percent on nights with rain, compared with 19 percent on nights classified as dry. Moreover, daytime road transect surveys over approximately seven months recorded a total of 175 roadkills, including kills of such potentially vulnerable species as bobcat, rufous-crowned sparrow, rosy boa, and red diamond rattlesnake. Continued compilation and mapping of roadkill information will help identify unsuccessful animal crossing locations, and monitoring such records over time will result in more accurate analyses of impacts associated with urban development, road construction, and increased traffic (Swift et al. 1993). In addition, management strategies can reduce animal mortality on roads and hence improve functional connectivity. For example, wildlife underpasses can be a successful tool in forcing some animals under a roadway (Foster and Humphrey 1995; Clevenger and Waltho 2000; Haas 2000; Ng et al. 2004); some culverts now have been installed for wildlife within the corridor.

A different, yet crucial threat to the continued existence and management of the corridor has to do with financial viability (Morrison and Reynolds in press). The original design called for some parcels of land within the corridor, particularly in the connectors between nodes, to be sold with conservation easements to private buyers in order to recoup some of the costs associated with the purchasing of land in an expensive market. However, developing the terms of the easements and pricing the parcels in order to attract buyers has proved challenging. Although numerous inquiries from potential buyers have been received, few sales have actually been completed. Potential buyers are discouraged by the high assessments burdening the land to support road and water infrastructure development. For example, a property of 40 acres (16 hectares) (assembled from several 5-acre [2-hectare] and 10-acre [4-hectare] lots and marketed singly) will carry annual costs for taxes and assessments of $8,000 to $12,000, making it economically unattractive to a buyer who, because of the conservation easement, can erect only one house on the property.

Overall, the Tenaja Corridor represents a bold experiment in conservation planning. By establishing the corridor, designed on biological principles for a suite of target species and pieced together parcel by parcel, The Nature Conservancy and its partners have attempted to mitigate the future isolation of a world-class preserve by urban sprawl. However, to date, the enormous costs associated with purchasing the parcels and restricting development through conservation easements have not been adequately recouped because the strategy for reselling parcels to conservation buyers has been negated by economic trends. Thus, in the long run, if this model is to fail, it will likely do so for financial rather than biological reasons. The most important lesson for replicating this type of effort elsewhere is to conduct an economic analysis simultaneously with a biological design analysis (Morrison and Reynolds in press). Economics should not compromise good conservation planning, but in the California case economic models might have prompted conservation planners to look for alternative corridor routes that were effective from a biological perspective, but less daunting from an economic perspective. For example, rather than a corridor through Riverside County, where property assessments are high, economic analysis may have suggested a corridor through nearby San Diego County, where property assessments are lower.

MAINTAINING CONNECTIVITY IN DEVELOPING LANDSCAPES: ADDITIONAL CASE STUDIES

In this section, we review several additional case studies to elucidate approaches and challenges of connectivity conservation in developing landscapes. Although there are certainly many examples from which to choose, we feel these studies provide a representative and interesting sample across multiple spatial scales, target species, and ecological systems, and thus serve to reinforce the lessons learned from the California case study.

FLORIDA ECOLOGICAL NETWORK

As in coastal southern California, natural areas in Florida have been challenged with rapid human population growth, urban sprawl, and habitat destruction (Harris and Atkins 1991; Hoctor, Carr, and Zwick 2000). Florida's population, approximately 15 million people, is increasing annually by approximately 250,000, resulting in habitat loss of up to 232 square miles (600 square kilometers) a year (Harris and Scheck 1991; Harris and Silva-Lopez 1992; Hoctor, Carr, and Zwick 2000). As is the case with southern California, to conserve Florida's biological diversity effectively, the identification and protection of large-scale connectivity are essential. A comprehensive regional network of reserves has been proposed (Noss 1987b, 1991; Noss and Cooperrider 1994), endorsed, and funded by several environmental groups and state governmental agencies, including the U.S. Departments of Environmental Protection and Transportation (Noss 1991; Hoctor, Carr, and Zwick 2000). The stated goals of the reserve network are to (1) conserve critical elements of Florida's native ecosystems and landscapes, (2) restore and maintain essential connectivity among diverse native ecological systems and processes, (3) facilitate the ability of these ecosystems and landscapes to function as dynamic systems, and (4) maintain the evolutionary potential of the biota to adapt to future environmental changes (Florida Greenways Commission 1994, reviewed in Hoctor, Carr, and Zwick 2000).

Hoctor, Carr, and Zwick (2000) recently adopted a regional landscape approach to help guide the design of the Florida reserve network. Using GIS analysis, they developed a decision support model to identify areas of ecological priority and landscape linkages necessary for functional connectivity. Their models incorporated land-use data on important ecological areas in the state, including habitat for target species, priority ecological communities, wetlands, roadless areas, floodplains, and important aquatic systems. The resulting Florida Ecological Network, incorporating approximately half of the state's area, provides a reserve system that contains most major ecological communities and most known occurrences of rare species. More than half of the network is already in conservation lands and public-domain water. Much of the land identified in the ecological network, however, is managed for multiple human uses on both public and private lands and not solely for biodiversity conservation.

Although the reserve network represents an important step toward biodiversity conservation in Florida, many issues remain to be addressed, as Hoctor, Carr, and Zwick (2000) emphasize. For example, more information is needed on the requirements of area-dependent species, such as the black bear (*Ursus americanus*) and the endangered Florida panther (*Puma concolor coryi*), to assess if the proposed network provides adequate connectivity for their persistence. Moreover, the reserve model does not include all important sites and species, in particular such uncommon, yet ecologically significant natural communities as pine rocklands and oak scrub tracts that may support rare species. More analyses also are needed on identifying, protecting, and managing core areas and surrounding buffers within the reserve network. As with connectivity conservation anywhere, prioritization on how best to focus conservation dollars on a combination of core areas, buffers, and linkages will entail tough choices with relatively limited funds (Simberloff and Cox 1987; Hobbs 1992; Simberloff et al. 1992). Florida has committed at least $300 million a year since 1990 for land-acquisition and conservation efforts. At these funding levels, the entire reserve network would be protected in, at minimum, three or four decades (Hoctor, Carr, and Zwick 2000). Time is of the essence, however, because continued human population growth and sprawl in Florida, if left unchecked, will certainly destroy priority areas within the reserve before they all can be protected.

As in southern California, roadways represent a significant impediment to animal movement and a major barrier to functional connectivity across the Florida landscape. Vehicle collisions are a primary agent of mortality for the Florida panther, accounting for nearly half of documented deaths (Maehr, Land, and Roelke 1991; Maehr 1997). To that end, attention has focused on the use of underpasses to facilitate the movement of panthers and other wildlife along roadways that traverse panther ranges (Foster and Humphrey 1995). For example, the state installed 24 underpasses, each approximately 66 feet (20 meters) long and 6.5 feet (2 meters) high, along a 40-mile (64-kilometer) fenced portion of Interstate 75 traversing Big Cypress National Preserve, Fakahatchee Strand State Preserve, and the Florida Panther National Wildlife Refuge. During 2 to 16 months of sampling at four of these underpasses, Foster and Humphrey (1995) recorded a variety of wildlife, including 10 crossings by panthers, 133 by bobcats, 361 by deer, 167 by alligators, and 2 by black bears. The researchers inferred that the underpasses reduced mortality for some species and helped prevent the highway from becoming a mortality sink.

CORRIDOR USE BY THE MOUNTAIN PYGMY-POSSUM, AUSTRALIA

According to the literature review by Beier and Noss (1998), Mansergh and Scotts (1989) provided the best example of the experimental approach to assessing the functionality of corridors. Mansergh and Scotts studied two subpopulations of the endangered mountain pygmy-possum in southeastern Australia. This small, cryptic species, the only marsupial hibernator, is also the only Australian mammal restricted to alpine and subalpine regions. The possum's range is limited to habitat of rocky scree slopes and boulder fields in heathland communities; the total area of available habitat is less than 4.6 square miles (12 square kilometers). Mansergh and Scotts (1989) studied the subpopulations of the possum in the Mount Higginbotham area, Victoria. One subpopulation enjoyed a relatively intact landscape on an undeveloped slope of the mountain. In contrast, the previously contiguous slope of the second subpopulation, representing 40 percent of the total population, was severely fragmented by roads and other developments associated with a ski resort.

Adult female possums are sedentary and remain in high-altitude areas that provide quality food and shelter. In contrast, during the breeding season, adult males travel between these areas along rock substrates on lower slopes. Such dispersal is an essential element of the species's social organization. Mansergh and Scotts (1989) found that in contrast to those in the unfragmented subpopulation, males in the ski resort subpopulation did not disperse, resulting in skewed sex ratios and lower survival rates. To mitigate the effects of development associated with the ski resort, a funnel-shaped 197-foot-long (60-meter-long) corridor of basalt rocks was constructed between the largest remaining patches of habitat. Under the road bisecting the two areas, two adjacent tunnels (3 by 4 feet [0.9 by 1.2 meters]) were installed and filled with rocks.

After the construction of this corridor, males were able to disperse between the previously isolated habitat patches; as a result, sex ratios within the ski resort subpopulation became similar to those within the unfragmented subpopulation. Moreover, when males were allowed to disperse through the newly established corridor, overwinter survival rates in the ski resort subpopulation rose to levels observed in the undisturbed area. By carefully collecting data before and after the manipulation, Mansergh and Scotts (1998) provided strong evidence for the corridors' ability to improve population viability (Beier and Noss 1998), although their study is unreplicated. The study also demonstrates that resource managers should recognize that dispersal can play an important role in population persistence and that constructing corridors and roadway underpasses can be an effective mitigation measure for habitats fragmented by roads and development.

KITENGELA WILDLIFE CORRIDOR, KENYA

Nairobi National Park is a rarity. It is a true national park within the fringes of a metropolis. It is situated on the very edge of one of the largest cities on the African continent—Nairobi, Kenya. Any visitor to Nairobi by air flies over the park when landing at the airport, and it is not uncommon to see photographs of lions or cheetah in the park with the skyscrapers of Nairobi in the distant background. The park contains a full array of ungulates, including zebra, wildebeest, hartebeest, and gazelle, along with their attendant predators, such as lion, hyena, leopard, and cheetah. The park is fenced on three sides to keep wild animals out of the city and human activities away from the reserve. The southern border, however, is unfenced, and it is through this area that the migratory herds that once rivaled the more famous Serengeti–Mara migration move from the park into the 205-square-mile (530-square-kilometer) Kitengela dispersal area (Odhiambo and Becha 2000). This dispersal route allows the park to be managed as an open system and part of the Athi Plains ecosystem.

The Kitengela dispersal area is currently under serious threat. The area is close to a rapidly growing city and is dotted with human settlements. Activities such as subsistence farming, quarrying, flower farming, and, above all, fencing of individual plots of land are fragmenting the area and acting as a barrier to migratory herds moving seasonally into the park (Odhiambo and Becha 2000). Until recently, the pastoral Masai community communally owned much of the area. Legislative changes have granted property rights to individual owners, thus spurring subdivision, fencing, and selling of land to other tribes, all of which has signaled a transition from the pastoral lifestyle toward a more sedentary agricultural one. The Masai are in the process of losing a traditional lifestyle that was in many ways compatible with the migratory movements of wildlife. If this sprawl is left unchecked, it is likely that Nairobi National Park's southern and only open boundary will become impermeable to wildlife. The park will then likely lose much of its wildlife, with wide-ranging predatory and migratory animals being hit the hardest.

To prevent further fragmentation of the Kitengela dispersal area, several organizations (Wildlife Conservation Society, Friends of Nairobi National Park, Wildlife Foundation, Kenya Wildlife Service, Kitengela Landowners Association, African Wildlife Foundation, International Livestock Research Institute, Global Environmental Fund, and The Nature Conservancy, among others) are working to implement the Wildlife Conservation Lease Programme (WCLP). This effort began in 2000 as a pilot program. Its aim was simple — to provide a financial incentive through a lease payment to traditional landowners south of the park to continue to allow wildlife unrestricted access to their land. In return for not fencing their land and for abiding by several other pro-wildlife measures, landowners in the program receive regular payments, three times a year, coinciding with when school fees for children are due. Payments, equivalent to about U.S.$3 to $4 an acre per year, are made at a public ceremony to ensure transparency. The landowners are free to continue to graze livestock (Odhiambo and Becha 2000).

Three years into the effort, the program is a great success, with a long waiting list of landowners eager to enroll their parcels in the program. Currently, 8,000 acres (3,239 hectares) owned by a hundred or so families are enrolled, but plans are under way to expand the program to up to 60,000 acres (24,291 hectares), fully securing the migratory routes necessary for wildlife to access the park. A new organization, the Wildlife Foundation, with United States and Kenyan ties, has been established to implement the program. The Wildlife Foundation works with donors, local nongovernmental organizations, communities, and government agencies to ensure that the parcels are correctly identified, payments are made, and enforcement mechanisms are in place. The Wildlife Foundation has also implemented a predator-compensation program where confirmed conflicts between predators and livestock are partially compensated by payments in an attempt to reduce wildlife–human conflict.

This pilot program, aimed at private lands, is an innovative conservation effort in East Africa. It has proved popular with both landowners and donors and has attracted the attention of land managers in other areas such as the Serengeti. The program offers landowners the opportunity to derive tangible benefits from wildlife on their land, and its focused efforts help maintain a migratory corridor within a rapidly urbanizing area. Its careful design, its focus on identifying migratory routes and protecting them, its transparency in implementation, and its partnership model of action have helped make it a promising example of how wildlife movement can be protected on private lands so close to a major urban center.

CONCLUSION

Sprawl perpetuates habitat fragmentation, a leading and proximal cause of population extirpation and species extinction. The conservation of natural levels of connectivity can help mitigate the detrimental effects of fragmentation in urbanizing landscapes. Regional connectivity assessments such as those being carried out in California and Florida may prove to be relatively quick methods to determine the degree of landscape connectivity for multiple target species and ecological processes. Such regional efforts are useful in generating interest among scientists and managers; in educating lawmakers, funders, and the general public; and in providing general guidance as to the location and feasibility of establishing or securing landscape linkages. Of course, generating interest and identifying general priorities for corridors is one thing; actually implementing a plan either to develop or to secure a corridor is quite another. The approach and design used in the Tenaja Corridor may prove to be one model that can be replicated elsewhere—it is at least a model actually in use (rather than theorized) and as such can provide ample guidance as to major issues in corridor design and implementation. Perhaps the most important general lesson learned from the Tenaja Corridor is that securing a wildlife corridor in a rapidly urbanizing environment is far more difficult than is usually anticipated. Indeed, the socioeconomic landscape, not the biological landscape, is most likely to prove a hindrance to the corridor's long-term viability and to its replication as a concept elsewhere.

We caution that much is still unknown about wildlife corridors and connectivity, particularly in areas with pronounced human use where the potential for human–wildlife conflict is high. To best protect biodiversity, corridors should be specifically designed for the purposes of facilitating movement of focal species and ensuring the continuation of ecological processes. Corridors designed for alternative or even competing functions can be ineffective at best and detrimental at worst. For example, roadside corridors, designed for human safety or aesthetic reasons, can serve as de facto wildlife corridors, but also can have negative consequences for native species by increasing mortality on roads (Bennett 1991; Harris and Scheck 1991). Similarly, greenways, long a part of the suburban and urban landscape, can also function as wildlife corridors (Hay 1991; Smith and Hellmund 1993; Ahern 1995; Zube 1995), but also may act as mortality sinks—unsuitable habitat with high mortality and low reproduction—for both resident and dispersing animals (Soulé 1991a, 1991b). The key to success lies in the actual design of the corridor.

Habitat models and empirical evidence of animal movement can provide invaluable data on how animals respond to potential barriers to functional connectivity associated with urban sprawl, including both urban edges and roadways. This effort can be greatly enhanced by new technological advances in acquiring and analyzing remote-sensed data, GIS spatial information, and animal movement patterns through global positioning system (GPS) and satellite telemetry. Although corridors will continue to appear as part of management and land-use plans, we will often be flying blind in trying to design, implement, and monitor workable linkages without basic research on how organisms move through a landscape.

Looking into the future, we can see that even though the concept of landscape-scale connectivity is now firmly rooted in conservation biology, the real challenge for the future is putting theory into practice to implement connectivity conservation in urbanizing systems (Crooks and Sanjayan in press). The question remains: In the face of urban sprawl, how do we best protect connectivity in a manner that maximizes the utility for species and ecological processes while minimizing costs associated with procurement, maintenance, and human–wildlife conflicts? The task may seem daunting. However, with new research under way, case studies to guide us, and, above all, an increase in the level of cooperation across disciplines and political boundaries, landscape connectivity—in places as far-flung as the rapidly urbanizing landscapes of southern California and Florida, the mountain slopes of Australia, and the vast African plains of Kenya—is becoming a reality.

REFERENCES

Ahern, J. 1995. Greenways as a planning strategy. *Landscape and Urban Planning* 33:131–155.

Beier, P. 1993. Determining minimum habitat areas and habitat corridors for cougars. *Conservation Biology* 7:94–108.

——. 1995. Dispersal of juvenile cougars in fragmented habitats. *Journal of Wildlife Management* 5:228–237.

Beier, P., D. Choate, and R. H. Barrett. 1995. Movement patterns of mountain lions during different behaviors. *Journal of Mammalogy* 76:1056–1070.

Beier, P., and R. F. Noss. 1998. Do habitat corridors provide connectivity? *Conservation Biology* 12:1241–1252.

Beier, P., K. Penrod, C. Luke, W. Spencer, and C. Cabañero. In press. South coast missing linkages: Restoring connectivity to wildlands in the largest metropolitan area in the United States. In K. R. Crooks and M. A. Sanjayan, eds., *Connectivity Conservation*. Cambridge: Cambridge University Press.

Bennett, A. F. 1991. Roads, roadsides, and wildlife conservation: A review. In D. A. Saunders and R. J. Hobbs, eds., *Nature Conservation 2: The Role of Corridors*, 99–177. Chipping Norton, Australia: Surrey Beatty.

——. 1999. *Linkages in the Landscape: The Role of Corridors and Connectivity in Wildlife Conservation*. Gland, Switzerland: International Union for Conservation of Nature and Natural Resources.

Bureau of the Census. 2000. *Census 2000*. Washington, D.C.: Bureau of the Census.

Clevenger, A. P., and N. Waltho. 2000. Factors influencing the effectiveness of wildlife underpasses in Banff National Park, Alberta, Canada. *Conservation Biology* 14:47–56.

Clevenger, A. P., J. Wierzchowski, B. Chruszcz, and K. Gunson. 2002. GIS-generated, expert-based models for identifying wildlife habitat linkages and planning migration passages. *Conservation Biology* 16:503–514.

Cowling, R. M., R. L. Pressey, R. Sims-Castley, A. le Roux, E. Baard, C. J. Burgers, and G. Palmer. 2003. The expert of the algorithm? Comparison of priority conservation areas in the Cape Floristic Region identified by park managers and reserve selection software. *Biological Conservation* 112:147–167.

Crooks, K. R. 2000. Mammalian carnivores as target species for conservation in southern California. In J. E. Keeley, M. Baer-Keeley, and C. J. Fotheringham, eds., *Second Interface Between Ecology and Land Development in California*, 105–112. U.S. Geological Survey Open-File Report 00-62. Sacramento, Calif.: U.S. Geological Survey.

——. 2002. Relative sensitivities of mammalian carnivores to habitat fragmentation. *Conservation Biology* 16:488–502.

Crooks, K. R., and M. A. Sanjayan, eds. In press. *Connectivity Conservation*. Cambridge: Cambridge University Press.

Crooks, K. R., and M. E. Soulé. 1999. Mesopredator release and avifaunal extinctions in a fragmented system. *Nature* 400:563–566.

Dobson, A., K. Ralls, M. Foster, M. E. Soulé, D. Simberloff, D. Doak, J. A. Estes, L. S. Mills, D. Mattson, R. Dirzo, H. Arita, S. Ryan, E. A. Norse, R. F. Noss, and D. Johns. 1999. Corridors: Reconnecting fragmented landscapes. In J. Terborgh, ed., *Continental Conservation: Scientific Foundations of Regional Reserve Networks*, 129–170. Washington, D.C.: Island Press.

Dobson, A. P., J. P. Rodriguez, W. M. Roberts, and D. S. Wilcove. 1997. Geographic distribution of endangered species in the United States. *Science* 275:550–553.

Estes, J., K. Crooks, and R. Holt. 2001. Ecological role of predators. In S. Levin, ed., *Encyclopedia of Biodiversity*, 857–878. San Diego: Academic Press.

Fisher, R., and K. Crooks. 2001. *Baseline Biodiversity Survey for the Tenaja Corridor and Southern Santa Ana Mountains: Final Report*. San Diego: Biological Resources Division, U.S. Geological Survey.

Florida Greenways Commission. 1994. *Creating a Statewide Greenways System for People ... for Wildlife ... for Florida: Florida Greenways Commission Report to the Governor*. Tallahassee: Florida Department of Environmental Protection.

Forman, R. T. T., and L. E. Alexander. 1998. Roads and their major ecological effects. *Annual Review of Ecology and Systematics* 29:207–231.

Foster, M. L., and S. R. Humphrey. 1995. Use of highway underpasses by Florida panthers and other wildlife. *Wildlife Society Bulletin* 23:95–100.

Gilpin, M. E., and M. E. Soulé. 1986. Minimum viable populations: Processes of species extinction. In M. E. Soulé, ed., *Conservation Biology: The Science of Scarcity and Diversity*, 19–34. Sunderland, Mass.: Sinauer.

Haas, C. D. 2000. Distribution, relative abundance, and roadway underpass responses of carnivores throughout the Puente-Chino Hills. M.S. thesis, California State Polytechnic University.

Haddad, N. 2000. Corridor length and patch colonization by a butterfly, *Junonia coenia*. *Conservation Biology* 14:738–745.

Harris, L. D., and K. Atkins. 1991. Faunal movement corridors in Florida. In W. E. Hudson, ed., *Landscape Linkages and Biodiversity*, 117–134. Washington, D.C.: Island Press.

Harris, L. D., and J. Scheck. 1991. From implications to applications: The dispersal corridor principle applied to the conservation of biological diversity. In D. A. Saunders and R. J. Hobbs, eds., *Nature Conservation 2: The Role of Corridors*, 189–220. Chipping Norton, Australia: Surrey Beatty.

Harris, L. D., and G. Silva-Lopez. 1992. Forest fragmentation and the conservation of biological diversity. In P. Fielder and S. Jain, eds., *Conservation Biology: The Theory and Practice of Nature Conservation*, 197–327. New York: Chapman and Hall.

Harrison, R. L. 1998. Bobcats in residential areas: Distribution and homeowner attitudes. *Southwestern Naturalist* 43:469–475.

Hay, K. G. 1991. Greenways and biodiversity. In W. E. Hudson, ed., *Landscape Linkages and Biodiversity*, 162–175. Washington, D.C.: Island Press.

Hobbs, R. J. 1992. The role of corridors in conservation: Solution or bandwagon? *Trends in Ecology and Evolution* 7:389–392.

Hoctor, T. S., M. H. Carr, and P. D. Zwick. 2000. Identifying a linked reserve system using a regional landscape approach: The Florida Ecological Network. *Conservation Biology* 14:984–1000.

Hunter, R., R. Fisher, and K. R. Crooks. 2003. Landscape-level connectivity in coastal southern California as assessed by carnivore habitat suitability. *Natural Areas Journal* 23:302–314.

Lambeck, R. J. 1997. Focal species: A multi-species umbrella for nature conservation. *Conservation Biology* 11:849–856.

Lembeck, M. 1986. Long term behavior and population dynamics of an unharvested bobcat population in San Diego County. In S. D. Miller and D. D. Everett, eds., *Cats of the World: Biology, Conservation, and Management*, 305–310. Washington, D.C.: National Wildlife Federation.

Lindenmayer, D. G., A. D. Manning, P. L. Smith, H. P. Possingham, J. Fischer, I. Oliver, and M. A. McCarthy. 2002. The focal-species approach and landscape restoration: A critique. *Conservation Biology* 16:338–345.

Lyren, L. M. 2001. Movement patterns of coyotes and bobcats relative to roads and underpasses in the Chino Hills area of southern California. M.S. thesis, California State Polytechnic University.

Maehr, D. S. 1997. *The Florida Panther: Life and Death of a Vanishing Carnivore.* Washington, D.C.: Island Press.

Maehr, D. S., E. D. Land, and M. E. Roelke. 1991. Mortality patterns of panthers in southwest Florida. *Proceedings of the Annual Conference of Southeast Association of Fish and Wildlife Agencies* 45:201–207.

Mansergh, I. M., and D. J. Scotts. 1989. Habitat continuity and social organization of the mountain pygmy-possum restored by tunnel. *Journal of Wildlife Management* 53:701–707.

McCaull, J. 1994. The Natural Community Conservation Planning Program and the coastal sage scrub ecosystem of southern California. In R. E. Grumbine, ed., *Environmental Policy and Biodiversity*, 281–292. Washington, D.C.: Island Press.

McEuen, A. 1993. The wildlife corridor controversy: A review. *Endangered Species Update* 10:1–12.

Miller, B., R. Reading, J. Strittholt, C. Carroll, R. Noss, M. Soulé, O. Sanchez, J. Terborgh, D. Brightsmith, T. Cheeseman, and D. Foreman. 1998. Using focal species in the design of nature reserve networks. *Wild Earth* 8:81–92.

Moore, F. R., and T. R. Simons. 1992. Habitat suitability and stopover ecology of neo-tropical landbird migrants. In J. M. Hagan III and D. W. Johnston, eds., *Ecology and Conservation of Neotropical Migrant Landbirds*, 141–157. Washington, D.C.: Smithsonian Institution Press.

Morrison, S. A., and M. D. Reynolds. In press. Where to draw the line: Integrating feasibility into connectivity planning. In K. R. Crooks and M. A. Sanjayan, eds., *Connectivity Conservation*. Cambridge: Cambridge University Press.

Myers, N. 1990. The biodiversity challenge: Expanded hot-spots analysis. *The Environmentalist* 10:243–256.

Ng, S. J., J. W. Dole, R. M. Sauvajot, S. P. D. Riley, and T. J. Valone. 2004. Use of highway undercrossings by wildlife in southern California. *Biological Conservation* 115:499–507.

Noss, R. F. 1987a. Corridors in real landscapes: A reply to Simberloff and Cox. *Conservation Biology* 1:159–164.

——. 1987b. Protecting natural areas in fragmented landscapes. *Natural Areas Journal* 7:2–13.

——. 1991. Landscape connectivity: Different functions at different scales. In W. E. Hudson, ed., *Landscape Linkages and Biodiversity*, 27–39. Washington, D.C.: Island Press.

Noss, R. F., and A. Y. Cooperrider. 1994. *Saving Nature's Legacy: Protecting and Restoring Biodiversity*. Washington, D.C.: Island Press.

Noss, R. F., H. B. Quigley, M. G. Hornocker, T. Merrill, and P. C. Paquet. 1996. Conservation biology and carnivore conservation in the Rocky Mountains. *Conservation Biology* 10:949–963.

Odhiambo, P., and H. Becha. 2000. *Proceeding of a Roadmap Towards Sustainable Management of Kitengela Wildlife Migratory Routes and Dispersal Area Workshop.* Nairobi, Kenya: East African Wildlife Society.

Penrod, K., R. Hunter, and M. Merrifield. 2000. *Missing Linkages: Restoring Connectivity to the California Landscape.* San Diego: California Wilderness Coalition, Nature Conservancy, U.S. Geological Survey, Center for Reproduction of Endangered Species at the Zoological Society of San Diego, and California State Parks.

Reed, R. A., J. Johnson-Barnard, and W. L. Baker. 1996. Contribution of roads to forest fragmentation in the Rocky Mountains. *Conservation Biology* 10:1098–1106.

Riley, S. P., R. M. Sauvajot, T. K. Fuller, E. C. York, D. A. Kamradt, C. Bromley, and R. K. Wayne. 2003. Effects of urbanization and habitat fragmentation on bobcats and coyotes in southern California. *Conservation Biology* 17:566–576.

Rosenberg, D. K., B. R. Noon, and E. C. Meslow. 1997. Biological corridors: Form, function, and efficacy. *BioScience* 47:677–687.

Sauvajot, R. M., E. C. York, T. K. Fuller, H. S. Kim, D. S. Kamradt, and R. K. Wayne. 2000. Distribution and status of carnivores in the Santa Monica Mountains, California: Preliminary results from radio-telemetry and remote camera surveys. In J. E. Keeley, M. Baer-Keeley, and C. J. Fotheringham, eds., *Second Interface Between Ecology and Land Development in California*, 113–123. U.S. Geological Survey Open-File Report 00-62. Sacramento, Calif.: U.S. Geological Survey.

Schultz, C. B. 1995. Corridors, islands, and stepping stones: The role of dispersal behavior in designing reserves for a rare Oregon butterfly. *Bulletin of the Ecological Society of America* 76:240.

Simberloff, D., and J. Cox. 1987. Consequences and costs of corridors. *Conservation Biology* 1:63–71.

Simberloff, D., J. A. Farr, J. Cox, and D. W. Mehlman. 1992. Movement corridors: Conservation bargains or poor investments? *Conservation Biology* 6:493–504.

Smith, D. S., and P. C. Hellmund. 1993. *Ecology of Greenways: Design and Function of Linear Conservation Areas.* Minneapolis: University of Minnesota Press.

Soulé, M. E. 1991a. Conservation corridors: Countering habitat fragmentation. Theory and strategy. In W. E. Hudson, ed., *Landscape Linkages and Biodiversity*, 91–104. Washington, D.C.: Island Press.

——. 1991b. Land use planning and wildlife maintenance: Guidelines for conserving wildlife in an urban landscape. *Journal of the American Planning Association* 57:313–323.

Soulé, M. E., and D. Simberloff. 1986. What do genetics and ecology tell us about the design of nature reserves? *Biological Conservation* 35:19–40.

Soulé, M. E., and J. Terborgh. 1999. *Continental Conservation: Scientific Foundations of Regional Reserve Networks.* Washington, D.C.: Island Press.

Swift, C., A. Collins, H. Gutierrez, H. Lam, and I. Ratiner. 1993. Habitat linkages in an urban mountain chain. In J. E. Keeley, ed., *Interface Between Ecology and Land Development in California*, 189–199. Los Angeles: Southern California Academy of Sciences.

Taylor, P. D., L. Fahrig, K. Henein, and G. Merriam. 1993. Connectivity is a vital element of landscape structure. *Oikos* 68:571–573.

Wilcove, D.S., D. Rothstein, J. Dubow, A. Phillips, and E. Losos. 1998. Quantifying threats to imperiled species in the United States. *BioScience* 48:607–615.

Wilson, E.O. 1992. *The Diversity of Life*. New York: Norton.

Winker, K., D.W. Warner, and A.R. Weisbrod. 1992. The northern waterthrush and Swainson's thrush as transients at a temperate inland stopover site. In J. M. Hagan III and D. W. Johnston, eds., *Ecology and Conservation of Neotropical Migrant Landbirds*, 384–402. Washington, D.C.: Smithsonian Institution Press.

Woodroffe, R., and J.R. Ginsberg. 1998. Edge effects and the extinction of populations inside protected areas. *Science* 280:2126–2128.

Zube, E.H. 1995. Greenways and the US national park system. *Landscape and Urban Planning* 33:17–25.

12

THE ECONOMICS OF BIODIVERSITY
IN URBANIZING ECOSYSTEMS

Stephen Farber

W ith urban populations increasing at a rate four times that of rural areas, sprawl is becoming a worldwide phenomenon (World Resources Institute 1998). Growing populations, increasing incomes and levels of consumption, and the drawbacks associated with living in dense urban centers create economic forces that both push and pull people away from central cities, yet they remain connected to the urban metropolis economically and culturally. Biodiversity losses, in terms of both species and ecosystem variety, are occurring throughout the world at rates unprecedented in human history (Wilson 1988; Heywood 1995). These losses result from a number of factors, including overharvesting, urbanization, resource development, pollution, and agriculturalization (Barbier, Burgess, and Folke 1994; Johnson and Klemens, chapter 2, this volume). The largest single cause of the decline in biodiversity is habitat loss and degradation (Ehrlich 1988). Because sprawl is a significant modifier of natural habitats, it is a prime focus of policies to protect the diversity of species and ecosystems. Although some may argue that sprawl is the inevitable result of market forces, this chapter illustrates that sprawl is a result of imperfections in market forces; and the resultant loss of biodiversity has significant implications for economic conditions associated with human welfare.

Sprawling development across the landscape and increased impacts on land and natural resources are reflections, in part, of increased economic prosperity. This prosperity possesses both the seeds of biodiversity loss and the wealth to avoid losses. Naidoo and Adamowicz (2001) found that across countries, the number of plants, amphibians, reptiles, and invertebrates designated as threatened species increases with the countries' per capita incomes. Birds were the only taxonomic group in which the numbers of threatened species decreased with income, perhaps because of landscaping or higher-income persons' demanding more tree and bush vegetation. Urban planning, which establishes human impact patterns on the landscape, can ameliorate the effects on biodiversity. White and colleagues (1997) showed that effective planning in a rapidly urbanizing landscape in eastern Pennsylvania had the potential to diminish by half the proportion of habitats at risk from urbanization. They suggested using the cost savings in public infrastructure under more compact development scenarios to fund conservation efforts, including the purchase of easements.

So there is a connection between urban settlement patterns and loss of species and natural ecosystems. Why should we be concerned about this? Are not these settlement patterns simply a reflection of supply and demand that serve us so well? What are the implications of biodiversity loss? What are the associated losses to human welfare? Do we really need to manage growth with biodiversity in mind? The purpose of this chapter is to address these questions from an economic perspective. First, it proposes that biodiversity is an ecological asset, with associated economic benefits at risk from urbanization and sprawl. Just as we manage our financial diversity through portfolio selection, we must consider the implications of urbanization on our ecological portfolio. Second, it addresses the economics of urban sprawl and associated biodiversity losses; although sprawl is associated with market forces, certain failures in those forces result in more extensive sprawl than would otherwise occur.

MANAGING ECOLOGICAL ASSETS

Ecological assets are those features of natural systems that yield services that enhance human welfare. These assets exist in the form of various species and ecosystem types that compose the ecological "portfolio." Biodiversity can be thought of as the variation in asset components of this portfolio, representing the multitude and variety of genes, species, and ecosystems. Managing this ecological portfolio is analogous to managing a financial portfolio, except that we know less about the ecological system and how it works than we know about economic systems and how economic agents work. Biodiversity lies at the core of natural systems, determining their connectedness and resilience. Therefore, a loss in biodiversity—whether it is at the level of genes, species, or ecosystems—translates into losses in valuable ecosystem services and the insurance value typically provided by a diversified portfolio. Important dynamic properties of ecosystems, such as reliability of ecological functions and resilience to change resulting from biodiversity, are similar to features of a desirable financial portfolio and similarly depend on diversity (Walker 1995; Yachi and Loreau 1999).

Although losses in ecological assets and diminished diversity of the ecological portfolio may impose welfare losses and costs to urban economies, preserving this portfolio may also be costly. Restricting development to preserve ecological features may result in lost incomes or increased economic costs. Managing ecological assets is therefore often a trade-off between losses and gains. This is strikingly the case for urban sprawl, where economic development typically imposes significant ecological and landscape alterations, resulting in the diminution of ecological assets. Protecting those assets, in turn, places constraints on the locations and types of allowable development.

Managing ecological assets in the face of sprawl requires the recognition of the valuable features of ecosystems at risk under a particular development scenario. Losses in natural services must be identified under the development scenario and weighed against the potential benefits of that development. Identification may be the result of formal physical analysis, such as hydrologic modeling of impacts from alterations in vegetative cover or slope conditions. Or identification may come from community recognition of critical ecological features that must be preserved in the face of development pressures.

ECONOMIC VALUES OF NATURAL SYSTEMS

One can measure the value of an ecosystem on a number of levels. Table 12.1 illustrates the different categories of values of natural systems and their services. *Instrumental values* result from our direct, indirect, or passive uses of natural systems. An example of a *direct use* is the use of forests for timber or recreation. *Indirect uses* include nature's services that are instrumental in providing us indirectly with things we value, such as the stream-quality protection afforded by riparian buffers. *Passive uses* include *observation values*, such as bird-watching or landscape viewing, and *option values*, which stem from our desire to

TABLE 12.1. Categories of Values of Ecosystems and Biodiversity

			FORESTED ECOSYSTEM EXAMPLES
INSTRUMENTAL VALUES	Direct use		Forest is used for development and timber
	Indirect use		Timber is used to protect stream quality
	Passive use	Observation	Forest is used for bird-watching
		Option	Forest is preserved for future use
NONINSTRUMENTAL VALUES	Human	Cultural	Forest is important in community activities and folklore
		Spiritual	Forest is inspirational to spirit
		Existence	Forest has value just because it exists
	Intrinsic		Forest has a right to exist

preserve services for future use, even though we may not use them currently. *Noninstrumental values* are those that are not so narrowly useful to services we directly enjoy, but rather are more broadly important to us or to nature itself. The *human values* include *cultural values*, such as icons important to cultures and their folklore; *spiritual values*, which lift our hearts and minds; and *existence values*, which reflect the desire simply to know that some natural system exists independently of any intent to use it now or in the future. A final category of value, *intrinsic*, is purely nature oriented and refers to moral and ethical beliefs that nature has rights of its own. For example, a tree has a value in and of itself, independent of humans. If broadly embraced, the human policy manifestation of intrinsic value is to give nature legal standing.

Recent research on natural systems has highlighted the economic values of the services of these systems to humans and their economies (Baskin 1997; Daily 1997). Instrumental values have the greatest potential for economic valuation; people can envision how nature's services are instrumental to their well-being. And people can likely gauge the trade-offs between gains and losses in these services and economically meaningful sacrifices. For example, it is easy to illustrate to people that an acre of riparian forest will save them money in flood damages. Noninstrumental values, in contrast, may be difficult to place economic worth on because people have difficulty gauging these benefits relative to familiar economic sacrifices. Communities may claim that there is no amount of money they would sacrifice or that could compensate for the loss of an important cultural icon or a species, such as salmon, that provides the fabric for entire native peoples' communities. For them, economic and cultural "goods" exist in completely separate "moral" dimensions. The intrinsic value, by definition, has no economic counterpart because it stems from a perceived non-human-based right.

Observational values, such as aesthetics, refer to the sensory experiences provided by the diversity of life. Many of these values can be monetized; for example, the beauty of a forest will be reflected in land markets, just as a beautiful painting will command a high price. In these cases, biodiversity provides enhanced welfare that may be compared with other, more goods-oriented means of welfare enhancement.

Functional values of biodiversity stem from the extractive or nonextractive uses of nature's resources, the instrumental use of nature's properties, and the insurance values that biodiversity provides against catastrophic ecological or economic change. We harvest nature by either depleting it or using it for sustainable yields of goods. The instrumental value of nature is a result of the functional services that natural systems perform for themselves, but that also have value to humans. These services include flood protection, climate management, pollination, and so on. Such values have clear economic measures, at least in principle, because without them economic life would be more expensive or less enjoyable. Option, or insurance, values of biodiversity are a result of nature keeping itself within reasonable bounds, such as avoiding collapses, flips, and irreversibilities (Scheffer et al. 2001) that would jar economic life.

The economic valuation of biodiversity and nature's services is based on two goals: human welfare enhancement and cost savings. Both goals provide guidance to economic valuation, or monetization, of services. For example, aesthetic values of biodiversity enhance human welfare, making life more enjoyable than otherwise. The enhancement has economic value because other substitute forms of welfare enhancement are costly—for example, having to travel a longer distance to view a pleasant forest brook after your neighborhood has been converted into a parking lot. Instrumental values can be monetized because nature may provide goods or services more cheaply or comprehensively than alternatives; for example, the flood-protection values of forests are based on avoiding costly damages or other forms of hydrologic mitigation.

ECONOMIC VALUATION TECHNIQUES

Economic valuation refers to the monetary valuation of welfare changes that can arise because of gains or losses in nature's services. Value can be measured either by society's willingness to pay for a service or by its willingness to accept compensation for the loss of a service. These two measures of the same service can result in vastly different values (Hanneman 1991; Brown and Gregory 1999). The appropriateness of willingness to pay or willingness to accept compensation depends on the valuation context, especially the property rights associated with the altered natural assets. For example, if a developer is presumed to have the right to develop a natural area, the valuation of lost natural services would be based on society's willingness to pay to preserve that service. Alternatively, if society is presumed to own those services, as may be the case on public lands, the valuation of potentially lost services as a result of development would be a compensation measure. In general, willingness to accept exceeds willingness to pay.

Some natural functions provide services that are directly purchased in markets. For example, the primary productivity function of ecosystems yields services such as agricultural and forestry production where crops, trees, and the land that supports them are sold on markets. Valuing these services is simple because markets reflect society's willingness to pay for them. Impacts of urban sprawl on losses in primary productivity can be valued as the monetary loss in agricultural and forestry yields.

However, most natural services are not sold directly in markets. When there are no explicit markets for services, we must resort to more indirect means of assessing economic values. A variety of valuation techniques can be used to establish the willingness to pay for or willingness to accept compensation for these services. Six major economic valuation techniques can be used when market valuations do not adequately capture the social value of nature's services:

- *Avoided cost.* Services allow society to avoid costs that would have been incurred in the absence of those services: flood control provided by forests avoids property damages, and waste treatment by wetlands avoids health costs.
- *Replacement cost.* Services can be replaced with costly man-made systems: natural waste treatment of wetlands and vegetative cover can be replaced with costly treatment systems.
- *Factor income.* Services provide for the enhancement of incomes: water-quality improvements provided by streamside vegetation increase incomes of the water recreation–service industry.
- *Travel cost.* Service demand may require travel, whose costs can reflect the implied value of the service: urban recreation sites attract distant visitors, whose value placed on those sites must be at least what they were willing to pay to travel to them.
- *Hedonic pricing.* Service demand may be reflected in the prices people will pay for associated goods: housing prices are higher near parks and forested areas.
- *Contingent valuation.* Service demand may be elicited by posing hypothetical scenarios that involve some valuation of alternatives: people will be willing to pay for the aesthetics of a forested or an agricultural landscape.

Each of these methods has its strengths and weaknesses. Each service also has an appropriate set of valuation techniques. Some services may require that several techniques be used jointly. For example, the recreational value of an urban park or a clean stream includes the value that visiting recreationists place on the site (travel cost) and the increased incomes of the associated recreational industry (factor income). Furthermore, the amenity value may be reflected in higher property values adjacent to the sites (hedonic pricing).

NATURE'S SERVICES

In order to evaluate the welfare and cost-savings benefits of natural systems, we must first consider the types of functions performed by these systems. One typology suggests the following categories of functions (Costanza et al. 1997):

Regulation of natural processes
  Gas
  Climate
  Disturbance
  Water cycling and quality
  Soil formation and retention
  Waste treatment
  Pollination
  Biological control

Habitat availability
  Refugium
  Nutrients

Production
  Food
  Raw materials
  Genetic resources

Information
  Recreation
  Culture and spiritualism
  Knowledge

These functions have obvious direct and indirect values to human economies. The valuation problem is to translate these functions into quantifiable magnitudes, recognizing the complex interconnectedness within natural systems.

It is not a hopeless task to place economic values on biodiversity. Attempts to do so require three steps:

1. Determine the dimensions of biodiversity to be evaluated.
2. Establish how changes in that biodiversity alter the functions described previously.
3. Place economic values on the goods and services provided by those functions.

An example illustrates this evaluation process. Suppose there is a concern for the deforestation of an urban landscape; the biodiversity dimension is a *forested ecosystem*. Forested ecosystems perform water-storage, soil-retention, and nutrient-fixing functions in the hydrologic, soil, and nutrient cycles. Losses in these ecosystems will likely result in higher vulnerability to flooding, sedimenta tion of streams, and losses in soil fertility. Hydrologic and soil loss models can make predictions of these effects in the watershed. Given the human settlement patterns and use of aquatic resources in the watershed, flood damage and recreational or water-supply losses can be estimated from standard economic valuation procedures. The economic value of loss in soil fertility can be estimated by calculating the monetary cost of the nutrient replacement necessary to offset loss of leaf litter.

VALUING BIODIVERSITY AND NATURE'S SERVICES

Recall that biodiversity refers to the variety of genes, species, and ecosystems and the ecological and evolutionary processes that sustain that variety. At a species level, it can be characterized by counts, such as the number of different species, the relative abundance of different species, and the interspecies genetic variance. It is the abundance and variety of all these life-forms that permit ecological processes to be performed and that define the dynamics of these systems. Biodiversity is life itself, and the services we receive from nature by definition depend on that biodiversity. For this reason, valuing biodiversity requires making some connections among the diversity being considered, the ecological functions of that diversity, and the resulting services that humans receive from those processes.

We may consider a single species and its loss or change in population. This species is somehow connected to services we receive from nature. It may be a keystone species important to preserving a fishery, for example. As such, its loss may result in spectacular alterations of natural-system services from a human perspective. Or it may be a species whose loss may not have catastrophic impacts on its ecosystem, but may diminish ecological functions and their services substantially enough to be of concern, so it thereby has some economic value. Or it may be the complexity and variation in species that are requisite to nature's services, such as the multitude of nutrient-processing organisms in soils or the conjunction of aboveground biomass, root structure, and soil particles that define hydrologic and nutrient cycles.

Ecological functions depend on the diversity of life. The ecological functions that nature performs for itself generate the human-valued services that we often take for granted or do not recognize. For example, consider the following functions of ecosystem processes:

- Primary productivity
- Maintenance of soil structure and fertility
- Regulation of hydrologic and nutrient cycles
- Control of climate and quality of the atmosphere

These important functions provide the life support system on this planet. The total value of these functions' services to humanity is inestimable because they are critical for all human and nonhuman life. It would not be reasonable to ask what the economic value of nutrient cycles is, in total, to humans; without them, there would be no humans. We can ask, however, what the human welfare implications are for small-magnitude or local changes in the nutrient cycle, such as a percentage reduction in nitrogen uptake by plants or the reduction in soil fertility in an agricultural region.

Although these functions are critical to human survival, there are meaningful ways to consider their value economically and, by implication, the value of biodiversity. Obviously, primary productivity is essential for human food supplies, so the value of such a service is inestimable. However, variations in productivity levels can be evaluated economically, based on the values of food supplies lost or on increased costs necessary to maintain food supplies. For example, conversion of an agroecosystem to urban uses has a primary productivity cost, measurable by the value of lost crops or the increased costs of producing food supplies elsewhere. The aesthetic value of lands converted from agricultural use can be measured by the differences in property values of varying distances from these lands. This aesthetic value may include visual, auditory, olfactory, and congestion effects afforded by agricultural lands. The point is that although we cannot meaningfully value these services in total, we can value marginal changes in those services.

The biodiversity of macro- and microorganisms engaged in decomposition and nutrient-cycling processes is critical to maintaining the structure and fertility of soils (Carreiro, chapter 6, this volume). The services provided by these processes are inestimable in total. Development is likely to disrupt such processes through deforestation and landscape alteration. Altering slopes and hilltops for urban development will change soil and vegetation in ways that are likely to increase soil erosion and reduce the fertility of soils irreversibly. The economic valuation of this loss will be based on increased costs necessary to maintain vegetation through fertilization or on the adverse welfare impacts of sedimentation on fishable streams. Development processes also alter the aesthetics of landscapes, a positive or negative impact that can be measured economically using the techniques discussed earlier.

The regulation of hydrologic and nutrient cycles is a function of the complex web of life for nature's producers, consumers, and decomposers. Deforestation of urban ecosystems can dramatically reduce the ability of vegetation and soils to retain water. Streamside vegetation loss can result in the increased flow of both natural and human nutrients into streams. These impacts directly reduce stream quality and human welfare and may cause increased flooding and resulting damages or mitigation costs. For example, the experimental clearing of a

New Hampshire forest resulted in a 40 percent increase in average stream flow and, during a four-month period, increased rainfall runoff to five times above the normal average (Ecological Society of America 2001). Deforestation and vegetative loss can result in greater economic costs where landscapes are more steeply sloped or soils less porous. The losses of these services of nature can be meaningfully valued at local and marginal scales, and the losses of even marginal changes can be large.

Climate and atmospheric quality are related to the biodiversity of urban environments. The study of urban heat islands shows that urbanization and loss of vegetation have a dramatic impact on both temperature and hydrologic regimes (Filho 2001). These local and global effects clearly have economic implications for the costs of climate control and mitigation of extreme hydrologic events. The value of trees for maintaining atmospheric quality and climate conditions has been known for some time. For example, the economic value of using forests as carbon sinks to mitigate climate change (IPCC 1996) can be viewed in terms of alternative and, in many cases, more expensive means of emissions controls or in terms of the damages from global warming that would result from deforestation. Estimates that forests may sequester between 40 and 50 tons of carbon per acre (100 and 125 tons per hectare), combined with estimated costs of global climate change, suggest that keeping a forest standing is worth between $525 and $646 per acre ($1,300 and $1,625 per hectare) (Lampietti and Dixon 1995). All these functions result in services to humans and have value in the sense that costs will be increased or welfare diminished when the levels of these naturally provided services are reduced.

We may be able to determine the value of these functions, but the role of particular species in performing these functions may not be known with great confidence. For example, there is some understanding of the roles of trees in hydrologic and nutrient cycles or in atmospheric chemistry (Lampietti and Dixon 1995). However, understanding the roles of particular species in providing for the ecosystem health necessary to produce these functions may not be satisfactory at this stage in our understanding of ecosystems, which makes it difficult, if not impossible, to apply a valuation to particular species.

Valuing a particular species may be reasonable in some circumstances. This is true when the species has a market, as in the landscaping value of a Japanese maple (*Acer palmatum*). Or it may be true for charismatic species, such as the spotted owl (*Strix occidentalis*) and sea otter (*Enhydra lutris*), where society can be asked for information on what compensation it would accept for the loss of these species or what it would be willing to pay to preserve them. In fact, a wide variety of threatened and endangered megafauna—such as the whooping crane (*Grus americana*), gray whale (*Eshrichtius robustus*), bottlenose dolphin (*Tursiops truncatus*), and bighorn sheep (*Ovis canadensis*)—have been economically evaluated (Loomis and White 1996; Bulte and Van Kooten 1999). However, the vast majority of species does not fall into these marketed or charismatic categories, yet they are likely to be more important to ecological functions and their services than are the marketed or charismatic species. Microbes, bacteria, ants, and bees may garner little public response in queries about willingness to pay, but individually and jointly they are critical to life and its processes.

A further complicating factor in determining the value of biodiversity on a species-by-species basis is that we can hardly expect to know the roles of each species in all the ecosystem processes. Meaningful valuation requires knowledge, which we do not have in the majority of instances. Moreover, some economists are reluctant to value species on an individual basis because of what they refer to as the "embedding" effect. If we ask people what each species is worth, and there are N species, studies suggest that the valuation of N taken jointly is considerably less than the sum of the valuations of all N species taken individually (Bjornstad and Kahn 1996). Therefore, valuing biodiversity on a species-by-species basis has limited applicability and legitimacy. An alternative is to consider the values of the services performed by an ecological community. Knowing these values can reflect on the values of the species that compose a healthy community, even though it may not be possible to attribute a value to each of the component species. All species may be jointly needed for the valuable functions performed, or it may not be possible, given the state of ecological science, to assign weights to the roles of each species.

The insurance value of biodiversity is another reason to shift the assessment focus from individual species. One of the values we place on a healthy ecosystem is that we can predict to a reasonable extent the economic conditions provided by that ecosystem. For example, we value highly a limited range of climatic conditions because many economic processes and infrastructure are geared to operate within those conditions. However, we also know that very small changes in ecosystem conditions can dramatically alter the ecology of a community, perhaps irreversibly (Scheffer et al. 2001). These "flips" in nature can create havoc for human conditions. This relationship suggests maintaining a degree of biodiversity sufficient to sustain the complex interconnected web of a resilient ecosystem; such prudence has a positive insurance value in avoiding dramatic and likely unknown changes.

Recent studies have begun to highlight the importance of maintaining species redundancies in functional ecological groupings. This maintenance makes the services of the associated ecosystems more reliable (Naeem 1998) or resilient to change (Walker 1995). For example, Walker (1995) cites a case in Western Australia where only a single plant species provides nectar to honeyeaters during a crucial period of the year. Survival of the honeyeaters and the pollination services they perform depend on the survival of this one plant. A cascade effect of loss of the honey-eating pollinators would alter plant species diversity. The lack of species richness within a functional grouping then reduces this ecosystem's reliability and its resilience to external conditions such as drought. The insurance value of biodiversity is much broader and more complex than the values of individual species that make up the biodiversity of a community; it is the complex web itself that has value, in contrast to the individual species values.

Conservation of biodiversity, or the health and integrity of ecosystems, can also be motivated by the irreversibility of natural processes in the face of pressures from urban sprawl. When ecological functions may be lost forever, it is prudent to delay their loss until more information is available on what the values of those functions are. This "precautionary principle" forms one of the bases for European Community environmental policy (European Commission 2000). The avoidance of irreversibility can be implemented through "safe minimum standards" (Ciriacy-Wantrup 1963) that impose minimum conditions on ecosystem status, such as a minimum number of trees per acre or of vegetative buffers along streams. These principles are particularly important for the prudent management of human activities under the highly dynamic, uncertain, and complex conditions of ecosystems. We know some things about how ecosystems work; we know where some knowledge gaps lie; and we will only later discover the importance of other things. In the context of these types of uncertainties, precautionary and safe standards principles are critical elements to our management of human activities. Maintaining a variety of genes, species, and ecosystems provides an insurance equivalent of precaution; avoiding species extinctions is a type of safe minimum standard.

EXAMPLES OF VALUING LOSSES IN NATURE'S SERVICES RESULTING FROM SPRAWL

In addition to the well-documented effects of sprawl on transportation-related welfare and public-service costs (National Research Council 1998), sprawl has impacts on the health of ecosystems, thereby affecting natural functions and services. Changes in biodiversity are often the pathway through which these ecosystem impacts occur. Argueta and Farber (2001) illustrate this point in figures 12.1 and 12.2. Figure 12.1 shows the inverse relationship between population density and percentage of tree cover across townships in Allegheny County, Pennsylvania. Figure 12.2 illustrates the correlation between the loss of tree cover and the attainment by streams of Clean Water Act standards. Urbanization of previously forested areas may risk the loss of valuable stream-protection services provided by forested ecosystems.

The economic valuation of losses in ecosystem services is illustrated in the Allegheny County forest water-quality case. Economic studies have shown that

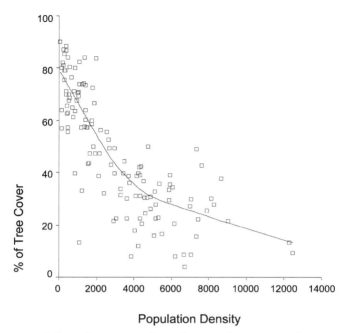

FIGURE 12.1. Relation between population density and percentage of tree cover across Allegheny County townships (Argueta and Farber 2001).

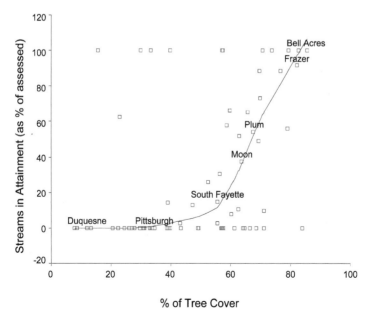

FIGURE 12.2. Relation between tree cover in Allegheny County townships and stream attainment of water-quality standards (Argueta and Farber 2001).

people are willing to pay for high-quality water, whether for drinking (Abdalla, Epp, and Roach 1990) or for recreation (Smith and Desvousges 1986; Farber and Griner 2000). Tying these economic losses precisely to forest degradation in the case of a particular development is problematic. However, figure 12.2 illustrates that cumulative losses of forest cover from 80 percent to 60 percent cover may reduce stream attainment of water-quality standards from nearly 100 percent to 20 percent, as in Allegheny County, clearly a significant reduction in local water quality. Farber and Griner's (2000) water-quality-improvement valuation suggested that typical households in western Pennsylvania were willing to pay between $26 and $51 per year for five years to improve impaired streams from moderately to unpolluted conditions. Assuming this figure is representative of residents' valuation of the loss in water quality, which is likely an underestimate (Hanneman 1991), and assuming roughly 4,000 households per township, losses in water quality of this magnitude are worth between $104,000 and $204,000 per year for five years, or between $0.52 and $1.02 million for the affected township. Assuming losses are proportional to loss of tree cover, each percentage reduction in tree cover from a development activity in this example would be worth from $26,000 to $51,000. This figure provides a nonarbitrary method to assess developers for ecological damages associated with deforestation and degraded water quality. The same size development in a large forested area will bear a smaller cost than one in a small forested area because the percentage loss of tree cover will be lower in the larger forested area. Increasing development will result in progressively higher ecosystem service levies per acre of deforestation as tree cover becomes a scarcer "good."

Water quality has direct impacts on property values. Leggett and Bockstael (2000) found that large increases in fecal coliform counts significantly reduced property values in the Chesapeake Bay area. In fact, a 100 count per 338 fluid ounces (100 milliliters) increase diminished property values between $5,114 and $9,824 per home. Of course, property prices do not reflect all the negatives associated with increased coliform counts because fisheries and water-supply costs would have to be included. Coupling suburban sprawl with water quality can be a means of valuing the ecologically related costs of sprawl.

This coliform study illustrates the economic valuation of the natural service of water-quality maintenance. Of course, other losses can be associated with deforestation, such as diminished water-storage capacity of the landscape because tree loss reduces infiltration, uptake, and evapotranspiration. Hydrologic studies can be used to illustrate how diminished capacity affects flooding regimes in a watershed. This diminished capacity may result in increased average or peak flows. Flood damages can then be assessed using traditional economic damage estimates from the Federal Emergency Management Administration or the U.S. Army Corps of Engineers. Increases in necessary flood-control structure costs can be estimated. Or cost increases for storm-sewer capacity can be estimated. Losses of urban forest amenities can be estimated using a hedonic pricing technique, such as that of Leggett and Bockstael (2000). For example, a study of Finnish urban forests revealed that a 0.62 mile (1 kilometer) increase in distance to the nearest forested area reduced the market price of a house by 5.9 percent, and homes with a view onto forests had market prices 4.9 percent higher than otherwise similar houses (Tyrvainen and Miettinen 2000).

Wetlands offer important natural services, such as flood control and water purification (Farber and Costanza 1987). They also provide habitat for diverse species, as a study of southeastern Ontario wetlands by Findlay and Houlahan (1996) shows. However, the quality of wetlands and their associated biodiversity depends critically on surrounding land uses (Miller and Klemens, chapter 3, this volume). Findlay and Houlahan (1996) found that greater density of paved roads in areas adjacent to wetlands reduced species richness in associated wetlands, whereas increases in the proportion of forest cover enhanced species richness. Sprawl diminishes wetland quality and associated biodiversity through road construction and deforestation. Because many wetland-dependent species rely on upland habitat and travel between local wetlands, maintaining sufficient wetland densities in the landscape is critical to those species' survival (Gibbs 2000; Calhoun and Klemens 2002). Loss in biodiversity will then reduce wetland ecosystem resilience, making it more likely that small changes can irreversibly alter wetland conditions. Road construction and deforestation then place at risk all wetland-related services. The value of urban wetland losses can be partially estimated through hedonic pricing techniques applied to housing markets. For example, Mahan, Polasky, and Adams (2000) have found that housing prices in Portland, Oregon, increase by $24 per house for each additional acre in size of the nearest wetland. Furthermore, reducing the distance to the nearest wetland by 1,000 feet (300 meters) increases the price of a home by $436. These valuations can provide some guidance in valuing degradations and losses of wetlands owing to sprawl. However, these hedonic values do not reflect the value of all wetlands services, such as water recharge or biodiversity benefits accruing to the community at large.

Songbirds, such as vireos, warblers, and thrushes, provide a direct benefit to people because of their diverse colors and sounds. These species are experiencing population declines (Keyser, Hill, and Soehren 1998). Members of these bird groups are especially at risk from urbanization. A variety of studies have shown that development that results in reduced forest cover and increased proximity to residential activities substantially reduces both species diversity and population abundance. For example, Friesen, Eagles, and MacKay (1995) showed that an increase in the number of houses adjacent to the habitat of neotropical migrant songbirds can reduce both species diversity and abundance up

to 50 percent. Odell and Knight (2001) found that birds sensitive to human disturbance—such as black-capped chickadees (*Poecile atricapillus*), black-headed
grosbeaks (*Pheucticus melanocephalus*), and Virginia and orange-crowned warblers (*Vermivora virginiae, V. celata*)—experienced increased population densities at greater distances from houses, and that higher housing densities reduced
bird population densities up to 50 percent. Keyser, Hill, and Soehren (1998)
showed that songbird nest predation increases as size of forest fragment decreases. About the only way to assess the economic valuation of losses or gains
in songbird diversity and abundance is through contingent valuation types of
studies. Such studies have been done for threatened and endangered charismatic species, such as the bald eagle (*Haliaeetus leucocephalus*), spotted owl,
and red-cockaded woodpecker (*Picoides borealis*) (Bulte and Van Kooten 1999).
For example, respondents to valuation questions for preserving the spotted owl
stated a willingness to pay ranging from $22 to $95 a year (1993 dollars). However, these values for threatened species may differ from valuations people place
on marginal changes in songbird species diversity and abundance. In addition,
the embedding problem in contingent valuation, noted earlier, requires very
careful construction of the valuation question to avoid having people implicitly
provide valuations for protection of a large variety of birds rather than of those
birds that are presumably the subject of the valuation study.

THE ECONOMICS OF SPRAWL AND BIODIVERSITY LOSS

An economic analysis of sprawl and biodiversity loss focuses on the following
elements:

- Market forces
- Subsidies
- Externalities
- Public goods

Each of these elements plays a role in helping us to understand the sprawl process and its impacts on biodiversity. Market forces drive land to its most profitable use in the short term. Agricultural land is crowded out by urban uses.
Forests are cut for housing developments. In the absence of market-distorting
subsidies, externalities, and public goods, many economists would not consider
sprawl and consequent biodiversity loss a social problem.

These market forces are guided not only by unfettered supply and demand,
however, but also by subsidies that alter supply and demand conditions. The
construction of highways, not fully paid for by users, and local taxation subsi-

dies of residential housing at the expense of commercial and agricultural land uses are examples of subsidies that enhance the demand for developable land. For example, a study of six Pennsylvania communities found that residential associated public-service costs (schools, sewers, highways) ranged from 3 to 111 percent more than associated revenues to the taxing community, whereas farmlands imposed public-service costs that were generally less than 10 percent of the tax revenues they generated (Kelsey 1995). Housing policies that offer low-interest loans to new residential housing rather than to redevelopment increase the pressures for urban areas to expand. Such policies, coupled with highway construction subsidies, are certain recipes for habitat fragmentation because settlement contiguity provides little benefit when highways can move people so quickly. However, agriculture has its own subsidies that artificially raise crop and agricultural land values.

Externalities are costs (or benefits) to third parties that arise from traditional market transactions. For example, the clearing of forests or the conversion of agricultural lands in market transactions affects the well-being of persons not party to those transactions. Markets incorporate the resource losses and development gains in determining who gets to do what to the land. But the externalities do not get incorporated into this loss/gain calculus. Losses in aesthetics and instrumental values of natural systems that the public would otherwise enjoy, such as recreation and flood protection, are costly externalities not incorporated into the prices of land or the transactions process. Externalities associated with biodiversity losses of species and of entire ecosystems contribute to making sprawl a major social problem. Too much development in the wrong places occurs because the biodiversity-related costs are not incorporated into the market transactions for land.

Public goods are benefits enjoyed by the public at large and are not easily marketable. A beautiful view is an example, and it may be impossible to charge all the beneficiaries for its use. As a result, beautiful views may be sold too cheaply from an economist's perspective. The same is true for other natural services that the public enjoys. Biodiversity itself is such a good; and because there are no effective ways of charging for it, it is undersold on markets. Land uses become determined through markets without due appreciation of the public-goods benefits of land in its natural state. It is encouraging, however, that some developers are beginning to factor in the amenities of untouched, or wild, lands in their development plans. Many are even doing it voluntarily, seeing the financial advantages. For example, wealthy residential communities are increasingly demanding open and natural spaces and are willing to pay price premiums for them. Studies of California housing markets suggest that properties within 1 mile (1.6 kilometers) of open space sell for nearly 10 percent more than similar properties elsewhere (Konrad 2003).

These subsidies, externalities, and public goods are the source of failures of traditional markets to incorporate all of nature's services into the costs of transactions. As a result, these services or the ecosystems that produce them are undervalued and are either sold too cheaply or simply destroyed for more profitable uses of land. Such undervaluation and destruction are the real culprits in biodiversity loss and result in sprawl's having far greater impacts on biodiversity. Although sprawl and biodiversity losses are a result of people's demands for what they anticipate as an enhancement in their quality of life, they are also a result of natural services being undervalued or not valued at all in development processes and transactions.

CONCLUSION

Sprawl is a global phenomenon, partially fueled by market forces reflecting desires for enhanced quality of life. The rise in incomes and the attempt to escape undesirable aspects of central cities are propelling people out of urban areas into previously undeveloped landscapes. The result is fragmentation of landscapes and ecosystems as well as increased threats to biodiversity and to the natural services provided by the diversity of species and ecosystems. These threats to natural services have direct economic implications, both as costs, such as increased water management, and as losses in benefits, such as an aesthetically pleasing landscape. These natural services are highly public, accruing to society in general. Therefore, their values are not incorporated into the largely private transactions that lead to sprawling and landscape-fragmenting development.

These values of natural-system services are not esoteric, theoretical concepts. They are as real as the incomes accruing to developers and as the taxes reaped by municipalities. Flood-damage costs from an imprudent development of steeply forested slopes or leveled hilltops are as real economically as earned incomes and taxes. Yet, unlike incomes and taxes, these natural systems are not typically valued monetarily in the public discourse surrounding development. Advocates of natural-system values rarely have the skills or resources to measure or articulate these services and their values, unlike the developers and municipalities that can readily quantify the incomes and taxes accruing from development. This disparity is tragic because it precludes a full analysis of the implications of development.

This chapter has sought to provide some guidance in the explicit consideration of natural-system values associated with the biodiversity losses resulting from urban sprawl. It suggests that valuing natural services and gauging the threats to these services from sprawl are feasible endeavors and should become a part of the development decision-making process. Species-by-species valuations may not be as important or effective in reflecting the values of lost natural services as consideration of the functional values of entire ecosystems placed at risk by development. Economists have developed a variety of tools for natural-service valuation, and ecologists are increasingly considering the functional values of ecosystems and their properties, including biodiversity. So it is possible to introduce these values into the sprawl debate and to incorporate them quantitatively into the full consideration of development and its implications for natural systems and human welfare. Not to do so is a tragedy and will only result in the eventual diminution of the health and integrity of those ecosystems and landscapes on which we so dearly depend. We must begin to think of nature as a valuable portfolio of assets, to be considered and managed just as prudently as we would manage our own personal finances. Maintaining biodiversity is the ecological equivalent of diversifying our personal portfolios, and we would want to do both for the same reason: the world is a dynamic, uncertain place, and it is not prudent to place all our eggs in one basket.

REFERENCES

Abdalla, C.W., D.J. Epp, and B. Roach. 1990. *Valuing Changes in Drinking Water Quality Using Averting Expenditures*. Environmental Resources Research Institute Report, no. ER9004. University Park: Pennsylvania State University.

Argueta, J.R., and S. Farber. 2001. *The State of the Environment in Allegheny County: Land, Water and Air*. Pittsburgh: University Center for Social and Urban Research, University of Pittsburgh.

Barbier, E.B., J.C. Burgess, and C. Folke. 1994. *Paradise Lost? The Ecological Economics of Biodiversity*. London: Earthscan.

Baskin, Y. 1997. *The Work of Nature: How the Diversity of Life Sustains Us*. Washington, D.C.: Island Press.

Bjornstad, D.J., and J.R. Kahn. 1996. *The Contingent Valuation of Environmental Resources: Methodological Issues and Research Needs*. Cheltenham, England: Elgar.

Brown, T.C., and R. Gregory. 1999. Why the WTA–WTP disparity matters. *Ecological Economics* 28:323–335.

Bulte, E.H., and G.C. Van Kooten. 1999. Marginal valuation of charismatic species: Implications for conservation. *Environmental and Resource Economics* 14:119–130.

Calhoun, A.J.K., and M.W. Klemens. 2002. *Best Development Practices: Conserving Pool-Breeding Amphibians in Residential and Commercial Developments in the Northeastern United States*. Metropolitan Conservation Alliance Technical Paper, no. 5. Bronx, N.Y.: Wildlife Conservation Society.

Ciriacy-Wantrup, S.V. 1963. *Resource Conservation: Economics and Policies*. Berkeley: University of California Press.

Costanza, R., R. D'Arge, R. de Groot, S. Farber, M. Grasso, B. Hannon, K. Limburg, S. Naeem, R.V. O'Neill, J. Paruelo, R.G. Raskin, P. Sutton, and M. Van den Belt. 1997. The value of the world's ecosystem services and natural capital. *Nature* 387:253–260.

Daily, G. C. 1997. *Nature's Services: Societal Dependence on Natural Ecosystems*. Washington, D.C.: Island Press.

Ecological Society of America. 2001. Ecosystem services: Benefits supplied to human societies by natural ecosystems. Available at: http://esa.sdsc.edu/daily.htm.

Ehrlich, P. R. 1988. The loss of diversity: Causes and consequences. In E. O. Wilson, ed., *Biodiversity*, 21–27. Washington, D.C.: National Academy Press.

European Commission. 2000. Communication from the Commission on the Precautionary Principle, COM (2000) 1. 02.02.2000. Brussels, Belgium.

Farber, S. C., and R. Costanza. 1987. The economic value of wetland systems. *Journal of Environmental Management* 14:41–53.

Farber, S. C., and B. Griner. 2000. Valuing watershed quality improvements using conjoint analysis. *Ecological Economics* 34:63–77.

Filho, A. J. P. 2001. Paradoxo das enchentes. *Ligação* 4:6–11.

Findlay, C. S., and J. Houlahan. 1996. Anthropogenic correlates of species richness in southeastern Ontario wetlands. *Conservation Biology* 1:1000–1009.

Friesen, L. E., P. F. J. Eagles, and R. J. MacKay. 1995. Effects of residential development on forest-dwelling neotropical migrant songbirds. *Conservation Biology* 9:1048–1414.

Gibbs, J. P. 2000. Wetland loss and biodiversity conservation. *Conservation Biology* 14:314–317.

Hannemann, W. M. 1991. Willingness to pay and willingness to accept: How much can they differ? *American Economic Review* 81:635–647.

Heywood, V. H., ed. 1995. *Global Biodiversity Assessment*. Cambridge: Cambridge University Press.

Intergovernmental Panel on Climate Change (IPCC). 1996. *Climate Change 1995: Impacts, Adaptations, and Mitigation of Climate Change*. Cambridge: Cambridge University Press.

Kelsey, T. W. 1995. Fiscal impacts of different land uses: The Pennsylvania experience. Report, Pennsylvania State University Cooperative Extension.

Keyser, A. J., G. E. Hill, and E. C. Soehren. 1998. Effects of forest fragment size, nest density, and proximity to edge on the risk of predation to ground-nesting passerine birds. *Conservation Biology* 12:986–994.

Konrad, W. 2003. Where nature is an amenity. *New York Times*, August 1, D1.

Lampietti, J. A., and J. A. Dixon. 1995. *To See the Forest for the Trees: A Guide to Non-timber Forest Benefits*. World Bank Environment Department Paper, no. 013. Washington, D.C.: World Bank.

Leggett, C. G., and N. E. Bockstael. 2000. Evidence of the effects of water quality on residential land prices. *Journal of Environmental Economics and Management* 39:121–144.

Loomis, J. B., and D. S. White. 1996. Economic benefits of rare and endangered species: Summary and meta-analysis. *Ecological Economics* 18:197–206.

Mahan, B. L., S. Polasky, and R. M. Adams. 2000. Valuing urban wetlands: A property price approach. *Land Economics* 76:100–113.

Naeem, S. 1998. Species redundancy in ecosystem reliability. *Conservation Biology* 12:39–45.

Naidoo, R., and W. L. Adamowicz. 2001. Effects of economic prosperity on number of threatened species. *Conservation Biology* 15:1021–1029.

National Research Council. 1998. *The Cost of Sprawl-Revisited*. Report no. 39. Washington, D.C.: National Academy Press.

Odell, E.A., and R.L. Knight. 2001. Songbird and medium-sized mammal communities associated with exurban development in Pitkin County, Colorado. *Conservation Biology* 15:1143–1150.

Scheffer, M., S. Carpenter, J.A. Foley, C. Folke, and B. Walker. 2001. Catastrophic shifts in ecosystems. *Nature* 413:591–596.

Smith, V. K., and W.H. Desvousges. 1986. *Measuring Water Quality Benefits*. Boston: Kluwer-Nijhoff.

Tyrvainen, L., and A. Miettinen. 2000. Property prices and urban forest amenities. *Journal of Environmental Economics and Management* 39:205–223.

Walker, B. 1995. Conserving biological diversity through ecosystem resilience. *Conservation Biology* 9:747–752.

White, D., P.G. Minotti, M.J. Barczak, J.C. Sifneos, K.E. Freemark, M.V. Santelmann, C.F. Steinizt, A.R. Kiester, and E.M. Preston. 1997. Assessing risks to biodiversity from future landscape change. *Conservation Biology* 11:349–360.

Wilson, E. O., ed. 1988. *Biodiversity*. Washington, D.C.: National Academy Press.

World Resources Institute. 1998. *World Resources, 1998–99: A Guide to the Global Environment*. Oxford: Oxford University Press.

Yachi, S., and M. Loreau. 1999. Biodiversity and ecosystem productivity in a fluctuating environment: The insurance hypothesis. *Proceedings of the National Academy of Sciences* 96:1463–1468.

13

CONSERVING BIODIVERSITY THROUGH STATE AND REGIONAL PLANNING

Jessica Wilkinson, Sara Vickerman, and Jeff Lerner

Habitat destruction, degradation, and fragmentation are the most pervasive threats to biological diversity in the United States. All are associated with the growing impacts of poorly planned development, or *sprawl*, which results in excessive land consumption. The obvious way to curtail the threat of sprawl to biodiversity is through good land-use planning. Land-use planning that keeps sprawl in check is sometimes referred to as *smart growth* and should help conserve biodiversity. If only it were that simple. Smart growth is growth that fosters economic vitality in community centers while maintaining the rural working and natural landscape. Implementing smart-growth land-use planning principles is never easy, and it becomes even more difficult when communities try to address biodiversity as part of that process. Most communities lack the policies, institutions, and political will to address conservation needs effectively through land-use planning. Consequently, incorporating biodiversity considerations into land-use planning presents major challenges. This chapter explains the importance of regional and statewide conservation planning to provide an ecological context for making environmentally sound local land-use decisions. It also provides some examples of broad-scale conservation plans.

The goal of most land-use planning laws in this country is to protect public health and welfare. Americans have come to rely on this aspect of land-use planning and on its ability to provide a degree of predictability and economic stability. Americans also have a healthy distrust of top–down government regulations and have traditionally preferred that land-use planning decisions be made locally. Most states have delegated the authority to prepare plans and implement land-development regulations to the municipal, county, or other local-level government. The principles that guide our current approach to land-use planning, however, are seriously at odds with the principles that guide ecosystem health. Unlike government agencies, ecosystems are dynamic and depend on disturbance and function at many different timescales (Ecological Society of America Committee on Land Use 2000). Perhaps most important, biodiversity must be planned for and protected on a scale different from that we typically see in land-use planning.

This chapter discusses the recent emergence of state and regional biodiversity conservation planning as a promising strategy for protecting biodiversity in the United States. We discuss the barriers to broad-scale planning and describe some well-established and innovative biodiversity conservation tools. Several state and regional biodiversity programs that work across jurisdictional boundaries and involve diverse interests are provided as examples of pioneering efforts to address biodiversity conservation through sound land-use planning.

BARRIERS AT ALL SCALES

It is not surprising that biodiversity conservation was not high among the nation's priorities during the first two or three centuries of U.S. history. Taming wilderness to suit human needs was part of the value system European settlers brought to this continent. The new nation's vast natural resources were valued, but early settlers were concerned primarily with exercising control over the landscape, its indigenous human inhabitants, and its natural resources (Nash 2001). Rivers were altered to reduce flooding and to facilitate navigation and irrigation. Fire was suppressed whenever possible. Wild animals and plants were more often seen as threats or competitors than as objects worthy of protection.

In the United States, resource exploitation reached its peak in the late nineteenth century. It was during this era of exuberant natural-resource exploitation that most state and federal resource agencies were established. They were designed to facilitate the orderly management of forests, rangelands, minerals, water, fish, and wildlife, but primarily for commodity purposes. Most of the lands they protected are at high elevations and have poor soils. By contrast, more biodiversity occurs at lower elevations on productive soils in floodplains and stream valleys—prime areas for agriculture and human habitation (Scott et al. 2001). Each of the newly established agencies pursued a narrow mission. Even the National Park Service and National Wildlife Refuge System were established to conserve and manage natural resources and to meet recreational needs (16 U.S.C. § 1; 16 U.S.C. § 668dd). By the time scientists and conservationists began to worry about the loss of biodiversity, these agencies' missions had become well entrenched. Although institutions are slow to change, some of these agencies have broadened their missions to address the burgeoning list of endangered species and other environmental problems. For example, the Forest Service and Bureau of Land Management's Northwest Forest Plan established late-successional reserves to conserve a broad range of old-growth forest species threatened by widespread conversion to younger forests as a result of logging.

Despite some positive state and federal programs, only 6 percent of the land in the coterminous United States is under permanent protection from being converted (Scott et al. 2001), and no single state or federal agency is responsible for conserving the nation's biodiversity. Many states have natural-areas programs, but these programs tend to focus on specific lands and generally do not address biodiversity values on a landscape-wide scale. The first state natural-areas program was established in Wisconsin in 1951 to preserve areas "harboring all types of biotic communities, rare species, and other significant natural features native to Wisconsin" (Wisconsin Department of Natural Resources 2002). Many more state programs have been established since then, but most have been able to protect only small remnant patches of habitat. Wisconsin's program has protected 100,000 acres (40,468 hectares) across 324 sites, a fraction of 1 percent of the state's land area.

Similarly, many cities and towns were developed before land-use planning became common, and many states still operate under planning provisions that date back to the 1920s (American Planning Association 2002). After World War II, even where development was planned, its primary goal was to provide housing for a growing nation. Where zoning was used to allocate land to different purposes, it was to accommodate human settlement—residential, agricultural, industrial, and commercial. Although the occasional park or natural area was squeezed in, very little land in the United States has been specifically allocated for biodiversity preservation, with the exception of private conservation reserves.

The emergence of the smart-growth movement as defined in the 1990s has drawn attention to the economic, social, and environmental benefits of compact development and the adverse impacts of sprawl. Many of the smart-growth principles—in particular, the focus on minimizing the amount of land consumed by development—directly support biodiversity conservation principles. Yet although smart-growth principles address *how much* land is consumed for development and what that more compact pattern should look like, they do not address *which* land should be developed and which land should be managed primarily for conservation values. Habitat and ecological concerns are rarely integrated into community development plans, and under some compact-growth scenarios adverse environmental impacts can be inadvertently exacerbated by forcing development into sensitive areas such as wetlands, riparian zones, and floodplains (Budnick 2001).

For growth to be "smart," it must include conservation principles that direct development away from sensitive areas and that minimize the fragmentation of existing intact habitats. For example, most of our major cities have been developed in riparian areas (i.e., along rivers), but such riparian systems often harbor a disproportionately large percentage of biodiversity (Scott et al. 2001). In arid landscapes such as the southwestern United States, as much as 75 percent of native biodiversity occurs in riparian areas (Pima County 2000a). Environmentally sensitive subdivisions (e.g., conservation clusters with dedicated open space) may provide greater ecological benefits than conventional large-lot subdivisions. However, if these environmentally designed subdivisions are scattered across the landscape, they, too, may still contribute significantly to habitat fragmentation.

Coupled with these historical, cultural, and institutional realities is a powerful and growing property-rights movement in many parts of the country. Even people concerned about fish and wildlife habitat are likely to believe that Americans have an inalienable right to do what they want with their land. The Constitution's prohibition against the taking of private property for public purposes without payment of just compensation inhibits local governments from restricting development for fear of lawsuits or compensation requirements. Although the threat of takings claims may be more serious than the likelihood of actually being compelled to pay landowners, perceptions of liability can cause risk-averse decision makers to limit regulation.

Development, according to the conventional wisdom, increases local property tax revenue and fuels economic expansion. Conservation is thought to be expensive, particularly if land is purchased at high prices and economic activities are inhibited. In reality, land conservation does cause a short-term rise in property taxes, but communities with more protected land save tax dollars in the long term by needing fewer roads, schools, and other infrastructure, which ultimately lowers property taxes. A significant amount of work has been done recently to document the true costs of development. For example, it was determined that saving wetlands along the Charles River in Massachusetts for flood control would cost $10 million. The alternative was to build dams and levees at a cost of $100 million (Kusler and Larson 1993). In addition to saving money, the nonstructural alternative will provide an array of tangential ecological benefits. The aesthetic, recreational, ecological, and other values of conservation have yet to be quantified in a manner that presents local decision makers with reliable and balanced information on which to base their decisions (Farber, chapter 12, this volume).

With so many rare species found exclusively on private land, local land-use planning should be a key point of intervention for biodiversity protection (National Research Council 1993). However, in a 1994 review of the natural heritage programs that inventory state biodiversity, fewer than 15 out of 40 reported that biodiversity information was used regularly in land-use planning, local development proposals, or even subdivision review, and only 7 states require that local plans address sensitive natural elements (Cort 1996). More recently, a 2003 survey of 40 natural heritage programs found that no states have adopted land-use laws that explicitly require local governments to conserve biodiversity. Only 13 of the 40 states surveyed reported that they received requests for natural heritage data in response to land-use planning laws (Wilkinson and Kennedy 2003).

In many cases, state and local decision makers fail to incorporate biodiversity information into their decision making because data are inaccessible; they also lack the capacity to apply available information. Reliable information about the overall status and distribution of biodiversity and ecosystem function is often not easily obtained, and restrictions on data dissemination may obstruct its application. Even if the necessary political will exists, a lack of knowledgeable staff, adequate funding, and resources inhibits the use of otherwise valuable information (Kennedy, Gordon, and Wilkinson 2001). Local government agencies are unlikely to have staff trained in the biological sciences, and few communities can afford the staff and technology required to conduct their own biodiversity assessments.

As their training dictates, the scientists charged with collecting biodiversity information focus on ensuring that their methods are scientifically sound rather than on producing information products tailored to any given user. In addition, scientists are not in the business of "marketing" their findings. If local land-use planners are to use biodiversity information, conservation experts must first better understand what information they need and in what form it would be most useful. Others—conservation organizations and resource agencies—must then step in to make sure that the information reaches those who need to use it.

If biodiversity conservation is to be better integrated into land-use planning, state land-use laws must provide local governments with the authority to conserve biodiversity. In addition, how these laws are interpreted and carried out over time may influence their effectiveness. Existing state laws and policies very often *can* be interpreted to require biodiversity conservation (Breggin, George, and Pencak 2003). Whether or not the political will exists to support or reward agencies or communities to take full advantage of these laws and policies is another issue. Finally, decision makers must understand the extent of their authority under these laws and policies, have access to the relevant biodiversity information, and have the technical expertise to carry out their charge.

At the state level, no state has yet adopted a comprehensive law or policy that mandates the proactive conservation of biodiversity on a landscape scale sufficient to protect entire ecosystems and their processes (Center for Wildlife Law and Defenders of Wildlife 1996). Only nine states have land-use-enabling laws—those laws that delegate land-use planning and regulation to the local level—with specific requirements for local governments to plan for biodiversity conservation. For example, Colorado statute requires county, city, and regional master plans to consider designations of areas containing endangered or threatened species (Breggin, George, and Pencak 2003). State legislation regarding endangered species may address some biodiversity concerns, but these concerns come into play only when specific populations are at severe risk of extinction. Numerous state laws, however, provide authority for addressing biodiversity considerations, yet they tend to do so indirectly by focusing on specific resources, such as wetlands and floodplains, or through specific activities, such as transportation planning or logging. State environmental impact assessment laws do hold some promise, but they address biodiversity considerations only on a site-by-site basis (Wilkinson and Kennedy 2003).

The Endangered Species Act is the primary piece of federal legislation designed to protect biodiversity by focusing on the conservation of individual species and associated habitat. However, the act generally applies only in situations where species have reached crisis status and conservation options are limited. It also tends to focus on individual species rather than on proactive conservation of intact ecosystems. The National Environmental Policy Act (NEPA) applies to only federal activities, and the required environmental impact statements are often viewed as burdensome. The Clean Water Act has some positive impacts on aquatic ecosystems, but for the most part it fails to address aquatic biodiversity or land uses that contribute to habitat degradation. In addition, the act's wetland protection provisions have failed to achieve the national goal of no net loss of wetland functions and to consider cumulative impacts across the landscape (National Research Council 2001).

Road construction, a leading cause of habitat loss and fragmentation (Stein, Kutner, and Adams 2000), is often financed through federal legislation, but carried out primarily at the state level with little consideration of biodiversity beyond the site-specific impacts. It is estimated that 20 percent of the land area of the United States is ecologically affected by public roads (Forman 2000). Site-level review of road projects often fails to consider these impacts, and expensive retrofits such as wildlife underpasses are of limited effectiveness and do not compensate for poor road planning.

The federal government's primary role in biodiversity conservation is through its research, private-land incentive programs, public-lands management, and oversight of migratory species. However, none of these tools addresses the root causes of biodiversity loss or provides land-use solutions (Wilkinson 1999).

Perhaps the greatest barrier to protecting biodiversity is a paucity of political will at every level of government. This paucity contradicts national polling data that show that the American public cares about the environment and is concerned about the loss of habitat and the decline of fish and wildlife (Belden Russonello & Stewart Research 2002; Coffin and Elder, chapter 15, this volume). During the past decade, Americans have demonstrated their commitment to conservation by overwhelmingly supporting ballot measures that levy additional taxes on themselves to pay for the purchase and protection of open space. Just over the past six years, more than $23 billion has been thus committed (Trust for Public Land and Land Trust Alliance 2004).

There are many obstacles to developing consistent, definitive, and accessible scientific biodiversity information to use in land-allocation planning and management. As a result, it is not surprising that the public lacks a clear vision of how ecological principles can be applied locally to protect biological resources in a manner that can help to piece back together the fabric of the biological landscape. It may be that the public misunderstands the issues of scale and thinks that protecting a 50-acre (20-hectare) parcel provides an adequate toehold for biodiversity. Current scientific thinking dictates that land-use planners should strive to protect and maintain habitat patches larger than 135 acres (56 hectares), although minimum habitat patches for large-ranging mammals may be more than 540,000 acres (218,623 hectares) (Kennedy, Wilkinson, and Balch 2003). Perhaps the public is more concerned about aesthetic and quality-of-life issues than about biodiversity, but people are seldom presented with coherent alternatives to the fragmentation and degradation of our ecosystems that inevitably occurs with typical development. What is missing is a shared vision of our communities, our states, and our nation, in which the landscape is managed at a scale sufficiently large to protect its natural values while providing a healthy, attractive, and safe place to live.

TOOLS FOR ADDRESSING HABITAT ISSUES AT DIFFERENT SCALES

Scientists and conservation practitioners have learned that protecting biodiversity requires maintaining or restoring large, intact habitats that are connected to one another and to their associated ecological processes. Planning for such protection requires a landscapewide perspective. This broader vision has emerged in part with the availability of technologically sophisticated biodiversity information, such as satellite imagery and geographic information systems (GISs)—powerful computer programs with which data can be analyzed and presented spatially. With GISs, complicated concepts can be presented visually in ways that are intuitive, dramatic, and persuasive. State natural heritage programs and statewide gap analysis projects are two examples of nationally standardized data sources that use these methods for analyzing geographic biodiversity information.

Encouraged by the availability of new tools and information, conservation planners have been developing and testing regional biodiversity plans throughout the United States over the past 15 years. Their approaches vary considerably in primary emphasis, purpose, technical sophistication, level of participation, and scale. No single effort or tool emerges as the perfect solution, but varying approaches may be necessary to reflect the country's ecological and cultural differences.

As regional biodiversity plans begin to shift the perspective of conservation work from one that focuses on individual parcels to one that transcends political boundaries, it becomes more apparent that land-use planners and biologists work at different scales. However, in many parts of the country, natural-resource managers, land trusts, local planners, and others are beginning to meld their perspectives using new technologies and planning principles to examine current and historical patterns of species and ecosystem distributions. They can then use this information to determine how best to acquire land, develop zoning ordinances that protect specific resources, and manage public lands to foster biodiversity conservation at a meaningful scale. Following are some examples of planning strategies that incorporate these technologies to guide conservation efforts.

ECOREGIONAL PLANNING

The Nature Conservancy has taken a comprehensive approach to biodiversity protection by developing ecoregional plans throughout the United States. *Ecoregions* are large areas of the landscape defined by environmental conditions including moisture, solar radiation, and characteristic animals and vegetation (Groves et al. 2000). The plans follow these ecological rather than political boundaries and give priority to sites containing "at risk" species and ecosystems. Conservation goals are set for each of the sites and areas prioritized for conservation action. The planning teams rely heavily on data from the natural heritage programs and on local expertise for site selection. Eighty such plans were scheduled for completion by 2003 and were intended primarily to guide the land-acquisition activities of The Nature Conservancy. The advantage of this approach is that it is relatively expeditious. The disadvantage is that because one group is spearheading the effort, organizations not involved in the planning may not be committed to the implementation.

GREEN INFRASTRUCTURE PLANNING

Although the concept of conservation networks or *greenways* has existed since Frederick Law Olmsted was designing recreational parks in the nineteenth century, the Conservation Fund has actively promoted the idea over the past decade with a stronger ecological focus. Greenways have evolved into a more ecologically robust approach to community planning, balancing systems of green infrastructure (rivers, floodplains) with gray infrastructure (sewers, roads). A green infrastructure system consists of *hubs* and *links*, and it attempts to optimize ecological services such as flood control while protecting wild-life habitat. Hubs are large protected areas or reserves, agricultural preserves, and managed native landscapes that support some resource extraction. Links may be large protected areas that connect existing parks or refuges, conservation corridors, streams, greenbelts, trails, and sometimes even utility corridors (Mitchell and Klemens 2000; Benedict and McMahon 2002). All green spaces are not equal from a biodiversity perspective, and in order to protect sensitive resources from overuse by recreationists or from intensive agricultural or forest practices, trade-offs will sometimes have to be made. There is always a danger, however, that the process will return to its recreational roots and emphasize economic benefits over ecological needs. One of the greatest advantages of this approach is its potential to "provide a broad, unifying vision for the future that people and organizations with diverse backgrounds and interests can buy into" (Benedict 2000:1).

BUILDING ALTERNATIVE FUTURES

Over the past ten years, GIS technology has advanced significantly to become a powerful tool in land-use planning. A group of landscape architecvvts at the Harvard School of Design, working with others in academic institutions around the country, have developed and refined the technique of creating models that show communities alternative visions for their future. An early study offered hypothetical maps of different development patterns in Monroe County, Pennsylvania (Bilda et al. 1994). Another study evaluated differ-ent scenarios for the future of Camp Pendelton, California (Steinitz 1996). A significant investment has been made in modeling futures for Oregon's Willamette Basin, beginning with the Muddy Creek Watershed (Hulse et al. 1997) and later involving the entire basin (Pacific Northwest Ecosystem Research Consortium 2002).

FEDERAL LEGISLATIVE TOOLS

Federal agencies have been reluctant to become involved in local land-use decisions. However, several federal wildlife conservation and water-quality programs indirectly affect land allocation and thus have the potential to encourage state and local governments to conserve habitat. Coordinating federal agencies and programs is often even more challenging than working at the state level.

STATE AND TRIBAL WILDLIFE GRANTS PROGRAM

A new federal program established in 2001 offers grants covering 75 percent of planning expenses to state fish and wildlife agencies that agree to develop by 2005 comprehensive wildlife conservation strategies that address the full array of wildlife and habitats. The Fish and Wildlife Service, the International Association of Fish and Wildlife Agencies, and nonprofit conservation organizations interested in conservation planning are assisting and encouraging state agencies to engage a broad spectrum of interests in the process. In those states that already have a comprehensive biodiversity initiative under way, this planning requirement, and the funding associated with it, is an opportunity to build on existing programs. In other states, development of the strategy may be the first chance the wildlife agency has to proactively consider the conservation of at-risk species.

HABITAT CONSERVATION PLANS

The Endangered Species Act is the strongest legal mechanism we have for protecting species in the United States. Unfortunately, it is often difficult to apply the law in a preventative manner or to address the conservation needs of multiple species. However, as a mechanism for obtaining "incidental take" permits, the act does allow landowners, states, municipalities, and other entities to develop habitat conservation plans for individual and multiple species. Permits are needed to avoid prosecution for "taking" endangered species either by direct means or through destruction of habitat. Several communities in the United States, especially in California, have used habitat conservation plans to facilitate development of some habitat while putting other habitat in conservation status. The advantage of large, multiple species plans is that they are legally binding agreements in which local governments attempt to protect enough habitat for endangered species, sometimes including species not yet listed. The disadvantage is that the plans generally fail to address the full range of ecological community values. The plans are also often not integrated with land-use planning and therefore may fail to protect adequate amounts of habitat or may allow significant habitat loss or both.

STATE PROGRAMS

Comprehensive land-use planning and zoning carried out by local government can be effective in guiding biodiversity conservation and minimizing habitat loss and fragmentation. In most states, the legislature has delegated the authority to conduct comprehensive planning and adopt zoning ordinances to local governments (e.g., counties or municipalities), but legislatures often determine what elements local governments must or may include in their plans. Local governments have the authority to develop specific plans for the sites and conditions of development designed to foster economic growth while providing for a community's general health, safety, and welfare. Whether planning and zoning are explicitly required or simply authorized differs from state to state.

Comprehensive planning is mandated in 24 states; in at least 4 states, local plans must go through a state certification process (Meck 2002). Comprehensive plans do not regulate activities, but rather establish the framework for both regulatory and nonregulatory decisions. Where planning is mandated, it can be used to ensure that local decisions conform to state priorities. Planning can also give communities the opportunity to identify their most important resources and those that are most in danger of loss and degradation. The state laws that authorize local governments' development of comprehensive plans outline the elements that can or must be addressed. Common components of a comprehensive plan include land use, housing, economic development, transportation, community facilities (including utilities), natural hazards, and critical and sensitive areas (Meck 2002). Localities then enact regulatory tools—zoning and subdivision regulations—to implement the plan. However, unless local governments hold fast to those regulations and resist granting variances or rezonings, the plans will not be reflected in on-the-ground results.

As discussed earlier, no states have adopted land-use laws that explicitly direct local governments to conserve biodiversity (Breggin, George, and Pencak 2003). However, many existing laws provide ample *authority* for local governments to do so. Oregon has perhaps the most explicit requirement for local governments to consider biodiversity in land-use decision making. Local governments in Oregon are required to complete comprehensive plans that address specific goals and zoning regulations. One of these goals, stated in Oregon's land-use statutes, requires local governments to "protect natural resources and conserve scenic and historic areas and open spaces" ("Goal 5" 1996:1). The natural-resource goal compels localities to assess their natural resources, identify uses that may conflict, and adopt programs to protect these resources. As part of this process, local governments must conduct an inventory of natural resources, with a focus on riparian areas, wetlands, and wildlife habitat. Oregon's land-use laws are particularly strong, owing to the oversight role played by the state. The state's Department of Land Conservation and Development reviews local plans to ensure that they conform to statewide planning goals.

Even though the authority exists, Oregon's land-use planning system has still not effectively addressed biodiversity issues (Wiley 2001). Decision makers have not regarded protecting habitat for biodiversity as important as protecting farmland and containing sprawl. There are several possible reasons for this inequity. The first is that there has been political support from the agricultural and forest industries and urban planners for Oregon's land-use laws. These groups fear that addressing habitat through regulatory means might upset the apple cart. Another reason may be that environmental zoning has the potential to restrict economic uses of property, thereby encouraging takings claims. A third reason may be the lack of an organized and influential constituency for habitat protection, especially at the local level. Oregon is a perfect example of a state that has effectively contained sprawl but simultaneously failed to address biodiversity issues on private lands.

In Delaware, each county planning agency is required to prepare a comprehensive development plan that is updated every five years (Del. Code Ann. tit. 9, §§ 2660[a], 4960[a], 6960[a]). Zoning regulations adopted by Delaware counties must be in accordance with the comprehensive plan (§§ 2603[a], 6904, 6907[a]). Planning at the municipal level is permitted, but not mandated. Comprehensive planning in Delaware is intended, among other purposes, to "preserve, promote, and improve the pubic health, safety, comfort . . . and general welfare," as well as to "conserve, develop, utilize and protect natural resources" (§§ 2651, 4951, 6951).

A Delaware county comprehensive plan must include conservation and must be developed in consultation with and reviewed by the state agriculture and natural-resource agencies to ensure it will achieve "the conservation, use and protection of natural resources in the area and . . . [result] in the identification of these resources." The conservation plan must include, at a minimum, the classification of natural areas, such as "wetlands, wooded uplands, habitat areas, geological areas, hydrological areas, floodplains, aquifer recharge areas, ocean beaches, soils and slopes" (Del. Code Ann. tit. 9, §§ 2656[g][4], 4956[g][4], 6956[g][4]). The county plan must also include a specific future land-use plan that includes designation of land for conservation (§§ 2656[g][1], 4956[g][1], 6956[g][1]). The recreation and open-space element of the plan (§§ 2656[g][5], 4956[g][5], 6956[g][5]), which includes the identification of nature preserves, is an obvious tool for habitat protection and planning. The parts of the plan that address transportation, water, and sewage and the recommended community design can also be used to curtail sprawl and habitat degradation. Although Delaware's land-use planning laws do not require local governments to protect biodiversity, they clearly provide these governments with the authority to develop comprehensive plans and zoning tools that consider biodiversity. Whether or not officials use this authority and to what degree is a matter of political will and leadership (Wilkinson et al. 1999).

Although local land-use planning and zoning have the potential to be powerful conservation tools, the level at which localities conduct planning and enact regulations may not be at a scale compatible with conservation planning. As discussed earlier, statewide or regional efforts to identify critical habitats and links between habitats should ideally guide local decision making. Short of a plan set forth by the state, local governments should be required or encouraged through incentive programs to make their planning decisions on a landscape level. Although few states provide this authority or these incentives, and none requires regional coordination explicitly for conservation purposes, some states do provide authority for regional planning that can be used for biodiversity conservation purposes. For example, Florida law requires its eleven Regional Planning Councils to develop strategic regional policy plans that are consistent with the state comprehensive plan (Fla. Stat. 186.507). In addition, local comprehensive plans are required to be consistent with the regional policy plans (1000 Friends of Florida 1999). Among other reasons, the plans are needed to "identify natural resources of regional significance and promote the protection of those resources" (Florida Administrative Code, Rule 27E-5.003 [10]). A regionally significant natural resource is defined as a "natural resource or system of interrelated natural resources, that due to its function, size, rarity or endangerment retains or provides benefit of regional significance to the natural or human environment, regardless of ownership" (Florida Administrative Code, Rule 27E-5.002 [4]). The Regional Planning Councils must use the best available data and information to map the areas determined to contain these resources (Florida Administrative Code, Rule 27E-5.004 [3][a]). Although not regulatory in nature, the regional plans and development processes are designed to coordinate local, regional, state, and federal agencies and organizations.

The East Central Florida Regional Planning Council's *Strategic Regional Policy Plan* (1998) suggests that habitat corridors be identified and protected through public-land-acquisition programs and through the planning and development process at all levels of government. The plan states that natural vegetative communities and native plant and animal species "shall be conserved and protected to ensure that the full complement of such communities and species continues to exist in perpetuity" (10). The plan also states that local governments should protect "adequate conservation areas, open spaces, river buffers and other appropriate mechanisms" (10) through their comprehensive plans and land-development regulations.

PRIVATE-LAND AND LAND-USE PLANNING

Many of the nation's natural-resource agencies were established with conflicting missions: to provide a steady stream of resources for human consumption (game species, trees, and recreation), but also to act as stewards of those resources. For the most part, these agencies focus their attention on the public lands they manage and fail to acknowledge the impact of private-land-use activities on the resources for which the agencies are responsible. Most state agencies responsible for endangered species protection and recovery would say they are not in the business of regulating land use. However, when uses of private land adjacent to public lands and elsewhere across the landscape cause widespread and severe declines in species populations, it becomes a public-agency problem. A few enlightened state agencies have come to acknowledge the role they can and should play in the land-use arena. These states have committed resources and staff time to ensure that local governments are given the information they need to make land-use decisions informed by biodiversity. As discussed later, Massachusetts has demonstrated a commitment to providing local governments with biodiversity information to aid them in protecting these resources.

TECHNICAL ASSISTANCE

Several states—including Virginia, Wisconsin, and Maine—have programs designed to provide local governments with the technical information and expertise needed to incorporate biodiversity considerations into land-use planning. For example, Virginia's Division of Natural Heritage (housed within the Department of Conservation and Recreation) has established the Locality Liaison Program to provide local governments in the state's coastal zone with biodiversity information and to aid in land-use decisions that protect biodiversity and preserve open space. The program produces and distributes maps depicting the location of natural heritage resources for each coastal resource management area in Virginia. The program also assists local governments with local land-use planning and decision making, the development of open-space protection plans, and habitat restoration and protection initiatives.

Maine's State Planning Office initiated a slightly different approach in 2000 with a program called Beginning with Habitat. A collaboration among the State

Planning Office, the Maine Department of Conservation, and other partners, this program provides habitat maps, species descriptions, and guidance to local communities in southern Maine to help those communities integrate biodiversity into local smart-growth planning. This partnership acknowledges the Planning Office's strength in working directly with communities and frees up the state's natural heritage program to concentrate on inventory work.

Whether through a mandated program established by state law or a voluntary outreach program, state natural-resource agencies need to acknowledge their stake in land-use decisions regarding private lands. These agencies must show leadership and vision by reaching out to local governments and providing them with adequate biodiversity information—in a format they can use—along with technical expertise and assistance in making sound land-use decisions.

MODEL APPROACHES

Despite the challenges discussed in the previous section, there is cause for optimism. Many states, regions, and communities are engaged in comprehensive efforts to identify, conserve, and restore the local native biodiversity. In the sections to follow, we summarize a few of the most interesting and effective approaches. We begin with state-level efforts in Florida, Oregon, Massachusetts, and New Jersey and then examine some regional conservation plans in the Sonoran Desert in Arizona, the Willamette Basin in Oregon, and the Chicago metropolitan area.

FLORIDA ECOLOGICAL NETWORK PROJECT

Florida is a state with exceptional natural resources. Its tropical climate supports a tremendous diversity of plant and animal species that inhabit a rich variety of ecosystem types (Cox et al. 1994). Florida is also under tremendous growth pressure, adding an average of 650 people a day (Hoctor, Carr, and Zwick 2000). The state now supports 15 million people. Along with the population growth come pressures on the land—for more housing, roads, and shopping malls. Because 75 percent of the state land area is in private ownership (Jue, Kindell, and Wojcik 2001), most of it is vulnerable to development and conversion to utilitarian uses. The result is a large and growing number of threatened and endangered species, which in turn has created pressure from certain segments of the public to protect them.

In the early 1990s, biologists from the Florida Fish and Wildlife Conservation Commission tried something new. They compiled information about the distribution of selected endangered species, rare plant communities, and focal species throughout the state. They also mapped lands already managed for conservation, such as parks and refuges. The commission then used the most credible scientific information and the most sophisticated technology available to determine what the minimum habitat requirements would be to support most elements of the state's biodiversity over time. Based on the analysis, it was possible to map priority habitats that had to be added to the existing state-wide system of conservation reserves. The priority habitats are called Strategic Habitat Conservation Areas and encompass 13 percent of Florida's land area. The report *Closing the Gaps* (Cox et al. 1994) was one of the first of a new generation of statewide conservation plans. It has been used to help guide the investment of public funds for land acquisition and has influenced some land-use decisions at local levels. Nearly 1 million acres (404,858 hectares) (or 20 percent of the total land area identified) has been purchased at a cost of nearly $2 billion (R. Kautz, Florida Fish and Wildlife Conservation Commission, personal communication, 2001). *Closing the Gaps* represents a bold new approach to conservation from a state perspective.

Also in the early to mid-1990s, the Florida Department of Environmental Protection spearheaded an effort to expand the state greenways-planning project "to conserve native landscapes, ecosystems and their species, and to connect people to the land and their archeological, historic and cultural resources" (Florida Greenways Commission 1994:1). In what is now called the Florida Ecological Network Project (figure 13.1), scientists and planners used

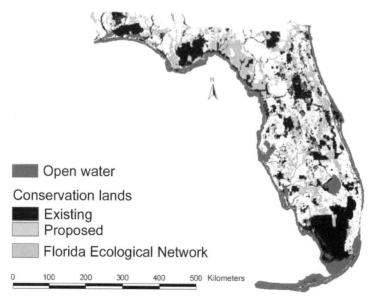

FIGURE 13.1. The Florida Ecological Network Project, a landscape approach to greenways planning that includes biodiversity. (Florida Greenways Commission)

an integrated landscape approach that employed GIS technology to identify large blocks of remaining habitat called hubs and narrower strips of land to link the hubs together to form a conservation and recreation network. The entire proposed system encompasses more than 57 percent of the state, of which nearly 11 million acres (4.45 million hectares) (27.5 percent) needed additional protection. It also includes many of the habitat gaps identified in the Florida Freshwater and Wildlife Commission's report *Closing the Gaps*. Both mapping efforts have been used to prioritize land acquisitions with public funds (Hoctor, Carr, and Zwick 2000) and are being integrated with early stages of state transportation planning.

OREGON BIODIVERSITY PROJECT

About the same time Florida's *Closing the Gaps* report was released, a group of private-industry and conservation interests in Oregon initiated a biodiversity project. The effort was inspired partially by the national Gap Analysis Program, which promised easy access to GIS-based statewide information on land cover, terrestrial vertebrate species, and land ownership and management. The Oregon Biodiversity Project was administered by Defenders of Wildlife, with active participation of The Nature Conservancy's Oregon Chapter and the Oregon natural heritage program. It involved more than 40 organizations, including representatives from academia; private industry; local, state, and federal agencies; and conservation groups (Defenders of Wildlife 1998).

The Oregon project focused more on habitat than on individual species. The partners created a historic vegetation map to determine which habitat types had declined significantly since European settlement and used the information to help select priority conservation areas. Forty-two "conservation opportunity areas" were identified. The conservation network in place before the completion of the project constituted approximately 10 percent of the state's land area. Adding the new sites would increase the percentage of land in conservation status to approximately 25 percent of the total land area. Unlike Florida, half of Oregon is currently in federal ownership, thus only approximately one-third of the newly identified areas were in private ownership when the strategy was released. However, public ownership and conservation of lands in Oregon (as it is in much of the West) disproportionately falls on high-elevation coniferous forests, whereas certain important ecoregions are almost entirely in private ownership. The biodiversity challenge is focused primarily on lands currently in agricultural use and ecologically significant areas now in the path of development.

Changes in land ownership and management are not systematically monitored to determine the impact of the Oregon Biodiversity Project on the ground.

However, several major land deals affecting "conservation opportunity areas" and a number of important policy decisions have resulted in part from issues raised by the project.

Incentives for private landowners became a major element of the Oregon conservation strategy because of the importance of the "working landscape" (agricultural and timber-producing lands) in conserving certain elements of biodiversity and maintaining ecological processes over time (Vickerman 1998). Project partners worked together in 2001 and 2003 to pass two pieces of comprehensive incentives legislation in the state legislature.

Because Oregon's land-use planning system is nationally recognized for its effectiveness in preventing sprawl, it is interesting (and disappointing) to note that the statewide Biodiversity Project has had little impact on local land-use decisions. This system has long prioritized the protection of farmland and promoted compact growth, but in its present form it does not readily accommodate or incorporate ecological goals. Moreover, the statewide scale of the Biodiversity Project does not easily adapt to local, site-specific decisions.

MASSACHUSETTS BIOMAP

Nearly a decade after Florida developed the first statewide biodiversity map, Massachusetts launched a multifaceted biodiversity program. This program has three objectives: (1) to build public support for protecting biodiversity in backyards, neighborhoods, communities, and watersheds; (2) to protect and restore ecosystems through land protection and ecological restoration projects; and (3) to promote the inclusion of biological conservation and ecosystem protection considerations in citizen, land-use, and government decision making (Massachusetts Executive Office of Environmental Affairs 2002).

A centerpiece of the program is the BioMap, accompanied by a full-color report with information on each of the state's ecoregions (Massachusetts Division of Fisheries and Wildlife 2001). The map contains core habitat areas and associated supporting natural landscapes. The core areas contain viable rare plant and animal habitats and viable exemplary natural communities. Overall, the BioMap identifies 23 percent of the state as core habitat and 19 percent as supporting natural landscape. At the time the BioMap was released, only 9 percent of the state was protected in core areas and approximately 4 percent in associated natural landscapes.

The map was developed as a tool to help set land-protection priorities, not for regulatory purposes. Although it is too early to tell what impact the program will have on biodiversity protection in Massachusetts, it represents an evolution in thinking about how to engage a broader public audience in the conservation effort than has been the case in Florida or Oregon.

The Massachusetts program also makes an explicit connection with local land-use planning. BioMap products are designed to integrate with open-space and recreation plans. The state-level Community Preservation Act also provides funding to assist communities in protecting natural areas, open space, affordable housing, and historic sites. In addition, the Executive Office of Environmental Affairs has contracted with the state's regional planning agencies and consultants to provide all 351 cities and towns in Massachusetts with a build-out map and analysis. Municipalities will now have maps that illustrate the community's current zoning, the land available for development and how it is zoned, and the maximum development possible in a particular community under current regulations. With the BioMap, local governments in Massachusetts now have the ability to consider the impacts of their land-use decisions on biodiversity. Through a series of ballot measures in 2001 and 2002, many communities in the state have voted to raise local property taxes to generate funds for land conservation, historic preservation, and affordable housing. Approving such a tax qualifies those communities to receive state matching funds under the Community Preservation Act.

NEW JERSEY LANDSCAPE PROJECT

Despite some of the most stringent land-use regulations nationwide, the suburbanization of the country's most densely populated state, New Jersey, is not only destroying important habitats, but also surrounding and isolating those habitats that remain. In an effort to protect New Jersey's rare wildlife species while helping to promote comprehensive growth management throughout the state, the Department of Environmental Protection's Endangered and Nongame Species Program launched its Landscape Project in 1994. This proactive, landscape-level effort is designed to move beyond the piecemeal protection of individual sites where rare animals occur.

The Landscape Project is based on a peer-reviewed methodology that uses wildlife to map the state's important habitat patches (Niles et al. 2001). Using GIS technology, project participants mapped every significant contiguous patch of field, woodland, and wetland in the state. Next, they used the presence of wildlife as an indicator of a habitat's value to create five categories of lands, depending on whether they are important to animal species that are federally endangered and threatened, state endangered, state threatened, or of special concern. The final category includes inadequately surveyed habitats suitable for rare wildlife.

The Landscape Project's maps are already serving land managers, land planners, environmental commissioners, land-development consultants, environmental groups, land-acquisition programs, and many other lay and professional people whose decisions affect the land. State regulators use the maps as the basis for deciding which lands provide habitat for endangered and threatened wildlife species and have to be protected through the state's Coastal Zone Management and Freshwater Wetlands Protection Act Rules (New Jersey Coastal Zone Management Rules 2001; New Jersey Freshwater Wetlands Projection Act Rules 2002.)

In the future, the maps promise to play a larger role in determining land-use patterns. The state is now working on a major antisprawl initiative that uses the project maps as one of several data layers to delineate "environmentally sensitive areas" where growth and development will be strictly regulated. Concurrently, and as part of this initiative, the New Jersey Department of Environmental Protection is also developing regulations that will extend statutory protection of endangered and threatened wildlife species to include habitat protection similar to federal endangered species regulations. Landscape maps are featured in this regulation as determining where the state presumes that specific rare animal species habitats occur.

Although not addressing the full complement of biodiversity, the Landscape Project is an important conservation endeavor. One of its strengths lies in the fact that the maps can be used at a scale suitable for municipal planning. Municipalities now have access to information about the possible presence of habitats for federal and state threatened and endangered wildlife in their areas down to the site level. The Landscape Project is also the only example nationwide where statewide biodiversity-assessment mapping is incorporated into state regulations that guide land-use decisions.

WILLAMETTE BASIN CONSERVATION STRATEGY

The Willamette Basin in Oregon covers 12,000 square miles (31,080 square kilometers), is home to 70 percent of the state's population, and supports 75 percent of the state's economic activity. The region offers one example of a spatially explicit regional conservation strategy that can be used to help guide land-use and land management decisions for the next 50 years. A team of 40 scientists in the Pacific Northwest Ecological Research Consortium (2002) concluded that even with a projected doubling of the region's population by 2050, habitat and environmental quality can actually improve over the coming decades if appropriate decisions concerning land use and management are made and implemented. The research project was funded by the U.S. Environmental Protection Agency (EPA).

Scientists involved in the Pacific Northwest Ecological Research Consortium worked with stakeholders to develop three alternative growth scenarios. One emphasized more development and a relaxation of land-use and environmental controls. Another projected the impacts on the region's ecosystems if existing land-use plans and strategies were fully implemented. A third emphasized conservation measures and included a map of essential habitats that can be conserved to help maintain viable populations of native fish and wildlife (figure 3.2). The conservation strategy also proposed using wider riparian buffers along streams, avoiding development in floodplains, and clustering rural residences to conserve and restore large parcels (Pacific Northwest Ecosystem Research Consortium 2002).

Concurrently, the Willamette Restoration Initiative, a group appointed by the governor to address water-quality and habitat issues in the basin, has adopted a strategy that incorporates the conservation priority areas from the conservation scenario described here (Willamette Restoration Initiative 2001). In 2001, the strategy was presented to state agencies, industry groups, the governor, and the state legislature. Despite the participation of a broad range of interests in the strategy's development, the strategy is strictly advisory and useful to decision makers only if they are motivated to use it. No single agency is responsible for its implementation. The EPA invested more than $10 million in the scientific analysis; however, funds were not available for outreach or implementation. Fortunately, several stakeholders who had been involved took responsibility for the outreach and implementation, preventing the scientific analysis and strategy from becoming stale and irrelevant. Additional funds were obtained for an outreach effort, focusing on local government and citizen groups. The scientific information has been repackaged for a lay audience. The Northwest

FIGURE 13.2. Willamette Valley habitat: oak savanna. (Defenders of Wildlife)

Planning and Conservation Council contracted with the Willamette Restoration Initiative staff to develop a specific sub-basin plan, based on the conservation scenario and incorporating more information from the Oregon Biodiversity Project and The Nature Conservancy's ecoregional plan. The plan will guide investments in land conservation by the Bonneville Power Administration, state agencies, local governments, and some private interests.

SONORAN DESERT CONSERVATION PLAN

The Sonoran Desert in Arizona is one of the most biologically rich areas in the United States. It hosts more than 2,500 known pollinators, and nearly two-thirds of the bird species in the country occur in this 55-million-acre (22-million-hectare) ecoregion. It is also under phenomenal growth pressure, with in-migration of up to 30,000 people each year, which consumes 7 to 10 square miles (18–25 square kilometers) of land annually. Not surprisingly, endangered species conflicts have caused great turmoil and provided political impetus for development of a far-reaching conservation plan in 1.6 million acres (647,773 hectares) of Pima County, Arizona, in the heart of the Sonoran Desert (Huckleberry 2001a).

The process led by Pima County was called *bioplanning*, or natural-resource assessment and planning, by its proponents, who believe it is a "necessary first step in defining and determining urban form" (Huckleberry 2001a). It differs from traditional planning by integrating the often independent and separate natural-resource planning and protection activities into one plan. The plan addresses six elements: ranch conservation, riparian restoration, mountain parks, historical and cultural preservation, critical habitat, and biological corridors. It is similar to such other efforts as the Florida Ecological Network and Massachusetts's BioMap in that it emphasizes the connectivity of essential habitats and addresses long-term species viability. The plan was initiated by county officials who wished to address endangered species issues in a comprehensive manner while allowing development to proceed (Pima County 2000b). Although the plan was conceived outside the traditional planning process, efforts are being made to align the conservation plan with local comprehensive plans.

The plan does not attempt to stop growth. It simply directs growth into the areas with the least natural, historic, and cultural resource values. It identifies both conservation and development reserves. The county has now adopted an updated comprehensive plan based on the conservation plan to avoid impacts to important habitats and to direct growth to less-sensitive areas (Huckleberry 2001a).

Although many people and organizations have played important roles in the effort in Arizona, as in Massachusetts, the leadership of a bold and visionary public official has given the project much greater visibility than it would otherwise have had. The plan has not been without controversy. Developers have objected to the level of protection proposed for sensitive areas and ranchlands (Huckleberry 2001b). The plan has resulted in several important land-use decisions and policy changes, but it remains to be seen whether this new approach will ultimately succeed in protecting the viability of the area's ecosystems along with traditional social and economic values.

CHICAGO WILDERNESS

Chicago Wilderness is a model example of an alliance of organizations that have worked together to develop a conservation strategy and plan that includes impressive public involvement—all within one of the nation's most urbanized regions. Chicago Wilderness is a "regional nature reserve" comprising hundreds of natural areas totaling more than 200,000 acres (80,972 hectares) in the metropolitan region. The region encompasses the crescent of land around southern Lake Michigan, including parts of southeastern Wisconsin, northeastern Illinois, and northwestern Indiana.

In 1999, Chicago Wilderness produced the *Biodiversity Recovery Plan* (1999), the region's first comprehensive biodiversity plan, following on the heels of a vibrant publication, *Chicago Wilderness: An Atlas of Biodiversity* (Sullivan 1997), that documents the region's varied natural communities and species. The effort also pools the expertise and resources of 140 federal, state, county, and local governments and nongovernmental scientific and environmental organizations. This unprecedented partnership has united disparate groups to work together to protect the region's rare natural communities and to restore them to long-term viability. Perhaps most important, Chicago Wilderness offers thousands of citizens the opportunity to become involved in biodiversity conservation in their own backyards.

CONCLUSION

Integrating biodiversity into planning at multiple scales has been and continues to be difficult, given the number and complexity of plans and land-use decisions that evolve and occur daily. Creating new planning mechanisms, especially at the state and regional level, is also difficult. The existing jurisdictional, policy, economic, and social barriers to the conservation of biodiversity and habitat have accumulated over the course of decades. It may take decades to overcome them.

A broad vision is needed to protect this country's ecological heritage, to avoid contentious debates over endangered species and habitat loss, to provide a more predictable business climate, and to protect our quality of life. Encouraging signs include improved technology and policy tools and the impressive number and diversity of citizen groups, state and local governments, and academics working to address ecological issues through planning.

A few tentative conclusions have become apparent to us in the course of reviewing dozens of state, regional, and local conservation-planning efforts and of participating in a handful of them. We consider these conclusions "tentative" because most broad-scale plans are fledgling efforts, and the ultimate outcomes have yet to be evaluated. Florida is an obvious success story. Florida's conservation plans have been used to determine what lands to acquire and which ecologically significant areas developers should avoid. As broad-scale, multiagency conservation planning becomes more common, it will be helpful to be clear about what success looks like and to track plan implementation and effectiveness.

Political leadership is critical, as is a broad base of political support. A champion for conservation planning with access to funding, the power to shape and implement policy, and an effective public voice can make or break a program. A conservation plan that addresses aesthetic, recreational, quality-of-life, economic, and ecological needs simultaneously will inspire more people and make it easier for policymakers to be advocates. Scientific credibility is important as well. The presumed benefits of a conservation plan are meaningless unless they actually materialize. By the same token, the most detailed and credible scientific proposal is irrelevant if the public does not see it, understand it, or care about it.

RECOMMENDATIONS

1. Planning should be viewed as a powerful state and local conservation tool. To be successful, it must be concerned about *which* lands to protect, must address conservation needs at multiple scales, and must consider a broad range of complementary values. According to the Conservation Fund, "As communities need to address haphazard development, they also need to address haphazard conservation—conservation activities that are reactive, site-specific, narrowly focused, and/or not well integrated with other efforts. To strategically direct our nation's conservation practices, we need 'smart conservation,' which promotes resource planning, protection, and management activities that are proactive, systematic, holistic, multi-functional, and multi-scale" (Benedict 2000:2).

2. Every state should consider developing an integrated conservation plan.

State plans can be used to guide public- and private-land-acquisition programs, identify critical areas for state and local regulatory purposes, direct state and federal conservation incentive programs to key areas, and give local governments the direction they need to utilize their land-use planning authorities for the greatest conservation good. Federal funding is available to address wildlife habitats of "greatest conservation need" through the Interior Department's State Wildlife Grant Program. Related values—such as water quality, recreation, and the protection of farm and forest lands—can be addressed by appropriate agencies and interests using public or private funding. If federal, state, local, and private interests work together, statewide plans will be of higher quality than if each issue is addressed separately and each interest works on its own. With a broader base of political support, the commitment to implementation may be strengthened.

3. State and local officials must provide leadership to encourage local governments to use their existing conservation authorities to integrate biodiversity conservation into local land-use planning and zoning.

4. States must provide local governments with incentives or requirements to make land-use decisions on a landscape or regional level. To improve efficiency and increase the range of options, local conservation needs can be addressed through regional planning. A statewide plan can provide context. Local implementation plans can provide the larger-scale plans with detail and refinement. Formation of regional councils may be an efficient way to address implementation challenges.

5. State agencies that collect, manage, and disseminate biodiversity information must play a role in marketing and outreach. They must ensure that the content and organization of the information is useful to land-use planners and that the information is provided to the key individuals.

6. States must provide technical support to assist agency personnel, local planners and officials, and private landowners in understanding and addressing conservation needs. This support should include science-based information, training, and user-friendly technical tools. For planners and policymakers who lack the time and inclination to develop a deep understanding of ecological principles, more interpreted information is needed—such as environmental assessments, overall habitat priorities, and help in accessing federal programs.

7. States and federal agencies also need to develop and fund incentives for private landowners to conserve habitat. Supplementing land acquisition and regulation with less-threatening approaches may go a long way toward alleviating local governments and landowners' concern that conserving habitat is politically dangerous.

8. Some level of public engagement is important to make conservation plans politically viable. Most people, given an opportunity, will not choose to

destroy or degrade the environment. If the choices are not offered, society will continue to make decisions piecemeal with unfortunate results. The term *biodiversity* is not critical, but ecological concepts are. The public must connect with nature on a practical level in order to understand and support the larger vision.

9. States need to designate a lead agency to facilitate conservation planning and to create meaningful opportunities for the public to participate in the process, which will likely require agencies to work more effectively with one another.

10. The private sector, including the conservation community and private industry, must play a more active role in broad-based conservation efforts. Government seldom leads and rarely advances new visions for the future for fear of criticism. Given the potential for federal laws to be weakened, it is especially important for the private sector and states to be involved in conservation efforts locally.

REFERENCES

American Planning Association. 2002. *Planning for Smart Growth: 2002 State of the States Summary Report.* Chicago: American Planning Association.

Belden Russonello & Stewart Research and Communications. 2002. *Americans and Biodiversity: New Perspectives in 2002.* Madison, Wis.: Biodiversity Project.

Benedict, M. 2000. Green infrastructure: A strategic approach to land conservation. *Planning Advisory Service (PAS) Memo* (October): 1–4.

Benedict, M.A., and E.T. McMahon. 2002. *Green Infrastructure: Smart Conservation for the 21st Century.* Sprawl Watch Clearinghouse Monograph Series. Washington, D.C.: Sprawl Watch Clearinghouse.

Bilda, E., J.S. Ellis, T. Johnson, Y. Hung, E. Katz, P. Meijerink, A.W. Shearer, H.R. Smith, A Sternberg, D. Olson, and C. Steinitz. 1994. *Alternative Futures for Monroe County, Pennsylvania.* Cambridge, Mass.: Harvard University Graduate School of Design.

Breggin, L.K., S. George, and E.H. Pencak. 2003. *Planning for Biodiversity: Authorities in State Land Use Laws.* Washington, D.C.: Environmental Law Institute and Defenders of Wildlife.

Budnick, N. 2001. Fight sprawl, kill salmon: Is the Portland area's zeal for urban density hurting endangered fish? *Willamette Week,* October 31. Available at: www.wweek.com/story.php?story=2107.

Center for Wildlife Law and Defenders of Wildlife. 1996. *Saving Biodiversity: A Status Report on State Laws, Policies, and Programs.* Washington, D.C.: Defenders of Wildlife.

Chicago Wilderness. 1999. *Biodiversity Recovery Plan.* Chicago: Chicago Wilderness.

Cort, C. 1996. A survey of the use of natural heritage data in local land-use planning. *Conservation Biology* 10: 632–637.

Cox, J., R. Kautz, M. MacLaughlin, and T. Gilbert. 1994. *Closing the Gaps in Florida's Wildlife Habitat Conservation System: Recommendations to Meet Minimum*

Conservation Goals for Declining Wildlife Species and Rare Plant and Animal Communities. Tallahassee: Florida Game and Freshwater Fish Commission.

Defenders of Wildlife. 1998. *Oregon's Living Landscape: Strategies and Opportunities to Conserve Biodiversity.* Lake Oswego, Ore.: Defenders of Wildlife.

East Central Florida Regional Planning Council. 1998. *Strategic Regional Policy Plan.* Maitland: East Central Florida Regional Planning Council.

Ecological Society of America Committee on Land Use. 2000. *Ecological Principles for Managing Land Use.* Washington, D.C.: Ecological Society of America.

Florida Greenways Commission. 1994. *Creating a Statewide Greenways System for People . . . for Wildlife . . . for Florida: Florida Greenways Commission Report to the Governor.* Tallahassee: Florida Greenways Commission.

Forman, R. T. T. 2000. Estimate of the area affected ecologically by the road system in the United States. *Conservation Biology* 14:31–35.

Goal 5: Natural resources, scenic and historic areas, and open spaces. 1996. In *Oregon's Statewide Planning Goals and Guidelines*, 1–3. Salem: Department of Land Conservation and Development. Also available at: www.oregon.gov/LCD/goals. shtml#The_Goals.

Groves, C., L. Valutis, D. Vosick, B. Neely, K. Wheaton, J. Touval, and B. Runnels. 2000. *Designing a Geography of Hope: A Practitioner's Handbook for Ecoregional Conservation Planning.* Arlington, Va.: Nature Conservancy.

Hoctor, T. S., M. H. Carr, and P. D. Zwick. 2000. Identifying a linked reserve system using a regional landscape approach: The Florida Ecological Network. *Conservation Biology* 14:984–1000.

Huckleberry, C. H. 2001a. Pima County Board of Supervisors memorandum: Sonoran Desert Conservation Plan, March 19. Tucson, Ariz.

———. 2001b. Pima County Board of Supervisors memorandum: Sonoran Desert Conservation Plan progress report and update, October 9. Tucson, Ariz.

Hulse, D., L. Goorjian, D. Richey, M. Flaxman, C. Hummon, D. White, K. Freemark, J. Eilers, J. Bernert, K. Vache, J. Kaytes, and D. Diethelm. 1997. *Possible Futures for the Muddy Creek Watershed, Benton County, Oregon.* Eugene: Institute for a Sustainable Environment, University of Oregon.

Jue, S., C. Kindell, and J. Wojcik. 2001. *Florida Conservation Lands 2001.* Tallahassee: Florida Natural Areas Inventory.

Kennedy, C. M., E. A. Gordon, and J. B. Wilkinson. 2001. *New York State Biodiversity Project: Needs Assessment.* New York: American Museum of Natural History.

Kennedy, C. M., J. B. Wilkinson, and J. Balch. 2003. *Conservation Thresholds for Land Use Planners.* Washington, D.C.: Environmental Law Institute.

Kusler, J., and L. Larson. 1993. Beyond the ark: A new approach to U.S. floodplain management. *Environment* 35:6–16.

Massachusetts Division of Fisheries and Wildlife. 2001. *BioMap: Guiding Land Conservation for Biodiversity in Massachusetts.* Boston: Commonwealth of Massachusetts.

Massachusetts Executive Office of Environmental Affairs. 2002. *Biodiversity.* Boston: Commonwealth of Massachusetts. Also available at: www.state.ma.us/envir/biodiversity.htm. Accessed March 12, 2002.

Meck, S., ed. 2002. *Growing Smart Legislative Guidebook: Model Statutes for Planning and the Management of Change.* Washington, D.C.: American Planning Association.

Mitchell, J.C., and M.W. Klemens. 2000. Primary and secondary effects of habitat alteration. In M.W. Klemens, ed., *Turtle Conservation*, 5–32. Washington, D.C.: Smithsonian Institution Press.

Nash, R. 2001. *Wilderness and the American Mind*. New Haven, Conn.: Yale University Press.

National Research Council. 1993. *Setting Priorities for Land Conservation*. Washington, D.C.: National Academy of Sciences.

——. 2001. *Compensating for Wetland Losses Under the Clean Water Act*. Washington, D.C.: National Academy Press.

Niles, L.N., J. Tash, M. Valent, and J. Myers. 2001. *New Jersey's Landscape Project: Wildlife Habitat Mapping for Community Land-Use Planning and Endangered Species Conservation*. Trenton: New Jersey Division of Fish and Wildlife.

1000 Friends of Florida. 1999. *Planning for Tomorrow: A Citizen's Guide to Smarter Growth in Florida*. Tallahassee: 1000 Friends of Florida.

Pacific Northwest Ecosystem Research Consortium. 2002. *Willamette River Basin Atlas*. 2d ed. Corvallis: Oregon State University Press.

Pima County. 2000a. *Riparian Protection, Management, and Restoration: An Element of the Sonoran Desert Conservation Plan*. Tucson, Ariz.: Pima County.

——. 2000b. *Sonoran Desert Conservation Plan: Preliminary Draft*. Tucson, Ariz.: Pima County.

Scott, J.M., F.W. Davis, R.G. McGhie, R.G. Wright, C. Groves, and J. Estes. 2001. Nature reserves: Do they capture the full range of America's biological diversity? *Ecological Applications* 11:999–1007.

Stein, B.A., L.S. Kutner, and J.S. Adams, eds. 2000. *Precious Heritage: The Status of Biodiversity in the United States*. New York: Oxford University Press.

Steinitz, C., ed. 1996. *Biodiversity and Landscape Planning: Alternative Futures for the Region of Camp Pendleton, California*. Cambridge, Mass.: Harvard University Graduate School of Design.

Sullivan, J. 1997. *Chicago Wilderness: An Atlas of Biodiversity*. Chicago: Chicago Region Biodiversity Council.

Trust for Public Land and Land Trust Alliance. 2004. *LandVote 2003: Americans Invest in Parks and Open Space*. Washington, D.C.: Trust for Public Land.

Vickerman, S. 1998. *National Stewardship Incentives: Conservation Strategies for U.S. Landowners*. Lake Oswego, Ore.: Defenders of Wildlife.

Wiley, P. 2001. *No Place for Nature: The Limits of Oregon's Land Use Program in Protecting Fish and Wildlife Habitat in the Willamette Valley*. Lake Oswego, Ore.: Defenders of Wildlife.

Wilkinson, J.B. 1999. The state role in biodiversity conservation. *Issues in Science and Technology* 15:71–77.

Wilkinson, J.B., S. L. Hsu, B. Rohan, D. Schorr, and J. McElfish. 1999. *Protecting Delaware's Natural Heritage: Tools for Biodiversity Conservation*. Washington, D.C.: Environmental Law Institute.

Wilkinson, J.B., and C.M. Kennedy. 2003. *Planning with Nature: Biodiversity Information in Action*. Washington, D.C.: Environmental Law Institute.

Willamette Restoration Initiative. 2001. *Restoring a River of Life: Willamette Restoration Strategy Overview. Recommendations for the Willamette Basin, Supplement to the Oregon Plan for Salmon and Watersheds*. Salem, Ore.: Willamette Restoration Initiative.

Wisconsin Department of Natural Resources. 2002. State natural areas program. Available at: www.dnr.state.wi.us/org/land/er/snas/info.htm (accessed March 13, 2002).

LEGAL REFERENCES

Del. Code Ann. tit. 9, §§ 2603(a), 2651, 2656(g)(1), 2656(g)(4), 2656(g)(5), 2660(a), 4951, 4956(g)(1), 4956(g)(4), 4956(g)(5), 4960(a), 6904, 6907(a), 6951, 6956(g)(1), 6956(g)(4), 6956(g)(5), and 6960(a).

Fla. Stat. 186.507.

Florida Administrative Code, Rules 27E-5.002 (4), 27E-5.003 (10), and 27E-5.004 (3)(a).

National Parks, Military Parks, Monuments, and Seashores. 16 U.S.C. § 1.

National Wildlife Refuge System. 16 U.S.C. § 668dd.

New Jersey Coastal Zone Management Rules. 33 *New Jersey Register* 3565, October 1, 2001. N.J.A.C. 7:7E-3.38. Available at: www.state.nj.us/dep/landuse/proposal/122701b.pdf.

New Jersey Freshwater Wetlands Projection Act Rules. 34 *New Jersey Register*, January 22, 2002. Subchapter 2, 7:7A-2.4. Available at: www.state.nj.us/dep/landuse/proposal/122701a.pdf.

14

INTEGRATING CONSERVATION OF BIODIVERSITY INTO LOCAL PLANNING

Jayne Daly and Michael W. Klemens

B iodiversity losses in both the developed and developing worlds are increasingly a topic of widespread concern. The focus, however, most often is on loss of species, and as a result the general public views biodiversity within the narrow definition of species diversity.

However, biodiversity is far more than a single population of a species. Instead, it encompasses the range of genetic variation contained within all populations of all species, the ecological communities into which these species are aggregated, and the landscape-scale functions and interactions among those communities. For the purposes of this discussion, *ecosystem* is broadly defined to include these landscape-scale functions, which are composed of a mosaic of individual habitats and systems, and the multitude of interactions occurring among these smaller units of diversity.

In short, *biodiversity* is what we so often refer to as "nature"—that integral "sense of place" that each of us experiences in and around our own village or town. Biodiversity is thus expressed in the rich tapestry of colors on an autumn day; the melodious songs of birds, frogs, and insects; the earthy aromas wafting through the damp forest; the movement of water from the mountains to the sea—the ebb and flow of all natural systems over time.

In the past, many people have relied on federal and state regulations to protect biodiversity. For example, the Endangered Species Act protects threatened and endangered species, and the Clean Water Act regulates the filling of wetlands. However, these regulations alone are insufficient to protect the entire range of ecosystem functions and interactions. When regulations are used in tandem with land-use planning principles and are informed by scientific data, comprehensive biodiversity protection is an attainable goal.

In this chapter, we explore the important role that local governments, grassroots organizations, and citizens' groups must play to protect the nature in their backyards and to become better stewards of biodiversity.[1] For the purposes of this chapter, we define *local government* as the level of government with decision-making authority that is closest to the people. In some states, such as New York and Connecticut, this means the village or town boards, whereas in other areas, such as Maryland and California, county governments are responsible for local decision making.

Although most of the case studies we describe in this chapter are taken from the northeastern United States, the issues presented are universal and represent challenges faced by communities across the nation and throughout most of the world. It is true that in some parts of the United States, as well as in parts of Europe, South America, Africa, and Asia, home rule is less relevant, and top–down government dictates many decisions, but the need to work with local people is widely recognized as a key (or often neglected component) to protecting successfully the complex and large landscapes needed to support biodiversity.

IMPORTANCE OF BIODIVERSITY

It is often argued that biological diversity has its own inherent value, that it is our obligation to preserve biodiversity for its own sake. These affirmations of stewardship are strongly rooted as expressions of many religious faiths and by secular ethicists. Yet in addition to philosophical and faith-based reasoning, it is important to take note that society receives many direct and tangible benefits from biological resources. Issues of water quality and quantity, rural aesthetics, recreational opportunities, tourism, and human health are closely intertwined and rest on a foundation of biodiversity.

Biodiversity has coexisted with human communities for centuries. In fact, humans have tended to settle in those very areas that are rich in biodiversity, including low-lying river valleys, coasts, protected harbors, estuaries, and the confluence of rivers. When an area is rich in biodiversity, it does not mean that humans must be excluded to preserve this biodiversity, but rather that attention should be paid to the human footprint on the landscape and the effect of that footprint on the natural systems. The human footprint is defined as not only the area of direct impact—for example, a housing subdivision or a road—but also

---

1. Our collective thinking for this chapter benefited greatly from the symposium "Integrating Conservation and Biodiversity into Local Planning: A Joint Initiative of Glynwood Center and the Metropolitan Conservation Alliance/Wildlife Conservation Society," which we held at Glynwood Center, Cold Spring, New York, April 3–5, 2002. At the symposium, we vetted many of these ideas and concepts to a focus group composed of local officials, planners, and scientists. Jayne Daly was director of programs at Glynwood Center from 1997 to 2004.

the effects of development or human-induced disturbance that often extend far beyond the actual developed area.

The biodiversity of wildlife and plant populations within a town or region is a direct measure of this footprint of ecosystem health and ultimately a measure of these ecosystems' ability to provide important services to local communities. A biologically diverse landscape is more resilient to change and can provide ecological services to our communities, now and into the future.

WHAT HAS TO BE CONSERVED

The full complement of biodiversity—species, genetic variability, ecological systems and functions—cannot be conserved within the existing networks of parks and protected areas. Ecosystems are just simply too large to be protected in this manner except in the most wild and remote regions, where the human footprint is minimal. And considering that humans already live in most ecosystems, including many that are ecologically diverse and species rich, it is essential to develop strategies that more fully integrate conservation into local land-use practices and planning.

The strategies utilized in rural and outer suburban areas will differ from those employed in urban and inner suburban areas. In most urban areas and associated suburbs, much of the biodiversity has already been lost or compromised. Therefore, the strategies in such areas tend to focus on restoration and rehabilitation. One should not underestimate these activities' ecological and public-education values, including unearthing and restoring buried streams in urban areas, restoring wetlands, and revegetating degraded wetlands and woodlands. However, most of these activities are beyond the scope of local planning, except where opportunities are created through urban redevelopment and brownfield rehabilitation.

In many rural areas, the native biodiversity template is still present and needs to be conserved through better local and regional planning. For purposes of this chapter, we define *rural* as disturbance levels 1 to 3, as defined by Klemens (1993), which connect clusters of human settlement, farms, and centers of commerce (see the box "Disturbance Factors"), as opposed to networks of roads that exist solely for the dispersion of people into housing developments.

The first step in integrating conservation and biodiversity into local planning is to identify the areas that are rich in biodiversity, which might include wetlands, woodlands bordering stream corridors, grasslands, and working landscapes such as farms and production forests. The second step is to identify the "vacant" spaces that connect these habitat nodes, allowing plants and animals to move across the landscape. These movements between habitat nodes are

DISTURBANCE FACTORS

All areas in New England have been modified by human activity, the present habitats largely resulting from these disturbances. This matrix focuses on both the severity and the frequency of these disturbances over the past 20 to 30 years and on the regularity of present disturbances to a site. In the case of aquatic habitats, the surrounding terrestrial habitats often give a good indication of the disturbance level.

The habitats can be characterized and coded as follows:

- *Low level 1.* These habitats are largely undisturbed, although they may be dissected by a road, trail, or railroad bed and usually contain a low density of human habitation. Passive recreational uses often occur in these areas. Large forested areas of Connecticut that are essentially rural fall into this category.
- *Intermittent level 2.* These habitats usually occur within low-level disturbance areas, but are periodically disturbed, with intervening recovery times. Examples include power line rights-of-way and selectively cut woodlots.
- *Regular disturbance 3.* These habitats, although essentially rural, are subject to annual disturbances most frequently associated with agriculture. These activities maintain habitats at a particular seral stage. Grazing, mowing, haying, and controlled burning are included within this category. Many areas of Connecticut that are a mosaic of agricultural land, fields, forests, and scattered human settlement are included in this category.
- *Suburban 4.* Although large open spaces may remain, human settlement predominates. One of the distinguishing features of this landscape is a road network designed solely to disperse humans to their residences, as opposed to roads linking settlements. The suburban road network is quickly distinguished on U.S. Geographical Survey topographic maps as a series of winding and twisting roads joining one another or terminating in cul-de-sacs. High-level disturbances occur at the edges of residential areas, and natural areas are often patchwork in distribution.
- *Urban 5.* This habitat is a more developed continuation of the preceding category, with large tracts of mostly built-on land. Remaining open space is usually heavily utilized and frequently abused. Introduced plants and feral animals are common.
- *Radically disturbed 6.* Severe disturbance and habitat alteration is the norm in these areas. Plowed, bulldozed, and scarified habitats; vacant lots; quarries; sand pits; and large dumps are terrestrial examples of this habitat type. Aquatic examples include quarry ponds, channelized streams, culverts, actively used swimming pools, settling ponds, and sewage-treatment plants.

Source: Klemens (1993).

essential in maintaining healthy and viable wildlife and plant populations. Although some of these connecting spaces—such as empty lots, edges of roadways, and land that has been used for dumping—may appear vacant and even unattractive to the untrained eye, they serve as vital connection points between habitat nodes and provide habitat for a variety of species specifically adapted to living on the transition zones between habitats. The rich diversity of species that occur in hedgerows that separate agricultural fields (Forman 1995) is one example of the ecological importance of such habitat strips and borders. Small strips of woodland bordering stream corridors are often species rich and help to guard the stream from both erosion and pollution, while also buffering it from fluctuations in temperature and dissolved oxygen.

THE ROLE OF COMMUNITIES

The escalating loss of biodiversity is the product of thousands of choices and decisions made over the previous centuries. It will take a concerted effort to make better, more informed decisions to begin to halt and ultimately to alter the current trajectory of environmental degradation. This effort will require enlightened leadership at all levels to make a commitment to change current practices. However, unlike traditional conservation strategies, which either resulted in total protection or assumed total destruction, the new paradigm we advance is that protection of biodiversity is not an either–or proposition; it is not a decision to be couched in absolutes.

Planners and communities must begin to see biodiversity as an important component to be incorporated into planning—one that will help to build more sustainable, higher-quality communities and regions. Development that embraces and respects biodiversity is often more attractive and at times less expensive to construct and maintain than development built in opposition to nature.

Some large-scale biodiversity protection, in addition to habitat protection for threatened and endangered species, is currently being achieved through the regulatory process. For example, federal and state floodplain laws regulate the placement of structures in flood-prone areas where they are subject to destruction. Although originally designed to protect against economic loss, these regulations also help to protect the rich biodiversity found in these areas: "The Federal Emergency Management Agency estimates that federal, state and local governments spent a total of $203 million acquiring, elevating or removing damaged properties from floodplains after the 1993 midwestern floods, saving an estimated $304 million in future flood damages" (Navota and Dreher 2000:6). And by allowing rivers to flood—unimpeded by man-made structures—these regulations help to maintain the natural dynamism of riparian (i.e., riverside) habitats, continuing the natural cycles of habitat disturbance and microhabitat creation.

Federal and state governments' role in environmental protection has led many citizens to believe that biodiversity is "already taken care of" or, even less true, already overprotected. These state and federal regulations are very important, but regulations alone will never successfully protect biodiversity. Community residents, professionals, and government officials must find a way to complement existing regulations that promote environmentally sound planning with some new tools and incentives. At the same time, the public must be educated about the connection between biodiversity and the quality of life in their communities. In short, a new paradigm is needed—one that advances the proposition that instead of developing land with the naive expectation that ecosystems will magically rearrange themselves around a new development (i.e., the old thinking), a community should first understand its ecosystems and then place development where it will minimize ecological impact. By doing so, we will bring biodiversity conservation fully into the smart-growth equation, creating quality communities that sustain both humans and the ecosystems on which all life ultimately depends.

CHALLENGES

Elected and civic leaders who are trying to integrate conservation and biodiversity into local planning face a number of significant challenges.

LACK OF AWARENESS

In most places, the issue of biodiversity is not part of the community's awareness, or, if so, it is peripheral to other discussions concerning tax reductions, downtown revitalization, traffic congestion, and growth. Where growth is an issue, there may even be conversations and studies about the need to protect open space for aesthetic or economic reasons, but rarely is the issue of protecting biodiversity raised. This neglect is a result of a variety of factors, the most prevalent being a lack of awareness of the biological diversity in the region. As indicated earlier, most people think of biodiversity as the need to protect rare and endangered species. Therefore, if there are not "protected habitats"—that is, habitats of rare and endangered species—in the area, or if those habitats will not be affected by a development, the public considers the issue of "biodiversity" to have been adequately addressed. Local decision makers and the public at large do not consider the impact that the development may have on migratory routes of birds and on mammals such as bobcat or bear, or the even more subtle habitat destruction that occurs when a lot is clear-cut, stream corridors are opened to erosion, or a road is widened and paved.

COMPLEX DATA AND LANGUAGE

Another barrier to communication and understanding at the local level is the lack of scientific data and meaningful professional advice. Few rural communities have the funding needed to develop the scientific data required to support new regulations or to hire the planning and legal professionals who can adapt innovative approaches to local circumstances. Large-scale, top-down conservation plans, including many state biodiversity strategies, contain data and recommendations at a coarse scale, often at a landscape level, and as such fail to provide the fine-grained detail to guide decisions at the local level.

Even if these data are made available, it is difficult and expensive to find a scientist who can translate those data into information that is meaningful for the average citizen and that can be incorporated into the planning process. Most scientists, like other specialists, use technical words or jargon that may only serve to confuse an already complicated situation. Instead, they have to assume the role of local interpreters, willing to extrapolate information and raise the public's awareness that important issues are at stake.

TIMING OF PROFESSIONAL ADVICE

Scientists are generally brought into the local planning process at too late a stage. In most cases, they get involved only when there is a development proposal under review. Sometimes they are asked to provide "a trump card"—a rationale to stop the development that is based on the need to protect biodiversity at the site. At other times, the situation is reversed, and the developer hires the scientist to prepare an environmental impact statement that minimizes biodiversity concerns. In the latter case, the community is often forced to rely on the developer's scientific findings because it cannot afford to hire its own consultant to verify the facts or to reach an alternative independent conclusion. Competing visions of how best to interpret and apply biodiversity information further confuse and polarize the local decision-making process. The debate becomes more about the quality of two different data sets than about the actual impacts of the proposed project.

COMPLEXITY OF TECHNOLOGY

There has been recent interest in providing a variety of environmental and ecological information to communities through the use of technology. The proliferation of geographic information systems (GISs) and companion mapping applications indicate a belief that the high-tech approach will provide a way to assimilate complex information into an understandable format that can be used at the local level. Although some communities have found these approaches extremely helpful in considering a variety of scenarios for development, many more find the expertise required to program the systems, along with the expense of gathering local data, to be prohibitive. Perhaps more fundamentally, the high-tech approach may fail to provide end users with a true understanding of the information being manipulated. These data layers may be rich and accurate, but they do not impart values or factor in other aspects of the difficult decision-making process, and they are often difficult to interpret.

LIMITS OF THE REGULATORY APPROACH

There are legal limits to what can be protected through the existing local regulatory process. For example, a vernal pool—a seasonally filled wetland depression that is important for production of amphibians and invertebrates—requires at least a 750-foot (229-meter) buffer in order to ensure its ecological function. However, in New York, most local wetlands laws, which are enacted in conjunction with state and federal legislation to protect water quality, require only a 100-foot (30-meter) buffer. If a municipality were to increase the buffer size to protect biodiversity adequately, it would be inviting a lawsuit because the regulation must be tied specifically to protecting water quality. In addition, because most vernal pools do not occur in isolation, but rather in clusters, increasing buffer zones from 100 to 750 feet (30 to 229 meters) would prevent development on significantly large parcels of land and might invite a regulatory takings challenge.[2] Therefore, although the intended goal of water-quality protection is met through these regulations, the biodiversity needs are not. One solution might be to enact specific regulations to protect biodiversity; however, though this approach may be laudable, the political barriers to enactment will be significant, and the approach may thus not be practical in the short term.

MISDIRECTED ZONING Some local governments have instituted large-lot zoning— for example, one residential unit on every 5 acres (2 hectares)—in an attempt to protect open space and biodiversity. This technique, however, does not accomplish its intended objectives. Rather, it spreads development across the landscape, interrupting migratory corridors, destroying habitat, and increasing the need for roads. Instead, biodiversity is best protected by concentrating development in high-density nodes. These nodes should be located so that they can be serviced by existing infrastructure and at densities that support the use of mass transit.

ENFORCEMENT AND MONITORING There is a serious lack of education, funding, and personnel dedicated to enforcing and monitoring local regulations.

---

2. The Fifth Amendment of the Constitution guarantees that "property shall not be taken for a public use without just compensation." Where local regulations have gone so far as to prohibit all economically beneficial use of a property, the courts have found that the regulations amount to a "total taking" and require that compensation be paid to the landowner (*Lucas v. South Carolina Coastal Council*, 505 U.S. 1003 [1992]).

Enforcement and monitoring fail in at least two phases: the application and development phase and the postdevelopment phase.

During the application phase, a significant amount of resource damage is incurred in simply gathering data about the site to assess the environmental impact of the development. Land clearing, percolation tests, and debris clearing can so severely damage the resources at the site that little is left to protect during the permitting process. Even if the municipality regulates land clearing, violations are not identified until after the fact, when the damage is done. At one development on Long Island, while the biologist and a representative of the Department of Environmental Conservation were walking the site to determine sensitive habitat areas for an endangered species, they noticed that a large road had been created by bulldozers within 100 feet (30 meters) of the habitat. The road had been cleared in order to conduct percolation tests required as part of the permit application process.

After the development is finished and the certificate of occupancy is issued, some landowners have work done to their property that they were not allowed to do during the development phase, such as clearing trees from a grove or disturbing vegetation along a stream corridor. These violations are difficult to detect until the parcel is put up for sale, and someone notices that the ecological resources have been altered.

Local judges, elected officials, and attorneys must be educated about zoning violations and the appropriate use of penalties. Although not all zoning violations are criminal, most codes provide criminal penalties for serious and repeat violations. However, many local judges and elected officials do not view code violations as "real" criminal offenses. When an offense such as filling a wetland comes before a local judge, his or her response is often a reprimand or an insignificant fine rather than the imposition of a criminal penalty or a sanction that can serve as an important deterrent if consistently enforced.

STRATEGIES TO PLAN FOR BIODIVERSITY

Despite the many obstacles to incorporating conservation and biodiversity into local planning, towns can take a variety of measures to ensure that biological resources are considered as their communities continue to develop and grow. By undertaking these measures, towns can maintain biodiversity while attaining tangible benefits for present and future generations.

BASELINE INVENTORIES

Towns have to know the land parcels and habitat corridors in their community that are important to protect, including habitats that support endangered, threatened, uncommon, and declining species. Identification of special habitat features (e.g., vernal pools, talus slopes) should also be incorporated into a town's biodiversity database. A biodiversity assessment or survey should be conducted by a qualified conservation biologist or landscape ecologist during appropriate seasons and utilizing standardized protocols (Miller and Klemens 2002). With this baseline of information, towns can then plan development around their natural-resource template—thereby keeping the fabric of habitats and connections between habitats relatively intact (Kiviat and Stevens 2001).

PROTECTING WORKING LANDSCAPES

Certain agricultural landscapes are especially valuable for the protection of biodiversity. For example, natural grassland communities are now very rare in the northeastern United States in part because the frequent fires required to maintain this habitat are considered incompatible with human settlement. In the lower Hudson Valley of New York, hayfields can provide a substitute habitat for natural grassland communities if they are managed properly—for example, by adjusting the timing of hay cutting to avoid the nesting season of grassland birds. Managed appropriately, hayfields can be important nesting areas for declining grassland birds, such as eastern meadowlarks (*Sturnella magna*) and bobolinks (*Dolichonyx oryzivorus*).

Wet meadows are another example of an ecological community currently maintained in large part by agricultural activities. Until the beaver (*Castor canadensis*) was exterminated by trapping in colonial and postcolonial times, it was the major agent of wetland change in the Northeast, including the creation of wet meadows. The cycle of wetland birth and renewal was closely tied to the flooding of mature forest by beavers' killing the trees and creating an open-water habitat. The beaver dam was eventually breached, creating an open, grassy wet meadow that reverted back to forest. Many species that require wet meadows are now intimately associated with agricultural lands. With the loss of beaver, agricultural activities such as mowing and grazing became the key force in keeping wet meadows open. Although the beaver has returned to parts of its former range and is once again beginning the cycle of wetland renewal, after a hiatus of two centuries, agricultural landscapes remain critical for the survival of wet meadow species. For example, the federally threatened bog turtle (*Clemmys muhlenbergii*) occurs almost exclusively on agricultural or immediately postagricultural landscapes (Klemens 2001). Prime farmland, however, is particularly attractive for development because it is relatively flat, cleared of forest, with deep and well-drained soils, and most often zoned for residential development.[3]

3. From 1992 to 1997, the national rate of land development more than doubled, to 3 million acres (1.2 million hectares) a year (Environmental Protection Agency 2001). More than 11 mil-

SCALE OF ECOSYSTEMS VERSUS SCALE OF DECISION MAKING

Ecosystems exist at the scale of thousands of acres, many at tens of thousands of acres, yet most of our decisions are made at a scale of 100 acres (40 hectares) or less, which is a small fraction of any given ecosystem. Decisions made at scales of hundreds of acres (or less) cannot be reassembled back into ecosystems totaling thousands of acres. Despite extensive environmental review at the state and local level, most development decisions contribute to biodiversity loss by fragmenting large ecosystems into smaller, less-functional units. Site-by-site reviews have a major cumulative impact on biological resources. To protect biodiversity adequately requires that communities plan at a scale that will protect these resources, which requires cooperation among neighboring municipalities because most ecosystems span multiple political jurisdictions.

WORKING AT AN INTERMUNICIPAL SCALE

Regional initiatives to protect biologically diverse resources can be accomplished through local government cooperation. An intermunicipal agreement (IMA) is a contractual arrangement between two or more local governments to conduct jointly those activities that each is authorized to perform alone. For example, several municipalities can enter into an IMA to protect the biodiversity in their region through a coordinated open-space plan, compatible local ordinances, and a regional conservation advisory board. The municipalities can also agree to hire or share inspectors or code enforcement officers. In 1995, 14 municipalities near Huntington, Long Island, entered into an IMA to protect the natural resources of the Cold Spring Harbor area. They agreed to develop a harbor management plan and to tailor zoning regulations to effectuate the plan (Nolon 1998).

COMPREHENSIVE PLANS

After the community has had an opportunity to learn about its resources, it can articulate the importance of biodiversity and the need for its protection in the community's comprehensive plan. The protection of biodiversity then becomes one of the specific objectives of the comprehensive plan. Because the comprehensive or master plan forms the foundation for local regulations, articulating the community's desire to protect species and habitat provides a rational for subsequent regulatory measures. Many communities include in the comprehensive

---

lion acres (4.5 million hectares) of rural land were developed during that time period, and more than half of that land was agricultural land—a conversion rate of more than 1 million acres (404,685 hectares) a year (American Farmland Trust 2002).

plan a natural-resources or environment section where information about bio-diversity is discussed. A recommendations section that allocates responsibility and lists the threats to biodiversity, the actions that should be taken, and the time frame for action is critical. What communities should avoid is creating resource-management plans for only certain parcels. The whole community—large land parcels, corridors, and special habitats—must be considered.

INNOVATIVE REGULATIONS

Once the community has incorporated biodiversity into its comprehensive plan, regulations such as those that protect wetlands, limit development on steep slopes, or promote clustering can help control environmental deterioration. A municipality can also adopt a conservation overlay zone to protect biologically diverse areas or significant habitat. To create a conservation overlay zone, the municipality can identify, based on scientific assessment, the area(s) in need of special protection. The areas can then be specifically identified on the municipality's zoning map. The overlay zone most often does not change the use and dimension requirements of the underlying land-use district, but rather provides more stringent standards.

For example, a municipality might adopt a stream corridor overlay district to preserve biologically sensitive areas, to preserve scenic character, and to protect water quality. The Town of Dover, New York, adopted a Stream Corridor Overlay District, which requires special site plan approval for certain activities and limits filling or excavation, clear-cutting of vegetation, and grading or altering the natural landscape. Dover's Planning Board may grant site plan approval if it finds that the proposed activity will not degrade the scenic character of the area, will not result in erosion or stream pollution, and is compatible with the surrounding landscape (Town of Dover Zoning Code 1999).

Other regulations, such as transfer of development rights (TDR), can be used to redirect development away from ecologically sensitive areas and toward areas that can sustain such development. Areas for conservation are identified as "sending zones," and areas for development are identified as "receiving zones." If one owns land in a sending zone, one's right to develop the land is restricted, but one can sell the development rights to a landowner in the receiving district. The development credit will allow a developer in the receiving district to build at a higher density than that allowed by zoning. TDRs are complex tools that can be very effective when administered properly, but they must always be considered as part of a larger comprehensive development and conservation plan.

In 1995, a TDR program was established in the Central Pine Barrens of Long Island to protect the ecological and hydrological resources of a unique pine barrens ecosystem. Under this TDR program, the development rights to

263 acres (106 hectares) in a 52,000-acre (21,053-hectare) preservation area have been transferred to a 47,500-acre (19,231-hectare) growth area (Central Pine Barrens Joint Planning and Policy Commission 1995). In exchange for selling their development rights, landowners must agree to put a conservation easement on their property that restricts any further development of the land.

INCORPORATING BIODIVERSITY INTO SUBDIVISION AND CONSTRUCTION PRACTICES

There exists a small, but growing literature on practices and designs that lessen the development footprint on the landscape. These publications not only promote biodiversity stewardship, but also provide designs for biodiversity-friendly structures and guidance (often in the form of decision-making trees) as to when and where it is appropriate to implement these designs. The placement of roads, the design of curbs and stormwater drains, pre- and postconstruction activities, and the location and design of accessory structures and lighting—all can be made more biodiversity-friendly (Calhoun and Klemens 2002).

INCORPORATING BIODIVERSITY INTO OPEN-SPACE PLANNING AND FARMLAND-PRESERVATION EFFORTS

Many communities and land trusts are attempting to manage growth and preserve quality of life and community character by acquiring land or development rights through fee simple purchase or conservation easements. The municipality or nonprofit group identifies certain parcels for protection based on factors that include opportunity, accessibility, economic feasibility, and the potential for public use or benefit. Because many of these parcels also contain significant wildlife habitat and natural resources, communities and land trusts should integrate biodiversity concerns into this prioritization process.

There is increased interest in the land trust community's becoming more strategic in its acquisition of lands that are part of townwide or regionwide biodiversity plans (Klemens 2002). By considering factors such as habitat quality, habitat diversity, habitat connectivity, and known locations of plant and wildlife populations, the preservation of open space and farmlands can help maintain biodiversity at a larger landscape level.

EDUCATION

Raising the community's awareness about its natural resources is an important first step to incorporating conservation and biodiversity into local planning. This education can be accomplished through a variety of techniques, including gathering and publicizing baseline information, engaging the community in discovering the nature in its backyard, implementing build-out analyses, conducting public-opinion surveys, and involving the community in visioning exercises. By understanding the needs of wildlife and ecosystem processes, residents can become informed advocates for planning that respects and promotes a community's natural-resource base. Such outreach has been significant in obtaining public support and buy-in for projects such as the Eastern Westchester Biotic Corridor, discussed more fully at the end of this chapter (Miller and Klemens 2002).

During the education process, it is important to speak about biodiversity in its broadest sense. Because most people still consider biodiversity as species protection, they should be educated to understand the bigger picture—that biodiversity is the "web of life" and part of larger issues such as water quality and habitat protection. By using language meaningful to a particular audience, planners or citizen advocates can incorporate biodiversity into the community's dialogue from the very beginning (Coffin and Elder, chapter 15, this volume).

The choice of who presents the information to the public is also an important consideration. If someone is perceived as a "No Growth" advocate, many residents may view the information with suspicion. However, if a business person in town or a respected appointed official is the messenger, the information will be more openly received (Coffin and Elder, chapter 15, this volume).

PARTICIPATORY TOOLS Citizens can gather habitat and species information. For example, a citizen group, land trust, or conservation advisory council can use aerial photos, maps, tours, and site visits to identify the types of habitats that exist in their community: on agricultural land, in woodlands, on public and private protected lands, in forests, along rivers, and in wetlands. Interviews with regional naturalists can provide information about the kinds of species that live or migrate through the region. Hunters and outdoor enthusiasts are also valuable sources of local information.[4] Although these data might not provide the entire scientific basis to conduct a development review, they do engage the community in learning about the nature in its backyard and build the constituency necessary for implementing protection strategies.

BUILD-OUT ANALYSES Another important tool that raises public awareness is the build-out analysis. This technique, which can be done with a GIS or by hand,

---

4. Glynwood Center in partnership with the Metropolitan Conservation Alliance, a program of the Wildlife Conservation Society, has designed a citizen tool to assess biodiversity: *Smart Agriculture: Connecting Communities, Farming, and Food*. For more information, contact Glynwood Center at www.glynwood.org.

is used to demonstrate what a given area will look like if everything permissible is developed under the existing zoning regulations. Most people are shocked by what their community will look like when they are shown a build-out scenario. It is important, however, to take the next step and not simply consider the visual impact of the build-out scenario, but also look at the development's impacts on biodiversity in the area.

PUBLIC-OPINION SURVEYS Collecting information about what the public values can also be an important tool in raising awareness about biodiversity. In Pound Ridge, New York, when considering how to fund open-space acquisition, the town's government conducted a public-opinion survey to learn if residents would agree to a small property tax increase and, if so, how the proceeds should be spent. The mailed surveys asked residents to indicate why they thought it was important to protect open space. When tabulated, the results enabled the town to identify three priorities for open-space acquisition: protecting water quality, maintaining the town's character, and preserving wildlife habitat. These findings became the foundation for the town's open-space plan.

VISIONING EXERCISES Often conducted in conjunction with the update of a master or comprehensive plan, this participatory technique brings residents together to consider alternative "future scenarios" for growth and conservation in their community. The most successful visioning exercises are preceded by an aggressive education of the public about the issues in the town. This education can be accomplished through a variety of techniques—including baseline inventories, build-out analyses, and public-opinion surveys—and by utilizing the press, private newsletters, or information meetings. When the public comes together to consider the issues facing the community, it is better prepared to address the subjects intelligently rather than simply react to the negative impacts facing certain neighborhoods.

There are many ways to conduct a visioning exercise,[5] but it is important to allow the residents enough time to consider the issues meaningfully, to build relationships, and to design alternatives. One town, in an attempt to respond to a tremendous frenzy of real-estate activity, conducted a unique visioning session by grouping citizens in committees based on interest affinity rather than on issues or community challenges such as downtown revitalization or recreation. The larger group was thus divided into committees made up of people with similar interests, such as large landowners, homeowners, youth, renters, busi-

5. See, for example, *Community Visioning*, a two-hour video and workbook to help planners, citizens, and elected officials understand and design visioning processes. It is available through the American Planning Association, Chicago.

ness people, and developers. Each of the ten committees was given three maps and a series of issues to consider. The committees met several times to design solutions to the community's identified challenges. When they reconvened as a full group for a two-night discussion, the results were astonishing. Developers took the lead in advocating for more conservation. Part-time summer residents said that the town needed affordable housing. In the end, the visioning resulted in the development of a variety of land-management plans to protect one of the largest expanses of coastal heath in North America on the island of Nantucket, Massachusetts.

INNOVATIVE APPROACHES

Local officials, planners, and interested citizens can look to several exciting examples for inspiration and verification that incorporating conservation and biodiversity into local planning not only is possible, but also reaps benefits beyond natural-resource preservation (figure 14.1). The three case studies presented here look at how a variety of places have successfully incorporated ecological design into their local efforts: the Eastern Westchester Biotic Corridor provides a framework for conservation planning within a biologically diverse region of New York; Eckenforde, Germany, demonstrates what can be achieved

FIGURE 14.1. A broad range of local interests and stakeholders are required to effect conservation at the local level, as illustrated by this operational diagram prepared by the Wildlife Conservation Society's Metropolitan Conservation Alliance (WCS/MCA).

by committed local officials who are determined to improve the biodiversity within a town on the Baltic Sea; and Jefferson Crossing in Connecticut illustrates how conservation design can be incorporated at the subdivision level in order to protect the natural resources at the site.

EASTERN WESTCHESTER BIOTIC CORRIDOR

Located less than 45 miles (73 kilometers) from Times Square, the towns of North Salem, Lewisboro, and Pound Ridge form an oasis of rolling forested hills and meadows, rocky ravines, and wooded swampland at the northeastern edge of the ever-expanding New York metropolitan region (Miller and Klemens 2002). Bounded by the Interstate 684 corridor to the west and the Connecticut state line to the east, these three towns have kept much of their rural flavor. Dirt roads bordered by ancient sugar maples wind through shaded forest, lichen-covered stone walls enclose grassy pastures, and small hamlets retain much of the ambience and vitality of a slower, gentler time. A rich diversity of wildlife remains in these towns because, despite recent and increased development, large tracts of unfragmented open space remain. These tracts are a legacy of relatively compact settlement patterns, rural land-use practices, and protected areas, including county parkland and watershed buffer lands surrounding the numerous public water-supply reservoirs located within these towns.

The Eastern Westchester Biotic Corridor (EWBC) project is a partnership between the Wildlife Conservation Society's Metropolitan Conservation Alliance (MCA) and the three contiguous towns of North Salem, Lewisboro, and Pound Ridge in northeastern Westchester County, New York (Miller and Klemens 2002). The goal of the project is to establish a regional, multitown approach to the conservation of wildlife and habitats. These towns were selected because they contain an impressive diversity of wildlife and habitats, because they are under development pressures that threaten those natural resources, and because there is an active interest within these towns to address these issues. The project commenced in late 1998 after MCA staff gave presentations to officials at town board meetings. In April 2002, the project concluded with the formal release of a detailed report supported by scientific data and maps showing the location of development-sensitive areas. The following recommendations were provided in the report:

1. Attempt to add area—through fee simple purchase or easement—to existing protected areas. This addition would buffer the existing habitat hubs from externally caused degradations. It would also reduce "edge effects," which have a negative impact on forest-interior and area-sensitive species. In addition, the buffers can often serve as additional habitat.

2. Consider enacting a conservation area overlay ordinance. Although this approach is not as effective as purchasing land (or obtaining easements to land), it does minimize and mitigate the impacts of development within designated zones. It is valuable in particular for maintaining wildlife habitat connectivity in developable parcels located between habitat hubs.

3. Consider formalizing intermunicipal relationships with other towns in the EWBC (and beyond) by establishing an intermunicipal council and adopting an intermunicipal agreement.

4. Consider extending the EWBC into Connecticut, joining with conservation initiatives in adjacent towns (Ridgefield, Wilton, New Canaan, and Stamford) and shared watersheds (e.g., Titicus and Norwalk Rivers).

5. Encourage better environmental review of projects by
   - Taking a hard look at impacts beyond individual project sites (i.e., considering cumulative impacts on townwide and regionwide scales).
   - Encouraging use of the generic environmental impact statement (GEIS) process. In this planning process, the town creates an environmental impact statement for a large block of land. Then, as individual development projects are proposed, they are evaluated against the GEIS findings. The town recovers the costs of the GEIS through a prorated fee assigned to each development project.
   - Requiring standards for wildlife surveys to ensure that adequate effort is being expended at appropriate times of year to assess on-site wildlife resources.

6. Integrate the recommendations of the EWBC study into the town's master plan.

In summary, the EWBC not only provides a framework for conservation planning within the towns of North Salem, Lewisboro, and Pound Ridge, but also creates a model with far broader applications. This model links traditional land-protection efforts with the rich and often untapped conservation potential presented by strategic engagement of the local land-use decision-making process.

ECKENFORDE: THE ECOLOGICAL CAPITAL OF GERMANY

Eckenforde, located in northern Germany on the Baltic Sea, is a small industrial city with a population of 23,000, surrounded by scenic agricultural landscapes and seashore.[6] Maintaining the landscape had always been a top priority, but elected officials did not always have the basic scientific information to distinguish between

---

6. Information on the ecological planning of Eckenforde was gathered during interviews with Michael Packschies (January 2002) and from his "Management of Urban Watersheds and Renaturalization of Derelict Lands as a Part of Holistic Ecological City Planning" (paper presented at Harvard University, Cambridge, Mass., November 2001).

acceptable and damaging development plans. In 1984, the city council hired an independent consultant, Michael Packschies, to conduct an environmental assessment of the city and to develop scientific guidelines that would form the basis for creating an ecologically sensitive land-use plan. During this year-long study, the vegetation and geological and hydrological attributes of the area (7 square miles [18 square kilometers]) were mapped and significant resource areas identified.

Upon the study's completion, Packschies was asked to consider the potential impact of the city's land-utilization plan (comparable to a town's comprehensive plan) on the identified resources and to propose alternatives for any potential impacts. He found that in many respects the land-use plan directly conflicted with the city's preservation objectives. Specifically, the assessment identified the northern edge of the city as the most biologically diverse and environmentally sensitive, but the land-use plan called for that area to be developed for housing. Packschies recommended that the plan for growth be reoriented, allowing development to proceed, but instead to the south, in less-sensitive areas. He also proposed that the city acquire some extremely sensitive land and implement other measures to improve existing natural areas. The city council agreed to implement 95 percent of Packschies's recommendations.

In 1993, the city adopted a land-use plan based on the environmental survey's findings and hired Packschies to oversee its implementation. During the past decade, while the city has continued to grow and develop, the ecology of the area has also improved.

The northern edge of the city was preserved, and the Lachsenbach Creek, which had been culverted, was renaturalized. Unearthing the creek in turn recreated wetlands and turned the entire landscape into an attractive recreational area for nature lovers. In one section, the culvert was simply plugged with a plastic bucket. The resulting wetland and the vegetation that surrounds it have become an attractive habitat for many animal species.

Two significant housing complexes have been built in the southern portion of Eckenforde to compensate for the lost development in the north. These developments were also designed to be ecologically sensitive and to incorporate innovative stormwater management to support nearby streams and habitat.

Over the past 15 years, the ecological planning for Eckenforde has had a tremendous impact on the quality of life in the region. The city has received many environmental awards, and its "eco-image" is used to attract tourists and to market residential housing.

JEFFERSON CROSSING: INNOVATIVE CONSERVATION DESIGN FOR A SUBDIVISION

On Talcott Mountain—a trap-rock ridge lying west of Hartford, Connecticut—a unique conservation subdivision was created, incorporating many innovative design principles (Calhoun and Klemens 2002). Unlike most subdivisions, where natural resources are expected to "fit" around a preconceived development pattern, Jefferson Crossing was designed with great sensitivity to the site's natural features. The subdivision is named for the rarest vernal pool–breeding amphibian found on the site, the state-listed Jefferson salamander (*Ambystoma jeffersonianum*), and for the fact that the salamanders will be able to cross freely through the site to their breeding pool. To accomplish this, all structures and infrastructure were placed more than 100 feet (30 meters) from the vernal pool. In addition, the design of the site maximized protection of the critical upland habitat zone through a combination of conservation easements and lot-clearing restrictions. Finally, the design allows for unimpeded movement of amphibians and other wildlife throughout the forested site.

The execution of this novel design required approvals from the town of Farmington, Connecticut, and a commitment from the developer to engage a team of professionals to integrate design, engineering, and natural-resource protection. For example, the proposed entrance road (using an existing access from a demolished single-family house) was determined to be too close to the vernal pool. The developer acquired an additional lot to enable relocation of the entrance road well beyond the vernal pool envelope. The houses were clustered several hundred feet away from the vernal pool. These actions, combined with lot-clearing restrictions (no more than 50 percent per lot) and conservation easements, resulted in 75 percent of the site being protected in its natural state.

The roadways internal to the site have curbing that is designed to allow salamanders to move freely over the road-edge structure. Stormwater is handled through swales and a single catch basin. To minimize mortality of amphibians and other wildlife caught in the catch-basin system, the water moves through a grassy swale and into an open, biofiltration wetland. By using low-gradient curbing and eliminating the need for hydrodynamic separators, amphibian mortality is minimized. Additional restrictions govern the design of individual driveways and exterior lighting, and the use of pesticides, herbicides, and salts.

Jefferson Crossing will incorporate its unique conservation design as part of its marketing strategy. The location of the homes tucked among the hemlock trees and nestled between trap-rock outcrops will attract a distinctive type of buyer, one who is looking to live in greater harmony with the natural world. The developer, who designed this project on the site of her family homestead, rejected conventional development patterns. Her vision has turned what many would consider a liability, a biologically diverse site, into an asset. At this time, the project has received all necessary approvals and includes a monitoring plan.

CONCLUSION

It is ultimately up to people to work individually and collectively to protect the biodiversity in their backyards. Local governments play an important part in protecting biodiversity by incorporating conservation into their planning and regulatory schemes and by cooperating with others to protect resources at the ecosystem level. Incentive schemes, whether private or public, will also spur interest and action to protect our natural resources. Protecting biodiversity will not be easy, but it is important. After all, what would a spring day be like without the bird's song or an autumn day without the changing leaves? Protecting biodiversity is simply about protecting the qualities that make our lives rich.

REFERENCES

American Farmland Trust. 2002. *Fact Sheet: Why Save Farmland*. Washington, D.C.: American Farmland Trust.

Calhoun, A.J.K., and M.W. Klemens. 2002. *Best Development Practices: Conserving Pool-Breeding Amphibians in Residential and Commercial Developments in the Northeastern United States*. Metropolitan Conservation Alliance Technical Paper, no. 5. Bronx, N.Y.: Wildlife Conservation Society.

Central Pine Barrens Joint Planning and Policy Commission. 1995. *Pine Barrens Credit Program Handbook: A User's Guide to the Central Pine Barrens Transferable Development Rights Program*. Great River, N.Y.: Central Pine Barrens Joint Planning and Policy Commission.

Environmental Protection Agency. 2001. *Our Built and Natural Environments*. Washington, D.C.: EPA.

Forman, R.T.T. 1995. *Land Mosaics: The Ecology of Landscapes and Regions*. Cambridge: Cambridge University Press.

Kiviat, E., and G. Stevens. 2001. *Biodiversity Assessment Manual for the Hudson River Estuary Corridor*. Albany: Hudsonia Ltd. and New York State Department of Environmental Conservation.

Klemens, M. W. 1993. *Amphibians and Reptiles of Connecticut and Adjacent Regions*. State Geological and Natural History Survey, bulletin no. 112. Hartford: Connecticut Department of Environmental Protection.

———. 2001. *Bog Turtle* (Clemmys muhlenbergii), *Northern Population, Recovery Plan*. Washington, D.C.: Fish and Wildlife Service.

———. 2002. Biodiversity protection: New opportunities for land trusts and public agencies. Paper presented at the Tenth Anniversary New York Land Trust Conference/Land Trust Alliance. May 31–June 1, Saratoga Springs, N.Y.

Miller, N.A., and M.W. Klemens. 2002. *Eastern Westchester Biotic Corridor*. Metropolitan Conservation Alliance Technical Paper, no. 4. Bronx, N.Y.: Wildlife Conservation Society.

Navota, J., and D. Dreher. 2000. *Protecting Nature in Your Community: A Guidebook for Preserving and Enhancing Biodiversity*. Chicago: Northeastern Illinois Planning Commission.

Nolon, John R. 1998. *Well Grounded: Shaping the Destiny of the Empire State*. White Plains, N.Y.: Land Use Law Center, Pace University School of Law.

Town of Dover Zoning Law. 1999. Available at: www.law.pace.edu/landuse/greatswa. html#I.%20Town%20of%20Dover.

15

BUILDING PUBLIC AWARENESS ABOUT THE EFFECTS OF SPRAWL ON BIODIVERSITY

Cynthia Coffin and Jane Elder

In a democracy, public engagement is critical for effective social change. Messages that seek to engage the public on growth and land-use issues compete for public attention with many other legitimate concerns and are sometimes lost in the background noise of modern media and our increasingly busy and complex lives. Professional practitioners—from new urbanist developers to regional planners to ecologists—are de facto messengers on issues of sprawl and biodiversity when speaking at a public meeting, talking to reporters, or contributing to a newsletter. These professionals need to ensure that their messages and strategies for communicating on smart growth and biodiversity conservation are clear, incisive, and consistent.

For too long, scientists and environmentalists have assumed that information alone will compel the public to act. Facts have been packaged with a dose of alarm to ensure that they grab the news media's attention. Information is only part of the equation, however. If powerful scientific information were effective on its own, Americans would have stopped smoking long ago, they would all be wearing seat belts every time they get in a car, and SUVs would be long extinct. Humans are complex beings and make decisions based on a variety of factors—some scientific, some experiential, and some emotional.

To tackle something as complex as the interaction between biodiversity and sprawl, communities and individuals need a greater understanding of how they will be directly affected by such problems as uncontrolled development, habitat loss, reduced open space, and invasive species. Messages must speak to values (the underlying beliefs that make people care) and concerns (the current or chronic worries that arise in the course of daily life). They must be accurate and supported by facts, but they are most compelling and effective when they appeal to values and concerns.

Although the public is concerned about the loss of biodiversity and habitat (in a 1996 national poll, 87 percent of Americans said that maintaining biodiversity was personally important to them), this broad public support is easily eroded in the face of concerns about jobs, property rights, or human comfort and convenience (Belden & Russonello and R/S/M Inc. 1996). Furthermore, expressed concern for biodiversity does not readily translate to action.

Americans associate a complex mix of values with the issue of sprawl: privacy, safety, choice, freedom, responsibility, and more. For 80 percent of Americans, the ideal home would be a single-family detached house with a yard on all sides (Hart and Teeter Research Companies 1992). Although this is old information, nothing suggests that these sentiments have changed. More recent data indicate that 29 percent of Americans would prefer to live in a small town, 27 percent would prefer a rural area, and 19 percent would prefer a newly built suburb. Much smaller percentages would prefer an older suburb or city (13 and 12 percent, respectively) (Belden Russonello & Stewart 1999).

Yet Americans are also worried about what is happening to the landscape. In a 1996 poll on attitudes about biodiversity, Americans ranked "the rate of land development and nature being lost" as a serious concern (Belden & Russonello and R/S/M Inc. 1996); only loss of rain forests and worries about toxic waste ranked higher among environmental concerns. Similarly, people want to protect open space: 76 percent of Americans think that their state should do more to manage and plan for new growth; 83 percent favor establishing zones for green space, farming, and forests that would be off limits to development (Belden Russonello & Stewart 2000).

When communicating about growth issues, biodiversity proponents run up against traditional perceptions of the American dream, fear about fundamental safety and security in neighborhoods, and a host of concerns that contributed to the sprawl phenomenon in the first place. To grapple with the problems associated with sprawl, communicators have to make a long-term, concerted effort to move the public from impasse to action. Messages must be very clear about the choices and solutions, and must make the environmentally sound choices more appealing than the status quo.

The remainder of this chapter is divided into two main sections. The first section provides an overview of the research and theory that can help inform communications about sprawl and biodiversity. This section includes a discussion of American attitudes about growth and biodiversity based on public-opinion research, and general guidelines for crafting a communications strategy. The second section provides specific recommendations for how to frame messages about sprawl and biodiversity, integrating the findings of the previous section.

USING AN INFORMED APPROACH

AMERICAN ATTITUDES

Public-opinion research provides important insights into crafting strategies that can help build a public constituency that cares about protecting biodiversity and promoting smarter growth. Research findings can help communicators identify values and concerns related to particular issues. They can provide information about the demographics and lifestyle choices of particular audiences and about where people get the information that helps shape their actions. The Biodiversity Project initiated several recent focus group and polling projects that identify American attitudes about both growth issues and biodiversity.

In the fall of 1997, the Biodiversity Project partnered with The Nature Conservancy of California to commission a series of 20 focus groups to assess public perceptions of sprawl, land use, and biodiversity. A year later, the focus groups were followed by a national poll on the same topic, commissioned by the National Trust for Historic Preservation. The polling firm Belden Russonello & Stewart conducted both research projects. The focus groups found that sprawl means many different things to Americans. For many Americans, the word *sprawl* evokes negative images, "such as traffic, congestion, concrete, pollution, ugly housing subdivisions, and strip malls." To others, *sprawl* suggests "a way out of current congestion, the ability to spread out, to move to a quiet, peaceful area, and economic growth" (Belden Russonello & Stewart 1998:22). The survey findings further illustrate the ambiguity of this term. When Americans hear the word *sprawl*, some are twice as likely to think it is something bad (21 percent) as good (10 percent), but most (64 percent) hear both good and bad in the term (Belden Russonello & Stewart 1999) (figure 15.1).

Many Americans believe that sprawl will help them solve many of their current problems. When asked about the most convincing reasons to allow sprawl development, people say that it will offer them more choices about where to live (77 percent say this is a convincing reason), provide affordable housing for young people (67 percent), and enable people to move to safer neighborhoods (76 percent), escape crowded cities (76 percent), and attend better schools (67 percent). More relevant to biodiversity, a number of people would support sprawl because it gives them the opportunity to live closer to nature (58 percent) or have larger yards (56 percent) (Belden Russonello & Stewart 1999).

Yet a strong majority of Americans (66 percent) believe controlling sprawl is personally important to them. When they are exposed to arguments about the pros and cons of sprawl, this concern increases to 74 percent (Belden Russonello & Stewart 1999). A poll conducted for the Pew Center for Civic Journalism

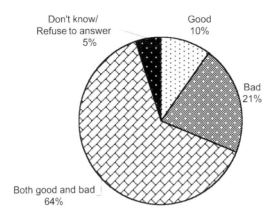

When you hear the term "suburban sprawl" do you generally think of it as describing something good, something bad, or something both good and bad?

FIGURE 15.1. Perceptions of sprawl (Belden Russonello & Stewart 1999).

shows that Americans rank sprawl and development as the single most important problem facing their community today, tied only with crime (Princeton Survey Research Associates 2000). People understand that sprawl creates traffic and longer commutes, destroys natural habitats and green space, abandons taxpayer investments in the city, and eliminates productive farmland. At the same time, many people (45 percent) feel that the problem is overwhelming and impossible to control (Belden Russonello & Stewart 1999).

Values help drive attitudes and behaviors related to sprawl and biodiversity. They are important factors in determining which arguments and rationales will be effective in building public support for smarter growth and habitat protection and in engaging people to take action on these issues. On sprawl, both the focus groups and the poll indicate that the key values associated with this issue include having a sense of community, enjoying privacy from one's neighbors, and the convenience of having shops and schools within walking distance (which many relate to freedom). When asked to choose the most important of these three values, Americans place the highest priority on having a sense of community (46 percent), followed by privacy (32 percent), and then convenience (21 percent) (Belden Russonello & Stewart 1999).

Other research identifies the core values related to protecting biodiversity. In a 1996 poll, Americans were asked to choose the most important personal reason to care about protecting the environment (in the context of biodiversity). A "responsibility to future generations" ranked highest, at 27 percent. Competing values included a respect for "God's work" (23 percent), a "desire for family to enjoy a healthy environment" (18 percent), and "the personal need to live in a healthy environment" (13 percent). Values more commonly drawn on by environmental advocates—"appreciation for the beauty of nature" and "nature's rights"—ranked much lower, at 9 percent and 8 percent, respectively (Belden Russonello & Stewart 1996:8).

When talking about the specific problems associated with sprawl, its impacts on the environment—loss of green space, habitats for wildlife, and wetlands that provide clean water—are the easiest links to make. Eighty-two percent of Americans believe that sprawl should be controlled because it destroys wetlands and forests that protect water quality (51 percent find this a very convincing reason, and the remaining 31 percent find it somewhat convincing); 80 percent believe that sprawl should be controlled because it destroys open space and natural areas (45 percent find this very convincing); and 79 percent believe that sprawl should be controlled because it destroys natural habitat for birds and other wildlife (47 percent find this very convincing) (Belden Russonello & Stewart 1999) (figure 15.2).

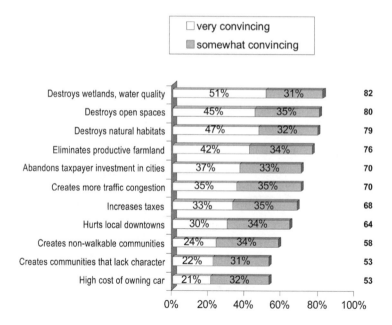

Please tell me how convincing each of the following is to you personally as a reason to control suburban sprawl: Is that very convincing, somewhat convincing, not very convincing, or not at all convincing reason to control suburban sprawl?

FIGURE 15.2. Reasons to control sprawl (Belden Russonello & Stewart 1999).

FIGURE 15.3. Support for smart-growth policies (Belden Russonello & Stewart 2000).

The data further show that there is widespread support for specific policies to protect the environment and to revitalize existing communities. Even when an issue's connection to sprawl is ambiguous, Americans will often support specific antisprawl policies because they believe that such policies make good sense. For example, as shown in figure 15.3, more than 7 in 10 Americans support

- Establishing zones for green space, farms, and forests outside existing cities and suburbs that would be off limits to development (83 percent)
- Using tax dollars to buy land for more parks and open space and to protect wildlife (77 percent)
- Having government give priority to maintaining services in existing communities rather than encouraging new development in the countryside (81 percent)
- Increasing coordinated efforts among towns to plan for growth (85 percent)
- Providing tax credits and low-interest loans for people to rehabilitate historic houses and to revitalize neighborhoods in cities and older suburbs (79 percent) (Belden Russonello & Stewart 2000)

THE ART OF COMMUNICATIONS

To use these research findings effectively first requires an understanding of basic communications principles. A good communications strategy can make the difference between a successful outreach effort and one that falls flat. Such a strategy requires patience, discipline, and creative thinking. On sprawl and biodiversity, the challenge is to convey the seriousness of the issue without overwhelming the public with too many facts or a sense of despair.

DETERMINE GOALS AND OBJECTIVES Before writing a message, one should clearly articulate the goals and objectives of an outreach effort. Be it broad-based education, public-policy change, fund-raising, or efforts to change the public's behavior, a communications campaign has a better chance of success if its designers are

- Clear about the goals
- Know what they are trying to accomplish within a given time frame
- Set objectives that can be measured

The goals help determine with whom to communicate to accomplish specific objectives. Some communications efforts may have to target very specific audiences, such as rural homeowners or parents of young children or seniors; other efforts may be more focused on influential civic leaders or the media. Multiple audiences are sometimes required. If the goal is to shape public policy, there are probably three key audiences: voters, key constituents, and decision makers.

DETERMINE AND LEARN ABOUT THE AUDIENCE Once an audience is selected, it is important to step back and learn as much about it as possible. The learning process can be as informal as having conversations with audience members to gain a more in-depth understanding of their beliefs and habits. Or, if resources permit, public-opinion research conducted by an experienced professional can be a valuable tool.

Investigating an audience entails listening for the core values its members bring to the issues at hand. People form their opinions on an issue by measuring it against their core values—those intangibles that drive decisions about where they live and what the future of their communities will be (e.g., choice and freedom). It is also important to be aware of the more immediate concerns an audience brings to the issue: current or chronic worries they may have about their own or their families' quality of life, health, economic status, and future. A message that leads with values provides people with a reason to care about a particular issue. Alternatively, a message will not be persuasive if it conflicts with values or fails to address concerns.

DEVELOP A MESSAGE After the audience has been researched, it is time to develop a message—typically a paragraph that provides the basic template for more specific communications. This message should be clear, compelling, and short, and it should do three basic things: give the audience a reason to care (appeal to values), describe the threat, and provide a solution. A slogan and a sound bite can be easily lifted from the message. A slogan—a short, pithy tagline used repetitively—is the kind of phrase that might be used on a bumper sticker, such as "Development is forever." A sound bite is a short statement that captures the essence of an argument and is the phrase one hopes will be quoted by reporters. It typically requires more context than a slogan—for example, "If developers get access to Smith Marsh, it will soon be gone forever. Protect our quality of life by voting 'No' tomorrow." These shorthand applications of the message can be useful in communications, but they are not a substitute for a thoughtful, well-constructed message paragraph.

When one is developing a message, it is important to be aware of how specific language can alter the impact of a statement. Because different audiences bring their own experiences to an issue, the communicator's intended meaning is sometimes not what the audience hears. For instance, a logger in the Pacific Northwest may have a different attitude toward the phrase "government regulation" than a suburban mom in New Jersey. No one set of "preferred" words or phrases may be appropriate for all circumstances.

USE ANECDOTES AND IMAGES Providing a human story illustrates and amplifies the message and makes it more salient and personal. In a debate over land use or other growth issues, the side that presents the more compelling human story first often comes out ahead because the other side never recovers. This story must be lined up before the communications effort begins. Likewise, pictures tell a story, evoke emotions, and appeal to values. Images should be chosen very carefully: an image that is too harsh may offend or be seen as extreme; one that evokes only beauty may send a message that all is well and no action is needed. Images should reflect the message and may include a positive appeal to values (with images of what is worth protecting) or a description of the problem (with disturbing images) or both (figure 15.4).

TALK ABOUT THE SOLUTIONS AND GIVE PEOPLE SOMETHING TO DO Every message should describe a solution to the problem at hand and provide individuals with practical steps they can take to help make a difference. There are at least two kinds of solutions. First, there are public policies and actions, such as public decisions to purchase conservation easements or to institute growth boundaries. Individuals can help support these actions by writing letters to public officials, making public comments, attending a planning meeting, or voting, just to name a few. Second, personal actions and behaviors (such as driving less frequently) help support public policies but also lead to changes in operating paradigms. Whether political or personal, messages must give people something to do—an action that allows them to respond to the threat they face—such as voting, driving less, or visiting a local nature center. People want to be helpful.

Don't let parking lots be the only open spaces we leave our children.

Uncontrolled development destroys nearly 1 million acres of parks, farms, and open space each year.
Sprawl not only threatens our environment, our health, and our quality of life, it's turning
our communities into strip malls, freeways, and parking lots.

Protect your choices. Fight overdevelopment. Fight sprawl.

Bi diversity
Life. Nature. You. Make the connection.

FIGURE 15.4. Effective use of images. (Biodiversity Project and Green Team Advertising)

ENLIST APPROPRIATE MESSENGERS The choice of a messenger for a communications effort depends on the message and the audience that will receive it. One of the biggest mistakes is to decide on a messenger before all the other elements are in place. Messages are typically most credible when they come from people affected by an issue or problem rather than from those far removed. Messengers can also be effective if they hold a respected position in society or represent an agency or organization that people believe to be trustworthy and honest. For example, a patient who suffers from asthma and a doctor from the American Medical Association might be very effective messengers for a message about smog and ozone pollution.

GET THE FACTS STRAIGHT A good communications strategy is backed up by facts. Developing fact sheets is an excellent way to identify the most convincing and relevant pieces of information and is handy for dealing with the media and for helping messengers stay on message. Journalists and the public have become increasingly skeptical of competing scientific information, so facts should be specific, not general, in order to be credible. For example, it is better to provide the number of acres of wetlands that will be lost because of a certain development than simply to say "acres of wetlands." At the same time, it can help to simplify statistics: it is more effective to say "three out of four" than "75 percent." Facts will also be more compelling if they relate to people's daily lives or experience, such as "the water we drink every day" or "the air our children breathe."

ANTICIPATE QUESTIONS AND CRITIQUES Even the best-laid communications strategy can go awry if it does not take into account the common concerns or critiques of a particular viewpoint and message. It can be extremely helpful to identify these concerns up front and prepare a response or raise the issue first and defuse any attacks. The two most common concerns about growth management have to do with cost and choice. These critiques appeal to Americans' innate expectation of freedoms, including freedom of choice, and of rights, including private-property rights. These values can be put to work legitimately for messages about growth management. For example, after much research and careful analysis, Smart Growth America rewrote its slogan several years ago to define itself as "a national coalition working towards better choices for our communities."

REACHING THE PUBLIC ON SPRAWL AND BIODIVERSITY

To grapple with sprawl and its impacts on biodiversity, communications can integrate the findings from the public-opinion research with the basic steps for crafting an effective communications strategy. With these guidelines in mind, the Biodiversity Project worked with national leaders in the smart-growth movement to develop a number of recommendations for communicating about sprawl. Two of the recommendations are key to a coordinated strategy. First, to address the ambiguity of the term, communications had to define *sprawl* clearly and frame it as out-of-control, irresponsible, or wasteful development that diminishes quality of life. Second, and more important, messages should draw on the values that Americans associate with the issue and emphasize that, contrary to expectations, this out-of-control development takes away choices and that controlling sprawl provides more choices for families and communities (Biodiversity Project 2000).

With regard to biodiversity, such control means more choices about where we recreate, about local mobility, about the character of our communities, and about the kind of landscape we want to leave our children. It means the choice to have clean air and water, flood protection, and erosion control. And it means the choice to live in a world where a rich variety of species shares our space and provides us with both essential resources and spiritual grounding.

Some additional recommendations emerge from the research. The focus groups indicate that people evaluate sprawl-related messages based on what the messages mean to their own quality of life. The impacts of growth and development on their local environment and community are not always clear to Americans, especially when they are presented with a number of sprawl-related issues at once (Belden Russonello & Stewart 1998). To make the problem less overwhelming and more clearly understood, curbing sprawl should be placed in the context of more specific actions, such as protecting productive farmland, protecting open space or critical habitat, protecting native species, relieving traffic congestion, or revitalizing communities.

The easiest way to demonstrate tangible impacts associated with sprawl is through the loss of open space, habitats for wildlife, and wetlands and forests that help provide clean water. Messages that draw on these links will be particularly effective in reaching a broad audience. In addition, communications should recognize that to the public, sprawl is a local problem and a concern only when it affects them personally. Messages about what is lost because of sprawl should be about communities and land where people live or other special places with which they identify.

Using consistent language will help advance a consistent message on sprawl that will resonate with the public and avoid confusion. Defining *sprawl* in a way that highlights the negative impacts, as discussed earlier, is a good start. Knowing what words to avoid is equally important. The research indicates that to most people *growth* is good. Communications should distinguish between *bad growth* (irresponsible, out of control, etc.) and *good growth* or better planning. Likewise, messages should talk about controlling sprawl rather than stopping sprawl. Other terms that resonate well include *balance, heritage, community, neighborhood, green space, open space,* and *productive farmland.* Terms to avoid include jargon such as *infill, density, brownfield, mixed use, urban growth boundary,* and *conservation easement.*

Communications should include a positive message along with warnings about sprawl. Communicate that people *can* make a difference and that the choices are not overwhelming. Be clear about how the choices will affect real people's lives, families, and communities. Describe the benefits that people will gain from controlling sprawl and adopting smart-growth alternatives. Even when a problem's connection to sprawl is ambiguous, Americans will often support specific smart-growth policies because they believe they make good sense. The public broadly supports limiting development in order to protect green space, farms, forests, and wildlife; giving priority to maintaining services in existing communities; and purchasing land to protect wildlife. Communications should emphasize these positive outcomes of smart growth.

Solutions that stress limits and boundaries run counter to the values of freedom, privacy, community, choice, and responsibility—especially when government is perceived as the one setting those limits. Alternatively, solutions that focus on protecting green space, enhancing environmental quality, reinvesting in neighborhoods, and giving priority to existing communities before tearing up the countryside reflect and reinforce those values. Communications should reinforce the values that Americans hold.

As discussed earlier, messages will be most effective when they give people something to do—as homeowners or renters, parents, consumers, and voters. At the same time, messages should not alienate them by suggesting things they cannot do easily or realistically. It is helpful to start with small steps. Instead of opening the conversation by first suggesting that they buy a house in the city rather than in a new subdivision, suggest that they combine their errands whenever possible, support locally owned businesses, or attend a local planning meeting. Over time, such messages can work up to home-buying choices for select audiences. As a starting point with the broader public, however, the message about home buying is likely to close more doors than it opens. Manageable actions that individuals can take to mitigate the impacts of sprawl on habitat and biodiversity include

- Joining a local community development or land conservation organization
- Supporting funding for public transportation to relieve the pressure on local roads
- Attending a planning meeting
- Calling their local leaders and asking them to support smart-growth policies
- Writing a letter to the editor making their views heard
- Getting to know and helping support their local parks and green spaces
- Introducing a child to these special places and visiting frequently
- Riding a bike, walking, or using public transportation whenever feasible to take advantage of local resources and reduce the demand for new roads

- Buying locally produced food and goods whenever possible to support local farms and to reduce the need for transportation of goods across the country
- Supporting small local businesses rather than new big-box stores that eat up open space and habitat

In most cases, the best messengers and spokespeople on sprawl issues will be those whose livelihood or future is compromised by the loss of recently developed land. They include the average citizen concerned about the community and farmers affected by the loss of productive land and their livelihood. Children are good messengers because their future will be affected by overdevelopment, and they can appeal to the values of an audience concerned about providing a better life for the next generation. Many other people are affected by the decline of urban neighborhoods. The elderly can talk about a time when their neighborhood had a sense of community and what they would like to leave behind as a legacy or about the difficulties of getting around without a car and the need for the independence provided by better public transit. Local business owners can talk about the economic pressures brought on by retail chains and superstores.

CONCLUSION

To engage the public on sprawl and biodiversity, messages must give people a reason to care and provide them with solutions that make them feel empowered and willing to take action. It is important to keep in mind that engaging the public is only one step in the larger process of effecting social change. True change will require a combination of tools and tactics. Environmental education—both formal (K–12) and nonformal (through zoos, museums, and nature centers)—can teach people critical thinking, basic ecological principles, and the impacts of human behavior on natural communities (Elder 2003). Grassroots organizing explicitly helps to empower and mobilize citizens in the political process (Sierra Club 1999). And community-based social marketing, in addition to developing media messages that appeal to values, identifies barriers to behavior change and seeks to address these barriers through community action and institutional change (McKenzie-Mohr and Smith 1999). Yet all these tactics will require effective messages, a well-developed communications strategy, and a clear understanding of the target audience.

Scientists, planners, and other professionals' best intentions to curb sprawl and protect biodiversity will fall short unless more people understand the issues, care about them, and are willing to make some easy and some tough choices to secure their own quality of life and that of future generations. Effective communication is critical to raise awareness and understanding of the issues and to help people identify real solutions and actions they can take to protect biodiversity and its benefits from the onslaught of sprawl development.

Professional practitioners increasingly find themselves in the public eye as they testify at public hearings, talk to reporters, and provide data and input for highly charged public debates. These professionals must develop basic communications skills and become more consistent in the messages they send to the public. The two key elements of a coordinated message are (1) always provide a label for sprawl, such as "irresponsible or wasteful development," and (2) always emphasize that smart growth is about offering more choices and that sprawl takes away choices. These messages eventually have to be carried by community leaders, homebuyers, and the media that speak to them, as well as, when possible, the development industry itself. Only then will the concepts of smart growth and biodiversity become engrained in the collective consciousness and guide everyday decisions and actions.

REFERENCES

Belden & Russonello and R/S/M, Inc. 1996. *Human Values and Nature's Future: Americans' Attitudes on Biological Diversity, an Analysis of Findings from a National Survey.* Washington, D.C.: Communications Consortium Media Center.

Belden Russonello & Stewart. 1998. *Choices Between Asphalt and Nature: Americans Discuss Sprawl, an Analysis of 20 Focus Groups Across the U.S.* Madison, Wis., and San Francisco: Biodiversity Project and Nature Conservancy.

——. 1999. *Personal Choices and Public Priorities: Understanding Americans' Attitudes Toward Suburban Sprawl, Results of a National Survey Conducted for the National Trust for Historic Preservation.* Washington, D.C.: National Trust for Historic Preservation.

——. 2000. *National Survey on Growth and Land Development.* Washington, D.C.: Smart Growth America.

Biodiversity Project. 2000. *Getting on Message: Making the Biodiversity–Sprawl Connection.* Madison, Wis.: Biodiversity Project.

Elder, J. 2003. *A Field Guide to Environmental Literacy: Making Strategic Investments in Environmental Education.* Rock Spring, Ga.: Environmental Education Coalition and American Association for Environmental Education.

Hart and Teeter Research Companies. 1992. *Preferred Types of Housing.* Washington, D.C.: Federal National Mortgage Association.

McKenzie-Mohr, D., and W. Smith. 1999. *Fostering Sustainable Behavior: An Introduction to Community-Based Social Marketing.* Gabriola Island, B.C.: New Society.

Princeton Survey Research Associates. 2000. *Straight Talk from Americans—2000.* Washington, D.C.: Pew Center for Civic Journalism.

Sierra Club. 1999. *Grassroots Organizing Training Manual.* San Francisco: Sierra Club.

16

■ ■

CREATING A FRAMEWORK FOR CHANGE

Michael W. Klemens and Elizabeth A. Johnson

reating a more scientifically informed land-use paradigm is essential to managing the biodiversity–sprawl interface. Although science can inform us of the dimensions of a problem, it rarely provides the road map required to find our way to a solution to that problem. One of the challenges we face as scientists, planners, and decision makers is bridging the gap between acquiring scientific knowledge and applying that knowledge to create change.

In this volume and at the conference "Nature in Fragments: The Legacy of Urban Sprawl," we have focused the attention surrounding the sprawl debate directly onto biodiversity and the interrelated issue of ecosystem quality (e.g., cycles of disturbance, decomposition, and pollination). We have framed the challenges from both human and biological dimensions, discussing the issues of both processes and scale. Our focus has been not only on ecological scales, but also on the levels of government (i.e., local, state, regional, national) where interventions might reverse the trend of wasteful, inefficient, and unsustainable consumption of ecosystems. Conserving biological diversity successfully will require weaving conservation into overall social and economic agendas, for if conservation continues to be looked on as yet another special interest, decision makers will invariably give it short shrift. However, if we can refocus the discussion of biodiversity to make it an integral part of discussions and decisions concerning community character, economic development, sustainable communities, and community self-determination, we can garner the support of other more established and powerful coalitions, increasing severalfold the likelihood of effecting biodiversity conservation as part of the land-use and governance processes.

Scientists have been able to raise the alarm concerning biodiversity loss and ecosystem degradation, yet have been frustrated by an inability to engage themselves and others constructively in solving land-use planning issues. Why?

Scientists are often reluctant to embark on the type of transdisciplinary work required to undertake on-the-ground land-use planning. This reluctance is in part a result of academic institutions' inability to reward (through advancement and tenure) the type of applied research and advocacy that will better inform and shape the land-use debate (Klemens 1993). In turn, decision makers' "corporate culture," requiring a "one size fits all" cookbook approach to managing natural resources, is anathema to the scientific understanding of the complexity and diversity of ecosystems. In addition, many academicians are reluctant to engage in what Funtowicz and Ravetz (1993a, 1993b) call *postnormal science*, the science of providing public-policy guidance where data are incomplete and decisions are urgent (i.e., even shorter time periods than the time frames of long-term, multiyear research projects). Postnormal science requires the skilled extrapolation of probable outcomes (trend analysis) at a level of scientific certainty sufficiently robust to shape decision response. Finally, even if many scientists are interested, they do not know how to communicate effectively with nonscientists.

The need for institutional change extends beyond the scientific community. We, the editors of this volume, recognize that the land-use planning system currently in place is moving forward like a juggernaut, fueled by standards, regulations, designs, and procedures largely bereft of ecological thinking. Therefore, if conservation biologists want more and better biological information folded in that process, *they* will have to redirect that process into an ecological framework. That redirection does not obviate the need for members of other disciplines involved in land use (e.g., planners, engineers, land-use attorneys) to recognize the failures of the current system, particularly as these failures pertain to the conservation of natural resources. Only through a partnership of land-use professionals can humans begin to reverse the trajectory of ecological waste that is the by-product of sprawl.

The chapter authors in this volume provided suggestions from their own particular disciplines and experiences to create this change. In addition, we offer the following thoughts and recommendations to the diverse readership of this volume as a catalyst to meet the challenge of becoming better stewards of our ever more urbanizing world.

1. *Redirect development into more compact human settlements with consideration of ecological landscape context and constraints.*

The habitat loss, fragmentation, and degradation that accompany sprawl are the primary causes of biodiversity loss in many regions. Land-consumption rates increasingly far exceed (in proportion) population growth (Yaro and Hiss 1996) (figure 16.1). The exodus into the suburbs and beyond and the strategies

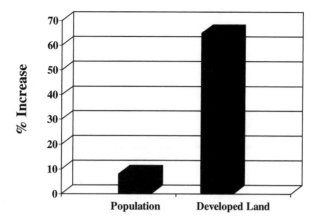

FIGURE 16.1. Developed land and population changes in the New York, New Jersey, and Connecticut region: 1925, 1940, 1960, and 1990. (Courtesy of Regional Plan Association)

to stabilize and reverse this trend are at the very core of the new urbanist and smart-growth movements. A deeper alliance between biodiversity conservation interests and these movements is essential, yet it will require the education of both communities. A central tenet of new urbanist communities is the clustering of homes into hamlets and the protection or preservation of visually pleasant open spaces and greenways (Arendt 1999). These open spaces are usually designed from an anthropocentric perspective, a vision of nature lush and green, but not necessarily biologically functional. Many of these developments in fact create abundant edge habitat, fragmenting the landscape into a patchwork mosaic of open spaces and dense development. Nonetheless, the new urbanist movement has tremendous potential to counteract the biologically deleterious effects of sprawl on both human and biological communities.

At the core of the new urbanist movement—or, as it is known in suburban and rural areas, traditional neighborhood design (TND)—communities are being created that build on traditional concepts of more compact urban and village settlement. By intensifying such development on smaller parcels of land, developments are created that are served by municipal services, such as community water and septic systems, thereby placing fewer demands on and causing less impacts to aquifers and wetlands by eliminating individual wells and septic systems. TND developments, by re-creating compact villages, encourage walking instead of driving, mixed uses where small retail establishments are intermixed with residential areas, and a diversity of housing options accessible to people of different incomes and ages. In short, TND developments can create anew the sense of community and the human interactions, intergenerational living, and generous public spaces that are absent from much of suburbia.

The promise of these types of developments for the conservation of natural systems is just beginning. They represent some very optimistic trends, and with increased interaction between ecologists and TND planners, the necessary thought required to add value to TND developments in the area of natural resources is occurring. One of the obstacles to be overcome is recognizing that open space protected through a TND development has to be located in such a manner that has ecological resonance—in other words, that it be connected ecologically (not just through a narrow constructed greenway) to other ecologically significant parcels. The town of Patterson, New York, has recently passed legislation mandating that open-space parcels on clustered developments ecologically interconnect with one another (Town of Patterson 2003).

Another potential benefit of TND developments is the opportunity presented by the many infill developments that occur on postindustrial or other sites, such as strip malls. Such developments have the potential to rectify and restore lost ecological functions through the redevelopment process. Madison Landing (figures 16.2 and 16.3), a TND redevelopment in coastal Connecticut, will replace a small airport adjacent to a large and ecologically significant salt marsh system with a compact village. The Madison Landing plan incorporates many ecological benefits, including removal of several acres of tarmac adjacent to the salt marsh, creating a 100-foot (30-meter) restored grassland between the salt marsh and the development site; protection of 75 percent of the site, including the ecological connections to the greater ecosystems in which the project is embedded; public access to the site through a system of trails in the protected upland; and creation of a state-of-the-art wastewater-management system instead of individual septic systems (individual septic system runoff from adjacent developments has been identified as a major source of pollution to ecologically significant salt marsh systems). Roof runoff will be directly infiltrated back into the ground, as opposed to being piped away through stormwater conveyance and treatment systems. Reinfiltration of stormwater in this manner protects the ecologically vital recharge relationship between uplands and wetlands that is often lost during conventional development.

Madison Landing creates a village node, using replications of existing Connecticut coastal architecture, at a streetscape density (figures 16.4 and 16.5) that is modeled on the existing village of Madison. The development includes public spaces and view ways, including a village green, and a variety

FIGURE 16.2. Aerial view of the Madison Landing site. At present, the site is a small, inactive private airport surrounded by development and salt marsh. (Photo courtesy of Leyland Alliance LLC)

FIGURE 16.3. Acres of tarmac at the edge of a tidal wetland impede ecological function and restrict the tidal marsh's ability to respond to sea-level rise by migrating inland. This runway will be restored to a 100-foot (30-meter) naturally vegetated upland zone bordering the tidal marsh. (Photo courtesy of Leyland Alliance LLC)

FIGURE 16.4. Aerial view of the proposed Madison Landing TND development. The ecological benefits of this development include more than 100 feet (30 meters) of restored upland bordering the tidal marsh, a state-of-the-art community wastewater-treatment plant, protection of 75 percent of the site as open space, and restoration of several acres of impervious tarmac to upland grass- and shrub land. (© 2000, 2002 Design and Watercolor — Michael B. Morrissey MRAIC)

of housing options designed for people at different life stages and family configurations. As such, Madison Landing blends the ecological and societal benefits of TND and is a model of what the integration of ecological thought into TND can accomplish.

As demonstrated by Madison Landing, the infusion of biodiversity knowledge into the new urbanist or TND process can yield major benefits to biodiversity conservation. This goal is readily attainable because the conversation about creation of a new development template is already ongoing, supported by a broad alliance of stakeholders. With biodiversity conservation "at the table," these developments can have added value by being placed into a larger ecological framework, which would ensure that open-space reservations on adjoining developments make ecological sense, connecting habitats and conserving key resources that extend onto parcels that have multiple ownerships or lie in more than one jurisdiction. To accomplish this, biodiversity conservationists must become more involved in the new urbanist, TND, and smart-growth movements, not only to inform the design of biodiversity-friendly devel-

FIGURE 16.5. Madison Landing replicates the architectural design and streetscape configuration of the existing village of Madison. This TND development creates a mix of housing types, encouraging multigenerational residency. Madison Landing also provides generous public spaces, broad view ways, and a trail system. By virtue of its compact design, pedestrian traffic is encouraged, fostering human interaction and less dependence on automobiles. (© 2000, 2002 Design and Watercolor—Michael B. Morrissey MRAIC)

opments, but also, on a larger philosophical basis, to understand that the promotion of compact developments in both urban and rural regions may present one of the best opportunities to counteract the deleterious effects of sprawl on the natural world. The creation of compact, livable, affordable, and pedestrian-friendly communities, served by sewers and public transportation, reverses the trend of dispersed development, resource consumption, and consumerism that have been the engines of sprawl. The effects of a reduction of resource consumption are far-reaching, extending conservation efforts well beyond national boundaries to the developing world, where so many of the resources that support the consumptive lifestyle of Western nations originate (Monro and Holdgate 1991).

2. *Raise awareness of the opportunities for biodiversity conservation as part of the land-use decision-making process.*

Many people believe that conservation still proceeds along a bifurcated path: habitat is either strictly protected or written off as developable. This simplified bipolar view has failed to protect biological diversity. Around the world, scientists and others have demonstrated time and again that protected areas cannot encompass the range of ecological and gene-flow processes required to sustain biodiversity. In addition, protected areas in most regions do not encompass the entire repertoire of ecosystems and other biodiversity. For example, in many areas of the northeastern United States, state and federal forests and state parks are located in scenic, mountainous areas. The ecosystems and wetlands that lie in the intermontane valleys, often on agriculturally valuable lands, are not well represented in the protected area portfolio. We must create opportunities to achieve conservation and development goals in tandem by creating pathways of information exchange between providers of scientific information and land-use and development decision makers. The land-use planning process is both institutionalized and accepted. Therefore, if biodiversity concerns are going to become part of the land-use and development process, it will be through the efforts of those scientists and conservationists who reach out to form partnerships and to create dialogue with professional planning organizations and their constituent communities. Such dialogue should educate planners and land-use decision makers about the ecosystems and about the actions necessary to protect ecosystem functions over time. Discussion about how best to integrate biological information into the planning process—that is, what tools planners need to do this work—is also critical.

3. *Increase biodiversity literacy among land-use decision makers: scale, scope, and complexity.*

This recommendation might seem to be a part of the second recommendation, but in fact it is a broader challenge. Before creating tools for land-use planners to create biodiversity-friendly land-use plans, those concerned about biodiversity have to create a market for such tools. It has been our experience that many communities actually feel that they have done a good job of protecting natural resources through cluster zoning and large-lot subdivisions. The reality is that these actions often create landscapes that are green, but ecologically dysfunctional, often dominated by subsidized plants and animals (DeStefano and Johnson, chapter 10, this volume). The first step is to educate those communities about the problems that these types of "conservation developments" have caused. Large-lot zoning is an accelerant of sprawl, dispersing fewer people over more land and creating large tracts of edge-dominated and disturbed land. Clusters designed in the absence of an ecosystem or a landscape context often fail to protect biodiversity. Instead, open-space reservations on individual subdivisions rarely connect with one another, creating a patchwork of open space and development. At the heart of this problem is the issue of the scale at which ecosystems can occur (thousands of acres) versus the scale of most land-use decisions (usually less than 25 to 50 acres [10–20 hectares]). Myriad small-scale decisions, no matter how thoughtfully each is made, cannot protect ecosystems or associated processes that function in an area many orders of magnitude larger than the piece of land about which those decision were made.

The full complement of biodiversity—encompassing genes, species, ecosystems, and ecosystem functions and services—should be articulated in a manner that indicates the various local and regional actions needed to protect them. For example, in New England, an individual township may be able to protect a vernal pool and the upland habitat used by its amphibian population, which is part of a landscape of 500 to 1,000 acres (202–405 hectares), yet no single township can protect (through land-use planning) the habitat and connections required by a small bobcat population that requires an interconnected habitat block of at least 10,000 acres (4,049 hectares).

Finally, education on the complexity of ecosystems must be done in a manner that not only educates, but also points toward solutions. Road design and stormwater management are activities where biological complexity is often compromised through ignorance and where biological information can provide a template for better development (Calhoun and Klemens 2002; Wenban-Smith 2003).

4. *Extend land-use review concerns beyond threatened and endangered species (in particular large, charismatic ones) to encompass a more complete suite of wildlife and plants and ecological communities.*

The protection of endangered and threatened species is a governmental mandate that affects development and management activities on both private and public property. The list of species in peril continues to grow, largely because of development, sprawl, and sprawl-generated consumption. Efforts to recover endangered species are often expensive and lead to conflict. All too often people equate biodiversity with threatened and endangered species. The focus on these species is important, but more attention should be placed on the entire range of species, in particular those species that respond negatively to development and sprawl. It is also important to focus on rarely considered species. For example, although invertebrates make up 95 percent of all known animal life, conservation of and research activities on invertebrates receive a fraction of the effort and resources devoted to vertebrates. Much more attention should be given to invertebrate resources, not only because of their abundance and intrinsic worth as species, but in recognition of the key ecological processes, such as pollination and decomposition, that are driven by invertebrates. The opportunities to advance conservation of a broad range of species that are declining should not be lost in our efforts to recover critically imperiled species.

5. *Integrate the protection of key ecological processes into the land-use planning process.*

Ecological processes are rarely addressed or even mentioned as important to a land-use planning goal. Yet, in terms of value, these processes have been the most quantified aspects of biodiversity in that many of them have been articulated in direct financial benefits or costs. For example, the value of crops and fruits that are insect pollinated is immense, yet rarely do decision makers think the processes that create these foods to be worthy of consideration. The costs of cleanup after natural disturbances such as coastal erosion, floods, and fire are well documented, yet these natural processes are a critical component of ecosystems and species maintenance (Farber, chapter 12, this volume). An intelligently developed suburban landscape can support thousands of invertebrate species that, in turn, maintain and support functioning ecosystems that are healthier, safer, and more sustaining to the people who live in them. Likewise, a fully functioning river ecosystem with associated wetlands and floodplain provides flood control, enhances soil fertility, and purifies groundwater. A better understanding of the values and functions of ecological processes such as pollination and decomposition, of disturbances such as flooding, and of the species associated with these processes is critical. Incorporation of this ecological knowledge is a key to more effective planning.

6. *Link top-down and bottom-up efforts to maximize effectiveness, and integrate conservation goals into local and regional decision-making processes.*

Conservation plans, including mandates to manage endangered species, are usually a top-down effort imposed by national or regional governments. Land-use decision making, in contrast, although operating within a national or regional framework, is primarily a locally driven, bottom-up endeavor. Many conservation groups are now working at the local level, realizing that effective stewardship of biological resources must become part of the local discussion, not a mandate from a higher tier of government. However, national and regional conservation and planning agencies have the ability to put local actions into a contextual framework by the very virtue of the large geographical areas that fall under their jurisdiction. Some of the most effective land-use and biodiversity programs have come from the synthesis of both the top-down and bottom-up approaches (Wilkinson, Vickerman, and Lerner, chapter 13, and Daly and Klemens, chapter 14, this volume). These efforts take the local "buy-in" and action and combines them with the larger vision and mandate.

7. *Create new partnerships to conserve biodiversity (e.g., biodiversity and local agriculture).*

In order for biodiversity conservation to become fully integrated into the land-use ethic, new partnerships must be formed with groups that influence how the nondeveloped landscape is managed. Farming and forestry are two industries that have great potential to become more effective partners in biodiversity conservation, particularly if one recognizes the importance of certain types of agricultural and forestry management in creating and maintaining certain types of open-canopy habitat. Such interactions will require some retooling of thinking, specifically recognizing the value of certain farming and forestry activities. For example, in the northeastern United States, small-scale grazing operations associated with dairy production support valuable biological resources, including wet meadow–dependent reptiles and grass-land birds. In fact, these farms are the primary habitat remaining for these species because many of the ecological processes that maintain open wet-lands and grassland habitats have been lost or altered in part by development. Recognition of the role of grazing as a surrogate for lost ecological processes has opened up a new network of collaborations, where conservationists are interested not only in the habitats on the farm, but also in the social and eco-nomic dimensions required to maintain the farmland production that in turn maintains these habitats.

8. *Incorporate adaptive management and flexibility into decision making.*

Ecosystems are highly variable; no two are exactly alike, and each has a dis-tinct set of stressors placed on it. One of the factors contributing to scientists' reluctance to become more involved in the public-policy process is regulators' and decision makers' desires to have uniform sets of standards and procedures to cover each decision. The application of uniform standards for biodiversity and ecosystem protection results in two outcomes: regulation that leaves sys-tems either underprotected or overprotected.

We suggest that an alternative public-policy paradigm may be more effec-tive at integrating biological information into the land-use planning process. Instead of providing absolute standards, regulations can provide the legitimacy to having an information-based decision-making process. The outcomes of that decision will be based on a formula (or decision-making tree) that will call out various required actions and standards according to the biological conditions and landscape health. Such a decision-making tree will also spell out the types of information required to make a credible and consistent determination. Such a system will ultimately better balance ecological stewardship with develop-ment by not underprotecting high-quality habitats or overprotecting degraded habitats that have reduced function and integrity owing to exogenous factors that disrupt natural processes. Calhoun and Klemens (2002) advanced such a three-tiered system for the protection of vernal pools in residential and com-mercial development settings. Pools are divided into three tiers based on their biological productivity and the condition of the upland landscape. Each tier is linked to a series of land-use planning and design measures.

In addition to the thorough planning steps outlined here, adaptive manage-ment requires that initial management decisions be modified as necessary as the project proceeds, particularly when additional information becomes available. Drafting rules and regulations that are sufficiently predictable yet adaptively flexible will be a challenge that will need to be addressed if we are to be successful in fully incorporating biodiversity conservation into planning.

9. *Monitor effectiveness and create measures of success.*

It is important that more effort and resources be devoted to measuring the effectiveness of strategies to integrate biodiversity and land-use planning activities. Measures of success have to be determined, and projects have to be adaptively managed based on the lessons learned. It is also essential to evaluate more fully the effectiveness of various smart-growth tools to control sprawl. For example, urban growth boundaries have been promoted as a smart-growth tool, yet they may have adverse environmental effects by forcing too much development and impervious surface coverage on steep slopes. As urban growth boundaries must be readjusted over time, significant speculation occurs on lands near the edge of these compact cities, anticipating a boundary expansion. With the values of lands inside the urban growth boundary increasing tremendously (because they are zoned for intense residential and commercial use), the relocation of the urban line becomes an issue of politics and speculation, where ecological issues may be overlooked. We should also realize that these boundaries are flexible and so must consider and monitor the repercussions to biodiversity as we continually expand these boundaries in the future. No-growth boundaries are not the solution to sprawl; they are but one tool that gives us time to develop even better ways to achieve sustainable solutions for living on Earth.

Many of the case studies and methodologies discussed in this book are experimental. They represent professionals' efforts to utilize the best available science and to integrate that information into a multidisciplinary model to better conserve biological values and ecosystem functions. As with any experiment, these novel approaches should be followed over time to judge their effectiveness at achieving meaningful conservation. A challenge for planners, developers, and decision makers is to consider the impacts of their plans and decisions at an ecological scale and over an ecological time frame. For the scientific community, the challenge is to foster more applied research that addresses land-use planning issues and to develop appropriate monitoring protocols and measures of success. Finally, it is clear from each chapter that many gaps remain in our knowledge and understanding about species and ecological processes in sprawl-impacted environments. We must focus more research efforts and dollars in this arena and to build research partnerships between scientists, land-use practitioners, and decision makers. Academic reward systems and grant makers must realize the legitimacy and importance of these efforts and provide professional advancement and financial resources to encourage the scientific community's fuller participation in land-use planning and decision making.

CONCLUSION

The genesis of sprawl comes from a multitude of decisions made by individuals of widely disparate professional backgrounds and interests; therefore, the solutions to sprawl must be multidisciplinary. In addition to opening the lines of communication between scientists and land-use planners, we have to broaden discussion among all the various constituencies involved in addressing sprawl and poorly planned development (economists, social scientists, lawyers, developers, realtors, etc.). This volume is offered as an important step in fostering a fuller dialogue about these issues among all stakeholders.

Flexibility and innovation in the land-use planning and decision-making arena are needed, yet the current legal and procedural system seeks security in consistency and in cookbook formulas to deal with specific issues. In contrast, it is the subtle and not so subtle differences in species assemblages and ecosystem processes, varying from site to site, that make the study of natural systems an intellectual passion for many biologists. Herein lies a conundrum: how to insert flexibility into a system that rarely values or allows it. How do we create a more flexible route to making land-use decisions that protects the interests of each stakeholder from the potential of abuse or manipulation by the other? Can we protect developers from growth opponents' unreasonable demands and from opponents' use of a more flexible review process to delay and halt legitimate projects, and can we ensure that developers in their turn will not use this flexibility to create more revenues at the expense of the environment? Unless we can develop a more open dialogue and ultimately better communication and trust between opposing factions, we cannot make the progress required.

Once a baseline of trust and communication has been established, we can attempt to correct some of the structural and procedural issues in the land-use decision-making system. We can recognize the need to make decisions based on incomplete knowledge, relying on trend analysis, but also recognize the obligation to monitor and manage these experimental projects adaptively. Successes must be shared, but so do failures. The lessons learned from projects that did not achieve what they set out to accomplish are as instructive as the success stories, yet we would rather tout our perceived accomplishments than relate these "failures" to our peers and colleagues. In a society that measures success in ego and financial rewards in both academia and the public and private sectors, how can we instill an ethos that says it is acceptable to misstep at times, that says those missteps are in fact the basis of societal progress, and that considers sharing these stories to be vital to our progress?

To whom does the future belong? It belongs to those communities that have the courage to foster innovation, to engage a broad constituency of interests within and beyond their political boundaries in the creation of a more sustainable future. As humans, we cannot live apart from our biological and ecological constraints. Ultimately, we lack the technological capacity to live beyond the sustainability of our planet's natural systems. We are a part of—not apart from—biodiversity.

REFERENCES

Arendt, R. 1999. *Growing Greener: Putting Conservation into Local Plans and Ordinances*. Washington, D.C.: Natural Lands Trust, American Planning Association, American Society of Landscape Architects, and Island Press.

Calhoun, A.J.K., and M.W. Klemens. 2002. *Best Development Practices: Conserving Pool-Breeding Amphibians in Residential and Commercial Developments in the Northeastern United States*. Metropolitan Conservation Alliance Technical Paper, no. 5. Bronx, N.Y.: Wildlife Conservation Society.

Funtowicz, S., and J. Ravetz. 1993a. The emergence of post-normal science. In R. von Schomberg, ed., *Science, Politics, and Morality: Scientific Uncertainty and Decision Making*, 85–123. Dordrecht, Netherlands: Kluwer.

——. 1993b. Science for the post-normal age. *Futures* 25:739–755.

Klemens, M.W. 1993. Can science bust loose? *Audubon* 95:112.

Monro, D., and M. Holdgate, eds. 1991. *Caring for the Earth—A Strategy for Sustainable Living*. Gland, Switzerland: International Union for Conservation of Nature and Natural Resources, United Nations Environmental Program, and World Wildlife Federation.

Town of Patterson. 2003. Subdivision of lands, additional requirements. Chapter 139 of the Code of the Town of Patterson, County of Putnam, New York, May 13.

Wenban-Smith, H.B. 2003. Wildlife and roads: A government perspective. In B. Sherwood, D. Cutler, and J. Burton, eds., *Wildlife and Roads: The Ecological Perspective*, 1–6. London: Imperial College Press.

Yaro, R.D., and T. Hiss. 1996. *A Region at Risk: The Third Regional Plan for the New York–New Jersey–Connecticut Metropolitan Area*. Washington, D.C.: Regional Plan Association and Island Press.

INDEX